Beyond Human Rights and the War on Terror

This edited collection provides a comprehensive, insightful, and detailed study of a vital area of public policy debate as it is currently occurring in countries across the world from India to South Africa and the United Kingdom to Australia. Bringing together academics and experts from a variety of jurisdictions, it reflects upon the impact on human rights of the application of more than a decade of the "War on Terror" as enunciated soon after 9/11.

The volume identifies and critically examines the principal and enduring resonances of the concept of the "War on Terror". The examination covers not only the obvious impacts but also the more insidious and enduring changes within domestic laws. The rationale for this collection is therefore not just to plot how the "War on Terror" has operated within the folds of the cloak of liberal democracy, but how they render that cloak ragged, especially in the sight of those sections of society who pay the heaviest price in terms of their human rights.

This book engages with the public policy strand of the last decade that has arguably most shaped perceptions of human rights and engendered debates about their worth and meaning. It will be of interest to researchers, academics, practitioners, and students in the fields of human rights law, criminal justice, criminology, politics, and international studies.

Satvinder Singh Juss, PhD (Cantab), FRSA, is a Professor of Law at King's College London, a Barrister-at-Law practising from 3 Hare Court, Temple, London, and a Deputy Judge of the Upper Tribunal (IAC) in London and Birmingham, UK. He is a former Human Rights Fellow at Harvard Law School, Boston, USA.

Routledge Research in Human Rights Law

Available titles in this series include:

International Human Rights Law and Domestic Violence
The Effectiveness of International Human Rights Law
Ronagh McQuigg

The Right to Religious Freedom in International Law
Between Group Rights and Individual Rights
Anat Scolnicov

The Right to Development in International Law
The Case of Pakistan
Khurshid Iqbal

Global Health and Human Rights
Legal and Philosophical Perspectives
John Harrington and Maria Stuttaford

Human Rights, Constitutional law and Belonging
The Right to Equal Belonging in Democratic Society
Elena Drymiotou

Dignity, Degrading Treatment and Torture in Human Rights Law
The Ends of Article 3 of the European Convention on Human Rights
Elaine Webster

The Right to Housing in Law and Society
Nico Moons

Human Rights and America's War on Terror
Edited by Satvinder Juss

Beyond Human Rights and the War on Terror
Edited by Satvinder Juss

For more information about this series, please visit: www.routledge.com/Routledge-Research-in-Human-Rights-Law/book-series/HUMRIGHTSLAW

Beyond Human Rights and the War on Terror

Edited by
Satvinder S. Juss

Routledge
Taylor & Francis Group
LONDON AND NEW YORK

First published 2019
by Routledge

2 Park Square, Milton Park, Abingdon, Oxfordshire OX14 4RN
52 Vanderbilt Avenue, New York, NY 10017

Routledge is an imprint of the Taylor & Francis Group, an informa business

First issued in paperback 2020

British Library Cataloguing in Publication Data
A catalogue record for this book is available from the British Library

Library of Congress Cataloging-in-Publication Data
Names: Juss, Satvinder S. (Satvinder Singh), editor.
Title: Beyond human rights and the war on terror / edited by Satvinder S. Juss.
Description: Abingdon, Oxon ; New York, NY : Routledge, 2019. |
Series: Routledge research in human rights law | Includes bibliographical references and index.
Identifiers: LCCN 2018030647 | ISBN 9781138543775 (hardback)
Subjects: LCSH: Terrorism--Prevention--Law and legislation. | Terrorism (International law)
Classification: LCC K5256 .B49 2019 | DDC 344.05/32517--dc23
LC record available at https://lccn.loc.gov/2018030647

ISBN: 978-1-138-54377-5 (hbk)
ISBN: 978-0-367-51976-6 (pbk)

Typeset in Galliard
by Taylor & Francis Books

Contents

Contributors

Abdullah K. Al-Saud is Director of Research at the King Faisal Centre for Research and Islamic Studies, an Assistant Professor at Naif Arab University for Security Sciences, and an Associate Fellow at the International Centre for the Study of Radicalisation, King's College London.

Roberta Arnold is an Attorney and Lecturer on "Law and Terrorism" at the University of Lucerne (Switzerland). An affiliated visiting scholar of Franklin University Switzerland, she has previously been a Public Prosecutor in Canton Ticino and a Military Investigating Magistrate (Switzerland).

Lord Carlile, CBE, QC, FRSA, is a crossbench member of the House of Lords and the former independent reviewer of terrorism legislation for the British government.

Willem Els is a Senior Training Coordinator at the Institute for Security Studies.

Martin Ewi is the Technical Coordinator and Regional Organised Crime Observatory Coordinator for Southern Africa for the ENACT Project at the Institute for Security Studies (ISS), Pretoria, having previously served as Senior Researcher for Counter-Terrorism with the Transnational Threats and International Crime Programme at the ISS.

Nadirsyah Hosen is a Senior Lecturer at the Faculty of Law, Monash University.

Satvinder S. Juss is a Professor of Law at King's College London and a former Human Rights Fellow at Harvard Law School, Boston.

Ivan Lidarev is a PhD student at King's College London and an advisor to Bulgaria's National Assembly.

Stuart Macdonald is a Professor and a Co-Director of Swansea University's EPSRC-funded £7.6m CHERISH Digital Economy Centre and Director of the university's multidisciplinary cyberterrorism research project.

Jeni Mitchell is a Teaching Fellow and postdoctoral researcher at King's College London specializing in civilian victimization by non-state armed groups.

Harsh V. Pant is Professor of International Relations in the Defence Studies Department and the India Institute at King's College, London. Presently, he is Director, Studies and Head, Strategic Studies Programme at Observer Research Foundation, New Delhi.

Sudha Setty is the Dean and a Professor of Law at Western New England University School of Law. She has been a visiting scholar at the University of Cape Town and a Fulbright Senior Specialist at the Chinese University of Hong Kong.

James C. Simeon is the Head of McLaughlin College and Associate Professor in the School of Public Policy and Administration, Faculty of Liberal Arts and Professional Studies, York University, Toronto.

George Williams is the Dean, the Anthony Mason Professor, and a Scientia Professor at the University of New South Wales Faculty of Law.

Foreword

When the terrorist attacks of 11 September 2001 occurred, I was judge at the Human Rights Chamber for Bosnia and Herzegovina in Sarajevo, a hybrid court established under the Dayton Peace Agreement of 1995 with the purpose of deciding on individual human rights complaints against the State of Bosnia and Herzegovina and its two entities. In October 2001, six Bosnian citizens of Algerian origin were arrested by the Bosnian police on suspicion of having planned a terrorist attack on the US embassy in Sarajevo. Since the Bush administration could not provide the Bosnian authorities with any evidence on which this suspicion (of the CIA) was allegedly based upon, a Bosnian court on 17 January 2002 ordered the release of these six men from pre-trial detention. However, instead of being released, they were again taken into custody by the Bosnian police and handed over to the US military forces, which were based in Bosnia and Herzegovina as part of the NATO-led Stabilization Force (SFOR) in accordance with the Dayton Peace Agreement. Since four of these men had also filed an application to the Human Rights Chamber, we had issued an interim order prohibiting the Bosnian authorities from allowing these men to be deported to the US. Despite various attempts by the High Representative for Bosnia and Herzegovina and European ambassadors to convince the US authorities to comply with a binding order by the highest court in Bosnia and Herzegovina, which was after all established on the basis of the US-brokered Dayton Peace Agreement with the task of developing the rule of law in this post-socialist and post-conflict country, the US forces ignored our binding order and transferred the six men to their military detention centre at Guantánamo Bay, which had been opened by Defense Secretary Donald Rumsfeld only a few days before. These six men spent many years in Guantánamo Bay without ever being formally charged with any criminal offence before their eventual release, one of them on the basis of a landmark judgment by the US Supreme Court (*Boumediene v. Bush*, 2008). In September 2002, the Chamber adopted a judgment in which it found various human rights violations by the State and the Federation of Bosnia and Herzegovina (we had no jurisdiction over the US), including the principle of non-refoulement, as there was at that time a serious risk that the applicants could have been subjected to the death penalty by US military courts.

This blatant violation of international law was my first professional encounter with the consequences of the so-called "War on Terror", in which the Bush administration would "take off its gloves". When I was appointed as UN Special Rapporteur on Torture in October 2004, the "War on Terror" was in full operation, and I got immediately involved in a joint investigation of the human rights situation at Guantánamo Bay. After long and sometimes absurd negotiations with the US government about international law and independent fact-finding methods, we were finally invited to visit this infamous detention centre in December 2005. However, since Defense Secretary Rumsfeld was not willing to give us the necessary assurances that we could speak in private with the detainees, we finally rejected this invitation and carried out our investigation on the basis of a thorough legal analysis and extensive interviews with ex-Guantánamo detainees. In February 2006, we published our joint report, in which we had established serious violations of international human rights law applicable at Guantánamo Bay, including arbitrary detention and torture. As a consequence, we urged the Bush administration to immediately close this illegal detention facility. Although President Obama, immediately after taking office in January 2009, had signed an Executive Order with the aim of closing this detention facility within one year, it is still in operation.

During my six years as UN Special Rapporteur on Torture, I was constantly confronted with allegations of torture in many parts of the world as a consequence of the so-called "War on Terror". The attempts of the Bush administration to justify torture as the "lesser evil" and to openly undermine the absolute prohibition of torture had devastating effects in many other democratic and less democratic countries. I vividly remember a fairly escalated and emotional dispute with the former British Home Secretary Charles Clark in the British Houses of Parliament in early 2006, in which he openly stated that defending British security against terrorism was far more important than the prohibition of torture and refoulement. During my fact-finding mission to Jordan in 2006, the speaker of the Parliament asked me why I was criticizing the practice of torture in his country when even the US, the alleged epitome of Western democracy and human rights, openly practised and advocated torture in its "War on Terror". During our joint investigation of secret detention in the fight against terrorism, which was published in 2010 and led to angry reactions by many states in the UN Human Rights Council, we identified not less than 66 states in all world regions that had used secret detention in combating terrorism. Many of these states had closely cooperated with the US government by having permitted CIA "black sites" on their territory, including European states such as Poland, Romania, and Lithuania, having actively participated in illegal CIA "rendition" practices or having applied the most brutal torture practices in their own secret detention centres for the purpose of providing intelligence information to the US ("detention by proxy"). Many of our findings were later confirmed by the US Senate Intelligence Committee's Report on CIA torture, a part of which was released in December 2014.

In a recently published book which I edited together with Anne Charbord (*Using Human Rights to Counter Terrorism*, Elgar Studies in Human Rights, 2018), we use many practical examples to argue that a state's lack of respect for human rights is counter-productive and hinders its fight against terrorism. The authors of this book, who have a wide breath of experience with counter-terrorism work at a national and international level, examined various counter-terrorism measures, including mass digital surveillance, the use of drones and the practice of torture. Our analysis shows that a lack of accountability for human rights violations in these areas can be conducive to an increase in terrorist activity.

The current crisis of democracy, the rule of law and human rights has many root causes, including the neoliberal economic policies in times of rapid globalization which led to a dangerous level of economic inequality, to the outsourcing of core governmental functions to the private sector, including to private military and security companies, to failed and fragile states, to insecurity, armed conflicts, organized crime, terrorism, and other forms of radicalization and violent extremism. One of the most obvious root causes for the erosion of human rights, democracy, and the rule of law is the so-called "War on Terror", both at the global and the local level. By reviewing the human rights implications of anti-terrorism laws in a variety of countries in different world regions, the authors of the book *Beyond Human Rights and the War on Terror*, edited by Satvinder Juss, provide many alarming examples of the extent to which the so-called "Global War on Terrorism" has had detrimental effects on the rule of law, democracy and human rights in these countries as well as on the basic values on which the post-Second World War international architecture has been built.

Manfred Nowak

Manfred Nowak is Professor of International Human Rights at Vienna University, Secretary General of the European Inter-University Centre for Human Rights and Democratisation in Venice, and Independent Expert leading the UN Global Study on Children Deprived of Liberty. Between 2004 and 2010 he served as UN Special Rapporteur on Torture.

Preface

The purpose of this compilation of highly topical essays is to elucidate and unravel the persistent influence of the "War on Terror" on both the domestic laws of the countries under consideration and on international law in general as it is today. This is important because the interface between the "Global War on Terrorism" and the "local war on terror" is one that needs constant assessment and evaluation if one is to keep an eye on how the erosion of civil liberties has become the "new normal", following the horror of 9/11. It is also important because of the readiness, not just of Western, but also of non-Western countries, to resort to violence in a way that moved the world "beyond human rights and the War on Terror" to something much more ominous and eerie. This is perhaps not so altogether surprising because the "War on Terror" was never simply a "war" of counter-terrorism. If so, it could have been waged through complex amalgams of criminal justice systems, administrative mechanisms, and internationally agreed rules and norms. What the "War on Terror" was also pivotally concerned with was the forcible installing of liberal regimes in countries where they had never existed, not realizing that not only do they not work, but they had not even worked in the post-Communist world after the fall of the Iron Curtain in 1989. But the "War on Terror" was also a "war" within the divine temple of liberalism itself.

On the one hand, it gave way to what has become well recognized now, namely the unleashing of populist forces on both the far left and the far right, so that leaders from across the political divide were able to rise, such as the Labour Party's Jeremy Corbyn in the UK and Pablo Iglesias from the anti-austerity *Podemos* party in Spain, to Matteo Salvini, the leader of the Anti-Immigrant League, and Luigi Di Maio of the Five Star Movement in Italy (the latter being a founding member of the European Union, the world's eighth-largest economy, but poised to threaten European stability itself). On the other hand, it gave way to what is so far barely recognized, namely a miscreation and malformation of the liberal ideal that was transfigured in a naked and blatant attack on Western civilization's liberal way of life, as epitomized by Donald Trump and Victor Orban, and further afield by Narendra Modi of India and Recep Erdogan of Turkey, so that a falling away from tolerance, diversity, and human rights has begun to take shape. They epitomize the battle between "nationalists" and "globalists" that is leading to the defeat of liberal and universalist values. The "War on Terror" was in this sense a very real "war" on the goods of liberal democracy, forcing progressive liberalism to beat a retreat everywhere. Small wonder, then, that the "Third Way" internationalist approach to the world, as characterized by leaders such as Tony Blair and Gerhard Schröder, is a thing of the past for many of today's vulnerable and embattled societies.

Political oppression anywhere in the world is hyped up and given a notoriety that has rarely been seen since the Cold War, so that for the military elites of NATO, the UN, the US, and the UK, it can serve as an intolerable affront and a standing *casus belli*. Yet, institutions such as NATO, the European Union, and the World Trade Organization were crafted following the carnage of the Second World War by the triumphant powers precisely in order to maintain peace, not just through collective military strength but also through mutual prosperity and well-being. For 70 years this model of geo-political affairs dominated the international system, but its credo is now being challenged by a deluge of nationalism, xenophobia and religious intolerance, which is leading to the rise of authoritarian impulses that make our representative institutions looking increasingly fragile and ineffectual. This digest *Beyond Human Rights and the War on Terror* is intended to show how historical and political developments are now challenging the very basis of human rights; and that the "War on Terror" is now constructed explicitly as a "civilizational conflict" between a radical Islamist foe and a Judeo-Christian "West". In fact, a "war" is now being waged exactly as Bernard Lewis and Samuel Huntington had "predicted".

It is against this background that the "War on Terror" needs to be understood. Terror is not some hazy and mysterious or boundless and infinite menace ready to engulf us from everywhere. It is a narrative of normal historical conflict.[1] In times past, this is precisely how it was understood by governments when they spoke of insurrections, political assassinations, and civil wars that were epoch-making. Governments did not intermix all forms of political violence into a single terrorist threat. Our military leaders understood – what our political leaders are reluctant to do today – that political violence can never be entirely eliminated. Terror cannot end. It is this flawed understanding that has led to armed forces being sent into foolhardy and blunderingly fought wars that have left Western cities in a state of endless terrorist alert. It is hard to think of any gain to Western foreign interests that has come from these wars. Yet, humanitarian interventionists almost daily remain on the look-out for some global horror or other by which they can justify the curtailment of civil liberties at home and usher in ever more harsher "anti-terrorist" laws. In many cases, there has not been the remotest threat to the national sovereignty of many of these countries by any other state over the last decade and half that the "War on Terror" has been waging. Yet, they have come to adopt a bellicose and aggressive posture that has laid a heavy cost on civil liberties and fundamental freedoms.

1 See Satvinder Juss, "Terrorism and the Exclusion of Refugee Status in the UK", *Journal of Conflict & Security Law* (Vol. 17, No. 33, Winter 2012, pp. 465–499) at p. 468.

The aim of this anthology, of different chapters written by different authors but that are linked thematically, is two-fold.

First, it aims to demonstrate to policy-makers how the normalization of war powers has meant that the liberties that we take for granted have been so much eroded today, and how the roots of liberal democracy and universal human values can be salvaged and reasserted. It is hoped that this approach will appeal to the increasing numbers rallying against the sweep to power of the "alt-right" in many democracies in the world that are currently facing a backlash because of a public distrust of institutions, where the masses feel that they have been abandoned. In this return to "great power" politics what is needed is not a rejection of the liberal order but its enrichment with government policies that provide for sustainable security and economic progress. There are now so many interest groups – from domestic law-enforcement agencies to national security agencies and to military sections – who now rely on the "War on Terror" for their raison d'être that unless the normalization of war powers is questioned by policy-makers, the "War on Terror" looks set to continue in perpetuity. For the avoidance of doubt, this is not because terrorism will continue to be a problem but because so many jobs everywhere rely on the "War on Terror" continuing.

Second, the intention behind this anthology is to provide a review of the human rights implications of anti-terrorism laws in different countries. Given the increasing interest even in the US in foreign law, this volume is intended to function as a strong entry-way for comparativists. University professors can assign such an anthology, together with a primary reading text (along with primary sources such as statutes and cases), in a seminar on national security law. An anthology such as this, with self-contained chapters of roughly equal length, will be ideal for a seminar whereby each chapter can be assigned to one student to lead a class discussion. This should prove particularly valuable given the diversity and range of expertise that this volume brings together with a combination of senior academics and professors from the UK, US, Australia and further afield, along with practitioners and politicians. The chapters are timely, moreover, given the arrival of the "Trumpian era". There is already in existence a large body of work on terrorism and violations of human rights going back to the 1970s and the chapters in this book feeds in and out of this literature, as they do with the political science literature post 9/11. However, most of the academic discussions on the "War on Terror" and the impacts on human rights have focused traditionally on the period between 2004 and 2008. After that, we became more concerned and preoccupied with the global financial crisis. In the age of ISIS and Donald Trump, the pendulum has now swung back. The effects of populism and anti-elitism on the "War on Terror" are beginning to emerge and these are addressed in several chapters in this work. Furthermore, this compendium considers the responses to the "War on Terror" in Arab states, in the East and the Far East, together with the human rights implications in those countries in the "gloves-off" approach to countering terrorism, and its exacerbation of the human rights abuses overseas and in these countries specifically. The universal impact of the discourse on human rights, moreover, means that it is essential that there are these chapters on non-Western states who are at the forefront of the "War on Terror".

The book opens with three chapters on modernity's fixation with the terrorism label, and challenges the belief in modern societies that our present-day concerns with stability and sustainable security can be tackled through the prism of "terrorism"-targeted laws. Chapter 1 asks what qualifies as terrorism, Chapter 2 suggests that we risk undermining the values of negotiation and reconciliation if we are not careful, and Chapter 3 calls for a disaggregation of the violence that lies behind conflict-induced displacement and gives the example of refugees today. We may consider these three chapters first.

Chapter 1 opens with Sudha Setty's "Assessing Unconventional Applications of the 'Terrorism' label", where she engages in an enquiry into what acts qualify as terrorism today in a general sense. The question is important because of the way that the enormous power of the law and government is ratcheted up to meet its "threat". It is also important because international law itself has failed to define it fully. Indeed, lawmakers and judges struggle to understand the parameters and the application of the term. Herein, however, lies the problem, in her view, because it is this very ambiguity that has been used by politicians and government officials to increase public fear, reduce levels of scrutiny by other branches of government, and treat traditional non-terrorism crimes as terrorism. Therefore, this chapter explores some non-conventional applications of the label of "terrorism" from the US point of view before the application of the label of "terrorism" more broadly, such as in India, which has led to a religious bias against Muslims and the targeting of disfavoured political minorities, combined with extraordinary powers granted to the government to deal with the threat of terrorism. The author makes out a case for why this poses a serious risk to due process and the rule of law because of the persistence of India's expansive definition of terrorism where India is more focused on prosecuting "terrorist" threats than proscribing human rights abuses. She traces the legal developments of the Terrorist Affected Areas Act 1984 ("TAAA"), the Terrorist and Disruptive Activities (Prevention) Act 1985 ("TADA"), and the Prevention of Terrorism Act 2002 ("POTA"), by the end of which selective prosecutions of Muslims, the poor, members of tribal groups, civilian protestors, and Dalits as "terrorists" were becoming commonplace. POTA was therefore repealed and replaced by Unlawful Activities (Prevention) Act 2004 ("UAPA"). This statute itself was amended in 2012, only to make the definition of "terrorism" even broader, so that the definition of "security" and a threat to it now includes "economic security", which means "financial, monetary, and fiscal stability" but even more remarkably goes on to include "security of means of production and distribution, food security, livelihood security". Unsurprisingly, the author is concerned with the proliferation in Indian law with the "unconventional applications of the label of terrorism".

In Chapter 2, Nadirsyah Hosen describes how self-determination movements are often castigated as terrorist in his "Separatist, Not Terrorist: Case Studies from Southeast Asia". Today, what matters most, he argues, is not so much a definition of terrorism, but rather the effect of what is labelled terrorism, because as a label terrorism promotes a greater attention from the media and policy makers in the West. This in turn helps people to associate the term "terrorism" exclusively with fanatical, radical Islamic sects, and it is this that has distorted views towards organizational violence after 9/11. The author makes good his thesis by looking at two case studies. These illustrate the difficulties in distinguishing between terrorism and religious-separatist movements in Southeast Asia. These comprise, first, the organized violence in Patani and, second, the Mindanao. Both involve Muslim separatist groups. A third case study involves the separatist movement in Aceh and Papua Indonesia. While the main source of conflict in Papua is not about religion, like in Patani and Mindanao, the tension in Papua leads to a separatist movement. However, the conflict in Aceh involved Islamic communities, which made the Indonesian government treat the Aceh differently from the Papua conflict. The three case studies reveal how the use of the label "terrorism" in the name of national security is misconceived. This is because the threats posed by separatist movements cannot be solved by labelling them as "terrorist groups/organizations". There has to be a better way of dealing with radical Islamist and ethno-nationalist/separatist struggles, where there is in any event the absence of an agreement on what terrorism is, this making it difficult to delineate the boundaries between using ordinary criminal law as against specific anti-terrorism law. The experience of the south-east region, may offer a valuable non-western perspective in determining what may or may not constitute "terrorism", because it takes into account the unique social, political, economic and historical factors against the background of which each of the three separatist movements that are considered exist. It is important, Hosen argues, that we identify organisational demands, assess our optimal approaches, and minimise their impact in the international arena. Western ethnocentricity has, on the other hand, has served only to produce definitions of "terrorism" that are sensationalistic. What would serve our interests best, he suggests, is a decisive move away from policies of counter-terrorism and states-of-emergency, to policies of negotiation and reconciliation.

In Chapter 3, "The 'Refugee Warrior' in an Age of Revolutionary Violence", Satvinder S. Juss and Jeni Mitchell develop this line of thought further and show that even refugees from war-torn areas of the world all too often become engaged in vindicating rights of self-determination against oppressive regimes, so that if refugees are to be given the protection they deserve, it is important to recognize the emerging phenomenon of the "refugee warrior". In fact, because this aspect of refugees' lives is shrouded in much obscurity and obscurantism, they are often nowadays feared and resented. We should not be surprised, however, if refugees are both victims and perpetrators of violence. But although they may be engaged in "refugee-based insurgency" this does not make them, by that fact alone, "refugee-terrorists". It is necessary once again to move away from conventional stereotypes in the West of such people and to disaggregate the violence that lies behind conflict-induced displacement. The authors look at the legal basis for the exclusion of refugees who have committed a crime against peace, a war crime or a crime against humanity. This is to be found in Article 1(F) of the Geneva Convention Relating to the Status of Refugees 1951, as well as the Qualification Directive (2004/83/EC) in European Law. Yet, neither of these provisions tell us anything about the level of "responsibility" required of a person before it can be said that there are serious reasons for considering their exclusion from refugee status. It is for this reason that the emerging case law has asked decision-makers to apply these provisions of exclusion cautiously and restrictively. The authors then go on to give consideration to the "War on Terror" itself and how the post-9/11 developments have led to no less than three Security Council Resolutions in September, November, and December 2001, and then another one in September 2005. The emphasis in all has been on "acts, methods, and practices of terrorism", their "financing and planning" being "regardless of their motivation" and requiring states "to take urgent action" so as to "eliminate the scourge of terrorism". Once again, precisely what is meant by "terrorism" is not clear. Moreover, there is no recognition of the right of oppressed peoples to revolt and take up insurgent action against an oppressor or aggressor entity. A series of cases discussed show the courts grappling with these difficult questions. It is noted how there is recognition in the British cases of the legitimate use of violence for political ends which is often overlooked even in legal circles. Finally, the reader is taken by the authors to the "age of revolutionary violence" and reminded how, in both law and security studies, the context of violent behaviour is critical. The complexity of contemporary political violence and lack of firm normative frameworks mean that decision-makers have difficulty in understanding violence and the role of participants in it. This is important because today "terrorism" is invoked in a vast range of ideological and political acts, whereas previously it was confined to the narrow acts of such groups as non-state armed groups targeting civilians. The durability of the "terrorist" label today has implications for the unfair treatment of both civilians and fighters involved in conflict situations, in the view of the authors. Accordingly, the answer lies today in characterizing contemporary violence as "revolutionary violence", when seen in campaigns in the Middle East today by violent sub-state actors, in a quest for the radical transformation of the existing political and social order. This would in turn help the international community to fully comprehend the legitimacy and legality of acts of violence in conflict-ridden societies around us.

After these three introductory chapters, which engage in a discussion of the problem of "terrorism" as a workable concept in an increasingly complex and multi-polar world, this compendium moves on to consider the specific threat from ISIS in the world today in the following three chapters. Chapter 4 deals with the origin and the nerve centre of ISIS in Saudi Arabia. Chapter 5 considers how when such terror is exported; for example, to a country like Switzerland, law-enforcement and anti-terrorism policies compete with each other for the attainment of peace and security. Chapter 6 considers how the UK has enacted "terrorism precursor offences", so that non-criminal methods of disrupting terrorist activity are prioritized, such as asset-freezing and proscription, but which it is argued need greater legislative restraint. We may now consider the next three chapters in more detail.

In Chapter 4, "The ISIL Jihadists of Saudi Arabia", Abdullah K. Al-Saud offers a rare and unique account from the Middle East of how jihadist groups have arisen, particularly ISIL in Saudi Arabia. He considers how we can explain the relative rise in recent years of radicalization and Salafi-jihadist ideology in the province of al-Qassim in Saudi Arabia. This has seen a sharp increase in the number of Saudi ISIL foreign fighters in comparison to other regions when the numbers are indexed to each region's population size. The province known as al-Qassim is at the heart of the Najd region in Saudi Arabia, and it is known as the "agricultural basket" of the country. It is one of the thirteen administrative regions of Saudi Arabia and the seventh most populated region in the country. It has come to be regarded as the centre of the Salafi movement. Al-Saud focuses on this area, not only because it has seen a high ratio of ISIL recruits from al-Qassim, but because of the nature of the upsurge in this region, which is qualitatively and quantitatively different from the earlier waves of Saudi Arabian foreign fighters. Given that the process of radicalization is complex and not reducible to a single cause or factor, Al-Saud explores three possible explanations for this difference. First is the *Fukkio al-'Ani* (set free the captive) campaign, which arose in the social media in the post-Arab Spring environment and sought to capitalize on the prevalent mood of rebellion at the time. Publically, the campaign focused on issues of human rights and the release of "political prisoners", but many of its organizers and supporters had more ominous and nefarious aims. It did not take extremists, who were longing for radical change in Saudi Arabia, long to join the campaign, and this resulted in marches and sit-ins that were mainly organized in the al-Qassim region and its main city of Buraydah. The second possible explanation is the role of facilitators and social networks, which argue that highly influential early travellers from the al-Qassim province to the Syrian conflict may have become very instrumental in garnering support, recruiting, facilitating, and connecting the local (al-Qassim) to the transnational (Syria and Iraq). Lastly, the role of a local group of Saudi neo-jihadi scholars, several of whom have come from the al-Qassim province, is explored as a reason for the distinct nature of this particular wave of jihadi fighters from the country. In the end, however, whereas terrorists come from different locations with different social backgrounds, and whilst they may have complex grievances, making them vulnerable and susceptible to recruitment, it is imperative, argues Al-Saud, to have deep contextual knowledge behind the complex process of radicalization if we are to be successful in devising solutions that can disrupt terrorist networks.

The challenge posed by ISIS is also considered in Chapter 5 by Roberta Arnold who provides a Swiss example in "The Criminal Implications of the 'War on Terror' and the Status of 'Foreign Fighters': A Swiss Perspective". The emphasis here is on prioritizing law-enforcement techniques over ant-terrorism mechanism. The Swiss government too, she argues, has made efforts to grapple with the geographical boundaries of the "War on Terror" and to inquire into the status of those involved in it. Accordingly, Arnold asks whether the "foreign fighters" supporting ISIS in Syria (where, as Al-Saud had shown, many Saudi fighters end up) also share the status of those promoting the movement elsewhere, such as in Europe. Her chapter analyses the legislative counter-terrorism measures adopted by Switzerland recently, including the Anti-IS Federal Act of 12 December 2012, the Federal Law on the Federal Intelligence Service of 1 January 2017, and the legislative amendment proposals of June 2017. It then discusses the outcomes of the first judgment of the Swiss Federal Criminal Tribunal based on the Anti-IS Federal Act, which was rendered on 15 July 2016 and confirmed on 22 February 2017 by the Swiss Federal Tribunal (FT). It concludes with the observation that the recent Swiss efforts are to be welcomed because, as highlighted in the Third TETRA (TErrorist TRAcking) Report, an interdisciplinary and global approach is taken to the fight against terrorism. This approach sets out to identify and solve the problem at its roots. It proposes solutions that have positive mid- and long-term effects (e.g. with regard to de-radicalization). The way this is done is by the effective exchange of information between law-enforcement authorities and the intelligence services because recourse to "armed conflict" norms is unhelpful given that the notion of the "War on Terror" has no legal foundation under international law, as noted by the ICRC.

In Chapter 6, "Disrupting Terrorist Activity: What Are the Limits to Criminal Methods of Disruption?", Stuart Macdonald and Lord Carlisle make a plea for the greater use of the criminal law. They draw attention to how the UK has enacted a large number of "terrorism precursor offences", which it is argued need greater legislative restraint. This is explained by an analysis of three non-criminal methods of disrupting terrorist activity: terrorism prevention and investigation measures (TPIMs); asset-freezing; and proscription. Four sets of concerns about them are then discussed explaining why they are regarded as less desirable in principle than prosecution. Whilst the authors agree that terrorism precursor offences are needed for the sake of prevention, the wide range of such offences currently in force in the UK go too far in pursuit of this objective. They argue that the same concerns that apply to the non-criminal methods of disruption apply also to terrorism precursor offences. This is counter-productive, for it risks undermining the very features of the criminal law that give such laws its unique moral authority and legitimacy. It is, in the authors' view, self-defeating to create offences in the name of prioritizing prosecution if those same offences undermine the basis on which prosecution is prioritized in the first place.

Finally, towards the end of this anthology, we return to how the fight against terrorism still prioritizes counter-terrorism initiatives through anti-terrorism laws, and this is most evident in countries like Canada, Australia, South Africa, and India. Chapter 7 shows that most advanced liberal democracies are converging in their laws so that they defer to the government to take the lead in the battle against terrorism, and the example of Canada is given. Chapter 8 gives the example of Australia, a latecomer to anti-terrorism laws, but which has had no qualms in imposing restrictions on freedom of speech, creation of new sedition offences and censorship rules, and introduction of detention without trial. Chapter 9 explains that even South Africa, which has experienced no major terrorist incident, now has systems, procedures, and governmental agencies that are responsible for the interception, investigation, prosecution, and adjudication of terrorist-related crimes. Chapter 10 focuses on India's experimentation with a muscular counter-terror policy, only for it to realize that not only has it been ineffective, but that there are now new terrorist threats from global organizations, such as al-Qaeda and ISIS, which it faces, requiring a more nuanced approach, thus bringing us full circle in this collection of essays to how we started off. So, let us consider in more detail the last four chapters.

Chapter 7 by James C. Simeon, titled "Terrorism Law in Canada: Combatting Terrorism through the Defense of Human Rights", is an excellent analysis of how terrorism should be understood. He explains how the legal definition of the crime of terrorism in Canada is found in the extensive provisions of the Canadian Criminal Code 1985, which covers everything from the definition of terrorism to the financing of terrorism, the freezing, seizing and restraint, and forfeiture of property, to a hoax regarding terrorist activity, proceedings and aggravated punishment, investigative hearing, and recognizance and conditions. The Canadian definition of terrorism is in two parts: terrorist activity and terrorist group. In Canada, the focus is on "an act or omission that is committed in or outside Canada". Canada appears to have the most international definition that draws explicitly on the UN Conventions and Protocols that deal with specific acts of terrorism. Defining what constitutes a terrorist activity by drawing on these international instruments certainly internationalizes the Canadian criminal code definition of the crime of terrorism. This is further reinforced by the explicit exclusion of such activities during an armed conflict provided that they are consistent with the applicable international laws. This is interesting as there are no such references to these in either the UK or the US legislation. The Canadian government is in the process of amending its terrorism laws with the introduction of a new 2017 National Security Act. Interestingly, in Canada mere membership of a terrorist organization is actually sufficient to make a foreign national or permanent resident inadmissible to Canada under IRPA s. 34(1)(f). Yet, what is surprising in this context is that the Canadian judiciary has still not failed to lay emphasis on the protection of human rights. The list of fundamental human rights set out in the Canadian Charter of Rights and *Freedoms* enabled the Supreme Court to ensure that an accused's constitutionally entrenched human rights and freedoms are not infringed. Given that the prosecution of terrorism cases is one of the most effective counter-terrorism strategies employed by states, the Supreme Court has required of the Canadian government that it does not exceed its legal and constitutional authority and that human rights are promoted to the highest degree. At the same time, however, it has recognized that national security too must be protected to the maximum degree possible. Nevertheless, in Canada it is the protection and advancement of fundamental human rights that has been the key to enhancing national security in a liberal democracy. Simeon's chapter is a much needed perspective for our modern polarized times when the maintenance of state security is often juxtaposed against the protection of fundamental human rights for all.

In Chapter 8, "Human Rights and Anti-Terror Laws in Australia", George Williams asks whether Australia needed to enact national anti-terror laws in the wake of September 11. This is because such laws have led to human rights being compromised. He undertakes a detailed examination of the laws actually enacted and the capacity of the Australian legal system to subject those laws to scrutiny on human rights grounds. The chapter is important because, as the author explains,

Australia came relatively late to enacting national anti-terror laws. It had no such laws prior to the September 11 attacks. Afterwards, however, it swiftly enacted new legislation of unprecedented reach. This has led to restrictions on freedom of speech through new sedition offences and censorship rules; the detention and questioning for up to a week by the Australian Security Intelligence Organisation (ASIO) of Australian citizens not suspected of any crime; the banning of organizations by executive decision; control orders that can enable house arrest for up to a year; detention without charge or trial for up to 14 days; and warrantless searches of private property by police officers. In fact, powers and sanctions once thought to lie outside the rules of a liberal democracy except during wartime have now become part of the Australian legal system. At the same time, these laws raise important questions about the protection of human rights, and the capacity of the Australian legal system to operate as a system of checks and balances on the unrestrained use of executive power.

The same concerns are raised in Chapter 9 by Martin Ewi and Willem Els in their "The Legacy of Apartheid and South Africa's Struggle to Contain Contemporary Forms of Terrorism and Violent Extremism", where they argue that although South Africa has not experienced a major terrorist attack in nearly 20 years now, there have been a series of warnings from foreign governments about the potential for terrorist attacks in South Africa. These have generated a great deal of debate, and sometimes panic among South Africans, about their capability to deal with such a terrorist threat. However, as they point out, South Africa's counter-terrorism measures, and the institutions of government that work tirelessly to avert the threat, has often gone unnoticed. Ewi and Els set out to fill this information void, by explaining how the South African government is organized internally to counter the prevailing threat of terrorism and violent extremism. They then identify and provide an overview of the systems, procedures, and governmental agencies responsible for the interception, investigation, prosecution, adjudication, and policy coordination on matters relating to counter-terrorism and the countering of violent extremism. Ewi and Els use the Henry Okah trial as a case study before concluding that South Africa has developed a reliable architecture for dealing with terrorism and violent extremism.

In Chapter 10, "Indian Counterterrorism and the Influence of the Global War on Terror", Harsh V. Pant and Ivan Lidarev suggest that India's approach to counter-terrorism has been influenced by the Global War on Terror (GWOT). This has meant that India has adopted a localized, defensive, law-and-order approach to counter-terrorism, using its internal security and legal apparatus. This approach itself has evolved in response to various attacks over the years. However, the authors argue that it still remains underdeveloped and incoherent due to domestic politics and bureaucratic resistance. Nevertheless, as a major target of Islamist terrorism, India has stood at the forefront of the GWOT. What is noteworthy is that India's terrorist threat has come primarily from local groups, either home-grown or Pakistan-based. For this reason, Delhi has refrained from combating global terrorism on the international stage, as the US and Britain have done. Instead, India has fought in the GWOT by waging its own "local war on terror". The question now, the authors ask, is whether the time has come for India to change its approach to counter-terrorism. One sobering thought, however, is that Indian counter-terrorism has produced few successes and it has neither checked home-grown terrorism, nor persuaded Pakistan to cease its support for terrorists. This is despite Delhi experimenting with a more muscular counter-terror policy, for instance after the Uri attacks in 2016. It is also noteworthy that the terrorist threat that India faces is changing. Global terrorist organizations, such as al-Qaeda and ISIS, now target the subcontinent, while militants returning from the Middle East threaten to revitalize India's home-grown Islamist movement. Pant and Lidarev conclude that presently it is not readily evident if Indian counter-terrorism policy as it stands currently can effectively address these threats. Indian counter-terrorism policy therefore increasingly stands at a crossroads today.

In ending this Preface, one could add to this chastening thought that so must it be true of a great many of the world's countries, as we go into an epoch "beyond the War on Terror", that counter-terrorism policy is increasingly and invariably at a crossroads today.

I would like to thank my authors for so ardently agreeing to participate in this project and I trust that readers will find these accounts enlightening, stirring and alarming in equal measure. I would like to record my praise and gratitude to Ghogi for the strategic support rendered in difficult circumstances. I would also like to thank my publisher Routledge, and especially Senior Editor Alison Kirk, as well as Seth Townley and Neil Dowden, for their abundant support for the production of two edited books of mine on terrorism at the same time. The other book, the prequel to this, is *Human Rights and America's War on Terror*, which tracks the development of anti-terror laws in America following 9/11 and the impact of these on human rights. I thank Alexandra Buckley for her attentive and conscientious overseeing of this project. And, finally, I would like to record my deep gratitude to Manfred Nowak, the former United Nations Special Rapporteur for Torture, for his impressive Foreword, written at my request at such short notice.

Satvinder S. Juss
4 June 2018

1 Assessing unconventional applications of the "terrorism" label

Sudha Setty[1]

Introduction

When the government deems a situation to involve anything labeled as "terrorism," a lot of things happen. Resources that are not available in other contexts are made available for the government to investigate and surveil suspects. The legal authority of the government to investigate, detain, interrogate, and punish increases dramatically. The right of the public to access information about the government's actions diminishes significantly. The willingness of legislatures and judges to engage in meaningful oversight wanes. The sense of fear experienced by much of the public, as well as the societal stigma associated with the underlying suspect behavior, skyrockets.

Fully understanding what acts qualify as terrorism such that the enormous power of the law and the government ratchets up is essential. Yet international law has failed to define it fully, and lawmakers and judges in numerous countries struggle to understand the parameters and the application of the term. This ambiguity has been used by politicians and government officials for a variety of goals: sometimes to increase public fear and reduce levels of scrutiny by other branches of government,[2] sometimes to recognize a traditionally underfunded or politically marginal issue as "terrorism" in a good faith effort to increase public attention and resources, but sometimes for political manipulation such that non-terrorism crimes are redefined as terrorism, bringing with it all of the consequences that follow.

This chapter explores some non-conventional applications of the label of "terrorism" and considers calls for continued expansion of the definition of terrorism to encompass crimes that have not traditionally been considered terrorism.[3]

1 I am grateful to Matthew H. Charity and Surabhi Chopra for suggestions and comments, and to Renee Rastorfer for excellent research assistance. I thank the Fulbright Senior Specialist program and the Centre for Rights and Justice at the Chinese University of Hong Kong Faculty of Law for their support as I began work on this Chapter.

2 See A. Trevor Thrall and Erik Goepner, Trump's Terrorism Fearmongering vs. the Facts, Cato Institute (Feb. 22, 2017), available at www.cato.org/publications/commentary/trumps-terrorism-fearmongering-vs-facts.

3 Some analysis here is drawn from a previous work: Sudha Setty, What's in a Name? How Nations Define Terrorism Ten Years After 9/11, 33 *U. Penn. J. Int'l L.* 1 (2011) (analyzing definitions of terrorism as developed and used on an international, comparative, and domestic level).

The first part briefly lays out the working definition of terrorism on an international level, and the gray areas in which individual nations make their own determinations as to what constitutes terrorism and what is instead considered ordinary crime.

The second part focuses on the definitions of terrorism under a number of common counterterrorism statutes in U.S. federal law, and then considers contexts that fall outside of the common usage terrorism in the context of U.S. law, exploring instances in which gang violence and animal rights-based crimes are treated legally as terrorism.[4]

The third part briefly considers the application of the label of "terrorism" in India, where concerns that broad and vague definitions of terrorism, religious bias against Muslims, and targeting of disfavored political minorities, combined with extraordinary powers granted to the government to deal with the threat of terrorism, pose a serious risk to due process and the rule of law.

Some have called on governments to continue to broaden the reach of counterterrorism law to reach other issues, such as sex trafficking[5] or some mass shootings.[6] This chapter concludes that most such efforts are founded in a good faith belief that the resources available to counterterrorism efforts will benefit other social justice causes,[7] while some efforts are backed by powerful groups with

4 These issues serve only as exemplars of the many unconventional contexts in which the federal government has identified the threat of terrorism. See, e.g., Jerome P. Bjelopera, *The Domestic Terrorist Threat: Background and Issues for Congress*, Congressional Research Service, Jan. 17, 2013, available at http://fas.org/sgp/crs/terror/R42536.pdf (visited Oct. 16, 2014) (listing anarchism, white supremacy, anti-government ideals, black separatism, and anti-abortion beliefs as additional areas in which the government has evinced heightened concern over terrorism). Further, the question of whether counterterrorism statutes have unconstitutionally criminalized speech and expressive conduct is a related but separate question from what this chapter addresses.

5 Human trafficking is already conflated with terrorism in particular sections of U.S. law. See Intelligence Reform and Terrorism Prevention Act of 2004: Title VII—Implementation of the 9/11 Commission Recommendations, Subtitle B—Terrorist Travel and Effective Screening, §7202 (2004) (establishing a Human Smuggling and Trafficking Center, in accordance with recommendations of the 9/11 Commission). Calls for the treatment of sexual violence as "terrorism" go back at least two decades. See, e.g., Carole J. Sheffield, Sexual Terrorism, in Jo Freeman, ed., *Women: A Feminist Perspective* 409, 409–10 (5th ed., Mayfield Publishing Co., 1995). Sheffield analyzes rape, spousal abuse, sexual abuse of children, and sexual harassment as four forms of "sexual terrorism," and identifies several more, including threats of violence, stalking, coercive sex, pornography, prostitution, sexual slavery and femicide. Id. at 412.

6 See Brian Michael Jenkins and Richard C. Daddario, Think Mass Shootings Are Terrorism? Careful What You Wish For, *Politico* (Nov. 7, 2017), www.politico.com/magazine/story/2017/11/07/think-mass-shootings-are-terrorism-careful-what-you-wish-for-215797 (countering arguments that the October 2017 mass shooting in Las Vegas, in which 58 people were killed, should be considered a terrorist attack).

7 E.g., L.Z. Granderson, Treat Chicago Gangs as Terrorists, CNN, Apr. 24, 2013, available at http://edition.cnn.com/2013/04/24/opinion/granderson-chicago-terror/ (lamenting that the level of resources often allocated toward counterterrorism efforts is not also directed at gang violence).

political influence. However, because in many democratic nations terrorism is granted unique legal treatment as an area in which expansive government power with lessened oversight and protection for individual rights is considered acceptable, importing such standards into other contexts is inviting a distortion of the traditional limits on governmental power and would allow for increases in government abuse and overreach.

The Definitional Dilemma

The quest to establish a universal definition of terrorism is entangled in law, history, philosophy, morality, and religion. Many believe that the definitional question is, by nature, a subjective one that eludes large-scale consensus. However, to address the problem of terrorist activity, the law must first define terrorism's parameters. This foundational question is of the utmost importance in determining who a state, nation, or international body will consider a terrorist and, therefore, who will be subject to the stricter laws, diminished rights protections, and harsher penalties that are concomitant with the designation of "terrorism." For example, in different jurisdictions, the designation of terrorist activity could result in the criminalization of otherwise protected speech,[8] a significant delay in access to counsel and other criminal due-process protections,[9] trial in a specialized court with fewer protections for defendants,[10] and, if convicted, significantly enhanced sentences for crimes.[11]

8 See, e.g., *Holder v. Humanitarian Law Project*, 130 S. Ct. 2705 (2010) (holding constitutional under the First Amendment a Patriot Act provision which made it unlawful to provide material support and assistance to organizations deemed terrorists, even where such support was nonviolent).

9 For example, in 2010, U.S. Attorney General Eric Holder shifted the Justice Department's policy with regard to the public safety exception articulated in *N.Y. v. Quarles*, 467 U.S. 649 (1984). Quarles held that the obligation of law-enforcement officers to inform arrestees of their right to counsel, among other *Miranda* rights, was subject to a public safety exception under certain circumstances. Holder's new policy articulation focused on the "magnitude and complexity of the threat often posed by terrorist organizations" and concomitant need for leeway in interrogation procedures as justification for delaying the reading of *Miranda* rights to suspects. *See* Attorney General Eric Holder, Jr., *Guidance for Conducting Interviews without Providing* Miranda *Warnings in Arrests of Terrorism Suspects*, U.S. Department of Justice, Oct. 19, 2010. A high-profile application of this policy occurred in conjunction with the interrogation of Dzhokhar Tsarnaev, one of the attackers in the April 2013 bombing at the Boston Marathon. See Charlie Savage, Debate over Delaying of Miranda Warning, *The New York Times*, Apr. 20, 2013, available at www.nytimes.com/2013/04/21/us/a-debate-over-delaying-suspects-miranda-rights.html?_r=0.

10 See generally Sudha Setty, Comparative Perspectives on Specialized Trials for Terrorism, 63 *Me. L. Rev.* 131 (2010) (discussing how specialized trials for terrorism in India allow for otherwise inadmissible evidence to be used against the defendant, place unusual limits on the right of the defendant to consult with counsel, and, in some cases, allow for burden shifting on the weight of evidence before the court).

11 See, e.g., U.S. Sentencing Guidelines Manual, 18 U.S.C. Appx. 3A1.4 (allowing for sentence enhancement for federal terrorism crimes). See also Wadie E. Said, Sentencing

The definitional ambiguity surrounding terrorism, along with the heightened legal and societal consequences of being designated as a terrorist, gives rise to international concern that governments will undercut civil liberties and civil rights by defining terrorism in an overly broad manner, allowing them to unfairly punish those who would not, in most situations, be considered by the international community as "terrorists."[12]

The United Nations General Assembly has tried to establish an internationally accepted definition of terrorism numerous times since the 1960s,[13] with the belief that "the effectiveness of the struggle against terrorism could be enhanced by the establishment of a generally agreed definition of international terrorism."[14] Each effort, however, failed based on the perceived subjectivity of any such definition, with some countries seeking exemptions for freedom-fighting or anti-colonial violence,[15] and others seeking to ensure that state-sponsored violence is not categorized as terrorism.[16] Nevertheless, almost all nations agreed that the definition of "terrorism" included common core elements such as the purposeful killing of civilians.

With a strong post-September 11 mandate to establish robust counterterrorism measures,[17] but without universal definition of terrorism on which to depend, the United Nations Security Council has established partial measures, such as including general descriptions of acts that fall within the rubric of terrorist activity without purporting to fully define terrorism. One working definition used by the United Nations is:

Terrorist Crimes, 75 *Ohio St. L. J.* 477 (2014) (describing how terrorism-related crimes carry significantly greater sentences than their non-terrorism counterparts).

12 See U.N. Econ. & Soc. Council, Comm'n on Human Rights, Report of the Special Rapporteur on the Promotion and Protection of Human Rights and Fundamental Freedoms While Countering Terrorism, pp. 26–27, U.N. Doc. E/CN.4/2006/98 (Sept. 28, 2005), at 27 ("[R]epeated calls by the international community for action to eliminate terrorism, in the absence of a universal and comprehensive definition of the term, may give rise to adverse consequences for human rights").

13 The search for a supranational definition of terrorism dates at least back to 1937, when the League of Nations considered the Convention for the Prevention and Punishment of Terrorism, Nov. 16, 1938, 19 League of Nations O. J. 23. Article 1(2) of the proposed Convention defined terrorism as "criminal acts directed against a State and intended or calculated to create a state of terror in the minds of particular persons, or a group of persons or the general public." Id. art. 1(2).

14 G.A. Res. 42/159, U.N. Doc. A/RES/42/159 (Dec. 17, 1987).

15 Alex Schmid, Terrorism—The Definitional Problem, 36 *Case W. Res. J. Int'l L.* 375, 386 (2004).

16 See Bruce Hoffman, *Inside Terrorism* 35 (Columbia University Press, 1998) (arguing that state-sponsored actions may be distinguished from terrorism because such actions can be deemed violations of international law or military rules of engagement and prosecuted accordingly as war crimes).

17 See S.C. Res. 1373, U.N. Doc. S/RES/1373 (Sept. 28, 2001) (mandating that all U.N. harsher sentencing for terrorist acts, freezing funds of those financing terrorist acts, sharing intelligence information with other member nations, and tightening border controls to prevent the migration of terrorists).

> Terrorism is, in most cases, essentially a political act. It is meant to inflict dramatic and deadly injury on civilians and to create an atmosphere of fear, generally for a political or ideological (whether secular or religious) purpose. Terrorism is a criminal act, but it is more than mere criminality.[18]

Security Council Resolution 1566 offers this partial definition:

> criminal acts, including against civilians, committed with the intent to cause death or serious bodily injury, or taking of hostages, with the purpose to provoke a state of terror in the general public or in a group of persons or particular persons, intimidate a population or compel a government or an international organization to do or to abstain from doing any act, which constitute offences within the scope of and as defined in the international conventions and protocols relating to terrorism … .[19]

Although seemingly expansive, Resolution 1566 limits the use of the label of "terrorism" to offenses that are recognized in previously agreed-upon international conventions and protocols, thereby tethering the implementation of Resolution 1566 to offenses commonly understood to fall under the umbrella of terrorism. Further, the language of the resolution limits its application to acts that are intended to provoke terror and/or compel a political response from a government.

Even with these interpretive limitations, the Security Council went further in protecting individuals and organizations from inappropriate designation as "terrorists" given the harsh consequences of such a designation. The Security Council designated an Ombudsperson to field petitions from individuals and organizations seeking to be delisted from being subject to international sanctions as terrorists.[20] Concerned about the severe repercussions of being designated as a terrorist, various Member States also moved to make the designation process more transparent, allowing for a challenge and delisting process for individuals and organizations, and strengthening international security by bolstering the perceived legitimacy of the United Nations as a regulator of security matters.[21]

18 *Measures to Eliminate International Terrorism: Report of the Policy Working Group on the United Nations and Terrorism*, U.N. GA/SCOR, 57th Sess., Annex at para. 13, U.N. Doc. A/57/273-S/2002/875 (2002).

19 See S.C. Res. 1566, P 1, U.N. Doc. S/RES/1566, at ¶ 3 (Oct. 8, 2004) (condemning all forms of terrorism, regardless of its motivations).

20 See S.C. Res. 1904, P 20, U.N. Doc. S/RES/1904 (Dec. 17, 2009) (mandating that "when considering delisting requests, the [Counter-Terrorism] Committee shall be assisted by an Office of the Ombudsperson").

21 E.g., Press Release, Security Council, Security Council Amends United Nations Al-Qaida/Taliban Sanctions Regime, Authorizes Appointment of Ombudsperson to Handle Delisting Issues, P 14, U.N. Press Release SC/9825 (Dec. 17, 2009), available at www.un.org/News/Press/docs/2009/sc9825.doc.htm (noting the concern of delegations from various nations that the process of designating terrorists be made more accessible, transparent, and equitable).

Non-traditional applications of "terrorism" in the United States

In the United States, federal law and agencies utilize dozens of different definitions of terrorism based on the function of the agency and the purpose for which the definition is used.[22] Two commonly used federal definitions can be found in the Anti-Terrorism and Effective Death Penalty Act of 1996 (AEDPA)[23] and the USA PATRIOT Act ("Patriot Act") of 2001,[24] and they are worth considering here in terms of applying "terrorism" to conventional and unconventional contexts.

The AEDPA was enacted in response to the 1993 World Trade Center bombings and the 1995 bombing of the Alfred P. Murrah Federal Building in Oklahoma City as part of a broader plan to prevent material support to terrorists that was seen as essential to those bombings. Under the AEDPA, terrorism is defined as:

> An activity that involves a violent act or an act dangerous to human life, property, or infrastructure, and appears to be intended to intimidate or coerce a civilian population; to influence the policy of a government by intimidation or coercion; or to affect the conduct of government by mass destruction, assassination, kidnapping, or hostage-taking.[25]

The AEDPA is a wide-reaching statute, defining terrorism for the purpose of designating Foreign Terrorist Organizations (FTOs) and freezing the assets of such organizations.[26] The consequences of FTO designation can be severe—financial intuitions may block or freeze assets of an FTO,[27] individuals may be barred from entry into the United States,[28] and material support to such an

22 See Nicholas J. Perry, The Numerous Federal Legal Definitions of Terrorism: The Problem of Too Many Grails, 30 *J. Legis.* 249, 249–50 (2004) (examining 22 definitions of terrorism under U.S. federal law).

23 See Antiterrorism and Effective Death Penalty Act of 1996 (AEDPA), Pub. L. No. 104–132, 110 Stat. 1217 (codified in scatter sections of 8, 18, and 28 U.S.C.) (authorizing the Secretary to designate foreign organizations as terrorists if they engage in terrorist activity as defined by the statute).

24 Uniting and Strengthening America by Providing Appropriate Tools Required to Intercept and Obstruct Terrorism Act of 2001, Pub. L. No. 107–56, 115 Stat. 272 (codified as amended in scattered sections of U.S.C.) [hereinafter Patriot Act].

25 See Exec. Order No. 13224, 31 C.F.R. 594 (explaining Congressional findings and purpose).

26 See, e.g., AEDPA §§ 219(a)(1)(A)-(C), 219(a)(2)(C) (codified in 8 USC §1189(a)) (finding that anyone who interacts with FTOs is violating the statute, and authorizing the Secretary of the Treasury to freeze the assets of entities designated as FTOs). President Clinton signed Executive Order 12,947 in January 1995, which was geared toward facilitating a peace agreement in the Middle East, but gave broad authority to cabinet departments to designate Foreign Terrorist Organizations (FTOs) with the purpose of disrupting their financial and operational capabilities, thereby laying the foundation for the authority granted under the AEDPA.

27 18 U.S.C. § 2339B(a)(2) (2006).

28 8 U.S.C. §§ 1182(a)(3)(B)(i)(IV)–(V) (2006).

organization is a criminal offense carrying potentially lengthy prison sentences.[29] Therefore, the procedural safeguards for erroneous designation, however limited, are crucial.

One such safeguard in the FTO designation process is the opportunity to contest the designation proposed by the State Department. This layer of judicial review offers some protection against arbitrariness in the designation that might otherwise constitute a substantive due process violation, and requires some disclosure of the basis upon which the State Department made its determination.[30] A second important safeguard is the mandatory review and renewal process: at least every five years, the State Department must review the designation to determine whether it should be revoked based on changes to the organization's actions or in the national security assessment by the United States.[31] These safeguards echo the review and delisting process that the United Nations adopted to improve procedural protections against erroneously being labeled as a terrorist and suffering the ramifications of that inappropriate designation.

The Patriot Act is also a reactive statute, passed in immediate response to the September 11, 2001 attacks. It includes a panoply of counterterrorism resources for the government: an increase in surveillance powers and government authority to conduct intelligence-gathering operations in matters of suspected terrorism, allowing for the civil seizure of assets based only on probable cause, heightened punishments for any of the underlying crimes related to the newly broadened understanding of "domestic terrorism," and numerous other powers.

The Patriot Act definition of terrorism includes:

> [A]cts dangerous to human life that are a violation of the criminal laws of the United States or of any State [that] appear to be intended to intimidate or coerce a civilian population; to influence the policy of a government by intimidation or coercion; or to affect the conduct of a government by mass destruction, assassination, or kidnapping; and occur primarily within the territorial jurisdiction of the United States.[32]

This definition includes reference to some commonly understood elements of terrorism, such as acts that are dangerous to human life and that are intended to

29 18 U.S.C. § 2339B(a)(1) (2006). The constitutionality of the FTO designation process authorized by Executive Order No. 13,224 and various statutes was upheld by the U.S. Supreme Court in *Humanitarian Law Project v. Holder. Holder v. Humanitarian Law Project*, 130 S. Ct. 2705 (2010).

30 Under the AEDPA, courts have the power to set aside the State Department designation of an FTO if it is arbitrary, capricious, and an abuse of discretion, or if it is not based on substantial evidence. AEDPA § 302(b)(3) (codified as 8 U.S.C. § 1189(c)(3)). Courts have, however, been extremely deferential to the State Department, choosing not to review classified evidence in some instances, but relying instead on State Department affirmations of substantial evidence to support its designation decision. E.g., People's Mojahedin Org. of Iran, 327 F.3d 1238, 1244 (D.C. Cir. 2003).

31 8 U.S.C. § 1189(a)(4)(C), (a)(6) (2006).

32 Id. § 802.

intimidate a civilian population, and the definition offers examples of common underlying crimes, such as mass destruction, assassination, or kidnapping. Nonetheless, critics have noted that such language could encompass the work of numerous activist groups, including environmental advocates such as Greenpeace, protestors of the World Trade Organization, and anti-abortion organizations such as Operation Rescue.[33] Indeed, because the definition suggests, but does not require, politically motivated violence as an element, a literal reading of the statutory language suggests that almost any violent act toward a civilian could qualify as "terrorism."

The definition of terrorism used in the Patriot Act was imported from the Foreign Intelligence Surveillance Act of 1978 ("FISA").[34] Like other definitions already examined, the definition of international terrorism in FISA includes several elements: that it "involve violent acts or acts dangerous to human life that are a violation of the criminal laws of the United States or of any State, or that would be a criminal violation if committed within the jurisdiction of the United States or any State"; that it "appear to be intended to intimidate or coerce a civilian population; to influence the policy of a government by intimidation or coercion; or to affect the conduct of a government by assassination or kidnapping" and occur totally outside the United States, or transcend national boundaries.

Given the far-reaching consequences of being suspected of terrorism and the broad powers for surveillance authorized under FISA at the time of its enactment, Congress expressed significant concern over the implications of FISA on civil liberties, and the potential for government overreach. This concern led to numerous safeguards beyond the limited scope of application of the legislation, including the reporting requirements of the Attorney General to Congress regarding the nature and extent of FISA-based surveillance conducted,[35] the mandated minimization procedures to ensure that individual privacy rights are safeguarded to some extent,[36] and the penalties available to punish those who conduct unlawful and overreaching surveillance.[37]

The Patriot Act uses the FISA definition of terrorism without the concomitant FISA safeguards in place, an especially problematic footing in light of the limited original application of the FISA definition to intelligence gathering outside of the criminal prosecution context. The lack of parallel due process protections in the application of the Patriot Act exacerbates the problems inherent in applying

33 See How the USA PATRIOT Act redefines "Domestic Terrorism," *Am. Civ. Liberties Union* (Dec. 6, 2002), www.aclu.org/national-security/how-usa-patriot-act-redefines-domestic-terrorism (analyzing the effect of the Patriot Act definition of terrorism if the government applied the act to Vieques protesters).
34 See Foreign Intelligence Surveillance Act, 50 U.S.C. § 1801(c) (2006).
35 See 50 U.S.C. §§ 1807, 1808 (2006) (describing the reports required by the Attorney General and other congressional oversight measures).
36 See, e.g., 50 U.S.C. § 1801(h) (2006) (directing the use of minimization procedures to "minimize the acquisition and retention, and prohibit the dissemination, of non-publicly available information concerning unconsenting United States persons")
37 E.g., 50 U.S.C. §§ 1809, 1810 (2006) (describing civil liability and criminal sanctions for breaches of FISA).

conflicting definitions of terrorism, including the potential lack of notice to individuals as to whether they will be categorized as a terrorist and exactly what kind of conduct is prohibited.[38] Even with some safeguards in place, vagueness in these statutes opens up potential for abuse if definitions are repurposed to punish non-terrorist activity, precisely the concern when applying the label of terrorism to unconventional contexts.

Two unconventional applications of the term "terrorism" to law-enforcement and intelligence-gathering efforts—gang violence and animal rights activism—offer insight into the possibilities and concerns in re-contextualizing terrorism.[39]

Gang violence

There are two primary ways in which gang violence and terrorism are conflated under legal standards. The first is a concern that powerful U.S. gangs, who are known to smuggle drugs,[40] weapons, and other illegal items into the United States, will also smuggle terrorists into the United States.[41] However, research suggests that this nexus remains at most speculative,[42] and some reports on

38 See, e.g., Perry, supra note 22, at 270 (arguing that conflicting definitions of terrorism could result in confusion and ambiguity)

39 There are too many unconventional contexts to evaluate in one book chapter, but these serve as exemplars for the concerns of applying the term elsewhere. E.g., Michal Buchhandler-Raphael, What's Terrorism Got to Do with It? The Perils of Prosecutorial Misuse of Terrorism Offenses, available at http://papers.ssrn.com/sol3/papers.cfm?abstract_id=1909505 (arguing that the terrorism charges brought against a microbiologist who attempted to use toxic chemicals to harm another person as part of a personal vendetta were inappropriate).

40 A related area of concern is that of "narco-terrorism," in which a drug trafficking and terrorism nexus must be demonstrated to prosecute under counterterrorism statutes. See USA PATRIOT Improvement and Reauthorization Act of 2005, 21 U.S.C. §960a (criminalizing the funding of terrorist activity or an FTO through drug trafficking); John E. Thomas, Jr., Narco-Terrorism: Could the Legislative and Prosecutorial Responses Threaten Our Civil Liberties? 66 *Wash. & Lee L. Rev*. 1881 (2009) (arguing that the requirement of a drug trafficking–terrorism nexus is too easy to meet and may encourage government abuse of powers granted under the Patriot Act); see also Johnny Dwyer, The Threat of Narcoterror: How the Strange New Iran Case Affects the Definition, *Time*, Oct. 17, 2011, available at http://content.time.com/time/nation/article/0,8599,2096950,00.html (visited Nov. 18, 2014) (noting the political expedience of labeling drug trafficking as "terrorism" for U.S. politicians during a campaign season). Others have noted that the conflation of the "war on drugs" and "war on terror" on a policy level has sometimes resulted in unintended policy consequences that undercut the ability to undercut terrorism. See Chris J. Dolan, United States' Narco-Terrorism Policy: A Contingency Approach to the Convergence of the Wars on Drugs and Against Terrorism, 22 *Rev. of Policy Research*, 451, 467–69 (2005).

41 See Testimony of FBI Assistant Director, Criminal Investigative Division, Christopher Swecker, before the House International Relations Subcommittee on the Western Hemisphere, Gangs and Crime in Latin America (April 20, 2005).

42 E.g., Celinda Franco, *Youth Gangs: Background, Legislation, and Issues*, Congressional Research Service, Jan. 25, 2008, at 24 (noting that "no evidence has been found linking U.S. gangs...with the smuggling of terrorists into the country"); cf. Mark

domestic terrorism do not include discussion of gang violence at all.[43] In such a situation, it appears that the concern focuses on the prospect of gangs providing material support to terrorists,[44] not committing acts of terrorist violence themselves.

The second context is the legal treatment of gang violence itself as terrorism. Six days after the September 11, 2001 terrorist attacks, New York became the first state in the United States to pass its own general anti-terrorism statute,[45] the Anti-Terrorism Act of 2001.[46] This law ratchets up the potential penalties where an underlying criminal act is committed with the intent to "intimidate or coerce a civilian population; influence the policy of a unit of government by intimidation or coercion; or affect the conduct of a unit of government by murder, assassination or kidnapping."[47]

This statute was tested in *People v. Morales*, a case that deserves close examination not only because of the nature of the crimes committed, but for the judicial response to the broad definition of terrorism being put forward by the prosecutors. Edgar Morales was involved in a gang-related shooting at a 2002 christening

Randol, CRS Issue Statement on Organized Crime and Gangs in the United States, Congressional Research Service, Jan. 12, 2010, at 2 (noting that "[t]he potential nexus between [drug trafficking organizations], organized crime, and terrorist organizations may be of interest for Congress. Terrorists may collaborate directly with organized crime groups to secure funding for their operations. Terrorist organizations may also use the structure and activities of organized crime groups as models for structuring their own organizations and financing their operations").

43 See Bjelopera, *supra* note 4.

44 See *Holder v. Humanitarian Law Project*, 130 S. Ct. 2705 (2010) (holding that it is constitutional to criminalize the provision of material support and assistance to organizations deemed to be Foreign Terrorist Organizations, even where such support is nonviolent).

45 Many other U.S. states have passed anti-terrorism statutes as well; they are seldom used, and with mixed application and results. For example, Nevada's antiterrorism statute defines terrorism as violent or coercive acts of destruction, without a required nexus to political or religious motivation, such that a plain reading of the statute could characterize the October 2017 mass shooting in Las Vegas as a terrorist attack. See Nev. Rev. Stat., NRS 202.4415 ("Act of terrorism" defined). Likewise, an Illinois anti-terrorism statute was the basis for prosecuting three men for material support for terrorism and conspiracy to commit terrorism in conjunction with their protests of a 2012 NATO summit in Chicago. Those defendants were ultimately acquitted of terrorism-related crimes, but convicted of misdemeanor mob action and felony possession of an incendiary device. See Steve Schmadeke, Found Guilty of Mob Action and Arson, but Not Terror Charges, *Chicago Tribune*, Feb. 7, 2014, available at http://articles.chicagotribune.com/2014-02-07/news/chi-closing-arguments-underway-in-nato-3-trial-20140206_1_brian-church-jared-chase-brent-betterly. Other states have labeled gang-related violence as a form of terrorism for decades, but not as part of a general anti-terrorism law. See, e.g., California Street Terrorism Enforcement and Prevention Act, Cal. Pen. Code §186.22 (1988) (using the term "terrorism" in the title of the act, but not using or defining the term in the body of the statute).

46 Anti-Terrorism Act of 2001, 2001 N.Y. Laws, Ch. 300 (Sept. 17, 2001).

47 N.Y. Penal Law §490.25 (1) (defining the act of terrorism for the purposes of the Anti-Terrorism Act of 2001).

in the Bronx in New York City, in which a child was killed and another bystander was severely injured.[48] In this case, the Bronx district attorney indicted Morales on charges of murder, attempted murder, manslaughter, gang assault, and criminal possession of a handgun, but also indicted Morales on those same charges under the auspices of the New York terrorism statute under the theory that Morales acted with the intent to intimidate the Mexican-American civilian population living in the area of the shooting.[49] A jury convicted Morales of a variety of offenses, including manslaughter, attempted murder, weapons possession, and conspiracy, as well as the terrorism-related corollaries of these crimes; Morales was sentenced to 40 years to life in prison.[50]

The intermediate appellate court modified Morales' sentence based on its findings that Morales' gang-related activity in a civilian neighborhood did not qualify as terrorist activity.[51] In doing so, the appellate court looked to the language of the Anti-Terrorism Act itself, notably the examples given by the New York state legislature as prior terrorist activity that helped motivate the passage of the statute. In addition to the September 11 attacks, the legislature cited the 1993 attack on the World Trade Center, the 1998 bombings of U.S. embassies in Kenya and Tanzania, the 1995 Oklahoma City federal building bombing, the 1988 downing of Pan Am flight 103 over Lockerbie, Scotland, a 1997 shooting at the Empire State Building, and the 1994 murder of a teenager on the Brooklyn Bridge as acts of terrorism.[52]

The appellate court further considered examples of international terrorism that motivated the Foreign Intelligence Surveillance Act of 1978 (FISA),[53] since the New York terrorism act was informed by language from FISA. The legislative history of FISA included examples of terrorism such as "the detonation of bombs in a metropolitan area" and "the deliberate assassination of persons to strike fear into others to deter them from exercising their rights."[54] The appellate court further noted that a 1986 federal statute specifically distinguished terrorism from

48 See *People v. Morales*, 20 N.Y. 3d 240, 244–45 (NY 2012).

49 Id. at 245.

50 Id. at 246.

51 See *People v. Morales*, 86 A.D. 3d 147, 157 (NY 1st Dep't 2011).

52 See N.Y. Penal Law §490.00 (2001). Whether all of those acts should have been described as "terrorism" remains a matter of debate. See Shaila K. Dewan, U.S. Decides '94 Attack on Hasidim Was a Lone Act, *The New York Times*, Dec. 6, 2000, available at www.nytimes.com/2000/12/06/nyregion/us-decides-94-attack-on-hasidim-was-lone-act.html (noting that the U.S. Attorney had, in 2000, re-characterized the 1994 murder of Ari Halberstam on the Brooklyn Bridge as a "terrorist act"); but see Glenn Greenwald, New York's Top Court Highlights the Meaninglessness and Menace of the Term "Terrorism," *Guardian*, Dec. 16, 2012, available at www.theguardian.com/commentisfree/2012/dec/16/court-terrorism-morales-gangs-meaningless (critiquing the inclusion of all of these highly differentiated crimes as terrorist acts, opining that the single common theme for six of these seven acts is that they were committed by Muslims against non-Muslims, and suggesting that the label of "terrorism" is a tool used to create a lesser system of justice for Muslim defendants).

53 Foreign Intelligence Surveillance Act of 1978, 50 U.S.C. § 1801 et seq.

54 *People v. Morales*, 86 A.D. 3d at 158.

"nonterrorist violence" such as "normal street crime."[55] The appellate court considered Morales's crime against this backdrop of these examples and found that, although heinous, Morales did not commit acts of terrorism. Although the appellate court cleared Morales of the terrorism-related convictions, it let stand all of the underlying convictions, holding that Morales' trial was sufficiently untainted, despite the stigma associated with terrorism and the additional evidence that prosecutors were able to introduce due to the alleged terrorism nexus.[56]

The Court of Appeals[57] in New York went further, ordering a new trial for Morales based on the finding that the entire trial was tainted by the unreasonable categorization of Morales' acts as terrorism as opposed to "gang-on-gang street violence."[58] The Court offered further clarification of what does not constitute terrorism: drive-by shootings, "ordinary violent crimes" such as robbery or personal vendettas, or the orchestration of a murder by an organized crime family of another syndicate's soldier.[59]

The Court's language as to how a terrorism trial is substantially different than one for other crimes in terms of the prosecutor's ability to introduce evidence is helpful in considering the ramifications of labeling a crime as "terrorism":

> By proceeding on the terrorism theory, the People were able to introduce evidence about numerous alleged criminal acts committed by members of [Morales' gang] over the course of three years. Without the aura of terrorism looming over the case, the activities of defendant's associates in other contexts would have been largely, if not entirely, inadmissible. Based on the record, it is apparent that the volume of proof regarding unrelated assaults, murders and other offenses created a reasonable possibility that the jury's findings were prejudicially influenced. Hence, the spillover effect requires reversal and a new trial on the underlying offenses.[60]

After the Court of Appeals' decision, Morales was retried on the non-terrorism-related charges and was found guilty of manslaughter, attempted murder, gang assault, criminal possession of a weapon, and conspiracy. In early 2015, he was sentenced to 50 years in prison for those crimes.[61]

55 Id. at 159.
56 Id. at 163–64.
57 The Court of Appeals is the highest court within the New York State judicial system.
58 See *People v. Morales*, 20 N.Y. 3d at 248, 250.
59 Id. at 249.
60 Id. at 250.
61 See Press Release of Bronx District Attorney Robert T. Johnson, 50 Years in Prison for Gangbanger Twice Convicted in Shooting that Killed Little Girl, Paralyzed a Bystander, Feb. 20, 2015, available at www.bronxda.nyc.gov/information/2015/case16.htm.

Animal rights activism

The boundaries among constitutionally protected political protest, politically motivated non-violent crime, and domestic terrorist activity come into sharp focus in a number of criminal cases involving supporters of animal rights. Animal rights-related crimes, unlike most other types of domestic criminal activity (whether usually designated as "terrorist activity" or not), is an area in which Congress has seen fit to enact legislation that is unusual in its specificity and nomenclature.[62] The Animal Enterprise Terrorism Act of 2006 (AETA)[63] expands the federal government's legal authority to combat animal rights extremists who engage in criminal activity and, as the name of the statute suggests, looks to stigmatize and penalize criminal activity by animal rights groups[64] by designating a variety of animal enterprise[65]-related crimes as terrorism.[66] This effort was led by a coalition of advocacy groups finding support in various business interests (e.g., livestock farms; fur operations; cosmetic, pharmaceutical, and biomedical companies; as well as animal-based entertainment businesses such as circuses and rodeos) and academic institutions engaging in animal research.[67]

The AETA's definition of terrorism includes provisions for terrorist activity that are common to other federal statutes, but also has a variety of unique provisions that label non-violent crimes such as trespass, property damage, and vandalism as "terrorism" as well:

62 One context analogous to that of animal rights-related "terrorism" is that of "eco-terrorism," which has been treated by the FBI as a "serious terrorist threat," with the use of multi-agency taskforces and Joint Terrorism Task Forces to investigate alleged eco-terrorist organizations. Testimony of James F. Jarboe, Domestic Terrorism Section Chief, Counterterrorism Division, Federal Bureau of Investigation, Feb. 12, 2002, available at http://web.archive.org/web/20080311231725/http://www.fbi.gov/congress/congress02/jarboe021202.htm. See Federal Bureau of Investigation, Press Release, *Eco-Terror Indictments: 'Operation Backfire' Nets 11*, FBI, Jan. 20, 2006, available at www.fbi.gov/news/stories/2006/january/elf012006. But see Steve Vanderheiden, Eco-terrorism or Justified Resistance? Radical Environmentalism and the "War on Terror," 33 *Politics & Society* 425 (2005) (arguing that the conflation of counterterrorism operations and criminal investigations of "radical environmentalists" is misplaced).

63 Animal Enterprise Terrorism Act of 2006, P.L. 109–374.

64 See Statements on Introduced Bills and Joint Resolutions, 152 Cong. Rec. S9254–01 (2006) (discussing actions by "extremist activists, acting in the name of animal rights")

65 An "animal enterprise" is defined as any "commercial or academic enterprise that uses or sells animals or animal products for profit." 18 U.S.C. § 43 (d)(1)(a).

66 Signed into law in November 2006, the AETA amended the Animal Enterprise Protection Act of 1992, 18 U.S.C. §43 (2000) (enacted Aug. 26, 1992) (AEPA). The AEPA was amended in 1996 and 2000 to increase penalties and sentences. See Kim McCoy, The Animal Enterprise Terrorism Act: Protecting Profits of Animal Enterprises at the Expense of the First Amendment, in Jason Del Gandio & Antony J. Nocella II, eds., *The Terrorization of Dissent: Corporate Repression, Legal Corruption, and the Animal Enterprise Terrorism Act* 6–7 (Lantern Books, 2014).

67 McCoy, *supra* note 66, at 8–9.

a Travel[] in interstate or foreign commerce, or use[] or cause[] to be used the mail or any facility of interstate or foreign commerce—

(1) for the purpose of damaging or interfering with the operations of an animal enterprise; and

(2) in connection with such purpose—

(A) intentionally damage[] or cause[] the loss of any real or personal property (including animals or records) used by an animal enterprise, or any real or personal property of a person or entity having a connection to, relationship with, or transactions with an animal enterprise;

(B) intentionally place[] a person in reasonable fear of the death of, or serious bodily injury to that person, a member of the immediate family … of that person, or a spouse or intimate partner of that person by a course of conduct involving threats, acts of vandalism, property damage, criminal trespass, harassment, or intimidation; or

(C) conspire[] or attempt[] to do so[.][68]

Civil rights groups have challenged the AETA on behalf of criminal defendants based in part on this broad definition of terrorism.[69] Given the fact that the label of terrorism carries significant legal and societal consequences, challenges to this designation alleged a substantive due process violation in the labeling of crimes such as criminal trespass when there is no intent to injure a person and no such injury occurs, no explosive devices are used, and the behavior is otherwise criminalized under state or federal law.[70] Thus far, such efforts have been unsuccessful.

Looking at international working definitions and other definitions used by the U.S. federal government in its counterterrorism efforts,[71] the AETA definition of terrorism is a significant outlier. Although the international community has not achieved consensus on the definition of terrorism, the acts that the AETA includes as terrorist activity—trespassing, releasing animals, vandalism, and destroying records—do not comport with the usual definitions of terrorism that use politically motivated murder or hostage-taking meant to intimidate significant groups of civilians as exemplars for the types of crimes to be designated as "terrorism."

The AETA exploits the vagueness problems at the international and federal level to explicitly define terrorism as something it is not commonly understood to be. Also, whereas the international community and U.S. government have often sought to ameliorate the stigma and legal impact of being erroneously labeled a

68 18 U.S.C. §43(a).

69 See Defendant's Motion to Dismiss Indictment and Memorandum of Law in Support, *United States v. Johnson*, No. 14 CR 390 (N.D. Ill. Nov. 6, 2014), available at http://ccrjustice.org/ourcases/US-v-Johnson (viewed November 18, 2014).

70 See id.

71 For example, the FBI's website on its counterterrorism efforts lists multiple definitions of terrorism under federal law, none of which resemble the AETA definition. See Federal Bureau of Investigation, Definitions of Terrorism in the U.S. Code, available at www.fbi.gov/about-us/investigate/terrorism/terrorism-definition (visited Oct. 31, 2014).

terrorist by establishing safeguards against inappropriate designation as a "terrorist," the AETA moves in the opposite direction by explicitly attaching the "terrorist" label to crimes that are usually categorized as ordinary felonies and misdemeanors, without protections in place that would necessitate additional review to determine whether "terrorism" is the appropriate label for the act in question.

This problem of expansive labeling without thoughtful scrutiny and judicial review is not merely an issue in the United States; in fact, the history of and potential for abuse by Indian law-enforcement and intelligence officers involved in counterterrorism law and policy illustrates this dynamic as well.

India's broad treatment of "terrorism"

India has struggled with security threats since its independence in 1947.[72] India's legal response has relied on a framework of constitutionally and statutorily granted emergency powers, plus non-emergency criminal laws granting broad intelligence-gathering and police powers that in many ways operate similar to emergency powers.[73] This makes it all the more precarious for individuals or organizations labeled as terrorists, who often find themselves in a draconian criminal justice system that limits their rights and access to justice.[74] From a rule of law perspective, India should be ensuring that the legal definition of terrorism remains narrowly written and construed so as to avoid the potential for abuse. Yet the persistence of India's expansive definition of terrorism and its application to a variety of conventional and unconventional contexts suggests that the Indian government is more focused on maintaining broad authority to investigate and prosecute security threats as it sees fit to define them, and less concerned with the human rights abuses that follow.

After Emergency Rule ended in 1977, political, economic, and security-related pressures continued to undercut stability in India. In the early 1980s the Punjabi separatist movement fueled fears that separatist movements throughout India would gain strength, motivating Parliament to pass the Terrorist Affected Areas Act of 1984 (TAAA), which granted more structured

72 See Anil Kalhan et al., Colonial Continuities: Human Rights, Terrorism and Security Laws in India, 20 *Colum. J. Asian L.* 93, 99 (2006) (describing violence related to terrorism as a "chronic crisis of national security").

73 See India Const. arts. 352–56, amended by The Constitution (Ninety-fourth Amendment) Act, 2006 (stating the emergency powers provisions); see also Granville Austin, *Working a Democratic Constitution: A History of the Indian Experience* 295–97 (Oxford University Press, 2003) (discussing the era of Emergency Rule under Prime Minister Indira Gandhi).

74 See Surabhi Chopra, National Security Laws in India: The Unraveling of Constitutional Constraints, 17 *Or. Rev. Int'l L.* 1, 24–33 (2015) (describing the broad scope of India's antiterrorism laws, and the effects on individuals within their purview); Setty, Comparative Perspectives, *supra* note 10, at 164–71 (discussing rule of law concerns with regard to the specialized courts used to try some terrorists in India).

and comprehensive police and intelligence-gathering powers.[75] This statute contained the first legislative definition of a "terrorist," which required that a person kills, acts violently, disrupts essential services, or damages property; with the purpose of intimidating the public, coercing the government, endangering the sovereignty or integrity of India, or "affecting adversely the harmony between different religious, racial, language or regional groups or castes or communities."[76] This extraordinarily broad definition, although only applicable to designated "affected areas" within India, had the potential, like the Patriot Act or other U.S. legislation, to create "terrorists" out of those conducting protected activities. Yet the TAAA contained no restrictive language or ameliorating procedures to protect against improper designation, creating a genuine concern for the over-labeling of ordinary crimes or legal activities as "terrorism."

Due to the political furor over the assassination of Prime Minister Indira Gandhi in 1984, the Terrorist and Disruptive Activities (Prevention) Act (TADA) was passed in 1985.[77] This new act defined terrorism in even broader terms as TAAA, with no geographic restriction to "affected areas":

> Whoever with intent to overawe the Government as by law established or to strike terror in the people or any section of the people or to alienate any section of the people or to adversely affect the harmony amongst different sections of the people does any act or thing by using bombs, dynamite or other explosive substances or inflammable substances or firearms or other lethal weapons or poisons or noxious gases or other chemicals or by any other substances (whether biological or otherwise) of a hazardous nature in such a manner as to cause, or as is likely to cause, death of, or injuries to, any person or persons or damage to, or destruction of, property or disruption of any supplies or services essential to the life of the community, commits a terrorist act.[78]

The constitutionality of this vague and broad definition of terrorism has been upheld by the Indian Supreme Court,[79] despite reservations about potential abuse of power[80] and accusations that TADA was being employed against political

75 See Terrorist Affected Areas (Special Courts) Act, 1984, No. 61, Acts of Parliament, 1984 (India) [hereinafter TAAA] ("An act to provide for the speedy trial of certain offences in terrorist affected areas and for matters connected therewith").

76 See id. § 2(1)(h).

77 See The Terrorist and Disruptive Activities (Prevention) Act, 1985, No. 31, Acts of Parliament, 1985 (India) [hereinafter TADA] ("An act to make special provisions for the prevention of, and for coping with, terrorist and disruptive activities and for matters connected therewith or incidental thereto").

78 TADA, Part II, § (3)(1).

79 See *Madan Singh v. State of Bihar*, (2004) 3 S.C.R. 692 (India) (observing that it is not possible to provide a precise definition of terrorism).

80 See *Kartar Singh v. State of Punjab*, (1994) 2 S.C.R. 375 (India) (upholding the constitutionality of TADA after acknowledging potential problems of overreach).

enemies of the government.[81] TADA expired in 1995, but its definition of terrorism was reused and broadened further with the enactment of the Prevention of Terrorism Act, 2002 (POTA), which has a checkered legacy that, in some respects, continues to define Indian counterterrorism policy today.

Prevention of Terrorism Act 2002

POTA was passed quickly by the Indian parliament, partly resulting from post-9/11 international mandates to strengthen counterterrorism operations worldwide.[82] POTA defined a terrorist as one who:

> [W]ith intent to threaten the unity, integrity, security or sovereignty of India or to strike terror in the people or any section of the people does any act or thing by using bombs, dynamite or other explosive substances or inflammable substances or firearms or other lethal weapons or poisons or noxious gases or other chemicals or by any other substances ... of a hazardous nature or by any other means whatsoever, in such a manner as to cause, or likely to cause, death of, or injuries to any person or persons or loss of, or damage to, or destruction of, property or disruption of any supplies or services essential to the life of the community, or detains any person and threatens to kill or injure such person in order to compel the Government or any other person to do or abstain from doing any act ....[83]

The determination of who is considered a terrorist under this provision falls to the central government and the state governments that have adopted POTA. Those groups designated as "terrorist organizations" have the right to challenge their designation through a petition to the central government and to appeal unsuccessful challenges to a review committee.[84] Judicial review over the designation is explicitly barred under POTA,[85] but courts later suggested that some degree of judicial review may be available as a constitutional matter.[86]

The POTA definition came under critique for, among other human rights concerns, selective prosecutions of Muslims, poor people, members of tribal groups, protesters, and Dalits as "terrorists" in special courts with diminished

81 See Kalhan, *supra* note 72, at 177–78.
82 See S.C. Res. 1373, U.N. Doc. S/RES/1373 (Sept. 28, 2001) (mandating that all U.N. member nations take proactive steps to combat terrorism).
83 The Prevention of Terrorism Act, 2002 (POTA), No. 15, Acts of Parliament, 2002 (India) Chapter II, § 3(1)(a).
84 POTA, Ch. III, §19.
85 POTA, Ch. VI, §54.
86 See POTA's Review Panel's Recommendation Binding on Gujarat: Supreme Court, *The Hindu*, Oct. 22, 2008, available at www.thehindu.com/todays-paper/tp-national/pota-review-panels-recommendation-binding-on-gujarat-supreme-court/article1361671.ece (mentioning that although the review committee's designation was considered final, Article 226 of the Indian Constitution allows for High Courts to issue writs that could bring such matters under judicial review).

protections for defendants, whereas others accused of the same acts were often not prosecuted at all or were charged with ordinary criminal offenses and were tried in ordinary courts.[87] Perhaps the most graphic example of this occurred in conjunction with the 2002 train fire in the town of Godhra, Gujarat, in which 59 people, mostly Hindu activists who were part of the Vishwa Hindu Parishad, a group affiliated with the Hindu conservative political party, the Bharatiya Janata Party (BJP), died. A large group of Muslim residents of Godhra had surrounded the train at the time and were in a heated argument with those on the train; investigations by the Gujarat state government concluded that those outside of the train were a "mob" that lit the fire purposefully, whereas the Indian central government's investigators concluded that the fire originated accidentally.[88] Following the train fire, rioting and extreme violence broke out in multiple parts of Gujarat, and approximately 1,100 people, mostly Muslims, were killed.[89]

POTA was used to charge many of the Muslims who were part of the crowd outside of the train, and 79 of those suspects were held in POTA-authorized pretrial detention for approximately seven years.[90] Those detainees were transferred for ordinary criminal processing only in early 2009, after the POTA Review Committee found that the designation of "terrorism" was inappropriate under the

87 See Ujjwal Kumar Singh, *The State, Democracy and Anti-Terror Laws in India* 165–219 (Routledge, 2007) (documenting selective prosecution under POTA); see also Chopra, *supra* note 74, at 30–35 (discussing ways in which the powers granted under POTA were abused); Amos Guiora, Legislative and Policy Responses to Terrorism, A Global Perspective, 7 *San Diego Int'l L.J.* 125, 171 (2005) (noting that some described POTA as a "terrorist law [that would be] … used to terrorise minorities"); Sudha Ramachandran, Filling India's Anti-terrorism Void, *Asia Times* online, Sept. 23, 2004, www.atimes.com/atimes/South_Asia/FI23Df03.html (noting that while the majority of the 32 organizations banned under POTA were Muslim, none of the Hindu extremist groups were ever targeted); Sachin Mehta, Repeal of POTA Justified, Legal Services India, www.legalservicesindia.com/articles/pota.htm (last visited Oct. 10, 2011) (observing that POTA had been "abused to book, without lucidity and accountability, political opponents and underprivileged communities").

88 Compare Report by the Commission of Inquiry Consisting of Mr. Justice G.T. Nanavati and Mr. Justice Akshay H. Mehta, Part I, Sept. 8, 2008, at ¶227 (the Gujarat government's commission concluded that the train fire was a premeditated crime that was part of a larger conspiracy intended to kill Hindu activists); Fatal '02 Hindu Train Fire Laid to Accident, Not Mob, *The New York Times*, Jan. 18, 2005, available at www.nytimes.com/2005/01/17/world/asia/17iht-india.html (reporting that the central government's investigating concluded that the train fire was an accident).

89 See Celia W. Dugger, *Religious Riots Loom over Indian Politics*, *The New York Times*, July 27, 2002, available at www.nytimes.com/2002/07/27/international/asia/27INDI.html (describing the heinous ways in which many Muslims were killed and injured during the riots).

90 See Pota Not Applicable in Godhra Riots Case: Gujarat HC, *The Hindu*, Feb. 13, 2009, available at http://timesofindia.indiatimes.com/india/Pota-not-applicable-in-Godhra-riots-case-Gujarat-HC/articleshow/4120487.cms.

circumstances, and the Gujarat High Court affirmed that the starting of the train fire, although arguably criminal, was not an act of terrorism.[91]

Even in 2002, however, POTA was not used to charge Hindus involved in the violence and rioting, leading to allegations of selective prosecution.[92] Further charges were made that local law enforcement, the BJP-led Gujarat state government, and its chief minister at the time, Narendra Modi (now India's prime minister), were complicit in and, in some instances, encouraging and instigating violence against Muslims.[93] Some in the Gujarat state government were convicted of crimes related to communal violence;[94] Modi was not convicted, although concerns about his complicity persisted.[95]

POTA was repealed in 2004 over sustained concern of human rights abuses by the police and intelligence community, but the bulk of its powers were encapsulated in other statutes. The 2004 amendments to the Unlawful Activities (Prevention) Act (UAPA) adopted the POTA definition in its entirety.[96]

The UAPA definition of terrorism

This expansive Indian definition of terrorism was entrenched further after the Mumbai terrorist attacks of November 26, 2008 left more than 160 people dead and hundreds more wounded.[97] When combined with a lack of meaningful judicial scrutiny, the broad UAPA definition of terrorism exacerbated the potential for

91 See POTA Review Panel's Recommendations Binding on Gujarat: Supreme Court, *The Hindu*, Oct. 22, 2008, available at www.thehindu.com/todays-paper/tp-national/pota-review-panels-recommendation-binding-on-gujarat-supreme-court/article1361671.ece.

92 See Human Rights Watch, We Have No Orders to Save You: State Participation and Complicity in Communal Violence in Gujarat, April 2002, available at www.hrw.org/reports/2002/india/.

93 See id.

94 See Gardiner Harris & Hari Kumar, *Stiff Sentence for Former Gujarat Minister, The New York Times*, Aug. 31, 2012, available at http://india.blogs.nytimes.com/2012/08/31/stiff-sentence-for-former-gujarat-minister/ (describing the decades-long sentences for 32 Gujarat government officials in conjunction with the 2002 riots).

95 See Ellen Barry, U.S. Reaches Out to Indian Opposition Leader It Once Rebuked, *The New York Times*, Feb. 10, 2014, available at www.nytimes.com/2014/02/11/world/asia/us-reaches-out-to-indian-opposition-leader-it-once-rebuked.html (describing the diplomatic chill between the United States and Narendra Modi as a result of Modi's governance of Gujarat during the 2002 riots).

96 See Unlawful Activities (Prevention) Amendment Ordinance, 2004, No. 2, § 15, Acts of Parliament, 2004 (India).

97 See Somini Sengupta & Keith Bradsher, India Faces a Reckoning as Terror Toll Eclipses 170, *The New York Times*, Nov. 30, 2008, at A1 (questioning whether Indian authorities could have better anticipated the terrorist attack and ensured heightened security). Shortly after this attack and with little parliamentary debate, the government passed two pieces of counterterrorism legislation: further amendments to the UAPA, and the National Investigation Agency Act. See Human Rights Watch, *Back to the Future: India's 2008 Counterterrorism Laws* 1 (2010). Both statutes increased the amount of power conferred on the central government for investigating and

abuse in the government's decision as to whether to treat suspects as ordinary criminals or terrorists.[98] The difference in potential consequences between an ordinary criminal prosecution and that of a UAPA case is stark: for example, a UAPA prosecution against a prominent Communist Party leader accused of impersonation, cheating, forgery, and criminal conspiracy for assuming a fake identity and forging documents was dismissed because of a failure to follow proper procedures to authorize prosecution. As a result, a court ordered the terrorism-related charges against the defendant dropped; instead of facing a potential life imprisonment under the sentencing framework of the UAPA, the defendant faced a maximum of seven years' imprisonment for the same acts under the Indian Penal Code.[99]

Nonetheless, the UAPA was amended in 2012 such that the definition of terrorism is now even broader. First, the predicate definition of "security" includes "economic security," which in turn includes "financial, monetary and fiscal stability, security of means of production and distribution, food security, livelihood security, energy security, ecological and environmental security."[100] Second, the "person" who can be viewed under the UAPA as engaging in terrorist activity not only includes natural persons, but also can be "a company; a firm; an organization or an association of persons or a body of individuals, whether incorporated or not; every artificial juridical person …; and any agency, office or branch owned or controlled by any person falling within any of the preceding sub-clauses."[101] Third, the "production or smuggling or circulation" of "high quality" counterfeit Indian currency is defined as a terrorist act.[102]

This repeated expansion of the definition of "terrorism" is particularly noteworthy given the history and political platform of the BJP, the current ruling party in the Indian government. In 2014, the BJP gained control of the Lok Sabha, the lower chamber of the Indian parliament, based in part on voter perceptions that terrorism remains a major problem for India,[103] and that the BJP was better suited to combat terrorism than the Congress Party-led government that passed the

prosecuting terrorist acts, with the latter act also establishing the National Investigation Agency.

98 See Repeating the Mistakes of the Past, Human Rights Documentation Center (Jan. 22, 2009), hwww.hrdc.net/sahrdc/hrfeatures/HRF191.htm (noting that the UAPA definition institutionalizes the worst overreaching and missteps from TADA and POTA because it relates not only to counterterrorism policy, but to other "disruptive" activities).

99 See Jiby Katakayyam, Cops Goofed Up, Ghandy Cleared, *The Hindu*, Mar. 30, 2012, available at www.thehindu.com/todays-paper/tp-national/tp-otherstates/cops-goofed-up-ghandy-cleared/article3260527.ece.

100 The Unlawful Activities (Prevention) Amendment Act, 2012 (No. 3 of 2013), §2(i).

101 Id. at §2(ii).

102 Id. at §4(ii). These acts have long been criminalized under British colonial and Indian law. See Indian Penal Code (1860), §§ 465, 468, 489D.

103 A 2013–2014 Pew Research Survey found that 88% of Indians surveyed believed that terrorism is a "very big problem," with another 17% describing it as a "moderately big problem." See Pew Research Center, *Indians Reflect on Their Country and the World*, at 29 (March 31, 2014).

UAPA amendments in 2008 and 2012.[104] Modi's possible role in the 2002 riots in Gujarat and his alienation of Muslims were campaign issues that ultimately did not gain much traction,[105] and Modi continues to enjoy high approval ratings of his approach to combating terrorism.[106]

The 2014 pre-election BJP platform on national security called for increasing the counterterrorism powers that it claimed were "dismantled" under the previous government.[107] The Modi government has already sought to increase its counterterrorism powers with a massive expansion of domestic surveillance under its Central Monitoring System,[108] a development that has already raised concerns from civil society groups and private citizens.[109] Yet Modi and the BJP have extraordinary power to expand the reach of counterterrorism powers even further given the UAPA's sweeping definition of terrorism. Unlike the international working definitions discussed in the first part and the most commonly used U.S. federal definitions discussed in the second part, the UAPA definition is not tethered to the commonly understood elements of terrorism, such as political violence meant to intimidate a group of civilians, and often involving serious injury or killing, hostage-taking or large-scale destruction. Not only does the UAPA definition allow for investigation and prosecution of acts like gang-related violence and animal rights-related violence—the two unconventional U.S. contexts examined in the second part—as terrorist acts, but it would also allow for many other acts already criminalized under the Indian Penal Code to be legally treated as "terrorism." These factors not only allow for unconventional applications of the "terrorism" label in India, they virtually encourage it, as well as the concomitant abuse of power that has historically plagued such applications.

Conclusion

The international community has emphasized the need to label terrorism accurately for a number of reasons: to emphasize the gravitas of the security threat posed by a group, to ensure accurate allocation of resources to combating those groups, to protect against the improper stigmatization of those inappropriately labeled as "terrorists," and to combat the propensity of governments to abuse

104 Id. at 12 (56% of respondents favored the BJP to combat terrorism, whereas only 20% favored the rival Congress party).

105 Id. at 13 (78% of respondents had a favorable view of Modi).

106 See Bruce Stokes, *India and Modi: The Honeymoon Continues*, Pew Research Center (Sept. 19, 2016), available at www.pewglobal.org/2016/09/19/india-and-modi-the-honeymoon-continues/ (showing a 61% approval rating for Modi on dealing with terrorism).

107 See Bharatiya Janata Party, Election Manifesto 2014, at 38, available at www.bjp.org/images/pdf_2014/full_manifesto_english_07.04.2014.pdf.

108 See Sudha Setty, Neoliberal National Security: Wielding Counterterrorism Powers to Protect Economic Growth, in Sairam Bhat, ed., *Privatization and Globalization: Changing Legal Paradigm* (Eastern Law House, 2017).

109 See Mira Kamdar, The Question More Indians Ask—'Is My Phone Tapped?' *The New York Times* (Oct. 26, 2017), available at https://nyti.ms/2iEz5wx.

counterterrorism powers to the detriment of groups and individuals without political clout.[110] Broadening the label of "terrorism" to include additional societal and criminal issues to which fewer resources and less public attention are often given is tempting. After all, such labeling would arguably mean that politicians and the public would allocate more resources toward counterterrorism, that law enforcement could marshal additional powers to investigate and prosecute these crimes, and that undesirable criminal behavior is further stigmatized.

However, it is precisely for those reasons that we should be cautious about unconventional applications of the label of terrorism. The use (or misuse) of a terrorism statute for a gang-related prosecution, the labeling of vandalism by animal rights activists as terrorism, or the prolonged terrorism-related detentions of one religious group for violent acts that are ultimately deemed to be non-terrorist acts are exemplars of the potential problems that may occur as the definition of terrorism is stretched toward new contexts. Further, taking gang violence, vandalism, arson, assault, murder, sex trafficking, and other violent acts that are already criminalized, and relabeling them as "terrorism" is a misnomer and a substantive due process violation.[111] The appellate court in *Morales* also suggested that such mislabeling dilutes efforts to combat actual terrorism, noting that "the concept of terrorism has a unique meaning and its implications risk being trivialized if the terminology is applied loosely in situations that do not match our collective understanding of what constitutes a terrorist act."[112]

To the extent that advocates seek to increase the penalties or stigma associated with these criminal activities or to convince politicians and policy-makers to prioritize those issues, they should address those deficits directly, not by bootstrapping other issues onto vague, overly broad, and amorphous definitions of terrorism that have already been misused to the detriment of politically less powerful groups and the rule of law more generally.

110 United Nations Commission on Human Rights, *Report of the Special Rapporteur on the promotion and protection of human rights and fundamental freedoms while countering terrorism, Martin Scheinin*, E/CN.4/2006/98, December 28, 2005, at ¶42 ("It is essential to ensure that the term 'terrorism' is confined in its use to conduct that is of a genuinely terrorist nature").

111 See Odette J. Wilkens, The Animal Enterprise Act: An Unjust Law and the Case for Repeal, 54 *S. Tex. L. Rev*. 535, 557–58 (Spring 2013) (arguing that the overbreadth of the AETA runs afoul of the "true threats" doctrine that distinguishes particularized crime (non-terrorism) from crimes with public impact (terrorism)).

112 *People v. Morales*, 20 N.Y. 3d at 249.

2 Separatist, not terrorist

Case studies from Southeast Asia

Nadirsyah Hosen

In an international arena that is dominated by media-reported terrorist attacks, what matters most is not a definition of terrorism, but rather the effect of what is labelled terrorism. As a label, terrorism promotes a greater attention from the media and policy makers in the West. The term terrorism, which many associate exclusively with fanatical, radical Islamic sects, has distorted views towards organisational violence especially after 9/11. In turn, this has created the misconception that internationally based violence is synonymous with terrorism. However, there is no all-encompassing definition of terrorism; there are only common elements that are used to determine actions as such,[1] and accordingly promote fear. The very inadequacy of this classification of terrorism is exhibited prominently throughout Southeast Asia, and particularly upon analysis of the southern regions of Thailand and the Philippines, and also in Indonesia. This highlights the need for a shift away from the destructive connotations associated with such Western interpretations of terrorism to an inherently Southeast Asian approach that takes into consideration the unique social, political, economical, and historical background in which each of these organisations exists.

Following the Bali bombings of 12 October 2002, Southeast Asia found itself under the international spotlight as terrorism analysts and several governments began referring to it as the "second front" even as the ensuing global "War on Terror" gathered momentum. As events unfolded, this unfortunate reputation seemed to gain currency – terrorist attacks in the region repeated themselves in the bombing of the Marriott Hotel in Jakarta on 5 August 2003, the bombing of the Australian Embassy in Jakarta on 24 August 2004, and another spate of bombings in Bali on 1 October 2005. Meanwhile, al-Qaeda-inspired terrorist cells were uncovered in Indonesia, Philippines, Malaysia, and Singapore. Al-Qaeda is widely believed to have managed to penetrate Southeast Asia through a Southeast Asian "alumni network" of fighters who had fought alongside the Mujahideen in Afghanistan during the resistance to Soviet occupation in the 1980s. Institutionally, al-Qaeda's influence came in the form of the notorious *Jemaah Islamiyah* region-wide terrorist network that aimed to establish a "*Daulah Islamiyah*" or regional Islamic state through violent means.

1 Laura K. Donohue, "Terrorism and the counter-terrorist discourse" in Victor V. Ramraj, Michael Hor, and Kent Roach (eds), *Global Anti-Terrorism Law and Policy* (Cambridge University Press, 2005) 13, 22–24.

Notwithstanding the current fixation with the phenomenon in the region, the fact of the matter is that terrorism and political violence is not new to Southeast Asia. During the Cold War, Southeast Asia witnessed a proliferation of both communist rebellions and separatist insurgencies, leading to the region being infamously labelled a "region in revolt". Throughout this period, home-grown communist movements in Malaya, Indonesia, the Philippines, Thailand, South Vietnam, Laos, and Cambodia emerged and, in the course of their confrontation with both the colonial and post-colonial state, engaged in acts of terrorism. At the same time, many of these countries also faced ethno-nationalist secessionist and separatist movements that took up arms against central governments. Many of these movements remain active today, and while some have mutated and taken on different forms, mostly their political agendas remain unchanged. To be sure, tactics of terror, violence, and intimidation were hardly the monopoly of communist and ethno-nationalist groups and movements. In not a few instances, acts of terrorism were either condoned or, worst, endorsed by central governments, often against local populations that were suspected to be sympathising with precisely those resistance movements alluded to above. This was certainly the case at different times and in different contexts in Indonesia, Burma, South Vietnam, Thailand, and the Philippines. Notwithstanding Southeast Asia's record of encounters with terrorism and political violence, it was only in the aftermath of 11 September 2001, or more precisely 12 October 2002 of the first Bali bombing, that these issues came to the fore in academic and policy discourse.

This chapter provides two case studies below to illustrate the difficulties of distinguishing between terrorism and the religious-separatist movement in Southeast Asia. The inadequacy of what is deemed to constitute terrorism and the effect thereof will be further considered in light of the prevalent organised violence in Patani and Mindanao. Both involve Muslim separatist groups. The third case study involves the separatist movement in Aceh and Papua Indonesia. While the main source of conflict in Papua is not about religion, like in Patani and Mindanao, the tension in Papua leads to a separatist movement. However, conflict in Aceh involved Islamic communities, which made the Indonesian government treat Aceh differently from the Papua conflict. Understanding the different trajectory of individuals or groups, especially their motives for getting involved in any activities of political violence, is very critical to avoid lumping together all terrorism acts in the same box. The three case studies reveal how such labels of 'terrorism' in the name of national security could be problematic. All this is not to deny that acts of violence and terror remain a salient security threat, but the issue of separatist movement is a complicated one that cannot simply be solved by labelling them as 'terrorist groups/organisations'.

Problems with definition

The term terrorism can be loosely attributed to a form of psychological warfare that is designed to alter behaviours of the state and general public to that of inconvenience out of fear. Terrorism in the current oft-cited use of the "War on Terror" refers, in a general sense, to violent, fear-inducing attacks, especially on civilians, by revolutionaries, insurgents and marginalised groups who wish to upset the established national and international order. In this sense, it does not matter what the source of 'terror' is. What matters is that the definition is fluid and changeable. This suggests that there is no particular environment that generates the archetypal terrorist, or for that matter that the "archetypal terrorist" exists. In order to realise the drivers of such violence "we have to look behind the images of cruelty and fear, and understand that the violence cannot solely be explained by state suppression, economic, or other structural factors"[2] as these conditions occur both in regions of peace and violence.

It is the Western hegemony that has created the difficulty in pinning down what it exactly is that terrorism entails. The current standards for what is considered terrorist action are the actions of foregone American founding fathers and revolutionaries. Ultimately, this highlights the effect that perspective has on the dichotomy of what is considered "right and wrong". This issue is compounded by the lack of an international consensus on a definition of terrorism, with the League of Nations rejecting a draft in 1937, outlining terrorism as "all criminal acts directed against a State and intended or calculated to create a state of terror in the minds of particular persons or groups of persons or the general public".[3] However, the pervasiveness of fear and terror amongst the public is often promoted by the action, or inaction of a state. Draconian measures that usurp human rights in concurrence with continuous media coverage of a "war on terror" effectively fuel the notoriety required to sustain the premise of radical and violent ideologists; with the public,[4] sympathisers,[5] and potential funders alike.[6]

Therefore, with no official definition, what it is that terrorism entails is subject to the misinterpretations of ethnocentric populations. Donohue pointed out that there are seven identifiable elements that are common in terrorist acts: the use of violence, the creation of fear, the generation of fear in a broader audience, purposive actions, a political agenda, actions levied on non-combatants, and the intention to achieve a broader goal.[7]

Ben Saul, in his book *Defining Terrorism in International Law* (2006), proposes the following definition, which, he argues, would reflect existing agreement on the wrongfulness of terrorism:

> (1) Any serious, violent, criminal act intended to cause death or serious bodily injury, or to endanger life, including by acts against property; (2) where committed outside an armed conflict; (3) for a political, ideological, religious,

2 Sascha Helbardt, "Anatomy of Southern Thailand's Insurgency: Some Preliminary Insights" (Working Paper No. 1, University of Passau, 2010) 26.

3 United Nations Office on Drugs and Crime, *Definitions of Terrorism*www.unodc.org/unodc/terrorism_definitions.html (accessed 20 October 2010).

4 Moghaddan, above n. 3, 19–20.

5 Moghaddan, above n. 3, 3.

6 Javaid Rehman, *Islamic State Practices, International Law and the Threat from Terrorism: A Critique of the 'Clash of Civilisations' in the New World Order* (1st edn, Hart Publishing, 2005) 53.

7 Donohue, above n. 1, 22–24.

> or ethnic purpose; and (4) where intended to create extreme fear in a person, group, or the general public, and: (a) seriously intimidate a population or part of a population, or (b) unduly compel a government or an international organization to do or to abstain from doing any act.

Furthermore, he suggests an explicit exception for acts of advocacy, protest, dissent or industrial action that are not intended to cause death, serious bodily harm, or serious risk to public health or safety.[8]

Other definitions usually include: "the use or threat of action" where it endangers life, or poses a serious risk to health or to property, and is "designed to influence the government or to intimidate the public or a section of the public", and where "the use or threat is made for the purpose of advancing a political, religious or ideological cause" (Section 1 of the Terrorism Act 2000 in the United Kingdom). And yet, on each of these counts, the attempt to define terrorism is fraught with difficulties in distinguishing terrorism from what it is not such as legitimate state responses or counter-terrorism, national liberation struggles or freedom fighters, and ordinary criminal offences.

With regard to freedom fighters, one only needs to offer the examples of Yasser Arafat and Nelson Mandela. Nobel Peace Prize winner Yasser Arafat has been charged with the cold-blooded assassination of US Ambassador Cleo Noel in the Sudan in 1973. His PLO (Palestine Liberation Organization) is an umbrella group embracing organisations for defending their lands. Nelson Mandela, another Nobel Peace Prize winner, did not get life imprisonment on Robben Island for sitting in at lunch counters, but if memory serves for plotting terror to overthrow the regime. Is it then true that 'one man's terrorist is another man's freedom fighter'?

It is worth noting that half of all terrorist organisations have such 'liberation' aims. They wish to make an independent state for a minority (the Basque Fatherland and Liberty group, the IRA, the Kurdistan Workers' Party), an independent Islamic state (Abu Sayyaf Group, Moro Islamic Liberation Front), or an independent working class (Revolutionary People's Liberation Party/Front). Put simply, they struggle for the country's liberation. Are they terrorists or freedom fighters? With reference to these elements the inadequacy of what is deemed to constitute terrorism, and the effect thereof, will be further considered in light of the prevalent organised violence in Patani, Mindanao, Aceh, and Papua.

Terrorism, separatism, and criminals

Southern Thailand – Patani

The extreme south of Thailand shares a 600-kilometre border with Malaysia.[9] It is in these regions of Yala, Narathiwat, and Patani that a considerable proportion of

8 Ben Saul, *Defining Terrorism in International Law* (Oxford University Press, 2006) 65–66.

9 Peter Lleyland, 'Thailand's Troubled South: Examining the Case for Devolution from a Comparative Perspective' (2009) 11 *Asian Law* 1, 3.

the nation's Muslim population reside.[10] This area feels the effects of a heavily Bangkok-centralised Thai state through considerable social and economic inequality. Southern Thailand has a longstanding history of violence that can be seen as a response to the disenfranchisement of people by their state.[11] Accordingly, groups such as the Patani United Liberation Organization (PULO) and National Revolutionary Front Coordinate (BRN-Coordinate) have been the locus of a Southern Thailand separatist agenda, with a *modus operandi* of merciless violence. The key leaders of the insurgence have previous connections to the global conflict in Afghanistan in the 1980s. Some of these fighters built regional alliances upon their return to their home country. An interview with one of the authors of this report reveals that JI (Jemaah Islamiyah) sent its Afghan veterans to Southern Thailand in the early 2000s to build a regional Islamist network. Hambali, an Afghan veteran from Indonesia, the only non-Arab who was part of the inner circle of al-Qaeda, was arrested in Bangkok after the first Bali bombing in 2002. Thus, groups like PULO and BRN-Coordinate have been considered in differing regards, with many viewing the self-proclaimed separatist groups as terrorists,[12] in contrast with former Prime Minister of Thailand Thaksin Shiniwatra's claims that the groups were mere bandits and drug traffickers.[13] However, the determinations of these groups as terrorists, separatists, or common thugs are all correct in certain respects. When viewing the term terrorist as a characterisation within itself, both PULO and BRN-Coordinate might satisfy common elements prevalent in acts of terrorism. The issue is also a complex one involving problems with justice, politics education, and economics – to name but a few. This, in turn, exhibits the difficulties with the catch-all term and the need for the deconstruction thereof, to better determine demands and, accordingly, reconciliation or negotiation methods.[14]

Recent intensification of violence beginning in 2004 can be seen as a response to the inexcusable policies of Thaksin who led the passive-aggressive integration of a Buddhist population into an area that claimed Islamic autonomy in accordance with a previously once independent Sultanate of Patani.[15] Currently, Buddhists make up approximately 20 per cent of the population in this area, with a disproportionate amount of power both economically and bureaucratically.[16] What

10 Ibid.

11 Human Rights Watch, *No One Is Safe: Insurgent Attacks on Civilians in Thailand's Southern Border Provinces* (2007), Chapter IV, available at www.hrw.org/reports/2007/thailand0807/.

12 International Crisis Group, *Southern Thailand: Insurgency not Jihad* (2005) Asia Report no. 98, www.crisisgroup.org/en/regions/asia/south-east-asia/thailand/098-southern-thailand-insurgency-not-jihad.aspx.

13 Lleyland, above n. 11, 8.

14 See Rohan Gunaratna and Arabinda Acharya, *The Terrorist Threat from Thailand: Jihad or Quest for Justice?* (Potomac Books Inc., 2012).

15 Carlo Bonura, 'Geopolitical Articulations: Global Terrorism, Southern Thailand' in Nair Biswas and Sheila Shampa (eds), *International Relations and States of Exception: Margins, Peripheries and Excluded Bodies* (Routledge, 2009) 48, 61.

16 Lleyland, above n. 11, 6.

began as an overarching movement for autonomy by an oppressed people against colonial expansion in the nineteenth century has culminated in Muslim–Buddhist violence that has claimed over 4000 lives since January 2004.[17] This new wave of violence that has pervaded Thai culture represents a shift from traditional separatism to public concerns of the groups' participation in the "global terror network".[18] Although actual links between Patani radicals and global terrorist networks such as al-Qaeda are tenuous at best,[19] the fear that terrorist attacks in Western nations have promulgated seems to have aroused suspicion amongst scholars.[20]

Nonetheless, the violence within Thailand's south does not subscribe to the Western hegemony of terrorism, nor common elements of what terrorist actions commonly entail. Southern Thai violence fails to satisfy the seven common elements present in terrorist acts in their entirety.[21] That is, Patani extremists generally limit their attacks to military targets, thus not satisfying the crucial element of attack on non-combatants.[22] From 2004 there have been a slew of murders and bomb attacks focussed primarily on military and police, but also directed at Buddhist monks and teachers.[23] Prima facie, it seems that this violence contravenes the non-combatant element required to determine terrorist acts as such. However, when considering that this violence is a backlash to the institutional oppression of a people, a degree of agency is required in determining the status of legitimate state targets and their aides.[24] Thus, Buddhist monks and teachers are seen as civil servants of a discriminate state institution,[25] which becomes especially apparent when considering the status of southern Thai Buddhist *wats* (temples) as makeshift military bases.[26]

The military control of the deep south has given rise to a slew of new legislation. The area has been under martial law since 2004, subordinating all civilian agencies to the military and allowing for sweeping powers of search, seizure, and arrest. A year later, an Executive Decree on Public Administration in Emergency Situations was announced, absolving security forces acting in "good faith" of criminal liability and permitting preventive detention of suspects for up to 30 days without charge. Meanwhile, 2008's Internal Security Act further curtailed

17 Bonura, above n. 17, 60.
18 Bonura, above n. 17.
19 Rohan Gunaratna, Arabinda Acharya, and Sabrina Chua, *Conflict and Terrorism in Southern Thailand*, (Cavendish Square Publishing, 2006) 10.
20 Zachary Abuza, *Conspiracy of Silence: The Insurgency in Southern Thailand* (United States Institute of Peace, 2009) 16.
21 Donohue, above n. 1.
22 John Gershman, 'Is Southeast Asia the Second Front?' (2002) 81(4) *Foreign* Affairs 60, 67.
23 Lleyland, above n. 11, 9.
24 Donohue, above n. 1, 25.
25 Peter Chalk, 'Militant Islamic Extremism in Southeast Asia' in Paul J. Smith (ed.), *Terrorism and Violence in Southeast Asia: Transnational Challenges to States and Regional* Stability (M E Sharpe Inc., 2005) 19, 25.
26 Lleyland above n. 11, 9.

detainees' rights. Under its terms, individuals in military custody have no right to see a lawyer or relatives and no right for their whereabouts to be known. The legislative moves were put in place to maximise the government's ability to obtain information needed to fight terrorism. Once in military custody, detainees are often tortured in the hopes of extracting confessions.[27]

Further, there is difficulty in determining the current violence that has plagued Southern Thailand as separatist in nature. Recent bouts of violence lack an identifiable or published separatist agenda with demands becoming increasingly multifarious. The unified political agenda that previously characterised the separatist movement has diffused into various demands of 'an independent state, an independent Islamic state, some form of union with Malaysia, or merely increased autonomy within Thailand'.[28] Therefore, this violence can no longer be characterised as terrorism, a unified separatist movement, but rather as diverse insurgency organisations engaging in political violence. It is intended, with this distinction drawn, that human rights violations such as the overt use of force by Thai defence force[29] will be avoided with the added checks and balances of state executive and judicial involvement. However, it must be noted that this shift of burden cannot be without accompanying reform of legal infrastructure and reflection on pervasive corruption.[30]

Southern Philippines – Mindanao

The Abu Sayyaf Group (ASG) emerged in the southern provinces of the Philippines in 1989 as an Islamic separatist organisation. The organisation's raison d'être was the establishment of an independent Islamic State of Mindanao, through the systematic violent targeting of Christian Southern Filipinos.[31] The identifiable common elements of terrorist acts are clearly identifiable in ASG's actions.[32] The violent actions of the ASG between the years of 1991 and 1996 entail 67 attacks being carried out culminating in 58 deaths and the injury of 398 people.[33] Further enhancing the determination of ASG as a terrorist organisation is the link between the organisation and assistance received from al-Qaeda.[34]

27 Abby Seiff (2016) '"We Have No Freedom": Losing Hearts and Minds in Thailand's Deep South', 33 (4) *World Policy Journal* 51. doi: 10.1215/07402775–3813003.
28 Lleyland, above n. 11, 22.
29 Human Rights Watch (2007), above n. 13, Chapter V.
30 Gershman, above n. 24, 72.
31 Charles Donnelly, 'Terrorism in the Southern Philippines: Contextualising the *Abu Sayyaf* Group as an Islamist Secessionist Organisation' (paper presented at the 15th Biennial Conference of the Asian Studies Association of Australia, Canberra, 29 June–2 July 2004) 5.
32 Donohue, above n. 1, 22–24.
33 Zachary Abuza, 'Al-Qaeda Comes to Southeast Asia' in Paul J. Smith (ed.), *Terrorism and Violence in Southeast Asia: Transnational Challenges to States and Regional* Stability (M.E. Sharpe Inc., 2005) 38, 42.
34 Andrew Tan, 'The "New" Terrorism: How Southeast Asia Can Counter It' in Uwe Johannen, Alan Smith, and James Gomez (eds), *September 11 & Political Freedom* (Select Publishing, 2003) 86, 99.

Primarily, the claims of these ties to al-Qaeda centre on events in the early 1990s of armament training by Osama bin Laden's associate, Muhammad Jamal Khalifa,[35] and financial assistance received from Ustadz Abdurajak Abubakar Janjalani, Osama bin Laden's brother-in-law.[36] Although violent attacks attributable to the ASG have continued with a recent attack in Basilan with two casualties and 13 injured,[37] 'there is little evidence to suggest that the ASG is currently engaged in the wider al-Qaeda network'.[38]

Unlike in Southern Thailand, the conflict in Southern Philippines has attracted more foreign fighters from other neighbouring countries such as Malaysia, Singapore, and Indonesia. This tie among fighters in the region could be traced back to their involvement in the Afghanistan conflict in 1980s. For example, the leader of JI, Abdullah Sungkar, sent its members, especially the Afghan veterans, to establish a military training camp in the early 2000s with the Moro Islamic Liberation Front (MILF). Hundreds of JI members from Indonesia, Malaysia, and Singapore participated in a series of military training sessions. Some of these veterans of the training stayed in Southern Thailand, and some of them have joined ASG.

The separatist agenda that perpetuated the ASG in violent, non-discriminate attacks against Christian Filipinos has considerably diluted in recent times. With corruption remaining rife throughout the Philippines, the ASG can be currently seen more as a criminal organisation than either separatist or, for that matter, terrorist in nature. This becomes especially apparent in view of the shift of the organisation's focus on profitability and, accordingly, divergence from the ideological cause. The ASG engages in primarily criminal behaviour including kidnappings, extortion, and drug trafficking.[39] Effectively, ASG is blurring the lines between what is deemed crime and terrorism, becoming a criminal organisation with terrorist roots. This behaviour takes advantage of an enabling state that has notoriously lax immigration laws, widespread corruption, unstable political landscape, and collusion amongst a highly discretionary executive branch.[40] The Philippines is one of the most corrupt nations in the world, with approximately 15 per cent of the governmental budget lost through corruption and a further 20 per cent attributable to "personal services and pension payments".[41]

35 Lesley Brown and Paul Wilson, 'Putting the Crime Back into Terrorism: The Philippines Perspective' (2007) 2 *Asian Criminology* 35, 41.
36 Chalk, above n. 27, 20.
37 Jewel Reyes, '2 More Die in Abu Sayyaf Attack in Basilan' (2010) ABS-CBN News, available at www.abs-cbnnews.com/nation/regions/03/01/10/2-more-die-abu-sayyaf-attack-basilan.
38 Brown and Wilson, above n. 37, 41.
39 Human Rights Watch, *You Can Die Any Time: Death Squad Killings in Mindanao* (2009) Chapter IV, available at www.hrw.org/reports/2009/04/06/you-can-die-any-time.
40 Allan Jones Salem, 'Nexus of Crime and Terrorism: The Case of the Abu Sayyaf Group', Master Thesis, Naval Postgraduate School, Monterey, California, December 2016, 65–70.
41 P. Wilson, 'The Social and Political Basis of Terrorism in the Philippines' in Shlomo Giora Shoham and Paul Kepper (eds), *Terrorism and the International Community* (de Sitter Publications, 2005) 63.

The distinction drawn between terrorism and violent criminal behaviour may seem semantic; however, there is a considerable difference in the way that terrorist acts are regarded in comparison with criminal acts, both by states and civilians. The criminal acts that the ASG presently focus on are distinct from the actions of a once unified separatist (or terrorist) organisation. The lack of foundational ideology behind the surge in a criminal action can be seen to have four effects. First, criminal motivation with a primary view to profit represents a departure from the alliance to a movement that is heavily reliant on political and religious ideology.[42] Second, the shift in motivation from combating social oppression (or promulgating radical ideologies) to the profitability of criminal actions ultimately garners and recruits fewer sympathisers than organisations who seem to be fighting for a cause. Third, the determination of the ASG as a criminal organisation that partakes in gang-like behaviour represents an important symbolic shift away from the elements of terrorism, resulting in the restriction of prevalent fear, an important goal in terrorist action.[43] This abatement of fear can be seen as resulting in a more understandable psychology of greed in conjunction with the diminishing fear of the unknown, or previously randomised acts of violence.

Lastly, the shift from the categorisation of the ASG, and other similar organisations, as terrorists to that of a criminal organisation may be able to assist with the way in which offenders are dealt with. For example, during the Philippines military campaign against the ASG, there were more than 150,000 people displaced from the area accompanied by considerable allegations of human rights violations.[44] Although the Philippines can be seen as an enabling environment, both the Filipino and US military involvement is not assisting in rectifying the salient issues of[45] socio-economic disparity, political inequality, and lack of regional cohesion. In this regard, the institution of counter-attack merely exacerbates the situation by increasing the perceivable threat of an organisation that could be dealt with in a traditional criminal law approach or through negotiation. Further, the abandonment of the Western "War on Terror" will represent a move away from the controversial anti-terrorist legislation and emergency measures that many states have instituted.[46] Such measures may reduce the fears of civilians, but the costs are extensive damage to the foundations of a democratic rule of law and the confiscation of human rights – too large a price to pay.[47]

Up until 2007, terrorist attacks in the Philippines were tried under the common criminal law called the Revised Penal Code. On 6 March 2007, President Arroyo

42 Rehman, above n. 8, 4.
43 Donohue, above n 1, 22.
44 Human Rights Watch, above n 41, 27.
45 Brown, above n 34, 44.
46 Human Rights Watch, *Philippines: New Terrorism Law Puts Rights at Risk*, 17 July 2007, available at www.hrw.org/en/news/2007/07/15/philippines-new-terrorism-law-puts-rights-risk.
47 Simon Tay and Tan Hsien Li, 'Southeast Asian Cooperation on Anti-Terrorism' in Victor V. Ramraj, Michael Hor, and Kent Roach (eds), *Global Anti-Terrorism Law and* Policy (Cambridge University Press, 2005) 399, 422.

approved the Human Security Act (HSA). HSA penalises acts constituting terrorism and imposes a penalty of imprisonment for 40 years. HSA defines terrorism by stating that anyone "sowing and creating a condition of widespread extraordinary fear and panic among the populace, in order to coerce the government to give in to an unlawful demand shall be guilty of the crime of terrorism".[48] It outlines how terrorism is punishable under Philippine law, specifying that those convicted "shall suffer the penalty of forty (40) years of imprisonment, without the benefit of parole as provided for under Act No. 4103, otherwise known as the Indeterminate Sentence Law, as amended".

HSA provisions allow law enforcers to wiretap communications between members of judicially declared outlawed terrorist organisations and to detain any person charged with or suspected of committing terrorism for three days without a judicial warrant. Because of the broad powers that it confers on law enforcers, HSA has been criticised in the international community and raised fears that it may result in violations of civil liberties. Another area of concern is that the Act provides for restrictions on movement including the imposition of house arrest where the legal basis is simply "in cases where evidence of guilt is not strong" rather than positive suspicion or a higher evidentiary threshold.

The definition of terrorism as embodied in the HSA is considered vague and highly prone to abuse. Chester Cabalza claims that the HSA "is one of the most incoherent, disorganized, and disjointed laws the Philippine Congress has ever passed".[49] He argues that the law has no clear standard objectives that will guide law enforcers; thus, it allows the law enforcers to have their own preference and interpretation of who is engaged in terrorism or conspiracy to commit terrorism. Moreover, he notes, the crimes enumerated in the Human Security Act are already punishable under the Revised Penal Code of the Philippines.[50] Harry L. Roque, Jr shares the same concerns. Roque takes the view that the vagueness of the definition of terrorism in the HSA stems from the use of words and phrases such as 'widespread', 'extraordinary', 'fear', 'panic', and 'unlawful demand'. This qualifying phrase does not really qualify at all.[51] He is afraid that the creation of a condition of widespread and extraordinary fear and panic among the populace depends on how crime is sensationalised, either by the state, or by the mass media, or by anyone who wants a certain criminal conduct to be characterised as 'terrorist'. Roque concluded that "the core criticism against the HSA is that it does not satisfactorily define what is being prohibited".[52]

48 Human Security Act of 2007, Congress of the Philippines, www.senate.gov.ph/republic_acts/ra%209372.pdf.
49 Chester B. Cabalza, 'Deconstructing Human Security in the Philippines', www.academia.edu/2137055/Deconstructing_Human_Security_in_the_Philippines
50 Ibid.
51 H. Harry L. Roque, Jr., 'The Human Security Act and the IHL Law of the Philippines: of Security and Insecurity' in Victor Vridar Ramraj et al., *Global Anti Terrorism Law and Policy* (Cambridge University Press, 2nd edition, 2012) 317
52 Ibid.

This law, passed under strong US influence, could lead to an increase in the number of acts of torture and extra-judicial killings in the framework of the fight against terrorism.[53] There was a school of thought that the Human Security Act is not likely to be used in practice. The main reason is that it contains some provisions to prevent abuse by the army and the police; in particular, 500,000.00 PhP a day (approximately 12,500 US dollars) shall be paid to the person charged with terrorism upon his acquittal or the dismissal of the charges against him. The prosecution may consequently keep relying upon the Revised Penal Code to avoid facing such risks. Members of civil society expressed deep concern that this provision could have an adverse effect: members of the law-enforcement agencies could prefer to kill the suspect instead of taking the risk of having to face the financial cost of an acquittal.

Though this approach of distinguishing violent and often radical organisations from their counterparts seems naive, it is not intended as an overarching approach to the treatment of all terrorist organisations. Further, there is no suggestion that terrorist organisations who *occasionally* engage in actions that are more criminal than terrorist in nature should be dealt with as a criminal organisation. However, this is an appeal to shift the terrorist paradigm from the uncertain, broad definition of an indiscriminate pool of "terrorists" that often share alternative ideological views, to a set of differentiable organisations. Such an approach will not only assist the identification of organisational demands, but also the assessment of the optimal approach to overcome issues at hand, while minimising the impact of this on the international arena.

Aceh and Papua conflict – Indonesia

The third case study is a conflict in Aceh and Papua Indonesia. The Papua conflict is an ongoing conflict between the Indonesian government and portions of the indigenous populations of West Papua in the Indonesian provinces of Papua and West Papua on the island of New Guinea. The long-running separatist movement in West Papua remains a sensitive issue for Indonesia, with pro-independence rebels the Free Papua Organisation (Organisasi Papua Merdeka – OPM) continuing to resist Jakarta's authority. Historically, the former Dutch colony, previously called Irian Jaya, had been preparing for independence before Indonesia asserted its claim in 1962.[54] The West Papua region officially became part of Indonesia after the Act of Free Choice in 1969, a referendum that was overseen by the United Nations. Since the decision was made to join Indonesia, a near-constant friction has continued with reports of violent crackdowns and human rights abuses committed by Indonesian authorities against pro-independence supporters. Since

53 Pauline E. Eadie, 'Legislating for Terrorism: The Philippines' Human Security Act 2007', *Journal of Terrorism Research* (2011) 2(3). DOI: http://doi.org/10.15664/jtr.226.

54 See Pieter Drooglever, *An Act of Free Choice; Decolonisation and the Right to Self-Determination in West Papua* (Oneworld Publications, 2009).

2003 Irian Jaya province was divided into Papua and West Papua. Both provinces are the poorest provinces of Indonesia despite being one of the most mineral-rich regions in the world.[55]

Following the Bali bombing, the Indonesian Anti-Terrorism Law began with the issuance of Government Regulation in Lieu of Law (GRL) No. 1 of 2002 concerning the Eradication of Criminal Acts of Terrorism on 18 October 2002 (Anti-Terrorism Law). On the same day, the government issued GRL No. 2 of 2002, which made GRL No. 1 retroactively applicable to the Bali bombings. In 2003, the Anti-Terrorism Law and GRL No. 2 became law after being confirmed by the legislature. Since its promulgation in 2002 there has been no amendment or revision to the Anti-Terrorism Law.[56] The question is: should the Anti-Terrorism Law be applied in the Papua conflict? Since the Bali and Jakarta hotel bombs, Indonesia has assumed a higher profile in the "War on Terror". The international focus on terrorism tends to highlight Jakarta's rather different security priorities. Although the Bali bomb forced the government to take more seriously the activities of Indonesian terrorist organisations, within the government the most pressing threat was thought to be separatism not terrorism. But in the case of Papua, such a line is blurred.

According to Jason Macleod, historically, the Indonesian government has not distinguished between armed and unarmed groups, classifying both violent and non-violent resisters as 'separatists' or 'terrorists' intent on destroying the Indonesian state.[57] Indonesia employs both military and police to deal with the OPM that caused many incidents. For instance, the OPM unit responsible for the Freeport shootings (18 shooting incidents with three fatalities from late 2009 to early 2010, and 12 shootings with ten fatalities between October 2011 and February 2012) appears to have wanted to terrify the company into shutting down and leaving Papua. They are not just going after police and military but also after civilians, including non-Papuan Indonesian migrants, workers for the gigantic gold and copper mine Freeport; and most recently tourists.[58] While officially the Indonesian government never declares that the separatist movement in Papua are terrorist groups, Indonesia does not use the local police. Instead, it uses Special Detachment 88, the Indonesian anti-terrorism police squad, to deal with the Papua conflict. This fact revealed that the line between separatists and terrorists is blurred.

55 See Esther Heidbüchel, *The West Papua Conflict in Indonesia; Actors, Issues and Approaches* (Johannes Herrmann, 2007).

56 Nadirsyah Hosen, 'Emergency Powers and the Rule of Law in Indonesia' in Victor V. Ramraj and Arun K. Thiruvengadam (eds), *Emergency Powers in Asia* (Cambridge University Press, 2010) 287–289.

57 Jason Macleod, *Merdeka and the Morning Star: Civil Resistance in West Papua* (University of Queensland Press, 2015) 15.

58 Sidney Jones, 'Papuan "Separatists" vs Jihadi "Terrorists": Indonesian Policy Dilemmas', a lecture at International Policy Studies program of Stanford University, 5 December 2012.

However, it is important to note that so far the Indonesian government has not used the Anti-Terrorism Law to deal with the OPM. A group involved in the killing of two soldiers and the theft of guns in Wamena in 2003 were given sentences ranging from 18 years to life; the men involved in killing security officers at a demonstration in Abepura in 2006 got 15 years. All have been sentenced using the Criminal Code; not the Anti-Terrorism Law. However this creates a different response. Sidney Jones revealed that Islamic jihadis in Indonesia questioned why the OPM had not been officially labelled as terrorists despite the fact that both jihadis and separatists do the same thing, but with different motives.[59] The jihadis accused that the government discriminates them due to the international pressure to label Islamic groups as terrorists.

Take the example of how the Indonesian government treats conflict in its northern province, Aceh, involving the Free Aceh Movement (Gerakan Aceh Merdeka – GAM). This was clearly a separatist movement seeking self-determination for Acehnese people.[60] While between 1976 and 1979 GAM's attacks were sporadic and not particularly effective, in 1989, after GAM's return from Libya, they had become better organised and forced the Indonesian security forces onto the defensive.[61] After 1998, GAM attacks on the security forces rose again. According to police figures, 53 policemen were killed from July to December 1999 and many more were injured. It was reported that the casualties between 12 March and 12 April 2001 included 33 military personnel and 36 police killed as well as 128 military personnel and 132 police injured. According to a military spokesperson, between June 2000 and April 2001 some 50 soldiers were killed while 206 were injured and eight were listed as missing. GAM sees the Javanese migrants as colonial settlers who are demographically shoring up Jakarta's claim to Aceh as well as potential collaborators with the Indonesian security forces. In June 2001, violence in the ethnically mixed Aceh–Gayo–Javanese areas of Central Aceh reached unprecedented levels with clashes between GAM and local village defence groups killing an estimated 64 people over a two-week period, of whom 50 were Javanese, and resulting in the burning of perhaps a thousand houses.[62] The conflict resulted in a large number of casualties, the deterioration of infrastructure, and psychological harm. However, after a series of failed peace efforts, the government of Indonesia and the GAM made a historic and dignified step by signing

59 Ibid.

60 On the conflict in Aceh see Edward Aspinall, *Islam and Nation: Separatist Rebellion in Aceh, Indonesia* (Stanford University Press, 2009); Michelle Ann Miller, *Rebellion and Reform in Indonesia: Jakarta's Security and Autonomy Policies in Aceh* (Routledge, 2009); Kirsten Schulze (2003) 'The Struggle for an Independent Aceh: The Ideology, Capacity, and Strategy of GAM' 26 (4) *Studies in Conflict and Terrorism* 241.

61 Richard Barber (ed.) *Aceh: The Untold Story* (Asian Forum for Human Rights and Development, 2000) 32.

62 Kirsten Schulze (2004) 'The Free Aceh Movement (GAM): Anatomy of a Separatist Organization' 2 *Policy Studies* 50.

a peace agreement on 15 August 2005 in Helsinki, ending the violent conflict after more than three decades.[63]

In this sense, it is important to note that the Indonesian government applied the Anti-Terrorism Law to GAM and labelled it as a terrorist organisation.[64] The Free Aceh Movement (GAM) has been characterised as being a radical Islamic organisation intent on establishing an Islamic state in northern Sumatra. However Damien Kingsbury explores GAM's relationship with Islam and shows that while GAM members are devout Muslims and that Islam pervades their political thinking, the organisation and its members are explicitly opposed to the creation of an Islamic state or the imposition of Islamic law.[65]

This is to illustrate how the issue has become complicated. The religious motive is seen as a vital point to distinguish between ordinary crime and terrorism. GAM was labelled as a terrorist organisation and some of its members were arrested and charged under the Anti-Terrorism Law. The motive in the Papua conflict is not a religious one despite the fact that there have been 144 reported fatalities between 2009 and 2014 in the separatist conflict in Papua. But should Jakarta officially follow Bangkok and Manila in dealing with Southern Thailand–Patani and Southern Philippines–Mindanao respectively, by declaring the Papua conflict as terrorism? However, to define "separatism" as "terrorism" would deepen Jakarta's targeting of peaceful dissent and the intimidation of Papuans generally. Use of the anti-terror law would enable the police to detain "separatist" suspects, including those engaging in peaceful protest, for a week rather than 48 hours. Ongoing efforts would strengthen the anti-terror law to give the police even broader powers to limit the freedom of speech and assembly. Sidney Jones has suggested not to apply the Anti-Terrorism Law in Papua, but rather to stop using it for crimes committed by jihadis that on the surface fall short of deliberate attempts to create fear, and for which there are adequate provisions in other laws, including the criminal code – crimes such as murder, robbery, and assault.[66] Jones suggestion reveals a dilemma faced by the Indonesian government.

President Widodo announced clemency for five Papuan prisoners while visiting Papua's provincial capital of Jayapura on 9 May 2015. The five men, convicted in 2003 for their alleged role in a raid on an Indonesian Armed Forces weapons

63 M.H. Ansori (2012) 'From Insurgency to Bureaucracy: Free Aceh Movement, Aceh Party and the New Face of Conflict' 1 (1) *Stability: International Journal of Security and Development* 31.

64 Kamarulzaman Askandar, 'The Aceh Conflict: Phases of Conflict and Hopes for Peace' in A.T.H. Tan (ed.), *A Handbook of Terrorism and Insurgency in Southeast Asia* (Edward Elgar, 2007). The US government did not put GAM on the list of terrorist organisations despite the Indonesian government's effort to convince the US. See Martina Klimesova, *Using Carrots to Bring Peace? Negotiation and Third Party Involvement* (World Scientific Publishing Co., 1st edition, 2015) 150; Edward Aspi nall and Harold Crouch, 'The ACEH Peace Process: Why It Failed', *Policy Studies*, No. 1 (East–West Centre, Washington, DC) 30.

65 Damien Kingsbury (2007) 'The Free Aceh Movement: Islam and Democratisation' 37 (2) *Journal of Contemporary Asia* 166–189.

66 Jones, above n. 60.

arsenal in Wamena on 4 April 2003, which resulted in the deaths of two soldiers, were serving prison terms ranging from 19 years to life imprisonment.[67] The Indonesian leader also announced the lifting of travel bans for foreign journalists there.[68] However, security forces for decades have acted with heavy-handedness and impunity to combat the low-level insurgency, which has resulted in widespread abuses. For the military, Papua is central to promotion advantages and their income – the government covers only 25 per cent of the military budget. Corruption and human rights abuses go hand in hand with this.[69] The conflict in Papua remains a problem for Indonesia.

Concluding remarks

This chapter has evaluated the dilemma facing three countries in the Southeast Asia region in dealing with radical Islamism and ethno-nationalism/separatism. Lack of agreement on what terrorism is reveals the difficulties of drawing a clear line using ordinary criminal law or anti-terrorism law. I would argue that the Southeast Asia region is in a better position, compared with Western governments and media, to determine what constitutes terrorism in the region by taking into account the unique social, political, economic, and historical background in which each of these separatist organisations/movements in Patani, Mindanao, Aceh, and Papua exist. Such an approach will assist the identification of organisational demands, and also the assessment of the optimal approach to overcome issues at hand, while minimising the impact of this on the international arena.

Effective categorisation, accompanied with increased integration within Southeast Asia via the Association of Southeast Asian Nations (ASEAN) and ASEAN Police (ASEANPOL), will assist in the progression of the Southern regions of Thailand and the Philippines, along with Indonesia, to a position that is better equipped to combat the violence. Although many of the member nations of ASEAN suffer considerable ideological differences,[70] which inevitably results in hesitation of unified action, states must put their differences aside in a utilitarian effort to stamp out enabling environments. Simply rectifying corruption and reforming legal infrastructure in nations with the limited governmental budget, such as the Philippines, is a task that is difficult, if not impossible, without external assistance. Western ethnocentricity has promulgated widely accepted connotations

67 Michael Bachelard, 'Papuans Face Ignorance, Corruption and Racism from Jakarta', *The Interpreter*, 26 June 2015, available at www.lowyinstitute.org/the-interpreter/papuans-face-ignorance-corruption-and-racism-jakarta.

68 Richard Chauvel, 'Papua: Dialogue as the Road to Peace', *Indonesia at Melbourne*, available at http://indonesiaatmelbourne.unimelb.edu.au/papua-dialogue-as-the-road-to-peace/.

69 Stephen Hill, 'Papuans and Jokowi Are Hostage to Indonesian Politics', *The Conversation*, 1 June 2015, available at http://theconversation.com/papuans-and-jokowi-are-hostage-to-indonesian-politics-42251.

70 Harald David, *Tension within ASEAN: Malaysia and its Neighbours* (1st edn, 1996) 79.

of "terrorism", which can be sensationalistic at best.[71] With the differentiation of organisations that were previously labelled terrorists, what was once a daunting and cumbersome task for policing states can be reformed into a discernible and, more importantly, targetable set of actionable areas. These actionable areas must be considered in conjunction with a decisive move away from counter-terrorism and states of emergency to policies of negotiation and reconciliation, to the creation of a new and inherently Southeast Asian criminal legal response to terrorism.

The definition of terrorism as determinable from prevalent Western hegemony is a term that inadequately describes much of the violence occurring in Southeast Asia. In particular, the organisations of PULO and BRN-Coordinate of Thailand, the ASG of the Philippines, and the OPM and GAM in Indonesia are a testament to this. Accordingly, through the formation of a classification system accompanied and tailored to inherently Southeast Asian solutions, states like Thailand, the Philippines, and Indonesia may be able to manage the threat of fear with the aim of controlling violence into the future.

71 M. Cherif Bassiouni, 'Terrorism, Law Enforcement and the Mass Media: Perspectives, Problems, Proposals' (1981) 72 (1) *Journal of Criminal Law and Criminology* 1, 3.

3 The 'refugee-warrior' in an age of revolutionary violence

Satvinder S. Juss and Jeni Mitchell

Introduction

Over the last score years, four wars have been fought in Afghanistan, Iraq, Libya and Syria. All involved foreign interventions, of varying types and scale. The countries in question all had pre-existing ethnic and religious cleavages, which were exacerbated by war and external meddling. In each case also, all or part of the opposition have included hard-core jihadi fighters. In each case the adversaries have committed 'war crimes' and 'crimes against humanity'. Although states have presented their interventions as humanitarian, and in support of popular forces against dictators and police states, in none of these four cases have foreign-supported actors succeeded in consolidating power and establishing stable states. The resulting carnage has been on an epic scale: these four conflicts alone have killed at least 600,000 civilians and forcibly displaced more than 20 million people.[1]

The most notorious of the barbaric acts in these regional upheavals, depicted in the daily diet of snuff movies, was the macabre sight of a rebel commander cutting open the body of a dead government soldier and eating his heart.[2] No one, one would hope, could expect such a person to be granted sanctuary anywhere, under international law. But what of less extreme cases, involving the 'foot soldiers' in

1 United Nations High Commissioner for Refugees, *UNHCR Global Trends: Forced Displacement in 2016* (Geneva: June 2017); United Nations Assistance Mission in Afghanistan, *Afghanistan: Protection of Civilians in Armed Conflict, Annual Report 2016* (Kabul: February 2017); Neta Crawford, 'War-related Death, Injury and Displacement in Afghanistan and Pakistan, 2001–2014', Brown University Costs of War Project (May 2015); 'UN Envoy Revises Syria Death Toll to 400,000', *Foreign Policy*, 22 April 2016; United Nations Support Mission in Libya, Human Rights Reports on Civilian Casualties, https://unsmil.unmissions.org/human-rights-report-civilian-casualties-0. Estimates of civilian casualties are notoriously difficult to authenticate, and the true death toll from these conflicts may be much higher. On the difficulty in assessing civilian casualty figures in Iraq, for example, see Section 17 of the Report of the Iraq Inquiry (the 'Chilcot Report'), www.iraqinquiry.org.uk/media/246676/the-report-of-the-iraq-inquiry_section-170.pdf.

2 Paul Wood, 'Face to Face with Abu Sakkar, Syria's "Heart-Eating Cannibal"', BBC News Syria, 5 July 2013, available at www.bbc.co.uk/news/magazine-23190533. Also see www.independent.co.uk/news/world/middle-east/isis-confessions-killer-british-jihadi-jihadists-a7501311.html.

this same revolutionary struggle, working to defeat President Assad's state forces? Would he or she succeed, notwithstanding acts of violence committed by them, if they find themselves having to flee their war-torn land? The answer to this question depends on what we would want the role of refugee law to be in the present world of regional conflict and religious rivalry, in wars where the West has taken clearly defined positions from the outset.[3] It would be unrealistic to ignore the context of the political violence embroiling the greater Middle East region today, arising directly from a succession of revolutions[4] and a series of gratuitous neo-colonial wars.[5] So the question is: should violent revolutionaries from today's blood-stained struggles be excluded from refugee status? Are they terrorists, or legitimate combatants?

We suggest that whereas once insurrections against oppressive state systems and tyrants were adroitly manipulated by external state actors, and their leaders often welcomed with open arms and afforded sanctuary from state-inspired persecution in their homelands, today the West in particular has lost control of revolutions, revolts and insurgent movements. Non-state armed groups and popular uprisings harness illicit trades and networks for funding and embrace new communications technologies for recruitment and propaganda, and their aims and narratives are no longer rooted in Cold War ideologies and power politics. With the decline of state leverage over armed groups, responsibility for asylum for their members has become more diffuse, and a more visible problem within international law. If this is so, then one question is whether international law today is sophisticated enough to embrace a right to revolution. And, if so, is there a right to seek sanctuary if one has participated in a failed revolution or revolt? Moreover, what role can the courts play in this context?

This discussion is timely for two reasons. First, much of the academic discussion on the 'War on Terror', and its impacts on human rights, took place between 2004 and 2008. After that, the focus shifted wholesale to the global financial crisis. In the age of Daesh and Donald Trump, the pendulum has now swung back again. In 2017 President Trump's Executive Orders[6] inaugurated a 'Muslim ban'

3 For a recent study, see Satvinder Juss, 'Terrorism and the Exclusion of Refugee Status in the UK', *Journal of Conflict and Security Law* (vol. 17, no. 3, Winter 2012) pp. 465–499.

4 Roger Own, *The Rise and Fall of Arab Presidents for Life* (Harvard University Press, 2012); Joshua Stacher, *Adaptable Autocrats: Regime Power in Egypt and Syria* (Stanford, 2012); Holger Albrecht, *Raging against the Machine: Political Opposition under Authoritarianism in Egypt* (Syracuse University Press, 2012); Hazem Kandil, *Soldiers, Spies and Statesmen: Egypt's Road to Revolt* (Verso, 2012).

5 One co-author has inquired into this question previously: see Satvinder Singh Juss, 'Refugee Law and the Protection of Children fleeing Conflict and Violence in Afghanistan', *Journal of Conflict and Security Law* (vol. 18, no. 2, Summer 2013) pp. 289–330.

6 *Executive Order Protecting the Nation from Foreign Terrorist Entry into the United States* (27 January 2017) at para 3. See www.whitehouse.gov/the-press-office/2017/01/27/executive-order-protecting-nation-foreign-terrorist-entry-united-states. Also see *Executive Order Protecting the Nation from Foreign Terrorist Entry into the United*

in America, which temporarily excluded from entry to the United States the citizens of the Muslim-majority countries of Syria, Sudan, Iran, Somalia, Libya and Yemen, resulting in a 120-day suspension of refugee resettlement to the United States and marked curtailment of refugees entering the county. President Trump's subsequent strengthening of the so-called 'Muslim bans', made effective from 18 October 2017, imposed further restrictions on Syrians, Libyans, Iranians, Yemenis, Somalians, Chadians and North Koreans. This was upheld by a 5 to 4 majority in the US Supreme Court in June 2018, with every Republican appointee upholding the ban and every Democrat appointee opposing it.[7] They also curtailed the movement of a small number of citizens of Venezuela and imposed additional screenings on Iraqi nationals. Some exceptions were allowed under the ban, such as for Iranian students or participants in cultural exchange programmes.[8] There is no explicit and clear focus, in any of the recent developments outlined above, of jihadi fighters alone being targeted rather than Muslims as a whole from named countries, none of whom are recorded as having posed a threat to the United States. As a result, an appreciation of the effects of populism and anti-elitism on the 'War on Terror' is now called for. Second, a discussion about what is meant by the 'War on Terror' is timely given that there is now a challenge to the very basis of human rights, in its historical and political developments, right across the world. The 'war' is now constructed explicitly as a 'civilisational conflict' between a radical Islamist foe and a Judeo-Christian 'West', and as such it is arguably now being waged exactly as Bernard Lewis[9] and Samuel Huntington[10] 'predicted' with the result that there is now the normalisation of 'war powers'. This normalisation, we argue, impacts on the application of the law of refugee status, especially to refugees who are from largely Muslim and non-Christian countries.

Where refugees have participated in internal armed conflict, there are two questions relevant to their recognition as refugees. First, were they personally involved in culpable acts and, if so, how is their 'individual responsibility' for any particular

States (6 March 2017). See www.whitehouse.gov/the-press-office/2017/03/06/executive-order-protecting-nation-foreign-terrorist-entry-united-states.

7 Adam Liptak, 'Trump's Travel Ban Is Upheld by Supreme Court', *The New York Times*, 26 June 2018, available at www.nytimes.com/2018/06/26/us/politics/supreme-court-trump-travel-ban.html.

8 See Press Release, 'President Donald J. Trump Strengthens Security Standards for Traveling to America' (available at www.whitehouse.gov/the-press-office/2017/09/24/president-donald-j-trump-strengthens-security-standards-traveling). Also see Clark Mindock, 'Trump's New "Muslim Ban": All You Need to Know about His More Extreme Replacement', 22 September 2017 (available at www.independent.co.uk/news/world/americas/us-politics/trump-muslim-ban-travel-new-changes-restrictions-what-are-they-differences-countries-list-a7962527.html).

9 Bernard Lewis, *What Went Wrong? Western Impact and Middle Eastern Response* (Oxford University Press, 2002). Also see Bernard Lewis, *The Crisis of Islam: Holy War and Unholy Terror* (Random House, 2004).

10 Samuel Huntington, *The Clash of Civilizations and the Re-making of the World Order* (Simon & Schuster, 2002).

acts to be attributed to them? The answer to this question defines the legitimacy and limits of acceptable 'revolutionary' conduct. Can we, for example, demonstrate a link between asylum decisions and determinations of the legitimacy of violence? It does appear that the judicial authorities, at the very least, are now beginning to require clear and credible evidence of the offending conduct, on the part of the asylum seeker threatened with exclusion, from the government authorities.[11] So much so that nearly every case where a refugee stands to be 'excluded' from the ambit of the refugee status involves this question.[12] Second, when can a person's actions in an armed conflict be said to be 'contrary to the purposes and principles of the United Nations'? The Supreme Court in *Al-Sirri* said this was a 'little used provision' of the Geneva Convention Relating to the Status of Refugees 1951[13] (hereafter 'the Refugee Convention').[14] The courts often have to 'construct' individual responsibility just as they 'construct' actions deemed contrary to the principles of the UN.

This chapter proceeds as follows. First, we identify and highlight the emerging importance of the 'refugee-warrior' in refugee law, as a feature that over recent years had become much shrouded in obscurity and obscurantism, but is of vital importance today if refugees are to be given the protection they deserve when being engaged in vindicating rights of self-determination against oppressive regimes. We explain that we should not be surprised if refugees are both victims and perpetrators of violence. Indeed, from strife-torn parts of the world it is unrealistic to expect them not to be so. Just because they may be engaged in 'refugee-based insurgency' does not make them, by that fact alone, 'refugee-terrorists'. It is important to disaggregate the violence that lies behind conflict-induced displacement.

Second, we look at the legal basis for the exclusion of refugees who have committed a crime against peace, a war crime or a crime against humanity. This is to be found in Article 1(F) of the Refugee Convention as well as the Qualification Directive (2004/83/EC) in European Law. Yet, neither of these provisions tell us anything about the level of 'responsibility' required of a person before it can be said that there are serious reasons for considering their exclusion from refugee status. It is for this

11 See below the discussion in the sections 'Acts contrary to the purposes and principles of the United Nations' and 'The legitimate use of violence for political ends'.

12 Notable cases include *SK (Zimbabwe) [2012] EWCA Civ 807; AN v. Secretary of State for the Home Department* (AA/06251/2008) (24 Sept. 2013); *Azimi-Rad* (Art.1F (a) – complicity – Arts 7 and 25 ICC Statute) Iran [2011] UKUT 339 (IAC); *DD* (AA/05707/2007) (9 September 2013); *AA-R (Iran) v Secretary of State for the Home Department* [2013] EWCA Civ 835; *AH* (Article 1F(b) – 'serious') Algeria [2013] UKUT 382 (5 August 2013); and the German case of in *BVerwG* 10C 48.07, discussed in this article.

13 The 1951 Convention relating to the Status of Refugees is the key legal document in defining who is a refugee. The 1967 Protocol removed geographical and temporal restrictions from the Convention. Available from www.unhcr.org/3b66c2aa10.html.

14 *Al-Sirri v. Secretary of State for the Home Department [2012]* UKSC 54, per Lady Hale at para. 1.

reason that the emerging case law has asked decision-makers to apply these provisions of exclusion cautiously and restrictively.[15]

Third, consideration is given to the 'War on Terror' and how the post-9/11 developments have led to no less than three Security Council Resolutions in September, November and December 2001, and then one in September 2005. The emphasis in all has been on 'acts, methods, and practices of terrorism', their 'financing and planning' being 'regardless of their motivation' and requiring states 'to take urgent action' so as to 'eliminate the scourge of terrorism'. Precisely what is meant by 'terrorism' is not clear. Moreover, there is no recognition of the right of oppressed peoples to revolt and take up insurgent action against an oppressor or aggressor entity. A series of cases discussed shows the courts grappling with these difficult questions. It is noted how there is recognition in the British cases of the legitimate use of violence for political ends.

Finally, the reader is taken to the 'age of revolutionary violence' and reminded how, in both law and security studies, the context of violent behaviour is critical. The complexity of contemporary political violence and lack of firm normative framework mean that decision-makers have difficulty in understanding violence and the role of participants in it. This is important because today 'terrorism' is invoked in a vast range of ideological and political acts, whereas previously it was confined to the narrow acts of non-state armed groups targeting civilians. The durability of the 'terrorist' label today has implications for the unfair treatment of both civilians and fighters involved in conflict situations. Accordingly, the answer lies today in characterising contemporary violence as 'revolutionary violence' when seen in campaigns in the Middle East by violent sub-state actors in a quest for the radical transformation of the existing political and social order. This would in turn help the international community to fully comprehend the legitimacy and legality of acts of violence in conflict-ridden societies around us.

The idea of the 'refugee-warrior'

Violence is central to the condition of the refugee, and not just because it is so often the reason for flight. A decade ago, the political science scholar Idean Salehyan argued that refugee flows have to be seen not just as 'the unfortunate consequences of violence and a humanitarian dilemma' but 'as part of the conflict dilemma itself',[16] so that one places 'forced migration squarely within the study of political violence'.[17] An extensive quantitative investigation by Salehyan and Kristian Gleditsch revealed that cross-border refugee flows are a primary driver of regional conflict clusters, with host states experiencing an increased risk of civil war.[18] Kelly Greenhill has demonstrated the ways in which weak states and

15 See section below on 'The refugee-warrior in international refugee law'.

16 Idean Salehyan, 'Refugees and the Study of Civil War', *Civil Wars* (vol. 9, no. 2, June 2007) pp. 127–141, at p. 128

17 Ibid., at p. 127

18 Idean Salehyan and Kristian Gleditsch, 'Refugees and the Spread of Civil War', *International Organization* (vol. 60, no. 2, Spring 2006) pp. 335–366.

non-state actors have manipulated actual or potential refugee flows to coerce more powerful states into favourable behaviour.[19] The militarised refugee was also the focus of the work of Sarah Lischer,[20] who demonstrated how the circumstances of refugee flight can help forecast the likelihood of subsequent violence and radicalisation within refugee populations. Research by Milton, Spencer and Findlay[21] on the radicalisation of refugees pinpoints conditions in the camps, together with the poor treatment of refugees by the host states when they arrive, and this has led the researchers to argue that 'the international community at large should take steps to address' both these problems urgently. These are just a few examples from an extensive literature within the fields of political science and conflict studies that approach refugees not just as passive victims, a sort of 'collateral damage' within war, but as conflict actors in their own right who help explain the causes, dynamics and outcomes of war.

Refugees can be both victims and perpetrators of violence, a fact often overlooked in legal analysis, but clearly evident in real-world case studies. In their book *Escape from Violence: Conflict and the Refugee Crisis in the Developing World*, Aristide Zolberg, Astri Suhrke and Sergio Aguayo introduced the term 'refugee-warrior' to describe conflict participants drawn from refugee populations, a phenomenon that becomes more likely as conflicts prove bitterly intractable and displacement endures for years, even decades. Refugee-warriors are 'not merely a passive group of dependent refugees' but 'highly conscious refugee communities with a political leadership structure and armed sections engaged in warfare for a political objective, be it to recapture the homeland, change the regime, or secure a separate state'.[22] The fact that the concept is problematic within international law, which generally establishes strict boundaries between civilians and belligerents for the purposes of refugee status, does not negate its manifestation in the real world, nor the debate over appropriate legal responses.

The concept of a 'refugee-based insurgency' has also become accepted within conflict studies, initially as a result of the successful examples of this type during several decades of conflict in Afghanistan. The mujahidin militias who fought the Soviets and their client regime in Kabul, and the Taliban forces who later captured the state until the Western intervention in 2001, both depended upon refugee populations for manpower and funding, as well as for non-material assets such as grievance and legitimacy. Islamo-democratic insurgents in the second phase of the Tajik civil war (1993–1997) were based within the refugee population across the

19 Kelly Greenhill, *Weapons of Mass Migration: Forced Displacement, Coercion and Foreign Policy* (Cornell University Press, 2010)

20 Sarah Kenyon Lischer, *Dangerous Sanctuaries: Refugee Camps, Civil War, and the Dilemmas of Humanitarian Suffering* (Cornell University Press, 2005).

21 Daniel Milton, Megan Spencer and Michael Findley, 'Radicalism of the Hopeless: Refugee Flows and Transnational Terrorism', *International Interactions* (vol. 39, 2013, pp. 621–645) at p. 621.

22 Aristide Zolberg, Astri Suhrke and Sergio Aguayo, *Escape from Violence: Conflict and the Refugee Crisis in the Developing World* (Oxford University Press, 1989).

border in northern Afghanistan. Following the Rwandan genocide of 1994, a Hutu extremist insurgency was waged from refugee camps across the border in the Democratic Republic of Congo (DRC), eventually precipitating Rwandan intervention in that country's complex civil war. And after the Khmer Rouge was removed from power by a Vietnamese invasion in 1979, its political and military cadres reconstituted themselves within the refugee camps established for Cambodians in Thailand. It is clear that any examination of the cross-border dynamics of insurgency, civil war and rebellion must take into account the status and activities of refugee populations.

This recognition of the refugee-warrior phenomenon has not made much headway within international legal circles. Instead, it seems to have expanded the desire of foreign governments to exclude potentially problematic refugee populations from entry. In relation to Iraqi refugees, Reinoud Leenders has shown how 'the label appears to have gained currency with the effect of helping to impose an "in-region solution" for refugees and drastically curbing refugees' access to direct asylum procedures in Western Europe'.[23]

It would be churlish to suggest that refugee-warriors would not ever be a source of instability or insecurity for receiving host states. As stated above, quantitative studies have indicated an increased risk of conflict within host states, and there have been cases of external intervention to eradicate militants, as in the case of the Rwandan intervention in the DRC and the Israeli invasion of Lebanon in 1982. One of the earliest scholars to write about international migration within the broad structure of security, the noted political scientist Myron Weiner, has described at length how migration has 'generated conflicts with and between countries'.[24]

In European countries, the greatest concern is the 'refugee-terrorist', a threat discourse that has poisoned national and international policy debates on migration policy in recent years. A 2017 report by the Danish Institute for International Studies was the latest of a number of studies to show that 'the great majority of individuals involved in perpetrating terrorist attacks in Europe within the last decade have been EU citizens', while also noting that most asylum seekers in Europe are actually fleeing terrorist violence in their home countries. Yet this reality struggles to penetrate public perceptions, and the use of migration routes by returning militants who *have* participated in European terrorist networks further complicates the picture.

Against the reality and the mythology of the refugee-warrior, the question remains: can such people be excluded from refugee protection when they flee persecution or indiscriminate violence in their home state? The question is a difficult one, and even more so when individuals seek asylum in states that have

23 Reinoud Leenders, 'Refugee Warriors or War Refugees? Iraqi Refugees' Predicament in Syria, Jordan and Lebanon', *Mediterranean Politics* (vol. 14, no. 3, 2009, pp. 343–363) at p. 343.

24 Myron Weiner, 'Security, Stability, and International Migration', *International Security* (vol. 17, no. 3, 1992–1993, pp. 91–126) at p. 91.

contributed to the interventions and wars driving most contemporary refugee flows. Violence, of course, has many forms, and many sources, not all of them localised. James Souter has already argued that modern refugee law should be re-conceptualised, expanding upon the two best-known objectives of refugee law (namely, to respond 'to a fundamental humanitarian imperative' and to express 'moral condemnation of the persecutory or otherwise illegitimate actions of refugee-producing states', which enjoyed its heyday during the Cold War). He argues for a third objective, which would also serve an 'important moral function: as a form of reparation for past injustice'.[25] This 'stems from a special obligation on the part of states to provide asylum to refugees for whose lack of state protection they are responsible, whether through their military interventions, support for oppressive regimes or imposition of damaging economic policies'. In this way, the institution of asylum can be used by states to 'rectify the harm they caused to individuals by turning them into refugees'.[26] This may be a radical thesis, but Susanne Schmeidl has studied the causes of forced migration cross-nationally from 1971 to 1990 and concluded that where there is foreign intervention, refugee flight is directly linked to instances of genocide, ethnic wars and civil wars. The fact that violent conflict, genocide and regime instability are the strongest predictors of refugee flight is also confirmed by Davenport, Moore and Poe,[27] and Moore and Shellman[28] have shown that the primary driver of forced migration between 1952 and 1995 was intrastate violence perpetrated by government and (particularly) non-state armed forces. When Eric Neumayer[29] looked at asylum applications to Western Europe he also found that it is political violence that is associated with a higher number of asylum applications, such that natural disasters, famines or foreign aid and trade are not significantly associated with asylum applications.

Yet most scholarship on conflict-induced displacement fails to disaggregate the violence that drives it. In the words of Sarah Lischer,[30] there is still a marked tendency of 'lumping all types of violence together or viewing displaced people as an undifferentiated mass'. All in all, therefore, it is surely high time that we focus on differentiating the causal drivers of refugee flows – for example, distinguishing between foreign interventions and localised violence, or between the revolutionary and counterrevolutionary use of force – before setting out to assess their implications for state security and refugee protection. This will surely yield more nuanced

25 James Souter, 'Towards a Theory of Asylum as Reparation for Past Injustice', *Political Studies* (2013, p. 117). DOI: 10.1111/1467-9248.12019.

26 Ibid. at p. 1.

27 Christian Davenport, Will Moore and Steven Poe, 'Sometimes You Just Have to Leave: Domestic Threats and Refugee Movements, 1964–1989', *International Interactions* (vol. 29, no. 1, 2003, pp. 27–55).

28 Will Moore and Stephen Shellman, 'Fear of Persecution: Forced Migration, 1952–1995', *Journal of Conflict Resolution* (vol. 40, no. 5, 2004, pp. 723–745).

29 Eric Neumayer, 'Bogus Refugees? The Determinants of Asylum Migration to Western Europe', *International Studies Quarterly* (vol. 49, no. 3, 2005, pp. 389–409).

30 Sarah Kenyon Lischer, 'Causes and Consequences of Conflict-Induced Displacement', *Civil Wars* (vol. 9, no. 2, June 2007, pp. 142–155) at p. 142.

and productive policy responses than adopting the simplistic position of labelling any form of non-state violence as 'terrorism', a label that today obscures far more than it clarifies, as we shall see below.

The refugee-warrior in international refugee law

Article 1F of the Refugee Convention stated that:

> The provisions of this Convention shall not apply to any person with respect to whom *there are serious reasons for considering* that:

(a) he has committed a crime against peace, a war crime, or a crime against humanity, as defined in the international instruments drawn up to make provision in respect of such crimes;
(b) he has committed a serious non-political crime outside the country of refuge prior to his admission to that country as a refugee;
(c) he has been guilty of acts contrary to the purposes and principles of the United Nations.

There were two reasons for the exclusion clauses.[31] First, to allow states to prosecute serious offenders, who may try to avoid extradition by claiming asylum elsewhere.[32] Second, to exclude from protection those who are not worthy of it.[33] Articles 1F(a) and (c) demonstrate the level of seriousness required to engage Article 1F(b), so the three limbs of Article 1F have a symmetry to them. This important principle comes directly from the Refugee Convention itself. The genus of seriousness has to be at a common level throughout, so that those who commit war crimes and act against the principles and purposes of the United Nations are those who are unworthy of protection,[34] provided only that a sufficiently high level of 'seriousness' can be shown, as confirmed by the UNHCR in the decision of the Court of Justice in Joined Cases C-57/09 and C-101/09 *Bundesrepublik Deutschland v. B und D*:[35]

31 Blake J. in *AH (Article 1F(b) – 'serious') Algeria [2013] UKUT 00382 (IAC)*.
32 Although Blake J. said this did not apply where the offence has been prosecuted and the offender has served his punishment.
33 Ibid., at para. 85.
34 Ibid., at para. 39.
35 Joined Cases C-57/09 and C-101/09 *Bundesrepublik Deutschland v. B und D* [2010] ECR I-000. Here the principal question referred by the Bundesverwaltungsgericht was whether mere membership of or support for an organisation listed in the Annex to the Council Common Position of 17 June 2002 on the application of specific measures to combat terrorism constituted a serious non-political crime within article 12(2)(b) or an act contrary to the purposes and principles of the United Nations within article 12(2)(c) of the Qualification Directive. The Court considered the authorities and said (at para. 94): 'It follows from all those considerations that the exclusion from

> All the types of criminal acts leading to exclusion under Article 1F of the 1951 Convention *involve a high degree of seriousness*. This is obvious regarding Article 1F(a) and (c), which address acts of the most egregious nature such as 'war crimes' or 'crimes against humanity' or 'acts contrary to the purposes and principles of the United Nations'. In light of its context and the object and purpose of the exclusion grounds highlighted above, a 'serious non political crime' covered by Article 1F(b) must *also involve a high threshold of gravity*. Consequently, the nature of an allegedly excludable act, the context in which it occurred and all relevant circumstances of the case should be taken into account to assess whether the act is serious enough to warrant exclusion within the meaning of Article 1F(b) and 1F(c).[36]

A second principle that arises directly from the Refugee Convention itself is that Article 1F can only be triggered if there are '*serious grounds for considering that*' Articles 1F(a), (b) or (c) have been engaged. There is a filter test to be applied in all cases. The Supreme Court in *Al-Sirri* [37] considered whether participation in armed uprisings amounted to acts contrary to the purposes of the United Nations under Article 1F(c), and it held that 'serious reasons for considering' had an 'autonomous' meaning to it. It was not dependent on another international instrument. What it meant were acts reaching '*a high threshold of gravity*', because 'serious reasons' is stronger than 'reasonable grounds' for which the evidence must be 'clear and credible' or 'strong', since '"considering is stronger than "suspecting"' and is also 'stronger than "believing"'.

European Union law too has made a contribution in this regard. The *Qualification Directive (2004/83/EC)* provides a common standard for the application of the Refugee Convention's requirements across the 28 Member States of the EU.[38] Article 12(2)(a) precisely mirrors article 1F(a).[39] Article 12(3), however, then ominously provides in addition that article 12(2) '*applies to persons who*

refugee status of a person who has been a member of an organisation which uses terrorist methods is conditional on an individual assessment of the specific facts, making it possible to determine whether there are serious reasons for considering that, in the context of his activities within that organisation, that person has committed a serious non-political crime or has been guilty of acts contrary to the purposes and principles of the United Nations, or that he has instigated such a crime or such acts, or participated in them in some other way, within the meaning of Article 12(3) of Directive 2004/83.' Also see *Joined Cases C-57/09 and C-101/09 Bundesrepublik Deutschland v B and D [2011] Imm AR 190.*

36 Quoted from Blake J. in *AH (Article 1F(b) – 'serious') Algeria [2013] UKUT 00382 (IAC)*, who cites the UNHCR view (at para 2.2.1) at para. 36 of his judgment; emphases added.

37 *Al-Sirri and another v Secretary of State for the Home Department [2012] UKSC 54.*

38 It states at the outset (at para. 1) that 'A common policy on asylum, including a Common European Asylum System, is a constituent part of the European Union's objective of progressively establishing an area of freedom, security and justice open to those who, forced by circumstances, legitimately seek protection in the Community'.

39 Article 12(2) states: 'A third country national or a stateless person is excluded from being a refugee where there are serious reasons for considering that: (a) he or she has

instigate or otherwise participate in the commission of the crimes or acts mentioned therein'.[40] There is a problem here because what does it mean to '*otherwise participate*' in the commission of a crime against humanity?[41] Lord Brown acknowledged in *JS (Sri Lanka)* that the language here is wider than joint enterprise liability under domestic law but that 'Article 12(3) does not, of course, enlarge the application of article 1F; it merely gives expression to what is already well understood in international law' so that 'criminal responsibility is engaged by persons other than the person actually committing the crime (by pulling the trigger, planting the bomb or whatever)'.[42] The result is that 'article 1F disqualifies those who make a *substantial contribution to the crime*, knowing that their acts or omissions will facilitate it. … responsibility will attach to anyone … contributing to the commission of such crimes by substantially assisting the organisation to continue to function effectively in pursuance of its aims'.[43] The Court settled for '*substantial contribution to the crime*' over actions that amount to a '*high degree of seriousness*'. So, it should still be possible to say that a person's conduct amounts to a 'high degree of seriousness' and meets the required 'high threshold of gravity' if he has made a 'substantial contribution to the crime' in question.

In carrying out this exercise, 'it is unnecessary to import … domestic standards of proof into the question' and, indeed, 'the circumstances of refugee claims, and the nature of the evidence available, are so variable'. Therefore, 'so long as the decision-maker is satisfied that it is more likely than not that the applicant has *not* committed the crimes in question or has *not* been guilty of acts contrary to the purposes and principles of the United Nations, it is difficult to see how there could be serious reasons for considering that he had done so'. The result is that in reality, 'there are unlikely to be sufficiently serious reasons for considering the

committed a crime against peace, a war crime, or a crime against humanity, as defined in the international instruments drawn up to make provision in respect of such crimes'.

40 The full citation of this provision (which was also referred to Lord Brown in para. 14 in *JS (Sri Lanka)*) is that: 'Paragraph 2 applies to persons who instigate or otherwise participate in the commission of the crimes or acts mentioned therein.'

41 The German Federal Administrative Court considered Article 12 (3) in *BVerwG* 10C 48.07, judgment dated 14 October 2008: '21. In the case of the activities of terrorist organisations in particular, the question additionally arises as to attribution. Under Article 12(3) of Directive 2004/83EC, the reasons for exclusion also apply to persons who instigate or otherwise participate in the mentioned crimes or acts. Thus the person seeking protection need not have committed the serious non-political crime himself, but he must be personally responsible for it. This must in general be assumed if a person has committed the crime personally, or made a substantial contribution to its commission, in the knowledge that his or her act or omission would facilitate the criminal conduct (see Paragraph 18 of the UNHCR Guidelines). Thus this principle covers not only active terrorists and participants in the criminal sense, but also persons who perform advance acts in support of terrorist activities … 22. 'In this Court's opinion, all three prerequisites of fact are met in the case of a person who actively supported the armed struggle of a terrorist organisation …' (cited in *JS (Sri lanka)* [2010] UKSC 15 by Lord Brown at para. 14).

42 *JS (Sri lanka)* [2010] UKSC 15 per Lord Brown at para. 33.

43 *JS (Sri lanka)* [2010] UKSC 15 at para. 35.

applicant to be guilty unless the decision-maker can be satisfied on the balance of probabilities that he is'.[44]

Accordingly, simply castigating a crime as 'terrorist' tells us nothing of the crime itself. It is more likely a misuse of language. This is why in one case, Sullivan LJ was critical[45] of the fact that 'the Tribunal did not give separate consideration to paragraphs (b) and (c) in Article 1F. While terrorism is a grave international threat, merely labelling an offence a terrorist offence is not sufficient, of itself, to establish that the offence is a serious offence for the purpose of Article 1F(b)'. Indeed, there was 'no discussion in the Tribunal's determination of either the seriousness of this particular terrorist offence, or the appropriate threshold of seriousness for the purpose of Article 1F'.[46]

Yet, if these are the strengths of the Refugee Convention, there are also weaknesses, for it is not clear from the Refugee Convention what level of 'responsibility' is required of a person, before the requirement of '*serious reasons for considering*' is triggered and the filter test is applied. Nor, is the required level of 'responsibility' clear after the requirement of '*serious reasons for considering*' is triggered and a person's illicit actions analysed. Under the Refugee Convention this too would presumably have an 'autonomous' meaning to be determined free of any other international instrument. Article 1F applied to those who had 'committed a crime' or been 'guilty of acts'. It applied to perpetrators themselves. After all, as *JS (Sri Lanka)* confirmed, Article 1F was to be applied restrictively and used cautiously, and although the 'crimes' themselves were defined by international instruments, the Refugee Convention did not define the 'responsibility' for such crimes by reference to international instruments. Yet, this is how 'responsibility' is being interpreted today. There are risks to such transposition into refugee law.[47]

Nevertheless, Western governments continue to resort to the denial of refugee status to asylum seekers who are associated with disagreeable actors, over which they no longer have any influence on the basis of the so-called 'knowing and personal participation' test. This was most famously expressed in the UK Supreme Court case of *JS (Sri Lanka)* [48] which explained the reasons for such a cautious approach given 'the serious consequences of exclusion for the person concerned'

44 Ibid., at para. 75.
45 *AH (Algeria) v Secretary of State* [2012] EWCA Civ 395.
46 Ibid., at para. 39.
47 Paragraph 18 of the *UNHCR Guidelines On International Protection: Application of the Exclusion Clauses*: Article 1F of the 1951 Convention relating to the Status of Refugees (the paragraph there referred to) reads: '18. For exclusion to be justified, individual responsibility must be established in relation to a crime covered by Article 1F … . In general individual responsibility flows from the person having committed, or made a substantial contribution to the commission of the criminal act, in the knowledge that his or her act or omission would facilitate the criminal conduct. The individual need not physically have committed the criminal act in question. Instigating, aiding and abetting and participating in a joint criminal enterprise can suffice' (cited by Lord Brown in *JS (Sri Lanka)* at para. 14).
48 *JS (Sri Lanka)* [2010] UKSC 15.

such that 'the article must be interpreted restrictively and used cautiously'.[49] When, therefore, a 28-year-old Sri Lankan Tamil member of the Liberation Tigers of Tamil Eelam (LTTE) was disqualified from the grant of asylum on the grounds that voluntary membership of an extremist group was tantamount to personal and knowing participation, or at least acquiescence, amounting to complicity in the crimes in question, given that he was the second in command of an LTTE combat unit of the Intelligence Division, the Supreme Court disagreed. In the words of Lord Hope there should be 'a close examination of the facts and the need for a carefully reasoned decision as to precisely why the person concerned is excluded from protection under the Convention'.[50] Following this decision in one case that subsequently reached the ECtHR in 2016, the Dutch government in relation to Afghanistan noted 'the applicant's steady career path in the KhAD'. The result was that 'the Minister excluded the possibility of the applicant not having known or not having been involved in human rights violations committed by the KhAD'. This was a case where reliance had been placed by the government of the Netherlands on an official report, on the basis of which 'the Minister underlined the widely known cruel character of KhAD, its lawless methods, the grave crimes it had committed such as torture and other human rights violations as well as the climate of terror which it had spread throughout the whole of Afghan society'.[51]

49 Ibid.

50 *JS (Sri Lanka)* [2010] UKSC 15 at para. 44. See also S. Singer, *'Terrorism and Article 1F() of the Refugee Convention: Exclusion from refugee status in the United Kingdom'* (vol. 12, no. 5, 2014), *Jn'l of Int'L Crim. Jus.*, at pp. 1075–1091 for the practice of the UK courts in this respect.

51 *A.G.R. v. the Netherlands* – 13442/08 (Judgment (Merits and Just Satisfaction): Court (Third Section)) [2016] ECHR 34 at para. 20. The Dutch government has used the 'knowing and personal participation test' in many cases routinely. In another case where the appellant had reached the rank of second lieutenant at an administrative department of one of the directorates of the Afghan security service KhAD/WAD ('*Khadimat-e Atal'at-e Dowlati/Wezarat-e Amniyat-e Dowlati*') during the former communist regime in Afghanistan, it proceeded to refuse asylum on the basis of 'an official report, drawn up on 29 February 2000 by the Netherlands Ministry of Foreign Affairs, on "Security Services in Communist Afghanistan (1978–92), AGSA, KAM, KhAD and WAD" ("*Veiligheidsdiensten in communistisch Afghanistan (1978–1992), AGSA, KAM, KhAD en WAD*")' which was not specific to the claimant, but which 'emphasised the widely known cruel character of the KhAD, its lawless methods, the grave crimes it had committed such as torture and other human rights violations and the 'climate of terror' which it had spread throughout the whole of Afghan society, including the army' (see *S.S. v. the Netherlands* – 39575/06 (Judgment (Merits and Just Satisfaction) : Court (Third Section)) [2016] ECHR 29 at paras 13–15). In another case involving a Turkish national, exclusion from refugee status was undertaken by the Dutch government based purely 'on the applicant's statements given in the course of the proceedings on his asylum request, connecting him with armed robberies and arson committed in support of Dev-Sol[1]/DHKP-C[2] which acts were classified as participation in and/or support of terrorist activities as described in Resolutions 1269 and 1373 of the United Nations Security Council concerning terrorism which stipulate that participants in and/or supporters of terrorist activities are to be excluded from the protection under the 1951 Refugee Convention' (see *H. v the Netherlands* – 37833/10 [2011] ECHR 1866 at para. 13).

The decision of the Dutch government was upheld but on a separate matter; namely, that the applicants had not demonstrated individual factors showing a real risk of persecution upon expulsion, given that since December 2010 the UNHCR no longer classifies former employees of the Afghan security service or soldiers in the Afghan army during the communist regime as specific categories of persons exposed to a risk of persecution in Afghanistan.

The 'War on Terror': from 'protection' to 'exclusion'

It is also the case that a number of post-9/11 developments have, however, shifted the focus of the international community away from 'protection' to 'exclusion'. First, there was *United Nations Security Council Resolution 1373 (28 September 2001)* [52] which expressly provided that 'acts, methods and practices of terrorism are *contrary to the purposes and principles of the United Nations* and that knowingly financing, planning and inciting terrorist acts are also contrary to the purposes and principles of the United Nations'.[53] This is further demonstrated by *United Nations Security Council Resolution 1377 (12 November 2001),* [54] the second major development, which recalled the earlier resolution and reaffirmed 'its unequivocal condemnation of all acts, methods and practices of terrorism as criminal and unjustifiable, regardless of their motivation, in all their forms and manifestations, wherever and by whomever committed'. It is significant that the 'motive' of a person involved in any 'methods and practices of terrorism' is deemed irrelevant. This is a monolithic view divorced from all reality that does not require one to consider the factual situation on the ground. In fact, all states are called on '*to take urgent steps to implement fully resolution 1373*' and to '*intensify their efforts to eliminate the scourge of international terrorism*'.[55] Indeed, in what is perhaps the leading trouble-spot of the world today, the International Special Assistance Force was early in Afghanistan authorised and mandated by *United Nations Security Council Resolution 1386 (20 December 2001)* [56] 'to assist the Afghan Interim Authority in the maintenance of security in Kabul and its surrounding areas, so that the Afghan Interim Authority as well as the personnel of the United Nations can operate in a secure environment' for a period of six months.[57] In fact, a third development from the UN Security Council required the promulgation of new stricter domestic laws because *United Nations Security Council Resolution 1624 (September 2005)* [58] called upon states to '*adopt measures, consistent with international obligations, to prohibit, by law, incitement to commit a terrorist act or acts and to deny safe haven to those guilty of such conduct*'. The recognition that states have to act 'consistent

52 Available at www.un.org/News/Press/docs/2001/sc7158.doc.htm.
53 Ibid., at p. 1.
54 Available at www.unhcr.org/refworld/docid/3c4e9456e.html.
55 Ibid., at p. 2.
56 Available at www.nato.int/isaf/topics/mandate/unscr/resolution_1386.pdf.
57 Ibid., at Article 1.
58 Available at www.un.org/News/Press/docs/2005/sc8496.doc.htm.

with international obligations' is significant, because it does mean that, given the international obligation to admit refugees,[59] states cannot act in a slap-dash unprincipled manner. Moreover, there are also General Assembly resolutions, such as 49/60 of 9 December 2004,[60] on 'measures to eliminate international terrorism' which set out to declare that 'acts, methods and practices of terrorism constitute a grave violation of the purposes and principles of the United Nations'[61] as well as 'including those which jeopardize the friendly relations among States' and 'hinder international cooperation'.[62]

If the suggestion here is that states impose a blanket ban on genuine refugees because of an obligation to adopt 'measures to eliminate international terrorism' the suggestion is wrong under international law. A discussion of these questions is now timely because legal decisions increasingly ignore individual acts of personal responsibility for particular activities in a disfavoured organisation in favour of the state interest in curbing terrorism. If a person is otherwise 'unworthy' or 'undesirable' he or she is at risk of being excluded from the protection of the Refugee Convention. To the extent that recent case law suggests that a person who is 'excludable' is not necessarily also 'undesirable', the converse must also be true, so that an 'undesirable' person should not necessarily be 'excluded' just because of his or her association with an unpalatable outfit or organisation. The logic is clear from the case of ***Ruhumuliza*** where it was explained that '[t]he fact that a person is excluded from the Refugee Convention does not of itself mean that his presence in the UK is undesirable within the meaning of the Immigration Rules'.[63] Here there had been concern about the claimant's activities during the period of genocide in Rwanda. However, the judicial tribunal concluded that, despite his history, he was at the present time not a person whose character, conduct and associations make it undesirable to grant him indefinite leave in the UK. This was even though he had been excluded from the Refugee Convention. Significantly, the judicial tribunal here was swayed by the fact that in the years immediately following the genocide, the claimant had returned to Rwanda in order to help with reconciliation. He had taken part in memorial events and had issued a statement acknowledging his failings and

59 Article 33 of the Refugee Convention imposes a duty of 'non-refoulement' on states when considering applications for refugee status: **Article 33. – Prohibition of expulsion or return ('refoulement')** 1. No Contracting State shall expel or return ('refouler') a refugee in any manner whatsoever to the frontiers of territories where his life or freedom would be threatened on account of his race, religion, nationality, membership of a particular social group or political opinion. 2. The benefit of the present provision may not, however, be claimed by a refugee whom there are reasonable grounds for regarding as a danger to the security of the country in which he is, or who, having been convicted by a final judgement of a particularly serious crime, constitutes a danger to the community of that country. Available at www2.ohchr.org/english/law/refugees.htm.

60 A/RES/*49/60* 84th plenary meeting 9 December 1994.

61 Ibid., at Article 2.

62 Ibid., at Article 1.

63 Ruhumuliza (Article 1F and 'undesirable': Rwanda) [2016] UKUT 284 (IAC) (19 May 2016).

apologising for the past.[64] Notwithstanding this, however, the tendency remains to confuse the two categories of 'undesirable/unworthy' with those who are 'excludable'. This is clear from the latest case law below.

'Acts contrary to the purposes and principles of the United Nations'

Terrorism does not appear in Article 1F. However, it best fits into Article 1F(c) of the Refugee Convention 1951 because of its reference to 'acts contrary to the purposes and principles of the United Nations'. Dr Sarah Singer has explained that, '"terrorism" is not a legal label, but an undefined political term: there is at present no internationally agreed definition of "terrorism", nor an internationally agreed list of "terrorist organisations". The discretion inherent in the undefined nature of the term "terrorism" therefore leaves the Refugee Convention's exclusion clause open to abuse by Member States seeking to exclude genuine asylum seekers from refugee status'.[65] We will examine the record of the Court of Justice of the European Union (CJEU) which has applied Article 12(2)(b) of the Qualification Directive,[66] which excludes a person from refugee status[67] who has committed 'a serious non-political crime outside the country of refuge.' In *Bundesrepublik Deutschland v. B und D* [68] the issue was whether membership of an organisation (the PKK and Dev Sol, which are now the DHKP/C) that was on a list of 'persons, groups and entities involved in terrorist acts' compiled pursuant to Common Position 2001/931/CFSP on the application of specific measures to combat terrorism was, of itself, a sufficient ground for exclusion under Article 12 (2) of the Qualification Directive. The Grand Chamber of the CJEU held that

64 At para. 14. Moreover, the judicial tribunal recognised that 'he had not at any time been regarded by the Rwandan government as a perpetrator of genocide, had never been indicted, did not appear on any of the lists of those wanted for genocide and was indeed looked upon by the Rwandan government as one of its leading expatriate citizens. He has had a number of important international posts, and whilst he has been in the United Kingdom has attended, by invitation, significant diplomatic events including official meetings with the president of Rwanda' (ibid.).

65 Dr Sarah Singer, 'Exclusion from Refugee Status: Asylum Seekers and Terrorism in the UK', CCJHR Working Papers Series No. 2, 2012 at p. 4 (available at www.ucc.ie/en/media/academic/law/ccjhr/workingpapers/SarahSingerRefugeeExclusionClausesandTerrorismCCJHRWPSNo2Dec2012updated.pdf).

66 This states that a person 'is excluded from being a refugee where there are serious reasons for considering that … he or she has committed a serious non-political crime outside the country of refuge prior to his or her admission as a refugee, which means the time of issuing a residence permit based on the granting of refugee status; particularly cruel actions, even if committed with an allegedly political objective, may be classified as serious non-political crimes'.

67 As Dr Sarah Singer has shown, this does not necessarily mean that a person 'excluded' from the protection of the Refugee Convention will necessarily be removed, because he or she may have human rights arguments to fall back on, which will prevent return; see S. Singer, 'Undesirable and Unreturnable Migrants in the United Kingdom' (vol. 36, no. 1, 2017) *Refugee Survey Quarterly*, at pp. 9–34.

68 *Bundesrepublik Deutschland v. B und D* [2010] ECR I-10979 at para. 83; also at [2011] Imm AR 190.

UN Resolutions 1373 and 1377 showed that international terrorist acts are contrary to the purposes and principles of the United Nations. The 'exclusion' clause applied in such cases. However, there had to be an 'international dimension'[69] to the act concerned. Nevertheless, the exclusion from refugee status of a person who had been a member of an organisation that used terrorist methods was conditional on an individual assessment of the specific facts, and that before a finding could be made, it must be possible to attribute to the person concerned a share of the responsibility for the acts committed by the organisation of which he or she was a member. Individual responsibility had to be assessed in the light of objective and subjective criteria.[70] The judicial trend in restricting the scope of state discretion in determining what constitutes terrorism and which persons are 'terrorists' when they apply to seek sanctuary from persecution at home is a positive one and has for the most part continued in a line of legal decisions since.

In *H.T. v. Land Baden-Wurttemberg*, [71] in 2015 the claimant, a Mr. T., challenged the revocation of his residence permit, on account of his fund-raising activities for the proscribed Turkish terrorist organisation the PKK and his conviction of terrorism for distributing their literature, even though he had earlier been granted refugee status in Germany. The decision follows that of *Dr. M. v. Federal Republic of Germany*, [72] by the Federal Administrative Court in Germany, in 2010. This concerned a Rwandan exile who had already been granted refugee status, but whose refugee status was also 'revoked' because he was the president in exile of a Hutu organisation that had armed combatant units in the eastern part of the DRC, to carry out rapes, killings and other human rights violations, deemed to amount to 'war crimes'. The court had concluded that, '*[t]he circumstances for exclusion are significantly based on the concept of unworthiness for asylum*'. Significantly, as has been discussed elsewhere,[73] the government had not blocked the decision on his status determination when he first applied for asylum in Germany. In addition, when the revocation of his refugee status was challenged the court below had found that in terms of his personal participation in the acts complained of, his responsibility had not been established by the government.

Unlike the case of *Dr M* in 2010, however, the case involving Mr. T's activities for the PKK went before the CJEU. It held that he could not be excluded from refugee status under Article 12 of the Qualification Directive,[74] which

69 Ibid., at para. 84.
70 Ibid., at para. 81.
71 C-373/13, *H.T v. Land Baden-Wurttemberg* [2015] ECLI:EU:C:2015:413.
72 Judgment of the 10th Division of 31 March 2011 – BVerwG 10 C 2.10.
73 Satvinder Juss, 'Complicity, Exclusion and the "Unworthy" in Refugee Law', *Refugee Survey Quarterly* (vol. 31, no. 3, 1 September 2012, pages 1–39), https://doi.org/10.1093/rsq/hds011.
74 Article 12(2)(c) of the Qualification Directive, for example, reflects Article 1F of the Refugee Convention, when it posits that an individual shall be excluded from eligibility for refugee status for acts contrary to the principles and purposes of the United Nations, which by implication includes acts of terrorism, and Article 12(3) of the Qualification Directive extends that exclusion to 'persons who instigate or otherwise participate in the commission of the crimes or acts' mentioned in Article 12(2).

mirrors the 'exclusion' clauses of Article 1F of the Refugee Convention,[75] because his actions were not serious enough, although he could be caught by Article 21 of the Qualification Directive, which applies if 'there are reasonable grounds for considering him or her as danger to the security of the state'[76] and echoes Article 33(2) of the Refugee Convention, which is to the same effect.[77] Although the CJEU did also add that 'the mere fact that the refugee supported' a disfavoured organisation in the European Union, 'cannot automatically mean that that person's residence permit is revoked pursuant to that provision'[78] and that 'the referring court must examine the role that Mr. T actually played in supporting that organisation, by ascertaining in particular whether he himself has committed terrorist acts',[79] the decision has been criticised for allowing existing refugee rights to be diminished.[80] Dr Sarah Singer has cautioned, however, that

75 The particular applicable provision of Article 1F here is Article 1F(c) of the Refugee Convention which provides that an individual is to be excluded from the benefits afforded by refugee status if 'there are serious reasons for considering that … he has been guilty of acts contrary to the purposes and principles of the United Nations'. Also see Thomas F. Lampert, 'Prioritizing National Security at the Expense of Refugee Rights: The Effects of *H.T. v. Land Baden-Württenberg*', *Boston College International and Comparative Law Review* (vol. 40, no. 3, 2017), available at http://lawdigitalcommons.bc.edu/iclr/vol40/iss3/2.

76 Article 21 of the Qualification Directive 2004/83 is entitled 'Protection from refoulement', and it provides that:

'1. Member States shall respect the principle of non-refoulement in accordance with their international obligations.

2. Where not prohibited by the international obligations mentioned in paragraph 1, Member States may refoule a refugee, whether formally recognised or not, when:

(a) there are reasonable grounds for considering him or her as a danger to the security of the Member State in which he or she is present; or

(b) he or she, having been convicted by a final judgement of a particularly serious crime, constitutes a danger to the community of that Member State.

3. Member States may revoke, end or refuse to renew or to grant the residence permit of (or to) a refugee to whom paragraph 2 applies'.

77 Article 33 of the Refugee Convention is entitled 'Prohibition of expulsion or return ("refoulement")', and it provides that:

'1. No Contracting State shall expel or return ("refouler") a refugee in any manner whatsoever to the frontiers of territories where his life or freedom would be threatened on account of his race, religion, nationality, membership of a particular social group or political opinion.

2. The benefit of the present provision may not, however, be claimed by a refugee whom there are reasonable grounds for regarding as a danger to the security of the country in which he is, or who, having been convicted by a final judgement of a particularly serious crime, constitutes a danger to the community of that country'.

78 *H.T v. Land Baden-Wurttemberg* , op. cit., at paras 85–87.

79 Ibid.

80 T.F. Lampert, 'Prioritizing National Security at the Expense of Refugee Rights: The Effects of *H.T. v Land Baden-Wurttemberg*', *Boston College International and Comparative Law Review* (vol. 40, no. 3, 2017), available at http://lawdigitalcommons.bc.edu/cgi/viewcontent.cgi?article=1776&context=iclr. There is also criticism on account of the scope of non-refoulement under EU law: see P. Boeles, 'Non-Refoulement: Is Part of the EU's Qualification Directive Invalid?', EU Law Analysis Blog, 14 January 2017,

criticism that it amounts to 'opening the door to a weakening of refugee rights by permitting revocation' must be balanced against the fact the CJEU here laid stress on the fact that 'a State's ability to define terrorism for the purpose of the exclusion clause is not unlimited' and that there is still the requirement of 'the necessity of establishing the individual responsibility for the individual concerned for the acts in question'.[81] Unfortunately, as she properly points out, 'the recent decision of the CJEU in *Mostafa Lounani* seems to have muddied the waters somewhat'.[82]

Mostafa Lounani[83] concerned a Moroccan national facing exclusion from refugee status in Belgium on the ground that he was guilty of acts contrary to the purposes and principles of the United Nations. He had been convicted in Belgium of participation in the activities of a terrorist group, namely the Belgian cell of Le Groupe islamique des combattants marocains (also known as the Moroccan Islamic Combatant Group – MICG), as a member of its leadership, as well as for criminal conspiracy, use of forged documents and illegal residence, leading to his being imprisoned for six years. The CJEU expressly applied the three most significant United Nations Security Council Resolutions. First, that of UNSCR 1373 (2001), which affirmed 'the need to combat by all means, in accordance with the Charter of the United Nations, threats to international peace and security caused by terrorist acts'. Second, USCR 1377 (2001), which '[s]tresses that acts of international terrorism are contrary to the purposes and principles of the Charter of the United Nations, and that the financing, planning and preparation of, as well as any other form of support for acts of international terrorism, are similarly contrary to the purposes and principles of [that Charter]'. Third, UNSCR 1624 (2005), that 'all States must cooperate fully in the fight against terrorism, in accordance with their obligations under international law, in order to find, deny safe haven and bring to justice … any person who supports, facilitates, participates or attempts to participate in the financing, planning, preparation or commission of terrorist acts or provides safe havens'.[84]

In what is surely a break with the jurisprudence developed so far, the Grand Chamber of the CJEU held that the 'application of the ground for exclusion of refugee status laid down in Article 12(2)(c) of Directive 2004/83 cannot be confined to the actual perpetrators of terrorist acts, but can also extend to those who engage in activities consisting in the recruitment, organisation, transportation or equipment of individuals who travel to a State other than their States of residence or nationality for the purpose of, inter alia, the perpetration, planning or preparation of terrorist acts'.[85] This was because '[a]mong the measures to be

available at http://eulawanalysis.blogspot.co.uk/2017/01/non-refoulement-is-part-of-eus.html.

81 Dr Sarah Singer, 'The War on Terror and Refugee Law', in Satvinder S. Juss (ed.), *Research Handbook on Refugees* (Edward Elgar, forthcoming 2019).

82 Ibid.

83 Lounani (Judgment) [2017] EUECJ C-573/14 (31 January 2017), www.bailii.org/eu/cases/EUECJ/2017/C57314.html.

84 Ibid., at paras 6–10.

85 Ibid., at para. 69.

adopted to counter' what it described as 'the growing threat posed by foreign terrorist fighters', it was necessary that 'States must ensure the prevention and suppression of activities consisting in the recruitment, organisation, transportation or equipment of individuals who travel to a State other than their States of residence or nationality' which is 'for the purpose of the perpetration, planning or preparation of terrorist acts'.[86] It held that 'it is not a prerequisite … that an applicant for international protection should have instigated a terrorist act or should have otherwise participated in the commission of such an act',[87] and that 'participation in the activities of a terrorist group can cover a wide range of conduct, of varying degrees of seriousness'.[88] In this way, it is entirely open for a judicial tribunal to determine that '[s]uch conduct may justify the exclusion of refugee status'.[89] The decision in *Mostafa Lounani* in 2017 reproduces the approach taken in *Dr. M* by the Federal Administrative Court in Germany in 2010 and as such negates a long line of both domestic and international jurisprudence – from *JS (Sri Lanka)* to *Bundesrepublik Deutschland v. B und D* – which had required there to be 'personal participation' and 'individual responsibility' for the acts in question, by opting in favour of the UN Security Council Resolutions which require governments to take all preventative measures to suppress terrorism. Given that this was a case where 'no finding was made that Mr. Lounani personally committed terrorist acts, or instigated such acts, or participated in their commission',[90] this is both a break with the past and a troubling decision for human rights and refugee law. Nevertheless, it does now seem that this is a flavour of things to come.

In *A and Others v. Minister van Buitenlandse Zaken*, [91] the Grand Chamber of the CJEU held that the fact that the activities of an organisation might be regarded as 'armed conflict' under international law did not prevent those activities being classed as 'terrorist acts' for the purposes of European Union law, such that its assets could be frozen. The case concerned a circle of persons and organisations involved in raising funds for the Liberation Tigers of Tamil Eelam (LTTE) who argued that the LTTE was not a terrorist organisation because its conflict with the Sri Lankan government had been an 'armed conflict' within the meaning of international law, and the inclusion of the LTTE on the list of those whose funds were to be frozen[92] was unlawful. The Grand Chamber held that following UN Security Council Resolution 1373 (2001), which was adopted to help combat

86 Ibid., at para 67.
87 Ibid., at para 70.
88 Ibid., at para. 71.
89 Ibid., at para. 75.
90 Ibid., at para. 65.
91 A and Others (External relations: Common foreign and security policy Fundamental rights: Charter of Fundamental Rights – Judgment) [2017] EUECJ C-158/14 (14 March 2017), available at www.bailii.org/eu/cases/EUECJ/2017/C15814.html.
92 This was under Article 2(3) of Council Regulation (EC) no. 2580/2001, and subsequently on the list of those whose funds were to be frozen appended to Council Implementing Regulation (EU) No. 610/2010.

terrorism, the European Council was required to establish a list of persons, groups and entities, committing, or attempting to commit, participating in or facilitating the commission of any act of terrorism. The decision can be criticised on a number of fronts. The reference to the Grand Chamber from the Raad van State (Council of State) of the Netherlands, in proceedings brought by the applicants was, however, whether the activities of the LTTE could be properly regarded as terrorist activities under European law, given that they arose in actions by armed forces during periods of armed conflict.[93]

It is arguable that they were not because the LTTE's actions were governed by international humanitarian law in accordance with the definition of those terms under that law. Actions by armed forces of a state in the exercise of their official duties were also covered by other rules of international law and not by international criminal law. By contrast, the purpose of UN Security Council Resolution 1373 (2001), and the subsequent European rules,[94] which followed the terrorist attack on the United States on 11 September 2001, was to prevent terrorist acts by means of the adoption of measures for the freezing of funds in order to hinder actions preparatory to such acts, such as the financing of persons or entities liable to carry out terrorist acts. The decision of the Grand Chamber effectively designates the LTTE a terrorist organisation in all but name, even though its activities were confined to an armed conflict with the government of Sri Lanka. The suggestion by the Grand Chamber that this[95] did not amount to a 'sanction' on the LTTE but 'rather a preventive measure' is a thin distinction between the two. Equally questionable was the Grand Chamber's conclusion that the rules of international humanitarian law did not prohibit the adoption, outside the framework established by that law, of such preventative measures, because if this is right the edifice of international humanitarian law stands easily to be undermined in this way. In fact, the Grand Chamber was clear in this respect when it held that actions by armed forces during periods of armed conflict, within the meaning of international humanitarian law, might constitute 'terrorist acts'. If this is right, then we may expect the conflation of international humanitarian law with international criminal law to continue, beyond European Union law, into international law more generally, and with worrying consequences for the future.

The legitimate use of violence for political ends

Three United Kingdom cases of 'exclusion' all concern 'actions contrary to the purposes and principles of the United Nations'. All three suggest that we should

93 Under common position 2001/931 and Regulation no. 2580/2001, their situation should be read in conjunction with Framework decision 2002/475, Recital II which specified that it did not govern actions by armed forces during periods of armed conflict.

94 As well as the purpose of Common Position 2001/931 and Regulation no. 2580/2001, passed pursuant to UNSCR 1373.

95 Given that under Article 2(3) of Regulation no. 2580/2001 designation of persons and entities who were to be included on the list.

be a little more understanding of 'political violence', and that when Western governments are less concerned about the relative loss of their foreign influence over revolutionary mechanisms, the question of legitimacy with respect to conflict actors and refugees is less complicated and altogether more clear. The first, from 2009, is *KJ (Sri Lanka)*. [96] The claimant, an LTTE member, had been involved in five battles with the Sri Lankan Army, even though he was a foot soldier and had not attacked civilians. Stanley Burnton LJ in the Court of Appeal observing of 'acts contrary to the purposes and principles of the United Nations', that 'it is clear that acts of terrorism – in particular the deliberate killing or injuring of civilians in pursuit of political objects – are such acts', but this is not true of 'acts of a military nature committed by an independence movement (such as the LTTE) against the military forces of the government'.[97] This suggests that combatants on the streets of Aleppo in Syria may kill other combatants and still qualify as refugees.

The second case, arising in 2010, is *SS*, [98] decided by the UK's specialist terrorism tribunal, the Special Immigration Appeal Commission. This involved a Libyan national who was an active member of the Libyan Islamic Fighting Group (LIFG). Mitting J. distinguished *KJ (Sri Lanka)* and the approach of Stanley Burnton LJ. He decided that[99] 'the fundamental definition of terrorism. ... is the use or threat of action designed to influence a government or to intimidate a population by serious acts of violence and some acts of economic disruption'.[100] Therefore, 'a definition of terrorism which had at its heart the use or threat of serious or life threatening violence against the person and/or serious violence against property, including economic infrastructure, with the aim of intimidating a population or influencing a government, except when carried out as a lawful act of war',[101] was adopted. Carnwath LJ in the Court of Appeal reversed this decision because it 'went too far [to say] that *KJ(Sri Lanka)* could not be relied on to support a distinction between different categories of violence for political ends'.[102] The confusion thrown up between the two approaches became obvious.

96 *KJ(Sri Lanka) v. SSHD* [2009] EWCA Civ 292.
97 Ibid, at para. 34.
98 *SS v. Secretary of State for the Home Department* (SC/56/2009), (30 July 2010).
99 Mitting J.'s decision was based on an analysis and comparison of Article 1.3 of the definition of terrorist act, adopted by the European Council on 27 December 2001, in a statement setting out their common position (2001/931/CFSP), and on the UK legislation where the definition of terrorism includes the threat of action, which is designed to influence the government, with the purpose of advancing a political or ideological cause, involving a serious damage to property or interference with or seriously disrupting an electronic system: see Section 1 of the Terrorism Act 2000 at www.legislation.gov.uk/ukpga/2000/11/contents.
100 *SS v. Secretary of State for the Home Department* (SC/56/2009), (30 July 2010) at para. 15.
101 *SS v. Secretary of State for the Home Department* (SC/56/2009), (30 July 2010) at para. 16.
102 *SS v. Secretary of State for the Home Department* [2011] EWCA Civ 1547 at para. 37.

The third case is *D.*[103] An Afghan national, aligned to insurgent groups, fought both against Afghan government and Coalition forces, present in the country pursuant to UN resolutions. Pill LJ in the Court of Appeal followed Stanley Burnton LJ in *KJ (Sri Lanka)*. Armed insurrection per se is not terrorism. Although 'the circumstances in which acts of violence against a government are acts of terrorism is a difficult question', nevertheless '*KJ* appears to be authority for the proposition that military action directed against the armed forces of the government does not as such constitute terrorism or acts contrary to the purposes and principles of the United Nations'. Accordingly, 'it is difficult to hold that every act of violence in a civil war, the aim of which will usually be to overthrow a legitimate government, is an act of terrorism'.[104] Given that 'the only findings were findings of acts against government forces', this meant 'acts of terrorism had not been committed on the findings made'.[105] Thus, revolutionary violence does not ipso facto exclude a person from refugee status, for that reason alone.

Indeed, in a judgment given by the High Court of Australia soon after the outrage of 9/11 in *Singh*, Kirby J. explained how the Courts have struggled to find a point that will allow decision-makers to differentiate between fugitives accused of a serious political crime and those in respect of whom there are 'serious reasons for considering' that they have committed a serious *non*-political crime.[106] The distinction has troubled courts for more than a hundred years. It was Viscount Radcliffe who warned[107] that it is now unlikely that the point of distinction will receive a definitive answer accepted by everyone as universally applicable. Even so, Kirby J. remained concerned that, where important rights and duties turn on the meaning of the expression, being rights and duties that must be considered by judges and other decision-makers, it is reasonable to demand that there should be a measure of clarity about the concept. Kirby J. was clear that even if the best that courts can do is describe the idea, and the appropriate ways to approach it, they should attempt to do so.[108] This is because the alternative is a negation of the rule of law and the surrender of such questions to idiosyncratic opinions that may have little or nothing to do with the context of the case at hand.

Whilst it is hard to disagree with that statement, it does seem that recent developments on the international plane – which have been replicated, and not without inconsiderable haste, by domestic legislatures in the Western world – may bring the day of universally accepted definitions closer home.[109] The developed

103 *Secretary of State for the Home Department v. D* [2010] EWCA Civ 1407.
104 Ibid at para. 55.
105 Ibid at para. 58.
106 See Mr Justice Kirby in *Mima v. Singh* (2002) 186 ALR 393 (at paras 64–67, esp. para. 67).
107 *R v. Governor of Brixton Prison, Ex parte Schtraks* [1964] AC 556 at 589 (quoted from Mr Justice Kirby in *Mima v. Singh* (2002) 186 ALR 393 at para. 66).
108 Mr Justice Kirby in *Mima v. Singh* (2002) 186 ALR 393 at para. 67.
109 Recent work has been conducted in Canada, for example, precisely 'in order to discern whether there has been an appreciable change in the application and interpretation of Article 1F(a)'; see James C. Simeon, 'Exclusion Under Article 1F(a) of the 1951 Convention in Canada', *International Journal of Refugee Law* (2009) pp. 193–217 at p. 195.

asylum systems of the western world have been worried, as Kirby J. pointed out, over the problem of defining a 'serious non-political crime', which has been described as one that presents 'the gravest difficulties'.[110] In an earlier manifestation of the phrase, it was said to present one of the 'most acute' dilemmas of extradition law.[111] A decade ago Kirby J. was concerned that the difficulties of definition derive, in part, from the absence of any settled international consensus about the expression and the changing views of national courts and tribunals about its meaning.[112] Can the same, however, be said a decade later? Kirby J. could not have been wrong when he observed: 'The content of the expression depends on an almost infinite variety of factors.[113] It has been influenced by the changing nature of crimes, of weapons, of the transport of criminals and of the global political order, and the increased vulnerability of modern societies to violent forms of political expression'.[114] The trend in the most recent case law, however, demonstrates a convergence in favour of exclusion on the basis that there is an understanding now of the kinds of people who deserve to be excluded from refugee status. This is clear from the 2016 case of *Youssef.* [115] Here the appellant had been a defence lawyer in Egypt, working on behalf of political prisoners. He had been a political activist in his own right. He was detained and tortured on two occasions in 1981 and 1982. In 1983 he was pressured by the state to speak out against his clients and when he refused to do so his office was destroyed and his files were stolen. He had been in the United Kingdom since 6 May 1994 where

See also Joseph Rikhof (Senior Counsel, Crimes against Humanity and War Crimes Section, Department of Justice) in 'Complicity in International Criminal Law and Canadian Refugee Law: A Comparison', *Journal of International Criminal Justice* (vol. 4, no. 4, September 2006, pp. 702–722). Available at SSRN: http://ssrn.com/abstract=1098768 or DOI: 10.1093/jicj/mql065. Others have been more forthright in concluding that some jurisdictions, like the United States, are now taking a strict approach to Article 1F: see Maryellen Fullerton, 'Terrorism, Torture, and the Refugee Convention in the United States', *Refugee Survey Quarterly* (vol. 29, no. 4, 2010) at p. 5.

110 Grahl Madsen, *The Status of Refugees in International Law* (vol. 1, A. W. Sijthoff, 1966) at p. 290 (quoted from Mr Justice Kirby in *Mima v. Singh* (2002) 186 ALR 393 at para. 64).

111 J. Reuben Clark, Jr., Frederick R. Coudert and Julian Mack, 'The Nature and Definition of Political Offense in International Extradition', *Proceedings of the American Society of International Law*, 1909, p. 94, cited in Garcia-Mora, 'The Nature of Political Offences: A Knotty Problem of Extradition Law' (1962) 48 *Virginia Law Review* 1226 at 1231 (quoted from Mr Justice Kirby in *Mima v. Singh* (2002) 186 ALR 393 at para. 64). The court went onto say that, 'so far as the Australian law on refugees is concerned, the scope of offences "of a political character" is not fixed' (at para. 64).

112 Mr Justice Kirby in *Mima v. Singh* (2002) 186 ALR 393 at para. 65.

113 Mr Justice Kirby in *Mima v. Singh* (2002) 186 ALR 393 at para. 65, where Mr Justice Kirby quoted from the British case of *Re Castioni* [1891] 1 QB 149 at 155; [1886–90] All ER Rep 640 at 644.

114 Mr Justice Kirby in *Mima v. Singh* (2002) 186 ALR 393 at para. 65, where Mr Justice Kirby quoted from the judgment of Lord Mustill in another leading British case of *T v. Home Secretary* [1996] AC 742 at 762; [1996] 2 All ER 865 at 876.

115 Youssef (Refugee Convention – Article 1F(c)) [2016] UKUT 137 (IAC) (2 March 2016).

he had claimed asylum on arrival. The tribunal held that the 'language used by the appellant is such that it can properly be characterised as explicit direct encouragement or incitement to acts of terrorism'.[116] It was argued on his behalf that the British government 'had not disclosed a single item in which the appellant had mentioned an act of terrorism in approving terms let alone stating that anyone should commit one'. He had made 'remarks about Osama bin Laden', but these 'had to be seen in the context of his belief that bin Laden 'did not kill civilians and did not say that', and it was pointed out that 'it was important to note his clear opposition to Islamic State on account of its brutal acts of terrorism'.[117] The judicial tribunal, nevertheless, held that: 'For a person to be excluded from refugee protection under Article 1F(c) of the Refugee Convention on the basis that they knowingly incited and encouraged acts contrary to the purposes and principles of the United Nations it is not necessary to show that such acts have actually been committed or attempted'.[118] This sits arguably at odds with what was said by the Supreme Court in *Al-Sirri,* namely, that '[i]n every case involving exclusion of protection under Article 1F of the Refugee Convention, the onus of proof is on the Secretary of State, a detailed and individualised examination of the facts is required, there must be clear and credible evidence of the offending conduct, and the overall evaluative judgment involves the application of a standard higher than suspicion or belief'.[119]

An age of revolutionary violence

In both law and security studies, the context of violent behaviour is critical. To the extent that courts are inconsistent in interpreting violent behaviour, across and within conflicts, it is largely due to the complexity of contemporary political violence and the lack of firm normative frameworks for understanding and evaluating its participants. The three cases described in the previous section indicate that there is indeed scope for enhanced flexibility within legal interpretations of previous participation in conflict by asylum seekers. Building upon these examples, we propose a new framework for evaluating non-state-actor violence within an armed conflict, one that shifts away from the monolithic label of 'terrorism' and enables more nuanced distinctions between legitimate and illegitimate violence during conflict.

In the search for an evaluative framework offering both utility and clarity, 'terrorism' is increasingly a dead end. As an analytical and legal concept, it has been eviscerated by self-serving politicisation and academic waffling. While it has always been a fundamentally normative concept ('one man's freedom fighter is another man's terrorist' having joined the ranks of statements too obvious to repeat), 'terrorism' has previously conveyed a more narrow set of acts and actors –

116 At para. 55.
117 At para. 50.
118 At para. 56.
119 Al-Sirri (Asylum – Exclusion – Article 1F(c)) Egypt [2016] UKUT 448 (IAC) (17 August 2016)

generally, non-state armed groups targeting civilians for some political purpose.[120] Today, however, terrorism is invoked in an enormous range of ideological and political acts: from propaganda campaigns and lone-wolf shootings, to elaborately staged massacres and large-scale insurgent attacks in active combat zones. The leading 'terrorism indices' enumerate thousands of deaths due to terrorism worldwide every year, and yet a sizable number of the incidents they include are insurgent attacks on military or police targets in a conflict-affected state, which in a previous era would have been considered within a framework of armed conflict rather than terrorism.[121] The elasticity of the 'terrorist' label may have some benefit in coordinating an international response to sub-state threats, but it also has a number of political and legal implications that generate unfair treatment of both civilians and fighters caught up in conflict situations.

For example, in 2014, the United Nations Security Council moved to stem the flow of foreign fighters, including those joining the Islamic State, by demanding that nations adopt laws to prevent their citizens from travelling abroad to join such groups. US intelligence officials had estimated that 15,000 citizens from 80 countries had been fighting with ISIS in Iraq and Syria in 2014, including more than 2,000 Europeans and 100 Americans. If they had passports permitting them afterwards to return to their home countries, they could carry out lethal attacks there. UN Security Council Resolution 2178 required countries to criminalise attempts to travel abroad to join a terrorist organisation and to prevent suspected foreign terrorists from entering or travelling through their territories. At one level, this was clearly important because, at the time, travelling to Syria or Iraq to join an extremist group was not a crime in many countries, and the resolution also therefore compelled governments to require airlines to share passenger lists and for nations to share information about terrorism suspects. But at another level, the Resolution once again threw up the thorny question of who was a 'terrorist'. It is readily comprehensible that ISIS and al-Qaeda are included, but the Resolution is not limited to these entities, referring to 'foreign terrorist fighters' without definition. As Human Rights Watch noted at the time,

> Resolution 2178 does not limit the actions that member states may designate as 'terrorism' or 'terrorist' – terms for which no universal legal definition exists. This has left governments to craft dangerously open-ended definitions that can capture a range of activities not generally considered terrorism. Those

120 On the evolution of terrorism in the modern era, see Bruce Hoffman, *Inside Terrorism* (Columbia University Press, 2006).

121 An insurgent group may use terrorism as a tactic, but this does not transform every insurgent act into an act of terrorism – a distinction that has become somewhat lost in recent years. Traditionally, an insurgent attack on a military convoy, for example, would not be considered terrorism, yet many such incidents are included in contemporary terrorism indices. The Global Terrorism Database, managed by the National Consortium for the Study of Terrorism and Responses to Terrorism, lists a total of 38,165 terrorist incidents in Iraq, Afghanistan, Somalia and Syria between 2003 and 2016, and yet 13,768 of these are attacks on military or police targets.

> already targeted by such laws include not only terrorism suspects but also peaceful protesters, journalists, political opponents, civil society, and members of ethnic or religious groups, many of them Muslims.[122]

Is it any wonder that more than 250 definitions of terrorism have been catalogued, when the term is used so loosely and in connection with such a wide range of disparate behaviour?[123] An unfortunate consequence is that there is a greater potential for exaggerating the terrorist threat, of transforming local or regional acts of war-fighting into a global menace that demands an overwhelming military and legal response. This heightens the likelihood of overreaching criminal laws within states, and of racial profiling targeting particular groups. The demonisation of Muslim populations expands worldwide, from President Trump's Executive Orders limiting immigration to xenophobic attacks on refugees in Europe; at the extreme end lies Myanmar's 'ethnic cleansing' of its minority Rohingya peoples, which has received only limited attention and approbation within the international community. In both democracies and authoritarian regimes, the global emphasis on counter-terrorism tends to elevate ethnic and religious identity over the realities of political and military behaviour.

The irony is that during the Cold War, when governments had greater involvement and leverage with non-state armed groups worldwide, they were less prone to 'lump together all forms of political violence into a single terrorist threat'.[124] We argue that it is time to deconstruct notions of terrorist violence into more specific and hopefully more useful concepts, in order to better capture the aims, effects and outcomes of political violence today. As part of this effort, we propose a new focus on a subset of political violence which we call *revolutionary violence*, as a way of capturing one of its most essential characteristics: the desire to radically transform an existing political, economic and social order.

By shifting from an analytical context of terrorist violence to a context of revolutionary violence, we recognise that today's non-state armed groups and social movements do not rely on singular modalities of violent (or indeed non-violent) action. The focus to date on a particular tactic (i.e. terrorism) does not specify so much as obscure the type of political violence of such concern today. In an age where non state armed groups can engage in conventional warfare, sponsor covert attacks in multiple countries, hack into global IT systems and craft savvy propaganda campaigns, how useful is the concept of terrorism? Whatever original utility it possessed has been further eroded by the increasing tendency to include within its remit violence against non-civilian targets, especially in Iraq and Afghanistan.

We argue that a better way of characterising contemporary violence in the greater Middle East today is the notion of *revolutionary violence*, which we define

122 Human Rights Watch, *Foreign Terrorist Fighter Laws: Human Rights Rollbacks under UN Security Council Resolution 2178* (New York, December 2016).

123 A.P. Schmid (ed.), *Handbook of Terrorism Research* (Routledge, 2011), pp. 86–87.

124 Satvinder Juss, 'Terrorism and the Exclusion of Refugee Status in the UK', *Jnl. of Confl. & Sec.* (vol. 17, no. 3, Winter 2012, pp. 465–499), at p. 468.

as campaigns of violent action by sub-state actors, intended to radically transform the existing political, economic and social order. The target may be more than just a regime: at times, it is the very structures and institutions of political, economic and social life, in a territory not necessarily perceived within existing borders. For this kind of fundamental reform, the revolutionary actor requires and seeks multiple forms of power. While the use of violence is key to the concept, there is no presumption that it is used in a specific way: it may be directed against government or civilian targets; it might be embedded within an elaborate political mobilisation or engaged in almost nihilistically. Often, violence is embedded within a broad range of *non-violent* activity, including anything from peaceful protest to propaganda efforts to extensive social service provision to local populations.

This diversity of action opens up a discussion of the legitimacy and legality of specific acts, which when viewed through the prism of the law of armed conflict may appear clearly illegal (e.g. the intentional targeting of civilians) or arguably legitimate (e.g. attacks on state military targets in accordance with international humanitarian law). It enables consideration of aims as well as methodology – for example, differentiating between self-defence militias and genocidal gangs. In essence, the centuries of ethical and legal development of the laws of war can be brought to bear upon the very modern question of whether an individual's acts within a conflict are legitimate, and thus clarify the appropriateness of asylum. We argue that this historically rich and consensus-driven framework is a far more appropriate one than the comparatively recent and divisive concept of 'terrorism', and more apt to produce ethically and legally rigorous outcomes.

Some may object to the use of 'revolutionary' in the context of protracted armed struggles, especially if one thinks of revolutions as discrete and fairly limited political events. But there are numerous historical examples of revolutions proving to be drawn-out and messy affairs, at times inchoate in their targets and trajectories, and often spiralling into armed conflict.[125] If one investigates the ideologies and aims of many of today's violent armed groups, revolutionary influences and ideals are not hard to find. For example, jihadist movements such as ISIS and al-Qaeda are often perceived in religious terms, but their use of violence in pursuit of power and worldly aims renders their ideologies inherently political. Unlike non-violent Salafi groups, many of whom share similar diagnoses and prescriptions for the world's ills but reject political involvement, jihadist groups overtly seek to acquire power and overturn the existing order in the Muslim world. The influence of Quranic scripture and scholars on their ideologies is clear – but so is the impact of more modern, indisputably revolutionary thought, especially in the writings of such important jihadi ideologues as Sayyid Qutb. The creation of a jihadi vanguard, for example, to lead and inspire the Muslim masses has obvious parallels with Leninist doctrine.

125 The French Revolution – so often the exemplar of modern revolutions – easily springs to mind.

Hezbollah and other Shi'a groups in the Middle East are descendants of a different revolutionary tradition, namely the 1979 Iranian revolution and the doctrinal innovations of Ayatollah Khomeini. While employing similar visions of the vanguard movement and the establishment of a shari'a state, their embodiment of Shi'a Islam places them in direct opposition to the Salafi-jihadi groups. The Taliban in Afghanistan represent yet another revolutionary strain, one that has evolved several times in the 20 years of conflict since Taliban militias first overthrew the Afghan regime. The secular political ideologies of two of the militant groups considered in the previous section, the PKK and LTTE, are clearly evident.

Finally, there are the numerous sub-state actors that emerged within the conflicts following the 'Arab Spring' revolutionary attempts. In both Syria and Libya, for example, armed groups not associated with jihadism or religious extremism became key actors in the revolutionary wars. This is another reason to shift the analytical prism from terrorism, which has become overwhelmingly associated with Islamic extremism, towards a broader conceptualisation of revolutionary violence.

These cases help support our final argument: that political violence in the greater Middle East today, while often ostensibly targeting Western actors, policies and ideologies, is in many ways interdependent with them. This is particularly pronounced in two aspects. First, as noted, their revolutionary ideologies have been influenced not just by theological or local traditions, but by Western ideologies and thinkers. Second, and more important, much of today's revolutionary violence has its roots in Western policies and behaviour.

There is a tendency in Western nations today, propelled by conflict fatigue and socio-economic woes, to perceive violence in the greater Middle East as more or less endogenous to the region – something for the afflicted states themselves to resolve, while Western policymakers try to somehow muddle through the complications for their own polities.[126] But this stance ignores the many ways in which contemporary violence and instability in the Middle East is interdependent with Western policy. This is clear by any timeframe chosen – certainly, from the direct colonial subjugation of the nineteenth and twentieth centuries, the Cold War support for authoritarian regimes, ongoing military and economic exploitation of the region, and most crucially the 2003 Iraq War. Revolutionary violence has at times targeted Western policy, and at other times been supported by Western governments. It has often been seen as a mechanism for the promotion of foreign interests in a region of important economic and geostrategic value.

What appears to be different today is that foreign governments have lost their sense of control of the revolutionary mechanism. This is true even for regional powers such as Saudi Arabia and Iran, who cannot always control the behaviour of their proxies, and even more so for Western powers, whose frequent shifts in support for sub-state actors betray a fundamental loss of vision and control in the region. External state control has been eroded by the increased complexity of conflict and the end of the bipolar international order; enhanced freedom of action for sub-state actors thanks to new technologies, global communications

126 See, for example, Jeffrey Goldberg, 'The Obama Doctrine', *The Atlantic* (April 2016).

tools and financing from criminal networks; and newly powerful and transnational ideologies that are proving more difficult to manipulate or combat.

This returns us to the argument of James Souter: that states have a moral imperative to offer asylum to those fleeing conditions for which said states bear some level of responsibility. The acknowledgement of varying levels of legitimacy within revolutionary violence – something that cannot be done with terrorism – allows a more nuanced consideration of conflict dynamics, including the root causes of oppression, rebellion and violence. While it is too simplistic to place all the blame for today's wars in the Middle East on Western states, it is also disingenuous for Western governments to pretend that decades of heavy intervention in the region have no connection to the violence from which millions have now fled. This is especially the case for countries like Afghanistan, Iraq and Libya, which have experienced overt military intervention followed by insufficient post-war reconstruction. On what ethical basis can states reject refugees from lands that they have invaded or attacked? And if it is ethically wrong to do so, should we not shape the law to correct this wrong?

In short, if we adopt a framework of revolutionary violence, in which a limited range of conflict behaviour can be deemed legitimate, and if we acknowledge the role of external state actors in creating the conditions for revolutionary violence to occur, it then becomes possible to envision an ethical and legal framework that would permit asylum for at least some refugee-warriors. The alternative is to require that every individual who contributes in some way to armed resistance against an oppressive or even genocidal regime must also sacrifice any future right to asylum; it also means agreeing that a state can invade another state yet wash its hands of the humanitarian consequences. Neither proposition sits easily within the ethical frameworks developed in relation to armed conflict in the modern era.

Conclusion: a right to revolution?

The international legal and political order is biased towards the status quo, state-centric system. There is no right to revolt; sub-state violence is usually characterised as illegitimate. It took many years for a consensus to emerge that the laws of armed conflict should also apply in intra-state conflicts. Recent events now raise the question of whether we should contemplate a 'right to revolt', and what this might look like from a legal/ethical perspective. In order to preserve legal norms related to human rights and the laws of war, it would need to stress that only violence directed towards non-civilian targets is legitimate. Subject to this, it is clear that, applying the ethical and legal tenets of international humanitarian law, those that engage in revolutionary movements are not necessarily beyond the pale, and are entitled to the right to asylum if in need of protection.

In the real world, notwithstanding international law's avowed establishment of strict boundaries between civilians and belligerents, refugee communities often manifest themselves as both victims and perpetrators of political violence. Historically, this has also been true legally. Such complications were recognised by astute lawyers in the past. This is clear from Kirby J's decision in Australia in 2002.[127] By the end of the twentieth century, therefore, it was recognised that the distinctions between permissible and impermissible violence were difficult to make. Even today, enlightened judicial decisions, such as *D*, [128] reflect the truism that 'the circumstances in which acts of violence against a government are acts of terrorism is a difficult question', but that 'military action directed against the armed forces of the government does not as such constitute terrorism or acts contrary to the purposes and principles of the United Nations'. This means that it 'is difficult to hold that every act of violence in a civil war, the aim of which will usually be to overthrow a legitimate government, is an act of terrorism'.[129]

What is clearly unacceptable, however, is the perpetration of violence directed towards civilian targets as this cannot on any ethical or legal standard be regarded as legitimate. It is in the interstices of these two polar opposites that the 'right to revolt' can be found in international law such that it can help develop a more cohesive and coherently strong basis for the application of modern refugee law to conflict situations across the world. The language of 'terrorism' in itself, as sometimes employed in more recent decisions, is distinctly unhelpful in this regard. No doubt the nuances of the 'refugee-warrior' are lost in the more than 250 definitions of terrorism that have been catalogued. The decision of the Grand Chamber of the CJEU in *A and Others v. Minister van Buitenlandse Zaken* [130] is a case in point, where it was held that the fact that the activities of an organisation might be regarded as 'armed conflict' under international law did not prevent those activities being classed as 'terrorist acts' for the purposes of European Union law, thus effectively designating LTTE a terrorist organisation rather than a revolutionary movement engaged in a struggle for independence against the government of Sri Lanka. This is despite the fact that historically it has always been difficult to determine when a person's actions in an armed conflict can be said to be 'contrary to the purposes and principles of the United Nations', which is why the Supreme Court in *Al-Sirri* said this was a 'little used provision' of the Refugee Convention.[131]

The confusion seeps into and begins to permeate the orderly application of refugee law. While, on the one hand, the landmark case of *JS (Sri Lanka)* draws upon historical understandings of conflict situations to decide that an Article 1F disqualification for refugee status only applies to those 'who make a *substantial contribution to the crime*, knowing that their acts or omissions will facilitate it',[132]

127 See note 111 above.

128 *Secretary of State for the Home Department v D* [2010] EWCA Civ 1407.

129 Ibid at para. 55.

130 A and Others (External relations: Common foreign and security policy Fundamental rights: Charter of Fundamental Rights – Judgment) [2017] EUECJ C-158/14 (14 March 2017), available at www.bailii.org/eu/cases/EUECJ/2017/C15814.html.

131 *Al-Sirri v. Secretary of State for the Home Department [2012]* UKSC 54, per Lady Hale at para 1.

132 *JS (Sri lanka)* [2010] UKSC 15 at para. 35.

on the other hand, the more recent decision of *Mostafa Lounani* [133] just simply concludes that 'it is not a prerequisite … that an applicant for international protection should have instigated a terrorist act or should have otherwise participated in the commission of such an act',[134] and that 'participation in the activities of a terrorist group can cover a wide range of conduct, of varying degrees of seriousness'.[135] The more the language of 'terrorism' and 'terrorist' is used the more likely it will be that the international community will fail in disaggregating contemporary violence in the greater Middle East today, and long-held distinctions between legitimate and illegitimate political violence will be eroded. This will lead to a number of unfortunate consequences for our understanding of modern conflict – and more important, for today's 'refugee-warriors' who may be denied the opportunity for asylum despite adhering to the laws of war.

133 Lounani (Judgment) [2017] EUECJ C-573/14 (31 January 2017), www.bailii.org/eu/cases/EUECJ/2017/C57314.html.
134 Ibid., at para. 70.
135 Ibid., at para. 71.

4 The ISIL jihadists of Saudi Arabia

Abdullah K. Al-Saud

Introduction

In early 2016, a cache of self-proclaimed Islamic State in Iraq and the Levant (ISIL) foreign fighter (FF) documents was leaked and obtained by a few media outlets and academic institutions. One of those institutions was the International Centre for the Study of Radicalisation and Political Violence (ICSR), King's College London, where I spent the past year and a half as a Visiting Research Fellow. I have taken an in-depth look at all the leaked documents of ISIL foreign fighters who came from Saudi Arabia, whether they were citizens or just residents.

At the outset, it is important to note that these leaked entry documents, while containing valuable information, neither give us the whole picture of the terrorist organization's structure nor the complete records of its recruits. Yet, they provide us with an important snapshot of its history at the time of its ascendance. Out of the total 759 records of Saudi ISIL foreign fighters in our dataset, 670 specified their exact date of entry into Syria, and 662 of them entered in the period between June 2013 and August 2014.

In this chapter, I will focus primarily on one aspect of the information contained in the leaked documents, namely the region/city of origin of those jihadists, compare it with previous available data of Saudi jihadists, and then provide an in-depth analysis and exploration of the possible reasons as to why a certain province/region in Saudi, namely al-Qassim, has a higher ratio of ISIL foreign fighters than the average of both the whole population and each of the other regions by a large margin.

But before embarking on our analysis, it is important to highlight that while those who hail from Saudi Arabia come first in the leaked entry documents and second in the overall foreign fighters in Syria and Iraq in terms of raw numbers,[1] the picture becomes completely different when such numbers are indexed against the overall Muslim population (see Table 4.1). The reason behind focusing solely on the Muslim population is that, although there are a number of new converts who joined the ranks of ISIL, the terrorist group attempts to target, predominantly, the Muslim population in each country.

1 'Foreign Fighters: An Updated Assessment of the Flow of Foreign Fighters into Syria and Iraq,' *The Soufan Group* (New York: December 2015).

Table 4.1 Ratio of foreign terrorist fighters from selected countries

Country	*Number of FF in Syria and Iraq*[2]	*Muslim Population*	*FF per 100,000*
Tunisia	6000	11.4 million	52.6
France	1700	4.8 million	35.4
Jordan	2500	9 million	27.7
United Kingdom	760	2.8 million	27.1
Russia	2400	9.5 million	25.2
Kosovo	232	2 million	11.6
Saudi Arabia	3244[3]	29 million	11.1

The data

The regional diversity of the Saudi ISIS contingent tells us that recruitment was not confined to a particular region or province of the Kingdom, as all 13 administrative provinces were represented in the sample. The largest represented province, in raw numbers, was Riyadh as 262 fighters of the total 735 who specified their city/region hail from there (the 24 fighters in our sample who did not provide any such information do not affect the percentages). The next most represented provinces were al-Qassim and Makkah (134 fighters each). However, a closer look through indexing the total number of fighters from each province to the province's population size allows us to understand the data in a substantially different light. The average ratio for the whole population was 2.6 foreign fighters per 100,000 residents.[4] Only four regions scored a higher ratio than the average and Riyadh is not the top one. Al-Qassim, which came second in raw numbers, is now first by a large margin, followed by Hail, Tabouk, and then Riyadh. The lowest ratio of fighters per 100,000 residents was scored in the three regions of the south of the Kingdom: Jizan, Najran, and Asir respectively (see Table 4.2).

Another way of looking at the data on the region of origin is by comparing the region of origin of the Saudi foreign fighters in Syria in our database to the region of origin of four earlier samples of Saudi militant jihadists, compiled by both Thomas Hegghammer and Aaron Zelin, and acquired through what has come to be known as the Sinjar Records. In 2007, Hegghammer had already published a brief report based on an analysis of 205 biographies of Saudis who died in Iraq between 2003 and 2005. He was able to know the geographical origin of 151 of

2 Ibid.
3 The Soufan Group has the number of Saudi foreign fighters at 2500. However, this is the official number of Saudi jihadists who travelled from 2011 until the end of 2016 as I obtained from a government official.
4 Overall and regional population figures were taken from The General Authority for Statistics, 'Statistical Year Book for 2013', www.stats.gov.sa/ar/1160. Note: 24 fighters in the sample of 759 have not provided any information regarding their city/region of origin and are not included in the Province totals.

Table 4.2 Administrative region origin of Saudi ISIL foreign fighters indexed to each region's population size

Region	*Population Size (end 2013)*	*ISIS Saudi Fighters per Region*	*Ratio of Fighters per 100,000 Residents*
All	29,195,895	759	2.6
Riyadh	7,309,966	262	3.5
Al-Qassim	1303,623	134	10.2
Makkah	7,471,975	134	1.7
Eastern	4,414,278	63	1.4
Hail	638,699	31	4.8
Tabouk	845,857	31	3.6
Al-Madinah	1,910,998	24	1.2
Asir	2,045,070	23	1.1
Al-Jawf	471,120	9	1.9
Al-Bahah	439,927	8	1.8
Najran	541,344	5	0.9
Jizan	1,460,540	6	0.4
Northern Borders	342,498	5	1.4

them and presented the shares of their distribution by the regions.[5] In 2008, the Combating Terrorism Centre at West Point published a detailed report based on the analysis of 590 records of foreign fighters entering Iraq through Syria from August 2006 to August 2007 (the Sinjar Records). Even though the report was not solely focused on Saudi foreign fighters, it provided detailed information regarding the region/hometown of 193 out of the 237 Saudis in the Sinjar Records.[6]

In 2010, Heggammer published his brilliant book on jihad in Saudi Arabia where he constructed a dataset of 539 biographies of Saudi militants who participated in violent activism in the period between 1980 and 2006. He divided them into three main categories: the first includes the biographies of 161 Saudis who participated in early jihad fronts (in Afghanistan, Bosnia, Tajikistan, and Chechnya prior to 1996) when the notion of jihad was classical and relatively uncontroversial. The second category includes a sample of 197 biographies of Saudis who went to Afghanistan and joined al-Qaeda between 1996 and 2001, when jihad became a more controversial and risky activity. The third category includes a sample of 259 biographies of Saudis involved with the al-Qaeda in the Arabian Peninsula (AQAP) between 2002 and 2006. While not all socio-economic data

5 Thomas Hegghammer, *Saudi Militants in Iraq: Backgrounds and Recruitment Patterns*, FFI Report (Kjeller: Norwegian Research Defense Establishment, 2007).

6 Peter Bergen, Joseph Felter, Vahid Brown, and Jacob Shapiro, 'Bombers, Bank Accounts, & Bleedouts: Al-Qa'ida's Road in and out of Iraq,' in Brian Fishman, ed., *Combating Terrorism Center at West Point Report* (West Point, NY: US Marine Corps, 2008).

were available throughout the dataset, Hegghammer was able to present the geographical origin of 369 militants.[7]

In 2014, Aaron Zelin published an article on Saudi foreign fighters in Syria based on a database he compiled on foreign jihadist 'martyrdom' notices from the autumn of 2011 up until late February 2014. According to him, 'exactly 300 Saudis have died in Syria as of late February 2014'. Out of this total, 203 'martyrdom' notices detail the city/origin of the deceased fighter.[8]

Taken together, all of these past data on the home city/region of Saudi militants involved in both domestic and foreign jihadist fronts can be very useful, especially when compared to our current sample of 759 Saudi ISIL foreign fighters in Syria. They provide longitudinal insight into how outflows of Saudi jihadists from different origins respond to different conflict paradigms and socio-political contexts (see Figure 4.1).

First of all, it is important to underscore the fact that, apart from Hegghammer's sample of AQAP jihadists 2002–2006, the combination of the data we have, especially our current one on the ISIL documents, reveals that Saudis who joined jihadist conflict zones abroad are a heterogeneous and diverse bunch, especially in terms of their geographical background, and they do not come predominantly from a specific socio-economically disadvantaged group or region.[9] The AQAP sample was unique in the sense that it was not a sample of foreign fighters, even though many of them were veterans of the Afghani jihad, but of domestic terrorists waging a violent terror campaign against their own government. Moreover, they had a lower average level of education and a higher average age at the start of the campaign than other samples compiled by Hegghammer as well as our current sample of Saudi ISIL foreign fighters, and they predominantly came from the province of Riyadh. One reason for the discrepancy in the AQAP sample is that the AQAP campaign was not a clear case of classical sanctioned jihad against an outside enemy, but a very controversial, contentious, and risky case of domestic insurgency. Nonetheless, even regarding the AQAP militants, Hegghammer writes that 'they cannot be described as poor or underprivileged', but are 'the least privileged group of the three samples' he studied.[10]

However, one of the most distinguishing features when we look at all of our data is that while the two most populated provinces (Riyadh and Makkah) have always provided the largest number of Saudi jihadists to conflicts abroad, al-Qassim, which in 2013 was the seventh most populated region in the country, started to see a sharp rise in the number of its own foreign militant fighters in

7 Thomas Hegghammer, *Jihad in Saudi Arabia: Violence and Pan-Islamism Since 1979* (Cambridge: Cambridge University Press, 2010).

8 Aaron Zelin, 'The Saudi Foreign Fighter Presence in Syria', *CTC Sentinel*, vol. 7, issue 4 (2014), pp. 10–14.

9 See a more detailed and extensive analysis of the Saudi contingent in the ISIL leaked entry documents in Abdullah K. Al-Saud, *The Saudi Foreign Fighters: Analysis of the IS Leaked Entry Documents*, International Centre for the Study of Radicalisation and King Faisal Center for Research and Islamic Studies report (forthcoming 2018).

10 Hegghammer, *Jihad in Saudi Arabia*, p. 189.

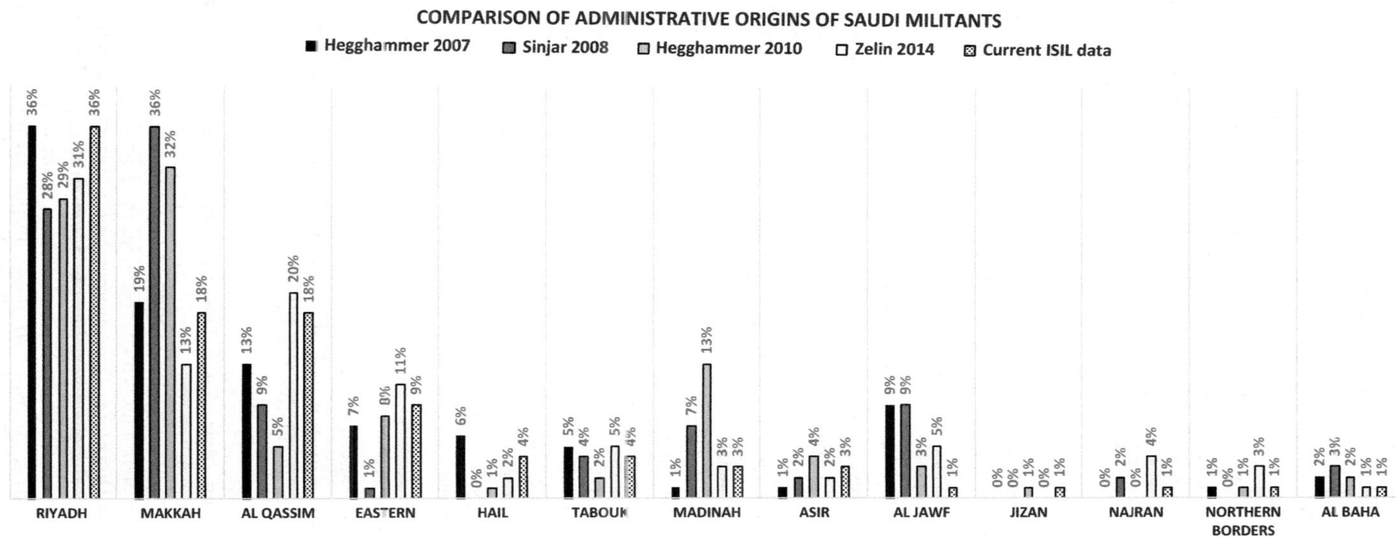

Figure 4.1 Comparison of administrative origins of Saudi militants

recent years, evident from the statistics from both our current ISIL documents sample and from Zelin's sample of 'martyrdom' notices of Saudis who died fighting for radical groups in Syria such as ISIL, now known as just the Islamic State (IS), or al-Qaeda's Jabhat al-Nusra (JN), which later became known as Jabhat Fateh Al-Sham (JFS) and then Hay'at Tahrir AlSham (HTS), between 2011 and 2014. In terms of raw numbers, fighters from al-Qassim in the Syrian conflict shared second place after those from the central region of Riyadh, but in terms of ratio of residents, al-Qassim actually came first in our sample by a large margin. The question here is what accounts for such an upsurge?

Analysis and discussion

Historically, al-Qassim has always been seen as the Saudi Kingdom's most socially conservative region. Religious figures from the region staunchly opposed and resisted girls' education when it was first introduced in the early 1960s.[11] During the 1980s and early 1990s, the region represented a strong base of support for the radical clerics of the *sahwa* movement, most prominent among them was Salman al-Awdah, whose arrest and imprisonment in 1994 instigated what has come to be known as 'the Buraydah Intifada' of 1995.[12] However, the religious conservatism of al-Qassim has never been homogeneous. Many well-known Saudi liberals have originated from the region such as Abdullah al-Qassimi (1907–1996), Turki al-Hamad, Ibrahim al-Blaihi, Mansour al-Nugaidan, and many more. But even if we are to argue that religious conservatism is the main characteristic of the majority of Qassimis, and that many of the aforementioned liberals have only left religious conservatism to liberalism after they moved out of al-Qassim, then why have Qassimis not figured predominantly in earlier samples of Saudi foreign fighters? In fact, in the two samples we have prior to 2001, they amounted to only 1 per cent and 4 per cent, where known, respectively.

What is more interesting is that the three regions that provided the largest numbers of Saudi ISIL foreign fighters in our database, Riyadh, Makkah, and al-Qassim, are the three regions with the lowest percentages of families living in absolute poverty, with al-Qassim faring even better than Makkah and Riyadh in this regard.[13] These figures further discredit the theory that radicalisation is mostly rampant in disadvantaged, underprivileged, and poor areas or regions, or at least that is not the case in Saudi Arabia. Nonetheless, the question still remains, how can we explain the relative rise in radicalisation and Salafi-jihadist ideology in

11 Abdullah Al Samti, *Awal Kitab Yunagish Fitnat Ta'leem Al Banat fi Al Saudiyyah* (First book discussing the trial of girls' education in Saudi Arabia), see Elaph website: http://elaph.com/Web/Culture/2009/7/458234.htm.

12 For more on the *Sahwa* movement see: Stephane Lacroix, *Awakening Islam: The Politics of Political Dissent in Contemporary Saudi Arabia* (Cambridge, MA: Harvard University Press); Hegghammer, *Jihad in Saudi Arabia*, pp. 70–78.

13 'Government Plans to Reduce Absolute Poverty from 13 Percent in 2009 to 2.2 Percent by 2020' (Ar.), *Al Sharq Al Awsat*, http://archive.aawsat.com/details.asp?section=43&issueno=11002&article=502441#.V_-OsJMrKu4.

al-Qassim, evident from the sharp increase in our sample in the numbers of Saudi foreign fighters from the Najd area in general, and al-Qassim in particular, in recent years?[14] While it is nearly impossible to know with absolute certainty what caused this recent upsurge, it is always fruitful to try and make smart speculations as to the reasons behind it. Three points might help give us some sort of an explanation.

(1) The Fukko al-A'ni (set free the captive) campaign

The most sinister campaigns are those that ostensibly uphold honourable, merciful, and noble slogans, but conceal more treacherous and ominous aims. One of those campaigns was the *Fukko al-A'ni* social media campaign that started in Saudi Arabia following the so-called 'Arab Spring' revolutions, trying to capitalise on the prevalent public mood of freedom and rebellion at the time. Outwardly, the campaign focused on the issue of human rights and, most specifically, the release of 'political prisoners'. Inwardly, along with its call for the release of a few constitutional reformists and activists, it called for the release of individuals who were detained in relation to any sort of terrorist activity—either through committing, supporting, funding, or enticing—and who were generally arrested after the 2003 AQAP terrorist campaign in the Kingdom.[15] Through anonymous social media accounts and platforms, most prominent among which were @almonaseron and @e3teqal, the campaign organisers coordinated with some of the relatives and friends of the detainees and staged marches, demonstrations, and sit-ins.[16]

14 Najd is the geographical central region of Saudi Arabia. While it is not an administrative province in itself, it incorporates the administrative provinces of Riyadh, al-Qassim, and Hail. According to our database, almost 58 per cent of the total 734 jihadists who listed their region/city of origin have come from Najd.

15 Among the most notable detainees the campaign advocated for were Suliman al-Ulwan, Khaled al-Rashid, and, most importantly, Haila al-Qusayyir who came to be known as 'al-Qaeda's lady'. In March 2010, the Saudi Interior Ministry announced her capture in Buraydah (al-Qassim region) on charges of lending logistical and financial support to al-Qaeda. In 2015, after her trial, she received a prison sentence of 15 years. According to reports, she renounced her radical views and support of al-Qaeda. See 'Haila al-Qusayyir Renounces her Support to the Organization and Refuses Daesh's Ideology', *Al Riyadh Newspaper*, 8 Nov. 2015, www.alriyadh.com/1098304.

16 For more background on the campaign see Mishari al-Thaydi's episode of his *Maraya* programme on al-Arabiya TV Channel 'Set Free the Captive ... or the Terrorist?' (Ar.), http://bit.ly/2dYxrS6. In 2014, Saudi courts started sentencing many organisers and participants in the campaign in Buraydah city to different prison terms. See, for instance, Huda al-Saleh, '13 Women on Trial for Buraydah Protests', *al-Arabiya*, 22 Nov. 2016, 'Imprisonment for a Yemeni Who Incited the Youth to Participate in Sit-ins in Buraydah' (Ar.), *Al Sharq Al Awsat*, 29 Oct. 2014, http://bit.ly/2dQSjYO; 'Supporting al-Qaeda and its Beliefs Calling for Stirring Up Sectarianism and Killing in Conflict Zones: Imprisonment for 3 Accusers Participated in "Buraydah Sit-ins" from Two to 4 Years' (Ar.), *Al Riyadh Newspaper*, 25 June 2014, www.alriyadh.com/947142. The *@almonaseron* platform on Telegram was run by the Saudi ISIL supporter Nadi al-Mudhayani who, along with Khalid al-Sirwani, blew themselves up

However, through crafty manipulation and employment of three different mechanisms or tools, the campaign was able to deceive some people and, at least until late 2013, mobilise many to its cause, including some well-known Islamist figures and activists[17] and many others, some possibly with good intentions not knowing the campaign's sinister side, who joined the social media hype at the time and started voicing their criticism of the government's handling of the prisoners/detainees cohort.[18]

The first tool the campaign employed was attempting to portray itself as a human rights campaign, to give itself a reformist aura through upholding benevolent, humanitarian, and appealing slogans that most people, especially prisoners' relatives and friends, can identify with.[19] Following the failure of the so-called '*Hunayn* revolution' to materialise in Saudi Arabia, which was supposed to start on 11 March 2011, Islamist and reformist radicals who longed for drastic change in the Kingdom found in this campaign the perfect vehicle through which to try and mobilise the masses and exert pressure on the Saudi government. After all, as Lacroix writes, the issue of detainees and prisoners is an issue 'for which there exists a core group of people who are easy to mobilize: the prisoners' relatives, some of whom, after years of waiting, are ready to do whatever it takes to get their loved ones back'.[20]

The second tool the campaign cunningly employed was its insistence on its peaceful nature. The campaign organisers and activists knew full well that demonstrations, marches, and sit-ins are prohibited by law in the Kingdom and, as a result, would generally lead to arrests. Even though arrests would usually only last for few days and did not lead to prosecution, whenever a police intervention happens, activists and radicals would agitate the public even more by highlighting

following a raid on their hideout in Jeddah on 22 January 2017. *@almonaseron* Telegram channel has been dormant ever since that raid. See Ibrahim Alawi, 'The Death of al-Mudhayani Closes the 'al-Munaseron' Account' (Ar.), Okaz, 26 Jan. 2017, http://bit.ly/2osFjBd.

17 Such as Nasir al-Omar, Salman al-Awdah, Abdulaziz al-Abdullatif, Yusuf al-Ahmad, Ibrahim al-Sakran, Abdulaziz al-Turaifi, Mohammad al-Ahmari, Mohammad al-Hudhaif, and Mohammad al-Abdulkarim.

18 For a sample of the tweets of those figures during the height of the campaign in early 2013, see https://twitter.com/0Strict/status/728574611823185920. In July 2011, Ibrahim Al Sakran released two videos called 'Except the Women Custodian of the Two Holy Mosques'. They were widely circulated; see http://bit.ly/2egGOi8 and http://bit.ly/2enXzUM.

19 The campaign was able to draw supporters from different points on the political spectrum, from liberal constitutional reformists to Islamist '*muhtasibun*' activists and militant jihadists. The reason behind this is that it intentionally and calculatedly, in order to draw as much support as it can, relied on vagueness and did not try to distinguish between different types of prisoners and detainees, painting all types in one colour: namely 'political prisoners'. For a more detailed account of the nature of the campaign and, especially, the role played by the *mutasibun*, see Stephane Lacroix, 'Saudi Islamists and the Arab Spring', *LSE Research Paper*, 2014.

20 Ibid., p. 16.

the state's injustice and aggression in the face of its peaceful and 'legitimate' demands.[21]

The third mechanism that the campaign capitalised upon was its overt focus on and publicisation of women detainees, most prominent among whom was Haila al-Qusayyir. It also sought to mobilise some of the wives and daughters of prisoners and detainees, most prominently Rima al-Jurayyish, Mai al-Talaq, Amina al-Rashid, and Wroud al-Rushudi, who, themselves, later became prominent voices, mobilisers, and advocates for the cause.[22] It is telling that all five were from the city of Buraydh in the heart of al-Qassim region, which made Buraydah, a city from which 100 foreign fighters in our sample come, a theatre for many demonstrations that culminated in what became known as the 'Buraydh sit-in' on 4 March 2013. When the state responded by arresting some participants in the sit-in, including women, activists and radicals alike seized the opportunity and produced videos decrying the state's 'mistreatment and oppression of innocent women' who, according to them, were merely calling for the release of their wrongfully imprisoned loved ones.[23] This was a wily tactic to arouse feelings of honour and pride among the conservative Saudi public and entice them into action. It is also telling that, as events transpired later, all of the women mentioned, apart from al-Rushudi, were al-Qaeda sympathisers and recruiters. While al-Qusayyir, from her prison in late 2015, came clean about her past role within the al-Qaeda organisation, al-Talaq and al-Rashid were caught, along with their six children, on the Saudi–Yemini border trying to be smuggled into Yemen in order to join the ranks of AQAP there. Al-Jurayyish, however, was able to smuggle herself into Yemen to join AQAP before deciding to switch allegiance and give *bay'ah* to Abu Bakr al-Baghdadi and join ISIL in Syria. Reports claim that in August 2015, al-Jurayyish married Abu Mohammad al-Shamali, the most prolific smuggler of Saudi foreign fighters into Syria according to our dataset, as his third wife.[24]

21 See, for instance, a lecture entitled 'Buraydah Sit-ins and the Peaceful Movement' that was delivered and videotaped on early March 2013 by Mohammad al-Qahtani and Mohammad al-Abdulkarim of the Saudi Civil and Political Rights Association (SCPRA) following what has come to be known as 'Buraydah sit-ins' that took place on 4 March 2013 and led to multiple arrests including women: www.youtube.com/watch?v=6hJ_PUWou8Q.

22 Many female relatives of detainees were filmed in highly emotional videos, some even crying, describing the 'aggression' and 'injustice' befallen them and their detained loved ones by the state. For instance, see the following videos: http://bit.ly/2ea8pis and http://bit.ly/2dZszwd.

23 See the following YouTube videos, for instance: 'The Ministry of Interior's Crimes Against the Free Women of Buraydah' (Ar.), http://bit.ly/2ea8pis; 'An Interview with the Father of the Kidnapped Aminah al-Rashid from Buraydah' (Ar.), http://bit.ly/2eKmXb3.

24 For full stories of all four women see the following articles: 'The Story of Haila Al Qusayyir …' (Ar.), *Ajel Electronic Newspaper*, 5 June 2010, www.ajel.sa/local/1125826; 'Haila Al Qusayyir Renounces her Support to the Organization and Refuses Daesh's Ideology' (Ar.), *Al Riyadh Newspaper*, 8 Nov. 2015, www.alriyadh.com/1098304; 'Mai Al Talaq and Ameena Al Rashid: From a Picnic in Al Qassim to the

While not all supporters or sympathisers of the campaign at the time were radical militants who espouse the Salafi-jihadi ideology, the campaign itself provided the perfect platform and the best opportunity for radical and terrorist groups to mobilise, recruit, and attract new followers.[25] Despite its, at least public, insistence on peaceful demonstrations and sit-ins, the campaign became an incubator of, rather than an alternative to, violent extremism. Extremist militant groups' strategy of capitalisation on this campaign in order to agitate and entice the masses against their rulers and security forces, despite ideological differences between them and some other activists in the same campaign, was very much in line with Osama bin Laden's instructions, in response to the 'Arab Spring', which he laid out in a letter just a week before his death. In the letter dated 25 April 2011, and recovered from the Abbottabad raid, bin Laden wrote:

> Initially, I would see that one of the most important steps of the oncoming stage is inciting the people who have not revolted yet, and encouraging them to get against the rulers, insisting that it is a religious duty and a logical necessity, so the arrows are concentrated on toppling the rulers without discussing the differences on issues.[26]

Even some known non-Saudi radicals, such as the UK extremist from Luton Abu Rahin Aziz (Abu Abdullah Al Britani) who later went on to join ISIL in Syria and died there, joined the campaign following the 'Buraydah sit-ins' and released a video in July 2013 entitled 'Haila al-Qusayr: Support our Sisters in Buraydah'.[27] Turki al-Binali (Abu Sufyan Al Sulami), a Bahraini who was one of ISIL's top religious figures, also released a video message to 'the free women of Buraydah' in March 2013 denouncing the 'assault' on them and declaring his solidarity with the 'Buraydah sit-in'.[28] Moreover, the most famous ISIL poet, a Syrian women who goes by the name of Ahlam al-Nasr (Dreams of Victory), wrote a poem in support of the cause entitled 'Release Haila al-Qusayyir'.[29]

Yemeni Borders' (Ar.), *Al Hayat Newspaper*, 7 May 2014, http://bit.ly/2dm79VZ; 'The Story of Rima Al Jurayyish From "Fukko al-A'ni" Until her Joining Daesh' (Ar.), *Al Arabiya*, 9 Feb. 2016, http://bit.ly/2ec3Xih.

25 Al-Qaeda and ISIL supporters and followers were quick to capitalise on the campaign and release multiple video and audio clips trying to mobilise the public against Saudi security forces and entice them into action. For examples see an archive of some of the clips that were made during that period: http://bit.ly/2dhOwYl.

26 *Osama Bin Ladin and Al Qaeda: Documents Captured at Abbottabad Compound*, SOCOM-2012–0000010, http://bit.ly/2e0FjFa.

27 'Haila Al Qusayr: Support our Sisters in Buraydah', www.youtube.com/watch?v=MHKs5nOlvgo; Adam Parris-Long, 'Luton Jihadi Abu Rahin Aziz "Dies in Drone Attack"', *Luton Today*, 6 July 2015.

28 'Abu Sufyan Al Sulami: A Message to the Free Women of Buraydah', www.youtube.com/watch?v=9CkJz_wLFd4.

29 This poem, among others, can be found in her own blog: http://ahlam-alnasr.blogspot.co.uk/search/label/%D9%82%D8%B5%D8%A7%D8%A6%D8%AF.

Mobilisation tools such as *nasheeds* (religious hymns) were used and employed by radicals in the midst of the *Fukko al-A'ni* campaign, especially around the theme of women.[30] The most famous *nasheed* that was used frequently during that period, as a soundtrack for many videos of sit-ins and interviews with female relatives of detainees, was intentionally very provocative and highly inflammable:

> The usurpers dishonoured our havens, and to captivity led our women. And the youth of creed are lost in slumber forgetting our misery. How can my people forget the virgins in the prisons of despots and Christians' lackeys? Our sister in prison cells is calling: O son of my religion you disrupted my heart.[31]

The main issue the campaign engineers used and capitalised upon was the issue of women detainees, and, as mentioned earlier, the most known women of the campaign were from al-Qassim province (Buraydah city). Whether the concentration on al-Qassim, and the city of Buraydah in particular, was a deliberate strategy on the part of the campaign's engineers in order to create an aggrieved and prone to radicalisation hot spot, or not, is unclear. What is clear however is that, in addition to the aforementioned women from Buraydah who became vocal during the campaign and later joined, or tried to join, radical groups, many of those who joined the campaign and were arrested for short periods in late 2012 and early 2013, for their part in the organisation and participation of some of the marches and sit-ins, became staunch radicals and violent terrorists later. The campaign tried adamantly, although sometimes indirectly, to engrave the notion of revenge from the state in the minds and hearts of many of its supporters and sympathisers. What happened later was that terrorist groups, such as al-Qaeda and ISIL, reaped the rewards of such a deliberate, albeit inexplicit, strategy.

We know of six confirmed cases of ISIL terrorist attacks, or foiled attacks—five in the Kingdom and one in Kuwait—perpetrated by individuals who were previously active participants in the demonstrations and sit-ins that took part in Buraydah city as part of the *Fukko al-A'ni* campaign. These individuals are: Adel Abdullah al-Mijmaj, who was killed in May 2016 (at 27 years old) in a government raid on an ISIL cell in the province of Makkah;[32] Salih al-Gash'ami who in May 2015 carried out a suicide attack on a mosque in al-Qudayh town in

30 For more on *nasheeds* as a messaging, mobilising, and recruiting tool in the jihadist scene, see Henrik Gratrud, 'Islamic State *Nasheeds* as Messaging Tools', *Studies in Conflict and Terrorism*, vol. 29, issue 12 (2016), pp. 1050–1070; Thomas Hegghammer, ed., *Jihadi Culture: The Art and Social Practices of Militant Islamists* (Cambridge: Cambridge University Press, 2017), pp. 22–81.

31 For instance, see the videos: 'The Free Women of Buraydah and the Scholars of the Land of the Two Holy Mosques: *Fukko al-A'ni* (Set Free the Captive)' (Ar.), www.youtube.com/watch?v=GYk8Ps0BMpE and 'Haila al-Qusayyir… Until When?' (Ar.), www.youtube.com/watch?v=m-dr0yaY9jM.

32 'Adel Al Mijmaj: 'From the Chaos of *Fukko al-A'ni* to a Suicide Bomber in Makkah' (Ar.), *Al Arabiya*, 6 May 2016, http://bit.ly/2dZfrak; 'Saudi Arabia Names Four Killed Terrorists', *Gulf News*, 6 May 2016, http://bit.ly/2em3et4.

al-Qatif;[33] Fahad al-Qabba' who carried out a suicide attack on Imam al-Sadiq mosque in Kuwait in June 2015;[34] Yousef Suliman al-Suliman who in August 2015 (at 21) carried out a suicide attack on a security forces mosque in Asir province;[35] Abdulrahman Abdullah al-Tuwaijri who in January 2016 (at 22) carried out a suicide attack on Imam Rida mosque in al-Ahsa province;[36] and Abdulrahman Salih al-Omar who in July 2016 (at 23), along with two others, attempted to blow up a mosque in the city of al-Qatif.[37]

This episode in the history of the Kingdom, which saw the city of Buraydah in the heart of al-Qassim province as its main theatre,[38] even while noting the several sit-ins in Riyadh as well, might help explain why, as opposed to previous samples of Saudi foreign militants in jihadist conflict zones, the ISIL entry documents data show al-Qassim province as the highest contributor of Saudi foreign fighters per capita. The ratio for Buraydah city alone is even higher than the overall al-Qassim province ratio (at around 15 fighters per one 100,000 residents, compared to around 10 for the whole province). As a result of the *Fukko al-A'ni*'s persistent negative campaign and the resultant skirmishes with security forces, some in the region, and elsewhere, especially friends and relatives of prisoners, were left with a deep sense of aversion and antipathy towards the government which they viewed as an unjust aggressor. It would be safe to assume that terrorist groups, especially ISIL which from April 2013 started making rapid military gains in Syria, preyed upon such a disenfranchised, aggrieved, and highly politicised group.

The link between the *Fukko al-A'ni* campaign and its advocacy for the prisoners and detainees, on the one hand, and recruitment to radical terrorist organizations such as ISIL and al-Qaeda's Jabhat al-Nusra, on the other, becomes very clear when we compare the names of the signatories of a public online 'Letter of the Detainees' Families', addressed to the former Saudi Minister of Interior prince Muhammad bin Nayif, with some of the names in the ISIL documents.[39] Names

33 'Perpetrators of Kuwait and Qudayh Attacks Participated in *Fukko al-A'ni*' (Ar.), *Al-Sakinah*, 29 June 2015, www.assakina.com/news/news2/72913.html.
34 Ibid.
35 'Saudi Says Its Citizen Carried Out Mosque Suicide Blast', *Al Jazeera*, 8 Aug. 2015, http://bit.ly/1Kb5Fag; 'The Danger of the *Fukko al-A'ni* Campaign and the Building of a Community Based Security System' (Ar.), *Okaz Newspaper*, 11 July 2016, http://bit.ly/2dijsri.
36 'Al Ahsa Mosque Suicide Bomber Identified', *Saudi Gazette*, 31 Jan. 2016, http://bit.ly/2ebgch7.
37 'The Danger of the *Fukko al-A'ni* Campaign and the Building of a Community Based Security System' (Ar.), *Okaz Newspaper*, 11 July 2016, http://bit.ly/2dijsri; 'Terrorists Named, Arrests Made in Madinah, Qatif Blasts', *Arab News*, 7 July 2016, http://bit.ly/2dimP1o.
38 See these videos as examples of different episodes in support of the campaign in Buraydah city: 'A Stand in Buraydah Entitled: *Fukko al-A'ni* Campaign' (http://bit.ly/2eFOWIU), 'A Man from Buraydah Writes *Fukko al-A'ni* on the King's Portrait' (http://bit.ly/2dOczdE), 'Supporters Write *Fukko al-A'ni* on the House of Buraydah's Emir' (http://bit.ly/2ekyYEv).
39 'Letter of the Detainees' Families' (Ar.), created 17 April 2014, https://justpaste.it/f4qs.

such as Ahmad al-Olayyan, Mu'ath al-Dubaikhki (both died, in 2014 and 2015 respectively), and Abdulaziz al-Duwiesh feature in both. Moreover, in both this letter and an earlier online open letter dated 26 February 2013 and addressed to the king, many of the signatories' family names, especially those who have large groups of signatories, can be found, in fewer numbers, in the ISIL entry documents, which can be indicative of kinship ties between them and of a possible causal relationship between the campaign and radicalisation.[40] In the earlier open letter, the signatories threatened that unless the detainees' 'security file' is closed, meaning 'the release of all prisoners even if on bail', the situation would soon explode.[41]

In one 'martyrdom biography' of a young foreign fighter from al-Qassim named Mohammad al-Rubaish (Faris al-Qassimi), it is claimed that he had a detained brother and was an active participant in the *Fukko al-A'ni* demonstrations and sit-ins in Buraydah after he 'started searching and asking about the reality of injustice befalling the detainees and the reasons behind their arrest, which made him realize the truth about this unjust tyrannical state'.[42] While he decided to head south and join AQAP in Yemen in July 2013 at the age of 18, others, as evidenced by our dataset, decided to go north instead and join ISIL in Syria.

(2) Facilitation and the role of social networks

Another hypothesis that might help explain the upsurge of foreign fighters from al-Qassim during the 2013–2014 period is that there were highly influential early travellers from the province to the Syrian conflict who became very instrumental in garnering support, recruiting, facilitating, and connecting the local (al-Qassim) to the transnational (Syria and Iraq). The average age of ISIL al-Qassim fighters in our dataset is 22.3, which is more than a year and a half lower than the average age of the whole Saudi contingent (23.9). In general, as evidenced by their average age and their responses to the question 'Have you participated in jihad before?', Saudi ISIL fighters represent a new generation of jihadists who most probably, prior to making the decision to travel to Syria, lacked any previous network connections or relationships with the jihadi world. So, how did they bridge the gap and make the connection from their local circumstances to terrorist organisations in foreign countries, in this case ISIL?

The answer can be found in the role of 'social networks' and 'facilitators'. As Timothy Holman writes, '[T]he initiation of relationships and expansion of social networks can come from those in the conflict zone traveling abroad or from early travellers going into the conflict zone.'[43] Furthermore, as Sageman finds out from

40 'An Open Letter from the Detainees' Families' (Ar.), 26 Feb. 2013, https://5etab.wordpress.com/.
41 Ibid.
42 'The Martyr Biography: "Faris Al Qassimi" Mohammad bin Ahmad Al Rubaish (May Allah Accept him)' (Ar.), 11 Jan. 2015, https://justpaste.it/iuiy.
43 Timothy Holman, 'Gonna Get Myself Connected: The Role of Facilitation in Foreign Fighter Mobilization', *Perspectives on Terrorism*, vol. 10, issue 2 (2016), p. 17.

his study of 150 Islamist terrorists, the vast majority of them were influenced by friendship, kinship, and the urging of family members to join jihadi expeditions.[44] While in the age of technology and multiple social networking platforms, recruitment and facilitation has been greatly influenced in the sense that physical and personal presence is no longer a necessity, as 'would-be travellers have new channels to sources of information and persons that can facilitate travel',[45] it remains the case that personal social and relational networks play a primary role in such a process, as 'radicalization does not occur in a vacuum [...] Offline relationships still matter a great deal.'[46] The question to ask then is: were there any early travellers from al-Qassim province who could have influenced their relational networks of kin, friends, and activists back home and facilitated their travel to Syria?

While it is impossible to accurately know the full catalogue of names, numbers, and exact entry dates of early travellers from al-Qassim, or the whole of Saudi for that matter, who made the journey to join jihadist groups in Syria, it would suffice to highlight the names of some early travellers from al-Qassim whose stories might have had an impact on their friends and acquaintances back home and facilitated their transition.

But before delving into that, let us take a closer look at two specific variables in our records, namely the date of entry and the name of the person who gave the fighter a *tazkiya* (recommendation), analysis of which could help draw a mind map of social networks within the al-Qassim ISIL contingent.

Responses to the question of *tazkiya* are not consistent in all forms. While most were recommended by one individual, others were given *tazkiya* by two, and a few by none. The other point that stands out here is the plethora of recommenders. There are around 100 recommenders for the 134 foreign fighters coming from al-Qassim, the vast majority of them are listed by their *kunyas* (aliases) only, with the exception of Turki al-Binali who recommended one fighter and Sheikh Nasir al-Thaqil who recommended two. These facts limit the investigative value of this field and makes it hard to analyse. However, it is worth highlighting that Abu Mohammad al-Shamali, the most prolific smuggler in our dataset, is also the recommender of the largest group of Qassimis, 12 out of the 134. Urwa al-Najdi and Abu Ali al-Tamimi come second as recommenders of six Qassimi fighters each. Alqamah (Abu Ali al-Swayyid) gave *tazkiya* to five, and Abu Suliman al-Khaboubi to four. Three other recommenders gave *tazkiya* to three individuals each, while all the rest have either recommended only one or two Qassimi fighters.

However, if we combine the date of entry of the fighters into Syria with the names of recommenders, we can get a better sense or an indication of prior friendship or kin relationship where a group has been given *tazkiya* by the same individual and travelled on the same day. Out of the 127 foreign fighters from

44 Marc Sageman, *Understanding Terror Networks* (Philadelphia: University of Pennsylvania Press, 2004), pp. 111–113.

45 Holman, 'Gonna Get Myself Connected', p. 16.

46 Seamus Hughes, 'To Stop ISIS Recruitment, Focus Offline', *Lawfare*, 7 Aug. 2016, http://bit.ly/2aDO965.

al-Qassim who listed their date of entry, 29 entered into Syria in small groups of two, three, or four, with each group entering on the same day and being recommended by the same individual or individuals. While few of them have the same family name, suggesting they are relatives (three out of four in one group), the majority have different family names suggesting a relationship of either friendship or maternal kin. Many of the remaining 98 Qassimi foreign fighters have travelled on the same day with other Saudi fighters in our dataset, suggesting that ISIL operated host houses (*ma'dhafat*) in Turkish border towns where newcomers from different cities, and probably countries, were hosted and assembled for a while before being smuggled into Syria together. A possible explanation of the relatively short list of foreign fighters entering into Syria on the same day, even in comparison to the list of those who were given *tazkiya* by the same person, is the security concern over smuggling recruits in large numbers.

While the data from these two answer fields gave us an inconclusive indication that any of the Qassimi foreign fighters had social links to individuals within ISIL that facilitated their travel and entry into the organization, it gave us a stronger indication that many of the fighters knew each other prior to their travel into Syria, evident from the facts that they come from the same city, some even the same neighbourhood, were recommended by the same individual, travelled together and entered on the same date, and are in the same age group. However, such trends or findings are not unique to the Qassimi fighters and can be found among many other Saudi, and non-Saudi, foreign fighters in the database.[47] Therefore, while their explanatory value in our case is not strong, it would be given more resonance if we review some early Qassimi travellers into Syria whose news, stories, or social networks might have formed a bridge for the recruitment of the province's youth and played a role in the rise of ISIL foreign fighters from their region/province in comparison to fighters from other Saudi provinces.

The highest profile early traveller to the Syrian conflict zone is the Qassimi Dr Abdullah al-Muhaisini. Even though al-Muhaisini used to live in Makkah prior to travelling to Syria, he was born and raised in Buraydah at the heart of al-Qassim province, where his family originated and where he spent most of his early years.[48] It is telling that one of the scholars he asserts to have studied under was Sheikh Suliman al-Ulwan, one of the radical *neojihadi* scholars from Buraydah who was first arrested in 2004, as we shall explore further below.[49] According to al-Muhaisini himself, it was al-Ulwan, whom he referred to as

47 For instance, a group of five foreign fighters from the small city of al-Wajh (Tabouk Province), two brothers and two others from the same family as the brothers, all between 18 and 22 at the time of entry, were recommended by the same two individuals who did not recommend any other fighter in the database but them, entered into Syria through the same entry point on the same date.

48 Dr Abdullah bin Mohammad al-Muhaisni, *Biography* (Ar.), undated, www.mohisni.com/index.php?option=com_content&view=article&id=59&Itemid=121.

49 Ibid.

'my sheikh', who actually encouraged him to travel and join the caravan of jihadists to Syria and requested that he stay in touch with him from there.[50]

In a familial/tribal society like Saudi Arabia, people still identify, although less strongly than in the past, with others on the basis of tribe/kinship/family/origin.[51] Therefore, the fact that al-Muhaisini left his city of origin early to live in Makkah does not mean that many in his city, or even region, of origin (Buraydah/al-Qassim) ceased to identify with him or view him as one of their own. A clear example of this is the case of the young foreign fighter with JFS (previously JN and currently HTS) from Buraydah Younis al-Qar'awi, the younger brother of the detained terrorist Salih al-Qar'awi.[52] In a video posted on his Twitter page on 28 October 2016, al-Muhaisini appeared beside the youth, who was to commit a 'martyrdom' operation against the Syrian regime's forces that same day, addressing Younis's mother and 'all our mothers in Buraydah, its surroundings, and the mothers of all *mujahideen*'.[53] The reason al-Muhaisini delivered this video message to Younis's mother – congratulating her for raising a 'hero' son who will 'be a groom in paradise tonight' and intercede on her behalf in heaven – is because Younis asked him to do so after he came up to him, following a sermon that al-Muhaisini gave about heaven, and told him, 'I am one of your relatives and from your same city [Buraydah].'[54]

Even though al-Muhaisini has distanced himself from ISIL since its infighting with JN began in early 2014, his role and influence, given his substantial online presence, over the jihadist community as a whole, especially in Syria, cannot be over-emphasised. According to his own posts, 'eager new jihadists

50 Al-Muhaisini related his story and testimony on the events that caused him to distance himself from ISIL in a debate with a Telegram group. The transcript of the conversation can be found here: 'Hiwar al-Shaikh Abdullah al-Muhaisini ma' Jama'at al-Dawla' (Conversation of Sheikh Abdullah al-Muhaisini with the Organization of the State), https://justpaste.it/jwvc.

51 For a more detailed discussion of the concepts of *asabiyya* (solidarity) and *qaraba* (closeness in social relations) in Saudi society, see Mamoun Fandy, *Saudi Arabia and the Politics of Dissent* (New York: Palgrave, 1999), p. 74; Daryl Champion, *The Paradoxical Kingdom: Saudi Arabia and the Momentum of Reform* (London: C. Hurst & Co., 2003), pp. 64–71; and Abdullah K. Al-Saud, *Religious Radicalization and Violence in Saudi Arabia*, unpublished PhD thesis (London: King's College London, 2012), chapter one.

52 Salih al-Qar'awi was one of 85 most-wanted terrorists announced by the Saudi government. He was handed over by al-Qaeda to the Saudi authorities following a drone strike in Pakistan in 2012 that resulted in the loss of both his legs, one of his arms, and one of his eyes. See 'Terrorist Designation of Saleh al-Qarawi', www.state.gov/r/pa/prs/ps/2011/12/178882.htm; Thomas Joscelyn, 'Online Jihadists Discuss Fate of Al Qaeda Operative Held by Saudi Arabia', *The Long War Journal*, 27 June 2013.

53 See the Twitter post at https://twitter.com/mhammadbbd/status/792040285341683714 and the video at www.youtube.com/watch?v=VO-YuZYI8HI.

54 Ibid. See also the Twitter posts at https://twitter.com/mhammadbbd/status/792039248044122112, and https://twitter.com/mhammadbbd/status/792039794314452993.

contact him daily'.[55] In a fast-changing jihadist environment such as Syria, it is very common to switch allegiances among the different factions fighting there. Some Saudis in our dataset have in fact indicated that they were members of JN or joined one of its training camps (*mu'askar*) prior to joining ISIL. This trend is arguably reversed nowadays with many ISIL members deserting it and defecting to other jihadist groups.[56]

Another influential figure from al-Qassim who was active online is Ahmad Abdullah al-Shayi', or 'the living suicider' as he came to be known. Al-Shayi' fought previously with al-Qaeda in Iraq during the leadership of Abu Mus'ab al-Zarqawi (died 2006) and suffered burns all over his body after a failed suicide-by-tanker attack in Baghdad in July 2005.[57] He was then handed to the Saudi authorities who treated him and then tried to de-radicalise and rehabilitate him through the counselling and rehabilitation programme. Al-Shayi' seemed to be rehabilitated after that and happy to be united with his family again in Buraydah.[58] However, as events revealed later, that was not the case. In 2013, he disappeared again from his family home only to appear in Syria this time, announcing, through his Twitter account, his joining ISIL, showing his picture there holding a Kalashnikov, and praising and promoting its fight against the Assad regime.[59]

Another early ISIL recruit from Buraydah was Mu'ath Abdulrahman al-Samil (died in January 2014) who, according to his entry document, joined the organisation in September 2012 at the age of 20.[60] According to a long-time member of a Saudi-based online de-radicalisation campaign that seeks to engage radicals in debates with the aim of moderating their views, Mu'ath, with whom he had a number of online chats and debates, was very active online around the issue of the detainees and the *Fukko al-A'ni* campaign and had links with the @almonaseroun and @e3teqal platforms.[61]

Another of the early travellers from Buraydah to the Syrian conflict zone was Abdullah Ibrahim al-Dakhil. Al-Dakhil died fighting for JN in the battle to capture Raqqa on 2 March 2013. Ironically, al-Dakhil's reach, impact, and influence only

55 Thomas Joscelyn, 'Popular Saudi Cleric Endorses Islamic Front, Calls for Cooperation with al Qaeda', *The Long War Journal*, 14 December 2013.

56 Mara Revkin and Jacob Olidort, 'Does ISIS Need Territory to Survive?', *New York Times*, 21 Oct. 2016.

57 See an interview with al-Shayi' right after his failed suicide attack in Iraq in the video: 'The Living Suicider Arrives into Syria to Aid the Militants' (Ar.), www.youtube.com/watch?v=tDjQ25IVKks.

58 See an interview with Al-Shayi' detailing his story and renouncing all of his 'previously-held' radical views: 'I Went for Jihad and they Made Me Bait to Kill the Innocent … And Our Travel [to Iraq] was a Grave Mistake' (Ar.), *Al-Riyadh Newspaper*, 21 Nov. 2007, www.alriyadh.com/295815.

59 Nasir Al-Hagbani, '"The Living Suicider" Ahmad Al-Shayi' from "al-Zarqawi's al-Qaeda" to "al-Baghdadi's Daesh"' (Ar.), *Al-Hayat Newspaper*, 11 Nov. 2013, www.alhayat.com/Details/571058.

60 See the Twitter post announcing his 'martyrdom' at: https://twitter.com/Mohmd199A/status/423451651262152704.

61 The individual wishes to remain anonymous.

started after his death, as a result of the emotionally charged video of his burial with his face shown and blood still gushing from his back.[62] Arguably, this video has had a great impact on many youths, especially those who already knew him in his hometown of Buraydah.

Lastly, there is the case of the famous *munshid* (singer) from al-Qassim, Maher Mish'al (Abu al-Zubayr al-Qassimi) (died July 2015), who was well known, especially among the religiously conservative circles in Saudi who prefer listening to *anasheed* (without musical instruments) rather than songs (with musical instruments). His relative fame came as a result of his earlier participation in a reality TV show on the *Bidaya* channel called *Shigatna* (our apartment).[63] On the anniversary of the late King Abdullah's ascendance to the throne in 2011, Maher dedicated a *nasheed* to him entitled *baya'nah* (we gave him our *bay'ah* or oath of allegiance).[64] However, that all changed in April 2013 when he pledged his allegiance to Abu Bakr al-Baghdadi and announced his travel to Syria to join the ranks of ISIL.[65] From there, he started appearing in many video clips, performing *nasheeds* in some, while talking about the situation in Syria and how he only felt happy and whole when he came to the 'land of jihad' in others.[66] He also appeared alongside another Saudi poet, Sa'ad al-Mutayri, and in the presence of the notorious Abu Waheeb (died May 2016)[67] and others, singing the infamous *nasheed* '*ya 'asib al-ras wainik*'.[68] The power, importance, and strong influence that *nasheeds* can have as a mobilising tool cannot be underestimated, and, arguably, so does the impact that Maher Mish'al, the young, dynamic, and charismatic *munshid*, had on some of his followers, friends, and fan base.

To sum up, while it is hard to know with absolute certainty the extent of the impact that certain individuals cast upon their social networks, it is safe to assume that they played a prominent role in the mobilisation and facilitation of new recruits who either know, relate, or identify with them. Let us move now to investigate the third possible explanation behind the disproportionate increase in the number of al-Qassim ISIL foreign fighters in comparison to others from the rest of the Saudi provinces.

62 See the videos at: www.youtube.com/watch?v=ulIiTYlzqDs and www.youtube.com/watch?v=TEelNX0B2cA.
63 '*Bidaya* Disassociate itself from the Radicalisation of the *Munshid* Maher Mish'al, and his Friends are Sad for his Fate' (Ar.), *AlKhaleej Online*, 13 July 2015, http://bit.ly/2fvi05j.
64 The *nasheed* video can be found at: www.youtube.com/watch?v=Dw4KJfwI3Nk.
65 Majid Al-Hazza', 'The Death of Daesh's *Munshid*. The Saudi Maher Mish'al' (Ar.), *Al-Arabiya*, 12 July 2015, http://bit.ly/2eOykKI.
66 See, for instance, the post: https://twitter.com/sshgge/status/789966682156634112; and the videos: https://www.youtube.com/watch?v=zde8fkJB5ZE and https://www.youtube.com/watch?v=cmGG6xy2ryo.
67 Colin Freeman, 'Islamic State Executioner Who Devised Deadly "Quranic Quiz" Killed by US Air Strike', *The Telegraph*, 9 May 2016, http://bit.ly/1T20eQ2.
68 The *nasheed* can be found at: www.youtube.com/watch?v=KcvNKE28IVw.

(3) The Saudi group of neo-jihadi scholars

During the late 1990s and early 2000s, a small group of very radical local Saudi religious scholars, from the cities of Buraydah and Riyadh, voiced very extreme opinions and adopted radical positions that made them central to the global jihadist movement and reigning Salafi-jihadi ideologues. The most prominent figures of this group are Hamoud al-Shu'aybi, Nasir al-Fahad, Ali al-Khudayr, Suliman al-Ulwan, and Ahmad al-Khaldi who to this day, apart from al-Shu'aybi who died late 2001, remain behind bars. The rise and radicalisation of this group of religious scholars, who have come to be known as the neojihadis,[69] or the scholars of the 'al-Shu'aybi school' in reference to their central, albeit mainly symbolic, figure Hamoud al-Uqla al-Shu'aybi,[70] was the result of many domestic, regional, and international factors that cannot be explored within the scope of this article.[71] However, what is important to highlight here is that their radical ideas and *fatwas* more than a decade ago, during the years preceding the outbreak of AQAP's violence and terror campaign in the Kingdom in 2003, contributed to the radicalisation of many Saudi Islamists and, most importantly, are still referenced and celebrated in radical militant circles both in and beyond Saudi Arabia.

In light of the influence that such radical scholars still hold in the jihadist scene and how they can convey a source of legitimacy on their organisation, it is not surprising that ISIL sources claimed in 2015 that Nasir al-Fahad, in a letter from his cell in *al-Hayer* prison, pledged allegiance to Abu Bakr al Baghdadi, while Jabhat al-Nusrah supporters online contested the authenticity of the letter, claiming it was a forgery.[72] Moreover, as Cole Bunzl writes, 'the Islamic State clearly is hoping for Khudayr's endorsement', as evidenced by a video released by the ISIL media office of Aleppo province that showed 'some of the Saudis [in Aleppo] seated before a well-placed copy of one of Khudayr's books'.[73]

It is important to remember that the average Saudi foreign fighter in our database is too young to remember vividly the 11 September 2001 attacks or even the 2003–2005 Saudi terror campaign. So when al-Qaeda and ISIL media propaganda, during the height of the *Fukko al-A'ni* campaign that adopted the release of 'political prisoners' as their rallying cry, started decrying the injustice befalling their respected and revered imprisoned scholars, they were able to draw the

69 Lacroix, *Awakening Islam*, pp. 249–255

70 See Hegghammer, *Jihad in Saudi Arabia*, pp. 83–98

71 For more on this group of scholars, the factors that contributed to their rise, and the role they played in the Saudi Islamist scene, and beyond, during that critical period of time, see ibid. and Al-Saud, *Religious Radicalization and Violence in Saudi Arabia*, Chapter 6.

72 Bridget Johnson, 'Saudi Cleric Who Issued Fatwa on WMD Permissibility Pledges Allegiance to ISIS', *PJ Media*, 25 August 2015, http://bit.ly/2eosGjw; Mu'ayyad Bajis, 'Al Dawla [ISIL] Organization Releases Nasir Al Fahad's *Bay'ah* to Al Baghdadi from Al Hayer Prison' (Ar.), *Arabi 21*, http://bit.ly/2eaNsqS.

73 Cole Bunzl, 'The Kingdom and the Caliphate: Duel of the Islamic States' (Washington, DC: Carnegie Endowment for International Peace, 18 Feb. 2016), http://ceip.org/2eoF3fg.

attention of this young aggrieved and angry demographic, possibly for the first time, to the intoxicating radical opinions and *fatwas* of these scholars.[74] Moreover, relatives of this radical group of scholars, as well as relatives of other main radical ideologues such as Walid al-Sinani, were successfully mobilised and became active proponents of the *Fukko al-A'ni* campaign, evident from their signatures on the 'Open Letter from the Detainees' Families' addressed to the king.[75]

Several of this group of radical neojihadis come from al-Qassim province, such as the group's symbolic leader, Hamoud al-Shu'aybi, who died in 2001; Ali al-Khudayr, who was arrested in 2003 and remains behind bars; and, most importantly, Suliman al-Ulwan, whose release from prison in early December 2012 after almost nine years of imprisonment was met with great joy and hype on social media platforms and among many influential Saudi Islamist figures.[76] That release was not final, but temporary awaiting the outcome of his trial. So when the judge sentenced him to 15 years in prison in October 2013 on charges related to his radical *fatwas* and support of terrorist groups,[77] agitation soared among the crowd gathered outside the court during that day[78] and among those already aggrieved and disgruntled as a result of the negative campaigning around the issue of detainees in the streets of his home city of Buraydah.

During his short time of freedom, even though he criticised al-Baghdadi's way of dealing with other jihadist factions and groups, al-Ulwan affirmed his support for the *mujahideen* in general in the land of the Levant (al-Sham), lambasting those who slander, attack, or abandon them and asking other scholars not to be quick and hasty in passing judgements on them before listening and hearing their words and communicating with their leaders.[79] Al-Ulwan's influence and outreach

74 See, for instance, the video '*Fukko al-A'ni*: Al Saloul Prisons' (Ar.), http://bit.ly/2dqygUH and 'A Message from Sheikh Nasir al-Whaishi to the Captive in Tyrants' Prisons' (Ar.), *Mu'assasat Al Malahim*, 1434 AH, transcript available at https://archive.org/details/Nasser.assir4.

75 Fourteen members of the al-Ulwan family signed the letter, including his father, brothers, and sisters. Twenty-six members of the Walid al-Sinani family signed the letter, including his mother and many of his children. The son of the late symbolic leader of the neojihadi group was a signatory to the letter, as well as the son of the actual leader of the group Nasir al-Fahad.

76 For a sample reaction from Saudi Islamist figures to the news of al-Ulwan's release, see 'Scholars' Comments on the Release of *Al Allamah* (The Most Knowledgeable) al-Ulwan' (Ar.), 6 Dec. 2012, http://bit.ly/2einvlS. For a taste of the reaction and mood among many Islamists upon the release of al-Ulwan, see Ibrahim M. al-Hugail, *With Sheikh al-Ulwan in his Release* (Ar.), https://www.saaid.net/Doat/hogail/34.htm.

77 '15 Years Imprisonment for Suliman al-Ulwan After Being Convicted of Violating the Fatwas of the Respected Scholars' (Ar.), *An7a*, 3 Oct 2013, www.an7a.com/119207/.

78 See the video: 'The Moment of Sheikh Suliman al-Ulwan's Exit from the Interior Ministry's Court After a 15 Year Verdict', http://bit.ly/2etWScx.

79 See the following videos: 'Comment from Sheikh Suliman al-Ulwan on ISIL' (Ar.), http://bit.ly/2e48e7G and 'An Advice and a Statement to the People of the Levant – Sheikh Imam Suliman al-Ulwan', (Ar.), http://bit.ly/2em7mvQ.

was not limited to the radicals and foreign fighters who have come from his hometown or even his country, as, according to an empirical research published by the ICSR, he was very popular among Western and European foreign fighters in Syria as well.[80]

In general, the emergence and rise of this group of scholars, who come predominantly from the central region of Najd (Riyadh and al-Qassim) during the early years of the new century, reinforced and strengthened a process of 'Najdification' of the jihadist community in Saudi Arabia that, as Hegghammer contends, started earlier with al-Qaeda in the 1990s.[81] During the AQAP terror campaign in the Kingdom 2003–2005, Riyadh and al-Qassim were central theatres for many terrorist attacks and government raids.[82] It seems that this tendency is still holding with regard to ISIL. According to Bunzl, 'The largest [ISIL] networks that Saudi security forces claim to have broken up were in Riyadh and al-Qassim.'[83] Our dataset from the Saudi ISIL entry documents certainly suggests a continuation of this trend, with most recruits, in raw numbers, coming from these two regions.

Conclusion

According to official Saudi estimates, while the year 2013 saw the travelling of nearly 1500 Saudi citizens and residents into Syria, to join various warring factions including but not limited to ISIL, that number dropped by more than half to only 650 in the year 2014, 383 in 2015, and only 56 in the last year of 2016.[84] While this pattern of flow followed and reflected, in part, practical developments on the ground, it was also the result of the Saudi government's more aggressive attempts at stemming this influx through, among other measures, its declaration of a penalty of imprisonment for all those who participate in conflicts abroad and its designation of Jabhat al-Nusra and al-Qaeda Organization in Iraq (now known as the Islamic State), among other groups, as terrorist organisations in both February and March 2014.[85]

80 Joseph A. Carter, *#Greenbirds: Measuring Importance and Influence in Syrian Foreign Fighter Networks*, ICSR Report, 2014.
81 Hegghammer, *Jihad in Saudi Arabia*, p. 131.
82 'Al-Qassim the Most Famous Saudi Province for Religious Conservatism Appeared on the "Domestic Terrorism" Map Last July' (Ar.), *Al Sharq Al Awsat*, 22 May 2004, http://bit.ly/2dsMgs8; 'Heroic Epics of the Security Forces in Al Qassim in the Face of Terrorists' (Ar.), *Al Riyadh*, 5 July 2006, www.alriyadh.com/168788; and 'Main Terrorist Attacks in Saudi' (Ar.), *Assakina*, 9 Feb. 2012, www.assakina.com/center/parties/21860.html.
83 Bunzl, *The Kingdom and the Caliphate*. In April 2015, the Saudi Interior Ministry announced the capture of a cell, connected to ISIL, of 15 Saudis called '*Jund Bilad al-Haramain*' (The Soldiers of the Land of the Two Holy Mosques) who used to meet regularly in al-Qassim Province; see 'Saudi Captures the *Jund Bilad al-Haramain* Cell that is Connected to ISIL' (Ar.), *Al Sharq Al Awsat*, 29 April 2015, http://bit.ly/2ebA31z.
84 Saudi Ministry of Interior official estimates as of November 2016.
85 'A Royal Order to Imprison any Saudi who Fights Abroad', (Ar.), *Al-Jazeera*, 3 Feb. 2014, http://bit.ly/2k55D1v; 'Full Text of the Saudi Interior Ministry Statement

Internally, Saudi security forces have also done an outstanding job thwarting many of ISIL's planned attacks and capturing many of its cells and supporters.[86] Other preventative initiatives aimed at countering terrorist propaganda and tackling the ideological side of radicalisation have been established by the Saudi government in the past couple of years, such as the Global Center for Combatting Extremist Ideology (*Etidal*) as well as the Ministry of Defence's Ideological Warfare Center.[87]

It is a fact that terrorists come from different locations and diverse social backgrounds. However, while turbulent backgrounds of political protests and grievances or relative economic deprivation cannot by themselves explain the motivational complex that lead individuals to join terrorist organizations, they are indications of vulnerability and susceptibility among a group of people in a specific area or location, which can be one of the motivational drivers behind the espousing of radical ideas and beliefs. Therefore, contextual knowledge is very important when trying to devise solutions that can disrupt the complex process of radicalisation. If hotbeds exist, then solutions must start at the local level to try and investigate, rectify and improve whatever ills or dogmatic fundamentalist cultures prevalent there.[88]

Designating Terrorist Organizations', *al-Sharq al-Awast*, 8 March 2014, http://english.aawsat.com/2014/03/article55329804/full-text-of-saudi-interior-ministry-statement-announcing-terrorist-list.

86 Abdullah bin Khaled Al-Saud, 'Deciphering IS's Narrative and Activities in the Kingdom of Saudi Arabia', *Terrorism and Political Violence*, 2017, http://dx.doi.org/10.1080/09546553.2017.1378645

87 The English-language accounts of both centres on Twitter are @etidalorg and @fekerksa_en. Etidal Centre website is: https://etidal.org/.

88 For an excellent account of the importance of the social dimension of radicalisation and the role played by extremist milieus and subcultures, see Manni Crone, 'Radicalization Revisited: Violence, Politics and the Skills of the Body', *International Affairs*, vol. 93, issue 3 (2016), pp. 587–604.

5 The criminal law implications of the "war on terror" and the status of "foreign fighters"

A Swiss perspective

Roberta Arnold

Introduction

With the launching of the "war on terror" by former US President G.W. Bush in response to the 9/11 attacks in 2001,[1] new issues have arisen under international law:[2] fifteen years later, some of these are yet to be solved. Whereas the term "terrorism" still lacks a universal legal definition,[3] the rise and growth of al-Qaeda and the Islamic State (IS)[4] have challenged the traditional distinction between criminal organisations and armed groups engaged in an armed conflict.[5] The means and methods used by these groups, along with the phenomenon of "Foreign Fighters" (FF),[6] has further contributed to this situation of uncertainty. One

1 See the speech addressed by former President George W. Bush to Congress on 11 September 2001, available online at https://georgewbush-whitehouse.archives.gov/news/releases/2002/01/20020129-11.html.

2 See R. Arnold, *The ICC as a New Instrument for Repressing Terrorism* (Ardsley: Transnational Publishers, 2004), at 1ss; Roberta Arnold, "Terrorism, war crimes and the International Criminal Court", in B. Saul (ed.), *Research Handbook on International Law and Terrorism* (Cheltenham: Edward Elgar Publishers, 2014), 282–297.

3 See J.M. Henckaerts et al. (eds), *How does law protect in war?* (ICRC: Geneva, 2014), chapter on 'Terrorism and terrorists', online at https://casebook.icrc.org/glossary/terrorism-and-terrorists.

4 For working purposes, "IS" in this essay will refer to the Islamic State of Iraq and the Levant (ISIL), also referred to as the Islamic State of Iraq and Syria (ISIS) or Daesh.

5 See ICRC, International humanitarian law and the challenges of contemporary armed conflicts – Report on the 32nd International Conference of the of the Red Cross and Red Crescent, Geneva, Switzerland, 8–10 December 2015, at 1, available online at www.icrc.org/en/document/international-humanitarian-law-and-challenges-contemporary-armed-conflicts.

6 See S. Kraehenmann, 'Foreign fighters under international law" (Geneva Academy of International Law), October 2014, online at http://psm.du.edu/media/documents/reports_and_stats/think_tanks/geneva_academy_foreign-fighters.pdf; Letta Tayler, "'Foreign terrorist fighter' law: human rights rollbacks under UN Security Council Resolution 2178", 2016 (18) 5 *International Community Law Review*, 455–482, at http://booksandjournals.brillonline.com/content/journals/10.1163/18719732-12341342; Human Rights Watch, "'Foreign terrorist fighter' laws – human rights rollbacks under UN Security Council Resolution 2178", December 2016; at www.hrw.org/sites/default/files/news_attachments/ftf_essay_03feb2017_final_pdf.pdf.

of the ongoing legal debates, for instance, revolves around the geographical boundaries of the "war on terror"[7] and the status of those involved: do the foreign fighters supporting IS in Syria share the status of those promoting the movement elsewhere? Depending on the answers, different legal consequences may arise under criminal law.

The aim of this chapter is to discuss the legal implications of the "war on terror" under criminal law, with a focus on the developments that took place in Switzerland. After the Introduction, the first section will address the applicable legal regime to acts of "terrorism" and its perpetrators, including FF.[8] The second section will illustrate the legislative counter-terrorism measures adopted by Switzerland in the last years, including the Anti-IS Federal Act of 12 December 2012 (hereafter: Anti-IS Act),[9] the Federal Law on the Federal Intelligence Service of 1 January 2017[10] and the legislative amendment proposals of June 2017.[11] The third section will discuss the outcomes of the first judgment of the Swiss Federal

7 See article 2 (definition of IAC) and article 3 (definition of NIAC) common to the four Geneva Conventions of 1949. Further definitions are contained in the two Additional Protocols of 1949. On this basis the ICRC has proposed the following definitions: "1. International armed conflicts exist whenever there is resort to armed force between two or more States. 2. Non-international armed conflicts are protracted armed confrontations occurring between governmental armed forces and the forces of one or more armed groups, or between such groups arising on the territory of a State [party to the Geneva Conventions]. The armed confrontation must reach a minimum level of intensity and the parties involved in the conflict must show a minimum of organization" (see www.icrc.org/eng/assets/files/other/opinion-paper-armed-conflict.pdf).

8 This term is generally used to describe individuals who leave their country of origin or habitual residency to join an armed insurgency abroad; it covers various forms of assistance to, support for or association with armed or *terrorist* groups. For details see S. Krahenmann, "Academy briefing no. 7 – Foreign fighters under international law" (Geneva Academy, October 2014), at 6, at www.geneva-academy.ch/joomlatools-files/docman-files/Publications/Academy%20Briefings/Foreign%20Fighters_2015_WEB.pdf. The term "FF" in this essay will refer to individuals who, moved by either personal or ideological reasons, join, support or promote movements like IS and al-Qaeda (which are forbidden in Switzerland).

9 See the Federal Act on the Proscription of the Groups "Al-Qaeda" and "Islamic State" and Associated Organisations of 12 December 2014 (SR 122), available in English at www.admin.ch/opc/en/classified-compilation/20142993/index.html.

10 On 16 August 2017, the Swiss Federal Council declared that the new Federal Law on the Federal Intelligence Service ("Intelligence Services Act", SR 121, at www.admin.ch/opc/it/classified-compilation/20120872/index.html) would enter into force on 1 September 2017. The following three directives also came into force on the same day: 1) the Directive on the Activities of the Intelligence Services (OAIN; SR 121.1, at www.admin.ch/opc/it/classified-compilation/20162430/index.html); 2) the Directive on the Information and memorisation of the Intelligence Services of the Swiss Confederation (SR. 121.2, at www.admin.ch/opc/it/classified-compilation/20162429/index.html); and 3) the Directive on the supervision of the intelligence service activities (SR 121.3, at www.admin.ch/opc/de/classified-compilation/20162713/index.html).

11 See Federal Office of Justice, press statement of 22 June 2017, "Le Conseil fédéral propose une série de modifications législatives pour renforcer la lutte contre le

Criminal Tribunal based on the Anti-IS Federal Act,[12] which was rendered on 15 July 2016 and confirmed on 22 February 2017[13] by the Swiss Federal Tribunal (FT). The fourth section will draw the conclusions.

The applicable legal regime

Introduction

In order to assess the legal status and conduct of those fighting along "terrorist" movements involved in an armed conflict (e.g. IS), it is first necessary to identify the applicable legal regime. In the context of an armed conflict, an act of violence that is subject to international humanitarian law (IHL) and complies with its principles may be lawful. Much will also depend on the classification of the armed conflict. Pursuant to art. 4 of the Third Geneva Convention of 1949 (III GC), in times of international armed conflicts (IAC) an individual participating to the hostilities may qualify as a combatant legitimated to fight. By default, all the others are civilians who are not allowed to take up arms, unless in case of self-defence or *levée en masse*. Otherwise, they will lose their immunity and may be prosecuted as ordinary criminals. This is even truer in times of non-international armed conflicts (NIAC), during which the applicable rules of IHL do not provide for combatant status. Thus, also the members of an irregular movement who fight in compliance with IHL may face prosecution under domestic law for having taken up arms. By contrast a combatant (in IAC) may only be prosecuted for breaches of IHL amounting to war crimes. This is an important discrimination to be retained.

War crimes are violations of IHL that are so serious as to entail individual criminal responsibility. They include acts that are *primarily* aimed at spreading *terror* among the *civilian* population of the adverse party.[14] The same conduct, however, if aimed at the military, does not fall under this ban. Thus, the notion of "terror" under IHL is not to be confused with the notion of "terrorism" addressed by the various conventions that have been adopted under the aegis of the UN.[15]

terrorisme", online at www.bj.admin.ch/bj/it/home/aktuell/news/2017/ref 2017-06-22.html.

12 See the "Federal Act on the Proscription of the Groups 'Al-Qaeda' and 'Islamic State' and Associated Organisations" of 12 December 2014 (SR 122), at www.admin.ch/op c/en/classified-compilation/20142993/index.html.

13 Judgment of 15 July 2016, SK.2016.9 (not published, online at https://entscheide.weblaw.ch/cache.php?link=15.07.2016_SK.2016.9&q=&sel_lang=en). The Federal Tribunal confirmed the Judgment of Federal Criminal Tribunal on 22 February 2017, Judgment no. 6B_948/2016, available online at http://relevancy.bger.ch/php/aza/http/index.php?lang=de&zoom=&type=show_document&highlight_docid=aza%3A%2F%2F22-02-2017-6B_948-2016.

14 See art. 33 IV GC, art. 51(2) of Additional Protocol I of 1977 (AP I) and articles 4 and 13 of Additional Protocol II (APII) to the Geneva Conventions of 1949.

15 See the website of the UN Office of Counter-Terrorism, at www.un.org/en/counter terrorism/legal-instruments.shtml. For an analysis see Arnold, *The ICC as a New Instrument for Repressing Terrorism*, at 7ss.

The applicable legal regime under international law

The applicable regime to acts committed in "wartime"

Depending on the context, two distinct legal regimes may apply to acts of violence.[16] In "peacetime", acts of violence are normally fought with traditional law-enforcement means (e.g. international legal assistance, criminal proceedings), which are subject to international human rights standards.[17] In "wartime", by contrast (i.e. scenarios that amount to an armed conflict under IHL), acts of violence are fought with military means and are subject to IHL. The standards differ, since the same act may be lawful in wartime, if it complied with IHL,[18] and unlawful in peacetime. As seen, unlike civilians, in times of warfare combatants have the right to fight and, under given conditions, even to kill.[19] The legality of an act, thus, will also depend on the context in which it was committed and by whom.

International criminal law (ICL) criminalised under the heading of war crimes[20] specific serious breaches of IHL.[21] Thus, in order to assess whether someone shall be liable for war crimes, the legal basis will be provided by (international) criminal law, which ensures that the requirements as to the elements of the crimes to be met are drafted in a sufficiently clear manner, in compliance with the principle of legal certainty.[22]

16 See ibid., at 111 ss.

17 E.g. the European Convention on Human Rights, the American Convention on Human Rights, the International Convention on Civil and Political Rights, the International Convention on Economic and Social Rights, the African Charter on Human Rights. See, e.g., Helen Duffy, "International human rights law and terrorism", in B. Saul (ed.), *Research Handbook on International Law and Terrorism* (Cheltenham: Edward Elgar Publishers, 2014), 335–360; R. Arnold, "Terrorism in international humanitarian law and human rights law", in R. Arnold and N. Quénivet (eds), *International Humanitarian Law and Human Rights Law* (Leiden: Martinus Nijhoff Publishers, 2008), 475–497, at 481.

18 In particular with the basic principles of military necessity, distinction and proportionality.

19 See Arnold, *The ICC as a New Instrument for Repressing Terrorism*, at 112 ss. On complementarity see the International Committee of the Red Cross in "What is the difference between IHL and human rights?", in ICRC, *International Humanitarian Law: Answers to Your Questions* (Geneva: ICRC Publications, 2015), at 35s; Duffy, "International human rights law and terrorism", 335–360; R. Arnold, "Terrorism in international humanitarian law and human rights law", in R. Arnold and N. Quénivet, *International Humanitarian Law and Human Rights Law* (Leiden: Martinus Nijhoff Publishers, 2008), 475–497, at 480.

20 War crimes can be divided into "grave breaches" and "other serious violations" of IHL. See Arnold, "The ICC as a new instrument for repressing terrorism", 168ss; Arnold, "Terrorism, war crimes and the International Criminal Court", at 285 ss.

21 The aim of IHL is to protect specific categories of persons and regulate the conduct of hostilities. It does not contain directly applicable criminal law provisions.

22 It is in consideration of this basic principle of criminal law that the criminalisation of the grave breaches of IHL was delegated to the member states of the four GCs and their Additional Protocols. For the same reason, in 2011 the Swiss legislator replaced articles 108–109 of the former Swiss Military Criminal Code (MCC) with the war

The classification of acts of terrorism

Only a restricted category of acts of "terror" falls under the heading of serious violations of IHL (war crimes). In general, an act of violence committed by an individual legitimated to join the hostilities (i.e. a combatant under art. 4 III GC) against a lawful (military) target will not constitute a war crime. By contrast, acts committed by civilians may be prosecuted as ordinary offences (and, according to some, depending on the circumstances, also as war crimes). Therefore, the *legal status* of the perpetrator will be pivotal.[23] The qualification becomes more complex when sympathisers of movements like IS or al-Qaeda committed an act of violence beyond the geographical boundaries of the territory of a state engaged in an armed conflict (e.g. Syria). The question, for instance, is how to classify the attacks that occurred in London and Manchester or in Barcelona in 2017. The current trend is to qualify them as "ordinary crimes". However, unless the domestic legislation of the state exercising jurisdiction over this type of acts provides for specific anti-terrorism provisions, these may have to be prosecuted under "ordinary" headings like murder and hostage taking. Accordingly, the sanction may not be adequate to the gravity of the act.

From a procedural point of view, another difficulty lies in the fact that, unlike war crimes, terrorism is a "treaty" as opposed to an "international" crime.[24] As such, it is not subject to universal jurisdiction.[25] The law-enforcement authorities faced with this type of act often lack the necessary legal basis and "teeth". As will be discussed later, Switzerland was confronted with this problem when its law-enforcement authorities had to investigate and adjudicate the first big case dealing with supporters of IS. The Federal Attorney General's Office had to rely on the Anti-IS Act,[26] which, however, was harshly criticised for its lack of clarity and for the limits posed by the foreseen sanctions (a maximum of five years of detention). The government also remarked that the intelligence services needed stronger investigative powers, reason for which a new Federal Act on the Intelligence Service (Intelligence Service Act, ISA) entered into force on 1 September 2017, following the positive outcome of the federal vote held on 25 September 2016.

crimes catalogue now contained in articles 264b ss CC and articles 118ss MCC (SR 321.0, online at www.admin.ch/opc/de/classified-compilation/19270018/index.html).

23 See Arnold, *The ICC as a New Instrument for Repressing Terrorism*, at 1ss and 57ss. It is beyond the scope of this essay to discuss whether acts committed by IS or al-Qaeda may qualify as crimes against humanity. On this topic see R. Arnold, "The prosecution of terrorism as a crime against humanity", 64 (4) ZAÖR 2004, 979ss, online at www.zaoerv.de/64_2004/64_2004_4_a_979_1000.pdf.

24 See Arnold, "Terrorism, war crimes and the International Criminal Court", at 283ss.

25 Unlike international crimes, treaty crimes are not subject to universal jurisdiction.

26 See the Federal Act on the Proscription of the Groups "Al-Qaeda" and "Islamic State" and Associated Organisations of 12 December 2014 (SR 122), at www.admin.ch/opc/en/classified-compilation/20142993/index.html.

Terrorism as a specific war crime

The following IHL provisions ban terrorism as a warfare method: articles 33 GC IV and 51(2) AP I (which apply in times of IAC) and articles 4 and 13 AP II (which apply in times of NIAC). These outlaw intimidating measures primarily aimed at targeting the civilian population (or, if AP II applies, also persons deprived of their liberty).[27] These must have been committed in violation of the principle of distinction. Acts aimed at the members of the armed forces of the adverse party, for instance, are not covered.[28] Breaches of these provisions are not "grave",[29] but they may nevertheless be prosecuted as other serious violations of IHL.[30] For instance, one may apply article 8(2)(c) (in times of IAC) or article 8 (2)(e) (in times of NIAC) of the ICC Statute.[31] The Statutes for the International Tribunal for Rwanda (ICTR) and the Special Court for Sierra Leone (SCSL) have gone even further, by including the breach of the above mentioned IHL provisions on terror in their war crimes catalogues (see art. 4 ICTR Statute[32] and art. 3d SCSL Statute[33]). Moreover, in the *Galić* case,[34] the International Tribunal for the Former Yugoslavia (ICTY) established that the use or threatened use of acts primarily aimed at "terrorising" the civilian population during an armed conflict is a serious *specific-intent* war crime, under customary law.[35] In the *Milošević* case,[36] it concluded that *every incident* of sniping and shelling by the Sarajevo-Romanija Corps (SRK) had been conducted with the deliberate intent to "terrorise" the civilian population of Sarajevo, and that it was in breach of art. 3 ICTY Statute.[37] On Appeal, the Appeals Chamber stated that indiscriminate attacks may also contribute to the climate of "terror",[38] finding Milošević ultimately guilty as a

27 Article 33 IV GC; Art. 51(2) AP I; Article 4(2) AP II; Article 13 AP II. Arnold, The ICC, at 78.

28 See Articles 48, 51(2) and 52(2) of Additional Protocol I, It

29 Article 50 GC I, Article 51 GCII , Article 130 GC III and Article 147 GC IV and Articles 11 and 85 AP I.

30 E.g. under the headings of wilful killing, hostage-taking, torture and inhumane treatment, wilfully causing great suffering, unlawful transfer and deportation, extensive destruction of property or unlawful confinement. The acts, however, must have been committed in times of IAC.

31 Arnold, *The ICC as a New Instrument for Repressing Terrorism*, at 197ss.

32 Contrary to Article 3 ICTY Statute, which is silent in this regard, Article 4 ICTR Statute explicitly outlaws acts of terrorism as a method of warfare.

33 Which is only applicable to NIAC. See Arnold, "Terrorism, war crimes and the International Criminal Court", at 286ss.

34 *Prosecutor v Galić* (IT-98–29-T), Trial Chamber, 5.12.2003, § 66.

35 *Prosecutor v Galić*, supra, §§ 582ss and 592–593. E.g. the nature of the civilian activities targeted, the manner in which they were carried out and the timing and duration thereof.

36 *Prosecutor v Milošević* (IT-98–29/1-A), AC, Judgment of 12.11.2009, §2ss (under count 1 of the indictment) ('*Milošević AJ*')

37 *Prosecutor v Milošević,* supra, §4, with ref. to *Milošević* TJ, § 910.

38 *Prosecutor v Milošević*, supra, at §§36/38. See also §66, which states that the indiscriminate character of attack can be indicative of the fact that the attack was directed against the civilian population.

commander[39] for having failed to prevent or punish those actions of the SRK that had been in breach of the prohibition of terrorist acts.[40]

In *Blagojević*, [41] for instance, the ICTY addressed the question whether the terrorisation of the Bosnian Muslim civilians in Srebrenica and Potočari could be prosecuted as the crime against humanity of persecution.[42] The Tribunal confirmed the conclusions reached in *Galić*, thus interpreting in the same fashion the war crime of "terror" and its elements.[43]

The *Galić* judgment[44] paved the way for the adoption of Article 3(d) SCSL Statute.[45] Breaches thereof have been prosecuted by the SCSL in the *Koroma* [46] and *Sankoh* [47] cases. These dealt with the role of two former leaders of the Armed Forces Revolutionary Council (AFRC) and the AFRC/Revolutionary United Front (RUF). Since both passed away,[48] unfortunately no judgment was rendered,[49] meaning that no precedents were made. In the *CDF* case,[50] however, the SCSL defined "serious violations" as cases "*where a rule protecting 'important values' is breached, resulting in 'grave consequence' for the victim*",[51] including acts of terrorism.[52] The Court held that the ban on terrorism under Article 4(2) AP II constitutes customary law[53] and that breaches thereof entail individual criminal responsibility.[54] It further defined the elements of the crime as follows:

i Acts or threats of violence directed against persons or property;
ii The Accused intended to make persons or property the object of those acts and threats of violence or acted in the reasonable knowledge that this would likely occur; and

39 *Prosecutor v Milošević*, supra, at §§ 281–282, 295.
40 Articles 3(d) and 7(3) ICTY Statute; *Prosecutor v Milošević*, supra, §116.
41 *Prosecutor v Blagojević*,(IT-02–60-A), TC, Judgment of 9 May 2007.
42 Count 5 of the indictment, *Prosecutor v Blagojević*, supra, at §§8/588.
43 *Prosecutor v Blagojević*, supra, at §589–591.
44 Prosecutor v *Galić* (IT-98–29-T), TC, supra, Judgment of December 2003.
45 This proscribes acts of terrorism as a serious violation of the LOAC applicable to the NIAC in Sierra Leone.
46 Indictment, Koroma (SCSL-2003.03.I), 7 March 2003, §32.
47 Indictment, Sankoh, (SCSL-03–02-I-001), 7 March 2003, §35, Count 1.
48 Tanu Jalloh, "Johnny Paul's dead body found in Liberia", *Concord Times* (Freetown, 11 September 2008); "Is ex-Sierra Leone junta leader Johnny Paul Koroma dead or alive?", *The Democrat* (25 October 2010) at http://allafrica.com/stories/201010260617.html.
49 See Arnold, "Terrorism, war crimes and the International Criminal Court", at 291ss.
50 *Prosecutor v Moinina Fofana & Allieu Kondewa*, TJ, 02.08. 2007, Case No. SCSL-04–14-T ('*CDF TJ*') and Prosecutor *v Moinina Fofana & Allieu Kondewa, AC*, 28.05.2008, Case No. SCSL-04–14-A ('*CDF AJ*').
51 *CDF TC*, § 94, with ref. to Decision on the Defence Motion for Interlocutory Appeal on Jurisdiction, *Tadić* (IT-94–1) AC, 02.10.1995, § 94 (*Tadić Appeal Decision on Jurisdiction*).
52 *CDF TJ*, supra, at §106.
53 *CDF TJ*, supra, at §96.
54 *CDF TJ*, supra, at §§88–89.

iii The acts or threats of violence were committed with the primary purpose of spreading terror among persons.[55]

The SCSL concurred with the ICTY by concluding that civilians enjoyed protection from terrorist acts *only as long as* they did *not* participate in the hostilities.[56] With regard to the required *mens rea*, it held that the author must have acted with either intent or recklessness[57] and that the intent to spread "terror" among the civilian population must be specific (by contrast, it does not need not to be the *only* purpose). The specific intent must be determined in each single case and it may be inferred from a) the circumstances, b) the nature of the acts or threats and c) the manner, timing or duration thereof.[58]

In the *Brima* case,[59] the SCLS found Brima, Kamara and Kanu guilty of acts of terrorism as a war crime under Article 3(d) SCSL Statute.[60] The prosecutor argued that the unlawful killings, sexual and physical violence, use of child soldiers, abductions and forced labour, looting and burning had been committed as part of a campaign to "terrorise" the civilian population of Sierra Leone.[61] On appeal, it argued moreover that the three 'enslavement crimes', i.e. the recruitment of child soldiers, the abductions and the forced labour and sexual slavery, should have also been included under this heading. The Court, however, dismissed this argument,[62] by holding that since these acts were directed towards the military effort,[63] the authors had lacked the specific intent to terrorise.

In sum, acts of terrorism may be prosecuted as a war crime under the ICC Statute in two ways: a) as a specific war crime; or b) as a non-specific war crime. The first option is precluded, for the time being, since the list of serious violations of IHL is exhaustive and does not encompass breaches of Articles 33 of GC IV, Article 51 of AP I and Articles 4 and 13 of AP II, yet. On the basis of the jurisprudence of the SCSL and the ICTY, according to which the use of terrorism as warfare method against the civilian population is a serious violation of IHL under customary law,[64] it is not to be excluded that in the future, the ICC's member states of may include it in the Statute as a specific war crime. Currently, though, the only viable solution is to prosecute such conduct under articles 8(2)(b) and 8(2)(e) ICC Statute.

55 *CDF TJ*, supra, at §170.
56 *CDF TJ*, supra, at § 132.
57 *CDF AJ*, supra, at §355 with ref. to *Galić TJ*, supra, at §54.
58 *CDF AJ*, supra, at §357.
59 Judgment, *Brima* (SCSL-04–16-T), TC, 20.06.2007 ('*Brima TJ*').
60 *Brima TJ*, supra, at §2113; 2117; 2121; para 2. of Annex A to the *AJ* Judgment (Procedural history). See Count 1 of the indictment.
61 *Brima*, TJ, supra, at §1434.
62 Brima *AJ*, supra, at §172.
63 *Brima TJ*, supra, at §1454/1468; Brima *AJ*, supra at §170ss.
64 *CDF TJ*, supra, at §96; *Brima TJ*, supra, at § 662; *Galić*, AJ, supra, at §98.

The legal status of "terrorists" engaged in an armed conflict

In times of IAC a major distinction is drawn between "civilians" and "combatants". The first are entitled to immunity from attacks (as long as they do *not* take a *direct part* in the hostilities) and to benefit from specific assistance.[65] The second, on the other hand, have the right to fight.[66] Article 4 III GC provides for a set of criteria that must be complied with by an individual upon capture, in order to enjoy prisoner of war (POW) status. It is inferred that whoever enjoys POW status, is a lawful combatant.[67] The doctrine is divided on the question whether the whole movement as such, or also the single individual member, shall comply with IHL in order to be granted POW (and thus combatant) status.[68] According to the author, if the whole group fails to comply, it will forfeit the whole movement's right to combatant status.[69] A key role is played by the requirement of "belonging" to a (state) party to the conflict. Emanuele Sommario, for instance, holds that a case could be made that al-Qaeda fighters captured by US forces in 2001 and 2002, i.e. during the first phase of the IAC between the USA and Afghanistan, met de facto the criteria of art. 4 III GC, in that they had a certain degree of organisation, they belonged to the Taliban army (NB: their military action was coordinated by the latter) and were commanded by Osama bin Laden. The only hurdle may lie in their lack of compliance with IHL rules and standards.[70] Whereas this might be true in times of IAC, in times of NIAC, though, no special status is bestowed upon fighters that have taken up arms against a government. These may be sentenced as common criminals based on the domestic legislation of the state who holds them in custody.[71] In this regard, the ICTY made the important statement that the failure by a non-state actor to comply with IHL has *no relevance* on the question whether the situation qualifies as an armed conflict. In the *Limaj* case,[72] the ICTY Trial Chamber concluded that the determination of the existence of an armed conflict is based solely on the intensity of the conflict and the organisation of the parties and that "the purpose of the armed forces to engage in acts of violence or also achieve some further objective is, therefore, irrelevant".[73]

65 Art. 51(3) AP I.
66 Art. 43(2) AP I.
67 See E. Sommario, "The status of foreign fighters under international humanitarian law" in A. de Guttry et al. (eds), *Foreign Fighters under International Law and Beyond* (The Hague: Springer, 2016), 141–160, at 147; Robert Heinsch, "Foreign fighters and international criminal law", in A. de Guttry et al. (eds), *Foreign Fighters under International Law and Beyond* (The Hague: Springer, 2016), 161–183, at 165.
68 See Sommario, "The status of foreign fighters", at 149 and 153.
69 See Arnold, *The ICC as a New Instrument for Repressing Terrorism*, at 127.
70 See Sommario, "The status of foreign fighters", at 150.
71 Ibid., at 153. He also addressed the question of nationality, which will be discussed briefly in the section dedicated to the status of foreign fighters.
72 ICTY, *Prosecutor v Limaj*, IT-03-66-T, Judgment of 30 November 2005, §§169–170. See on this also Sommario, "The status of foreign fighters", at 155.
73 *Prosecutor v Limaj*, supra, §§169–170. See Sommario, "The status of foreign fighters", at 155. He refers further to the UN Human Rights Council, Report of the

The specific case of foreign fighters supporting al-Qaeda and/or IS

With regard to movements like al-Qaeda or IS, the question is whether their involvement in the "war on terror" by the US qualifies as an armed conflict subject to IHL and, in the affirmative case, of what kind (IAC or NIAC). Accordingly, the status of their members and the qualification of their conduct may differ.

The ICRC rightly remarked[74] that, from a legal perspective, there is *no such thing* as a "war against terrorism". Thus, the legal assessment of each act of violence must be undertaken ad hoc. A difficulty lies in particular with the *geographical scope* of application of IHL and the fact that the "war on terror" seems to have spilled over the traditional boundaries of armed conflict scenarios. According to some, in principle, IHL applies *only* to the territory of the state in which the conflict is taking place. According to others, though, IHL also applies throughout the territories of states involved in a NIAC *extraterritorially*, even though the hostilities related to that conflict may not be taking place on their territory.[75] This would mean that acts carried out by a non-state actor (e.g. IS) on the territory of an assisting state (e.g. France) as part of the ongoing hostilities (e.g. between the US and Syria) would be penalised under the domestic law of that state (and probably qualified as a "terrorist act"), even if they were compliant with IHL. As suggested by the ICRC in its Report on its 32nd International Conference: "This would be the case, for example, if an attack by the non-State party concerned were directed at a military objective in the assisting State's territory."[76] By default: "If the attack were directed at civilians or civilian objects, it would also be criminal and prosecutable under IHL as a war crime."[77]

In this statement the ICRC concludes that the act would be prosecuted *under IHL* as a war crime, so the question arises as to whether, in this case, a state would apply its special war crimes provisions or, preferably, its domestic anti-terrorism provisions. The ICRC Report raises also the following question:

> a person who would constitute a lawful target under IHL moves from a State in which there is an ongoing NIAC into the territory of a non-neighbouring non-belligerent State, and continues his or her activities in relation to the conflict from there. Can such a person be targeted under the rules of IHL by a third State in the territory of the non-belligerent State?

According to the ICRC, the question may be approached in two different ways:

> Pursuant to the first view, there is no territorial limitation to IHL applicability as such (whether in IAC or NIAC). Under this approach, what is decisive is

independent international commission of inquiry on the Syrian Arab Republic, UN Doc. A/HRC/27/60, 13 August 2014.

74 ICRC Report on its 32nd Conference, supra, at 17.

75 See ibid., at 14.

76 See ibid.

77 See ibid.

> not where hostile acts occur but whether, because of their nexus to an armed conflict, they actually represent "acts of war." Therefore, any extraterritorial use of force for reasons related to an armed conflict is necessarily governed by IHL, regardless of territorial considerations.

Pursuant to the second and, in the ICRC's opinion, preferable view, based on reasons of law and policy, the outcome may be the following:[78]

> common Article 3 contains explicit provisions on its applicability to the territory of a State in which a NIAC takes place. Traditionally, this has been understood to cover only the fighting between the relevant government's armed forces and one or more organized non-State armed groups on its soil. However, as the factual scenarios of NIAC have evolved, so has the legal interpretation of the geographic scope of applicability of common Article 3. There have been numerous instances in which assisting States, which are fighting in the territory of a non-neighbouring host State alongside its armed forces against one or more organized armed groups, have accepted the applicability of common Article 3 and of other relevant provisions of IHL to this type of conflict. As already noted above, there are reasons to believe that, in this case, IHL also applies to the territories of the assisting States.[79]

The ICRC, however, rightly comes to the conclusion that:

> it is of a different legal magnitude to suggest that "territory" may be understood to mean that IHL – and its rules on the conduct of hostilities – will automatically extend to the use of lethal force against a person located outside the territory of the parties involved in an ongoing NIAC, i.e. to the territory of a non-belligerent State. This reading would lead to an acceptance of the legal concept of a "global battlefield." This, however, does not appear to be supported by the essentially territorial focus of IHL, which on the face of it seems to limit IHL applicability to the territories of the States involved in an armed conflict.[80]

To conclude otherwise, would mean that:

> a member of an armed group or an individual civilian directly participating in hostilities would be deemed to automatically "carry" the "original" NIAC wherever they go when moving around the world. Thus based on IHL, they would remain targetable within a potentially geographically unlimited space. With very few exceptions, State practice and *opinio iuris* do not seem to have accepted this legal approach and the great majority of States do not appear to

78 Ibid., at 14–15.
79 Ibid.
80 Ibid.

> have endorsed the notion of a "global battlefield." In addition, in practical terms it is disturbing to envisage the potential ramifications of the territorially unlimited applicability of IHL if all States involved in a NIAC around the world were to rely on the concept of a "global battlefield."[81]

The ICRC finally summarises its view by concluding that:

> it would be more legally and practically sound to consider that a member of an armed group or an individual civilian directly participating in hostilities in a NIAC from the territory of a non-belligerent State should not be deemed targetable by a third State under IHL. Rather, the threat he or she poses should be dealt with under the rules governing the use of force in law enforcement. These rules, which are part of international human rights law (IHRL) – and which are, of course, also applicable to the potential use of lethal force outside situations of armed conflict – would merit a separate examination.[82]

This conclusion reinforces the view that non-state actors whose supporters commit hostile acts from the territory of states that are *not engaged* in the battlefield shall be adjudicated under the law-enforcement regime of those states, including criminal law. The consequence is that their acts may qualify as a criminal conduct subject to that state's "counter-terrorism" legislation. The situation, however, may vary in the following scenario:

> if persons located in a non-belligerent State acquire the requisite level of organization to constitute a non-State armed group as required by IHL, and if the violence between such a group and a third State may be deemed to reach the requisite level of intensity, that situation could be classified as a NIAC. Thus, IHL rules on the conduct of hostilities would come into effect between the parties. The relationship under IHL of the two States would also need to be determined in this case, based on the relevant rules on the classification of armed conflicts between States.[83]

The US administration argued that between "al-Qaeda and its associated forces", on the one hand, and the USA, on the other, there is a "global NIAC". The main argument is that the rules governing use of force and detention of individuals for security reasons are generally less restrictive under IHL than under the law applicable to law enforcement.[84] However, this position has been severely

81 Ibid.
82 Ibid.
83 Ibid., at 16.
84 See S. Kraehenmann, supra, at 16, with reference to: J.F. Addicott, "Rightly Dividing the Domestic Jihadist from the Enemy Combatant in the 'War against Al-Qaeda' – why it matters in rendition and targeted killing", *Case Western Reserve Journal of International Law*, Vol. 45 (2012–13), 259ff.

criticised by most legal authorities, including the ICRC.[85] It should also be observed that in the case of Afghanistan, or Iraq, there have been phases when the presence of the USA armed forces on their territory arguably constituted an occupation bringing into play IHL and the customary rules applicable to IAC, pursuant to API. Also worth mentioning is the fact that the legal or political characterisation of an armed group as terrorist, or as a criminal gang, is *irrelevant* for the determination of the existence of an armed conflict. The purported aim or ideological motivation of the group is also immaterial.[86] As remarked by Sandra Krähenmann in her research paper on foreign fighters:

> in a situation that reaches the threshold of a NIAC, a "criminal" group whose aim is purely lucrative or a "terrorist" group whose ultimate aim is global jihad may be a party to the conflict. Unquestionably, Islamic State and al-Nusra (with their foreign fighters) are parties to the NIAC in Syria (and in the case of IS, Iraq).[87]

Her conclusion, thus, is that these movements qualify as parties to a NIAC (not an IAC), regardless of their motives or objectives. She refers to the *Boškoski and Tarčulovski* case, in which the ICTY held that even though some states – and even the UN Security Council – had condemned some of their acts as being "terrorist", both the Kosovo Liberation Army (KLA) and the (Macedonian) National Liberation Army were to be considered parties to the armed conflicts in Kosovo and Macedonia.[88] She recalls further the jurisprudence of the Special Court for Sierra Leone (SCSL), which determined that the RUF/Armed Forces Revolutionary Council (AFRC) was considered to be a party to the conflict in Sierra Leone, notwithstanding the fact that it had undertaken a campaign of "terror" against the civilian population, as its primary *modus operandi.* [89]

This jurisprudence suggests that in times of NIAC, the fact that a movement does not comply with IHL does not forfeit its status as party to the NIAC subject to IHL (in particular common art. 3 to the four GCs of 1949). What matters is whether de facto, because of the intensity and continuity of the hostilities, the overall situation amounts to an armed conflict. In sum, the legal status of the parties does not determine the legal qualification of the situation as a NIAC. This, however, does not imply a state's recognition of belligerency status to the non-

85 See S. Kraehenmann, supra, at 16, with references to: ICRC, "International humanitarian law and the challenges of contemporary armed conflicts", 2011, 10; M. Sassòli, "transnational armed groups and international humanitarian law", *HPCR Occasional Paper Series*, Winter 2006. See also C. Garraway, "Armed conflict and terrorist organizations", in van den Herik and Schrijver, *Counter-Terrorism Strategies in a Fragmented International Legal Order*, 452.

86 S. Kraehenmann, supra, at 23.

87 Krahenmann, "Academy briefing no. 7", at 23.

88 *Prosecutor v. Boškoski and Tarčulovski*, Judgment (Trial Chamber), 2008, §192.

89 Krahenmann, "Academy briefing no. 7", 24. She refers to SCSL, *Prosecutor v. Charles Ghankay Taylor* (SCSL-03–01-A), AC, Judgment of 26 September 2013, at §300.

state actor it is fighting: it might apply to the latter its domestic criminal laws, notwithstanding its compliance with IHL.

Per analogy, the same conclusion shall apply to IS and al-Qaeda: regardless of their motives and methods of warfare, if the clashes between them and a state reach the intensity of a NIAC, IHL will apply, regardless of the status to be granted to the movement's members. The latter will not be considered as combatants and it will be down to the affected state to decide what legal regime to apply.

A related issue is the status to be granted to foreign fighters (FF), i.e. supporters of IS or al-Qaeda, who decide to leave their homelands to join the fight conducted by these movements in Syria or elsewhere. In this regard, the ICRC observed that "foreign fighters" is not a concept of IHL and that the applicability of IHL to a situation of violence in which such fighters may be engaged

> depends on the facts on the ground and on the fulfilment of certain legal conditions stemming from the relevant norms of IHL, in particular common Articles 2 and 3. In other words, IHL will govern the actions of foreign fighters, as well as any measures taken in relation to them, when they have a nexus to an ongoing armed conflict.[90]

Thus, in the view of the ICRC, FF will be subject to IHL, regardless of their nationality, both in IAC and NIAC. Nationality, however, may play a role in order for a state to determine, under the III GC, whether to grant POW status to its *own* nationals captured fighting for a foreign army.[91] It will also play a role for determining whether a detained person may benefit from "protected person" status under the IV GC. In any case, if a FF will not be granted either POW or protected-person status under the III or IV GC, he or she will still enjoy the "safety net" protections provided by fundamental guarantees restated in Article 75 AP I , which has customary law status.[92]

In times of NIAC, the nationality of FF will have no relevance since there is no POW or protected person status. *Hors de combat* FF, however, will enjoy the basic guarantees foreseen by common art. 3 and AP II (when applicable). This means further, from the perspective of criminal law, that a person accused of having committed a crime shall be guaranteed the right to fair trial.

Conclusions on the applicable legal regime under international law

From a legal perspective, as highlighted by the ICRC,[93] there is no such thing as a "war against terror". The legal classification of the various situations of violence

90 ICRC Report on the 32nd International Conference, supra, at 19.
91 Ibid. State practice on this differs. On the issue of nationality see also Sommario, "The status of foreign fighters", at 152ss.
92 ICRC Report on the 32nd International Conference, supra, at 19–20.
93 Ibid., at 17.

needs to be undertaken on an ad hoc basis. Depending on the level of intensity of the clashes between the parties, and whether the regular armed forces of a state are involved, the situation may amount to either an IAC or a NIAC. Accordingly, members of movements like IS or al-Qaeda may invoke belligerency status. The fact that, as a policy, neither IS nor al-Qaeda comply with IHL standards nevertheless poses a major obstacle in this regard. Moreover, the movements should prove to "belong" to a party to the conflict, in order to claim that they are fighting an IAC. This might have been the case for al-Qaeda in the past, when they were still fighting on behalf of the Taliban, but not necessarily nowadays.

If they operate in a NIAC, failure by the affected state to recognise belligerent status for them means that they may be tried under the domestic ordinary criminal law provisions of the affected states for the mere fact of having taking up arms. The question, then, is whether a prosecutor would opt for the application of "ordinary" criminal law charges, such as murder, or for the "war crimes" provisions. This holds true, at least, for those members of movements like IS or al-Qaeda who have been involved in the hostilities taking place in the territory of a state in which the clashes have reached the level of a NIAC (or even of an IAC, depending on the context).

With regard to those individuals who decided to support these movements from third countries, the applicability of IHL on the basis that the "war on terror" has reached global dimensions[94] is not feasible, due to the fact that IHL does not spread its applicability beyond the territory of the parties to the conflict "in a way that would allow the targeting of individuals associated with armed groups around the world". Pursuant to IHL, NIACs are confined to the territory of each party to an armed conflict. This means that the acts perpetrated by supporters of IS *beyond* the geographical borders of a state affected by an armed conflict, would *not* qualify as an act of warfare. As observed by the ICRC:

> While such NIACs can spill over into neighbouring countries because of the continuity of hostilities, they cannot spread to third countries. The ICRC is of the view that the IHL criteria of intensity and organization required to constitute a NIAC would need to be fulfilled in the territory of each individual third State for the applicability of IHL to be triggered.[95]

Therefore, regardless of whether the acts of violence committed by the movement complied with the core principles of IHL (e.g. distinction), these would be adjudicated under ordinary criminal law and counteracted with traditional law enforcement tools. This, so far, seems to have been the approach of all the European states who have been targeted by IS's acts of "terrorism" (e.g. in France, Germany, Spain or Belgium).

94 Ibid., at 18.
95 Ibid.

At a symposium organised by the Swiss Military Academy at ETH Zurich on 9 September 2017, all the guest speakers,[96] who are generals in their respective countries (Switzerland, Belgium, Germany and France), agreed that the use of the armed forces is a subsidiary counter-terrorism measure that shall be the last resort upon the request of the civilian authorities, who have the leadership.

The prosecution of acts of terrorism as "war crimes" under the Swiss legislation

On 1 January 2011, important legislative amendments entered into force in Switzerland. The Cantonal Criminal Codes of Procedure were unified into a new Criminal Code of Procedure.[97] In order to fully implement the Rome Statute for an International Criminal Court (ICC) and comply with the principle of legal certainty, a new detailed war crimes catalogue was introduced in both the ordinary and the military criminal codes.[98] The Military Justice retained its competence over war crimes committed by members of the Swiss armed forces during an armed conflict to which Switzerland is a party,[99] whereas the general competence to adjudicate them was delegated to the federal civilian authorities. For this reason, on 1 January 2012 the Federal Attorney General's Office created its Centre of Competence for International Criminal Law.

The prosecution of acts of "terror" as a war crime, however, is challenged by the following difficulties: the war crimes provisions (articles 264b–264j of the Swiss Criminal Code)[100] require the determination, at a preliminary stage, as to

96 Major-General Johan Peeters (BEL), Generalleutnant a.D. Rainer Glatz (DEU), Général de brigade aérienne Hervé Bertrand (FRA), Korpskommandant A. Schellenberg (CHE). See the News of 9 September 2017, Swiss Television, at www.srf.ch/sendungen/tagesschau/hurrikans-armee-gegen-terrorismus-gold-fuer-schweizer-biker. See also: MILAK– Herbsttagung – Terrorismusbekämpfung in Europa: Der Beitrag der Streitkräfte, 9 September 2017, summary available at www.vtg.admin.ch/de/organisation/hka/milak.detail.event.html/verwaltung/2017/17-09/17-02-24_diplomfeier-militaerakademie-an-der-eth-zuerich.html.

97 SR 312, in English at www.admin.ch/opc/en/classified-compilation/20052319/index.html.

98 Swiss Criminal Code, SR 311, online in English at www.admin.ch/opc/en/classified-compilation/19370083/index.html; Swiss Military Criminal Code, SR 321.0, online at https://www.admin.ch/opc/fr/classified-compilation/19270018/index.html. Under the old MCC, war crimes could be prosecuted under articles 108 and 109. See R. Arnold, L. Boillat and S. Heinrich, "Challenges in prosecuting under universal jurisdiction", in (2012) 54 (2) *Politorbis* 40, at 41; A. Müller and S. Heinrich, "Die Strafverfolgung von Völkerrechtsverbrechen in der Schweiz", 2015 (10) *Zeitschrift für Internationale Strafrechtsdogmatik* 501, at 502, online at www.zis-online.com.

99 On the role of the Swiss Military Justice see, e.g., R. Arnold and S. Wehrenberg, "The criminal responsibility of the superior under article 264k of the Swiss Criminal Code", 2013 (52) MLLWR 241, at www.ismllw.org/REVIEW/2013%20ART%20Arnold%20Wehrenberg.php.

100 SR 311, available online in English at www.admin.ch/opc/en/classified-compilation/19370083/index.html.

whether the facts occurred during an armed conflict.[101] Art. 264a of the Swiss Criminal Code (CC) on crimes against humanity[102] does not provide for this context element, but the non-retroactivity principle bars prosecution under this heading for acts committed before its entry into force on 1 January 2011.

This problem, by contrast, does not arise with regard to war crimes since the latter were already encompassed prior to 1 January 2011 under articles 108 and 109 of the former Swiss Military Criminal Code.[103]

A third alternative is prosecution of acts of terror under one of the ordinary crimes provisions (e.g. murder); unlike international crimes, though, these are not subject to universal jurisdiction and are subject to shorter statutory limitations under art. 97 CC in combination with art. 10 CC. Finally, specific forms of terrorism (in particular its financing) may be prosecuted under art. 260ter CC (on organised crime) and art. 260cinquies CC (financing of terrorism), but their application is very difficult, due to the required elements of crime. Art. 260ter CC, for instance, provides that the organisation must be secret in its structures. The provision was thought primarily for structures in use by the Italian Mafia and there are now undertakings by the Swiss government to revise this provision, in order to facilitate its application. At the same time, art. 260quinquies on the financing of terrorism refers to the notion of terrorism contained in the existing international counter-terrorism treaties and it is limited to its financing.

In order to circumvent all these problems in the prosecution of acts of violence perpetrated by the members and/or supporters of movements like IS and al-Qaeda, the Swiss legislator decided to adopted emergency laws, which will be illustrated next.

The Swiss response

The Swiss counter-terror strategy: a new comprehensive approach

In April 2017,[104] the Swiss Federal Council reconfirmed its 2015 strategy and goal to increase the Swiss efforts in the fight against terrorism. In the same period

101 The Swiss Criminal Code does not provide for a definition of armed conflict, meaning that reference has to be made to the definitions provided under IHL.

102 SR 311, at https://www.admin.ch/opc/en/classified-compilation/19370083/201701010000/311.0.pdf. On the possibility to prosecute acts of terrorism as crimes against humanity see R. Arnold, "The Prosecution of Terrorism as a Crime Against Humanity" 64 (2004) *ZaöRV* 979–1000, at www.zaoerv.de/64_2004/64_2004_4_a_979_1000.pdf.

103 I.e. prior to the revision of 1 January 2011. An English version of the 2009 text is available online at www.admin.ch/opc/de/classified-compilation/19270018/index.html.

104 Press communiqué of the Swiss Federal Council: "Le Conseil fédéral maintient les mesures prises dans le cadre de la lutte contre le terrorisme", 12 April 2017, available in French at www.admin.ch/gov/fr/accueil/documentation/communiques.msg-id-66386.html.

the Federal Office of Justice (OFJ) released the Third TETRA Report,[105] which identified seven phases during which terrorism shall be addressed: 1) beginning of radicalisation; 2) detection investigations; 3) criminal proceedings; 4) sentencing/condemnation; 5) execution of sentencing; 6) reintegration.

The Report concludes that whereas law-enforcement and judicial authorities may play a key role in phases 3)–5), at an earlier, preventive stage a pivotal role may be played by the intelligence services and the cantonal immigration services in detecting "red flags". As a consequence, on 1 September 2017 the new Federal Law on the Intelligence Services came into force, granting these broader investigative powers.[106] The immigration services, on their part, who act on the basis of the Foreign Nationals Act (FNA),[107] may play an important role in the interviewing phase of asylum seekers and in reporting suspicious cases to the competent authorities.[108]

The federal police, on the other hand, will only come into play in phase 3), i.e. once the suspected "terrorist" has started carrying out suspicious activities that justify the opening of an investigation case. There is a current discussion on the necessity to grant to the federal police access to the data bank of flight passengers.[109] More specific preventive measures that may be adopted at this stage (which are yet to come into force) are the seizure of travel documents and the obligation to show up on a regular basis at a specific police station. The Foreign Nationals Act (FNA)[110] is currently under revision in order to integrate these measures. The latter only applies to foreign nationals, meaning that these measures would not be applicable to FF holding Swiss nationality. In this regard, the Third TETRA Report cites the case of two young Swiss French men who were apparently planning a trip to Syria. There were not sufficient elements of suspicion to justify the opening of criminal proceedings under art. 309 of the Swiss Criminal Code of Procedure (CCP). Therefore, the intelligence service, on a different legal basis, conducted a preliminary interview with the two suspects, who eventually left the country. Under the existing legislation, nothing more could be done. In the aftermath, criminal proceedings were initiated by the federal attorney general and, upon their return to Switzerland, the two young men were placed in preventive detention.[111]

105 TETRA is a coordination group that was originally born as a taskforce. See Troisième Rapport TETRA: Mesures prises par la Suisse dans la lutte contre le terrorisme à motivation djihadiste, April 2017, online at www.ejpd.admin.ch/dam/data/fedpol/aktuell/news/2017/2017-03-14/tetra-ber-f.pdf.
106 Loi sur le renseignment, SR 121, at www.admin.ch/opc/fr/classified-compilation/20120872/index.html.
107 SR 142.20, available in English at www.admin.ch/opc/en/classified-compilation/20020232/index.html.
108 Third TETRA Report, supra, at 11.
109 Third TETRA Report, supra, at 14.
110 SR 142.20, available online in English at www.admin.ch/opc/en/classified-compilation/20020232/index.html.
111 Third TETRA Report, spra, at 16.

During this preliminary phase, when no criminal proceedings have yet been opened, the federal police can only undertake a preliminary investigation aimed at corroborating the suspicions that have been reported to it by the intelligence services. The only preventive measures that might be undertaken are to be found and based on the Foreign Nationals Act (FNA),[112] i.e. the ban to enter the country or the expulsion from it. In 2016, for instance, banning the entry was ordered in 122 cases by the federal police. In 107 of these 122 cases, the decision was made against persons suspected of committing acts of terrorism or of extreme violence, or supporting forbidden groups and organisations.[113] "Support" means a personal or material support, such as recruitment or propaganda. Thirty-nine out of these 107 cases concerned persons who had been in conflict zones, i.e. travellers motivated by the jihad. As already mentioned, since some of these measures cannot be applied to Swiss nationals, the Federal Council entrusted the Federal Department of Justice and Police (FDJP) with the task to create a "package" of new measures that could be adopted beyond the context of criminal proceedings (e.g. the obligation to show up at a police station, the withdrawal of IDs or the enlisting of a person under scrutiny in a specific database).[114] There are, however, various other legal aspects that still need clarification.[115]

The fourth phase (opening of criminal proceedings and indictment), comes into play when the police or the intelligence services have collected sufficient elements to report the case to the competent authorities.[116] The legal bases lie in:

- art. 260ter Swiss Criminal Code (participation and support to a criminal organisation)
- Anti-IS Federal Act of 12 December 2012[117]

112 SR 142.20, available online in English at www.admin.ch/opc/en/classified-compilation/20020232/index.html.
113 Third TETRA Report at 15. Pursuant to art. 1 of the Federal law of 12 December 2014 (RS 122), these are al-Qaeda, Islamic State and the associated organisations.
114 A package of new legislative measures was proposed in June 2017 and the consultations will terminate on 13 October 2017. For more details see the Press Report of the Federal Office of Justice of 22 June 2017, "Le Conseil fédéral propose une série de modifications législatives pour renforcer la lutte contre le terrorisme", available online at www.fedpol.admin.ch/fedpol/fr/home/aktuell/news/2017/ref_2017-06-22.html.
115 Third TETRA Report at 17. These are: –adapting the provisions addressing the suppression of those websites that contain elements inciting violence against persons or things; –granting of a place of residence and interdiction to enter a specific region; –observation/preventive custody aimed at preventing the person from going abroad for terrorist purposes and creation of a new legal basis for the decision to detain someone in view of repatriation or expulsion; –the Border Guards should get facilitated access to the databank of Fedpol; –increasing legal measures available against the financing of terrorism.
116 I.e. the Federal Attorney General's Office (FAGO), the Tribunal of Coercive Measures (TCM) and the Federal Office of Justice (FOJ).
117 See the Federal Act on the Proscription of the Groups "Al-Qaeda" and "Islamic State" and Associated Organisations of 12 December 2014 (SR 122), available online in English at www.admin.ch/opc/en/classified-compilation/20142993/index.html.

- Swiss Criminal Code of Procedure (CCP): coercive measures (surveillance of means of communication, observation, interrogations, preventive custody, etc.)
- Mutual legal assistance and cooperation between the TETRA security authorities

In addition, the following measures are being planned:[118]

- revision of the Federal Law of 6 October 2000 on the surveillance of communication via mail and means of telecommunication (LSCPT)[119]
- Amendment of art. 260ter CC (organised crime) and extension of the ban on IS (art. rev260sexies CC)
- Approval and enforcement of the Convention of the European Council for the prevention of terrorism and its Additional protocol

The Third TETRA Report, in this regard, highlights the problem of the threat posed by a radicalised person enjoying freedom of movement. It cites the case of a young Swiss national who had returned from a journey to Turkey: depending on the gravity of the suspicions and the charges, an individual suspected of supporting IS may be released from preventive custody. Art. 237 of the Criminal Code of Procedure (CCP) provides for alternative subsidiary and softer measures to preventive detention (i.e. prevention of escape, collusion or reiteration of the crime, under art. 221 CCP). In the above-mentioned case, the young Swiss had been arrested and placed in preventive custody upon his return from Turkey in June 2016, following an arrest warrant from the Federal Attorney General's Office. The Tribunal of Coercive Measures concluded later that the requirements for maintaining this measure were no longer given, thereby lifting the provision. The Federal Attorney in charge of the case required the setting in place of subsidiary measures. These, however, required intensive cooperation between various cantonal authorities.[120] In sum, the Third TETRA Report highlights the need to reinforce cooperation between the existing federal and cantonal institutions and to strengthen the powers of the federal police and the intelligence services. Efficient measures may also be taken at administrative level, e.g. on the basis of the Foreign Nationals Act (FNA).[121]

118 Third TETRA Report, at 19 and FEDPOL, "Dossier de presse – Lutte contre le terrorisme: stratégie et projets en cours", available online at www.fedpol.admin.ch/dam/data/bj/sicherheit/gesetzgebung/terrorismus-europarat/rohstoff-f.pdf.

119 RS 780.1, available online at www.admin.ch/opc/fr/classified-compilation/20002162/index.html. The amended version will enter into force on 1 January 2018.

120 Third TETRA Report, at 19. Such alternative measures might be the obligation to report to a specific police station, to undergo medical treatment, the interdiction to entertain social relations with specific persons, etc.

121 SR 142.20, available online in English at www.admin.ch/opc/en/classified-compila tion/20020232/index.html.

The following section will illustrate some of the new legislative measures that have been adopted and proposed recently.

New legislative measures

The Anti-IS Federal Law

In November 2001, the Federal Council released a directive banning groups like al-Qaeda and related organisations. It extended it in 2003, 2005 and 2008. A final three-year-extension was made on 1 January 2012 by transforming it into a parliamentary directive, which expired on 31 December 2014. Since another extension was not possible, in consideration of the increased threats posed by these movements, the Federal Council proposed in its Message to the Parliament the adoption of an Emergency Law,[122] based on article 165 of the Swiss Constitution, which would also follow the recommendations made by the UN SC Resolution 2178 of 24 September 2014, calling Member States to cooperate urgently on preventing the international flow of terrorist fighters to and from conflict zones.[123] The Parliament, thus, followed the proposal by adopting the Federal Act on the Proscription of the Groups "Al-Qaeda" and "Islamic State" and Associated Organisations ("Anti-IS Act").[124] This came into force on 1 January 2015 and will expire on 31 December 2018.[125]

Art. 1[126] outlaws al-Qaeda, the group "Islamic State" and all other groups that may be either acting under their mandate, pursuing their objectives or sharing

122 Message concernant la loi fédérale interdisant les groupes "Al Qaïda" et "Etat islamique" et les organisations apparentées of 12 November 2014, reference nr. FF 2014 8755, available online at www.admin.ch/opc/fr/federal-gazette/2014/8755.pdf.

123 The full text of the Resolution can be found at www.un.org/press/en/2014/sc11580.doc.htm along with a commentary to the text. Through resolution 2178 (2014), which was unanimously adopted, the UN Security Council condemned violent extremism and decided that Member States shall, consistent with international law, prevent the "recruiting, organizing, transporting or equipping of individuals who travel to a State other than their States of residence or nationality for the purpose of the perpetration, planning of, or participation in terrorist acts". While most speakers acknowledged that a military and security approach to the international spread of terrorism was necessary in the short term, they stressed the need for a comprehensive approach that addressed marginalization, long-standing conflicts and other factors that helped attract individuals to extremism.

124 RS 122: Loi fédérale interdisant les groupes "Al-Qaïda" et "Etat islamique" et les organisations apparentées, available online in French, German and Italian at www.admin.ch/opc/fr/classified-compilation/20142993/index.html.

125 Loi fédérale interdisant les groupes "Al-Qaïda2 et "Etat islamique" et les organisations apparentées du 12 décembre 2014, at www.admin.ch/opc/fr/classified-compilation/20142993/index.html (French version).

126 Art. 1 Interdiction Les groupes et organisations suivants sont interdits: a. le groupe "Al-Qaïda"; b. le groupe "Etat islamique"; c. les groupes de couverture, ceux qui émanent du groupe "Al-Qaïda" ou du groupe "Etat islamique" et les organisations et groupes dont les dirigeants, les buts et les moyens sont identiques à ceux du groupe "Al-Qaïda" ou du groupe "Etat islamique" ou qui agissent sur son ordre.

their methods. A list of banned groups is contained in appendix 2 of the directive of 2 October 2000 on measures against persons or organisations related to Osama bin Laden and the groups al-Qaeda or the Taliban. The latter encompasses the measures adopted under UN Resolutions 1267, 1333, 1390, 1455, 1526, 1617 and 1735.[127]

Art. 2[128] provides that whoever, on Swiss soil, participates, puts human resources or materials at its disposal, organises propaganda actions, recruits members or otherwise promotes the activities of one of the groups or organisations outlawed under art. 1 may be punished with a maximum of five years of detention. If the accused committed the acts abroad, he or she may be equally punishable if arrested and not extradited from Switzerland. Pursuant to para. 3 the prosecution and adjudication of the acts are subject to federal jurisdiction.

Due to the foreseen expiry of the Emergency Law, the Federal Council, in June 2017, proposed a revision thereof.

The new package of measures proposed by the Federal Council in June 2017

On 22 June 2017 the Federal Council announced that it would propose a targeted revision of the Swiss Criminal Code and other relevant laws, in order to facilitate the role of the police and the judiciary in addressing activities that *increase the risk* of a terrorist attack. This proposal comes also in order to fully implement the Council of Europe Convention on the Prevention of Terrorism.[129] Consultations ended on 13 October 2017.

127 See the Message, at 8933, para. 2.

128 Art. 2 Dispositions pénales 1 Quiconque s'associe sur le territoire suisse à un groupe ou à une organisation visé à l'art. 1, met à sa disposition des ressources humaines ou matérielles, organise des actions de propagande en sa faveur ou en faveur de ses objectifs, recrute des adeptes ou encourage ses activités de toute autre manière est puni d'une peine privative de liberté de cinq ans au plus ou d'une peine pécuniaire. 2 Quiconque commet l'infraction à l'étranger est aussi punissable s'il est arrêté en Suisse et n'est pas extradé. L'art. 7, al. 4 et 5, du code pénal1 est applicable. 3 La poursuite et le jugement des actes cités aux al. 1 et 2 sont soumis à la juridiction fédérale.

129 Reference: CETS No. 196, available online at www.coe.int/en/web/conventions/full-list/-/conventions/treaty/196. From the official summary: "The Council of Europe has adopted this Convention to increase the effectiveness of existing international texts on the fight against terrorism. It aims to strengthen member States' efforts to prevent terrorism in two different ways: •by establishing as criminal offences certain acts that may lead to the commission of terrorist offences, namely: public provocation, recruitment and training •by reinforcing co-operation on prevention both internally (national prevention policies), and internationally (modification of existing extradition and mutual assistance arrangements and additional means). The Convention contains a provision on the protection and compensation of victims of terrorism. A consultation process is planned to ensure effective implementation and follow up." A detailed report was released by the Federal Department of Justice and Police in June 2017: DFJP, "Approbation et mise en oeuvre de la Convention du Conseil de l'Europe pour la prévention du terrorisme et de son Protocole additionnel et renforcement des normes pénales contre le terrorisme et le crime organisé – Avant-projet et rapport

One of the aims is also to sanction activities like training, recruitment and travelling abroad with terrorist goals, by extending the Anti-IS Federal Law of 12 December 2012[130] and formally integrating it in the federal legislation (which is no longer subject to time restrictions). The elements of the crimes should be defined more precisely, following the critiques raised by the Federal Tribunal and the Federal Criminal Tribunal in their first judgment based on this law.[131] For instance, one of the problems is a maximum sanction of five years of detention. This is in line with the sanctions foreseen by the Swiss Criminal Code in art. 260ter CC (organised crime) and art. 260quinquies CC (financing of terrorism), but it has been criticised as being inappropriate. In particular with regard to FF, the question is whether a FF who is arrested upon his or her return to Switzerland, may be de-radicalised and no longer pose a threat after such a (short) time. Expulsion, moreover, cannot apply to Swiss nationals.

At the same time, a working group has been entrusted with the revision of art. 260ter CC (organised crime),[132] in order to facilitate its application[133] and adapt the sanctions to the gravity of the offence (now a maximum of five years of detention).[134]

The Mutual Legal Assistance Act (IMAC)[135] shall also undergo amendments in order to improve international cooperation, especially with regard to the fight against the financing of terrorism. Last but not the least, the Federal Council launched two other counter-terrorism projects: a) before the end of 2017, a consultation will be undertaken on the preventive measures that might be adopted by the police against potential criminals *outside* the context of criminal proceedings;

explicative", available online at www.bj.admin.ch/dam/data/bj/sicherheit/gesetzgebung/terrorismus-europarat/vn-ber-f.pdf.

130 RS 122: Loi fédérale interdisant les groupes "Al-Qaïda" et "Etat islamique" et les organisations apparentées, available online in French, German and Italian at www.admin.ch/opc/fr/classified-compilation/20142993/index.html.

131 See the Judgment of the Federal Criminal Tribunal of 15 July 2016, Ref nr. SK.2016.9 and the Judgment of the Federal Tribunal, BGer 6B_948/2016.

132 Art. 260ter CC: "1. Any person who participates in an organisation, the structure and personal composition of which is kept secret and which pursues the objective of committing crimes of violence or securing a financial gain by criminal means, any person who supports such an organisation in its criminal activities, is liable to a custodial sentence not exceeding five years or to a monetary penalty. 2. The court has the discretion to mitigate the penalty imposed (Art. 48a) if the offender makes an effort to foil the criminal activities of the organisation. 3. The foregoing penalties also apply to any person who commits the offence outside Switzerland provided the organisation carries out or intends to carry out its criminal activities wholly or partly in Switzerland. Article 3 paragraph 2 applies."

133 An initiative for the revision of this provision was launched in the Swiss Parliament on 31 January 2014. Prévoir des dispositions pénales efficaces pour poursuivre le crime organisé (révision de l'art. 260ter CP), available online at www.parlament.ch/en/ratsbetrieb/suche-curia-vista/geschaeft?AffairId=20140401. The details of the problems attached to it are reported in this document.

134 Third TETRA, at 20.

135 SR 351.1, available in English online at www.admin.ch/opc/en/classified-compilation/19810037/index.html.

b) at the same time, a National Plan of Action shall be adopted against radicalization and violent extremism.[136]

Finally, another measure taken to implement the Council of Europe Convention on the Prevention of Terrorism has been the introduction of art. 74 in the new Federal Law on the Information Services,[137] which sets the criteria for banning specific organisations.

The new Federal Law on the Information Services

The Federal Law on the Information Services[138] was adopted by the 65.5 per cent of the Swiss population with the referendum of 25 September 2016 and entered into force on 1 September 2017. Pursuant to art. 1, the new law regulates a) the activities of the information services in Switzerland; b) its cooperation with other authorities and private individuals, both in Switzerland and abroad; c) the oversight over its activities. Its scope, as defined by art. 2, is to protect important national interests, and its aim is to contribute to the protection of the fundamental guarantees of the Swiss democracy and of its population, to increase the security of the Swiss population and Swiss nationals abroad, to support the power of action of Switzerland and to contribute to the protection of the national interests of the state. It defines the tasks of the information services (art. 6), in particular the collection and treatment of information that may prevent in time threats posed, among others, by terrorism, and its cooperation with the other authorities (art. 9–12). It specifies which information may be collected without (art. 13–16) or with (art. 26–33) prior authorisation. In general, it grants broader powers to the information services of the Swiss Confederation. Among these is the measure of permanent surveillance, which may be requested for the most serious cases. The request for authorisation must be addressed to the Federal Administrative Tribunal (art. 29), which will decide on the basis of the principles of legality, proportionality, opportunity and proportionality. The decision will be then submitted to the Chief of the Federal Department of Defence, who will decide upon consultation with the Chiefs of the Federal Department of Justice and the Federal Department of Foreign Affairs (art. 39).[139] The oversight is ultimately delegated to the Parliament (art. 81).[140]

136 For more details see the press statement made on 22 June 2017 by representatives of the Federal Office of Justice and the Head of the Federal Department of Justice and Police "Il Consiglio Federal propone modifiche di legge per combattere meglio il terrorismo", available online in German, French and Italian at www.ejpd.admin.ch/ejpd/it/home/aktuell/news/2017/2017-06-22.html.

137 LRens, SR 121, available in French, German and Italian online at www.admin.ch/opc/fr/classified-compilation/20120872/index.html. It entered into force on 1 September 2017.

138 LRens, SR 121, available in French, German and Italian online at www.admin.ch/opc/fr/classified-compilation/20120872/index.html.

139 Third TETRA Report, supra, at 13.

140 It is beyond the scope of the present essay to examine the pros and cons of this new law. Critiques have been expressed by HumanRights.Ch: "La nouvelle Loi sur le

Federal Law of 6 October 2000 on the surveillance of communication via post and telecommunications (LSCPT)

A new, amended version, of the federal law on the surveillance of communication[141] entered into force on 1 January 2018. It aims at improving the existing means of surveillance and to adapt the law to the new technologies.

Swiss jurisprudence

The Swiss Federal Criminal Tribunal (FCT) holds the competence to adjudicate those crimes that, pursuant to the Swiss Criminal Code (CC),[142] are prosecuted by the Federal Attorney General's Office. Pursuant to art. 2 of the Anti-IS Law, the prosecution and adjudication of violations thereof fall within the competence of the federal authorities. The Federal Attorney General's Office (FAGO) undertook a massive anti-IS intervention in February 2017 in Canton Ticino, leading to one arrest.[143] This followed the first trial held by the FCT in the capital of Canton Ticino, Bellinzona, in February 2016, on the basis of the "anti-IS" legislation. Charges were brought against four Iraqi nationals aged between 29 and 34 under the suspicion of being members or supporters of ISIS and for having tried to set up an IS cell in Switzerland.[144]

The judgment of the Federal Criminal Tribunal of 15 July 2016 (SK.2016.9)

On 15 July 2016 the FCT pronounced its first judgment[145] based on art. 2 of the Anti-IS emergency law,[146] condemning one of the accused for having *promoted* [147]IS, for the fact of having gone on board a plane in Zurich with the destination of Istanbul,

renseignement continue de soulever de l'opposition", at www.humanrights.ch/fr/droits-humains-suisse/interieure/protection/securite/suisse-loi-renseignement; or Amnesty International, Swiss Branch: "Loi sur le renseignement (LRENS) – Exploration du reseau câblé", Bern, 3 December 2015, online at www.amnesty.ch/fr/themes/surveillance/surveillance-en-suisse/la-loi-sur-le-renseignement-lrens.

141 RS 780.1, online at www.admin.ch/opc/fr/classified-compilation/20002162/index.html.

142 SR 311.0, online in English at www.admin.ch/opc/en/classified-compilation/19370083/index.html.

143 Federal Attorney General's Press Release, "Combating terrorism: Searches carried out in Ticino", 22 February 2017, online at: www.admin.ch/gov/en/start/documentation/media-releases.msg-id-65761.html.

144 Swiss trial begins of alleged Islamic State terror cell, 29 February 2016, SwissInfo, at www.swissinfo.ch/eng/plotting-attack-_swiss-trial-begins-of-alleged-islamic-state-terror-cell/41990190.

145 Judgment of the Federal Criminal Tribunal of 15 July 2016, SK.2016.9.

146 SR 122, Federal Act on the Proscription of the Groups "Al-Qaeda" and "Islamic State" and Associated Organisations, available online at www.admin.ch/opc/en/classified-compilation/20142993/index.html.

147 In German the term is *gefördert*.

Turkey, in order to travel further to the "Islamic State". The Federal Criminal Court was itself very critical of this legal basis, describing as "problematic" the vagueness of the term "support" in art. 2.[148] Also the Federal Tribunal, in its judgment of 22 February 2017, considers this "vagueness" as problematic from the point of view of the principle of legality, but nevertheless confirms the judgment of the Federal Criminal Tribunal.[149]

THE FACTS

In the autumn of 2014 the federal police (FEDPOL) received the information that several persons residing in Canton Thurgau were about to leave to Syria in order to join the Jabhat-aI-Nusra Front. On 18 December 2014, D and his sister E, both Swiss citizens, left their domicile at their parents' house with the aim to fly to Istanbul. After their first investigations, the FEDPOL concluded that the plan must have been to leave for Syria to join the IS. Several coercive measures of investigations were approved by the competent authority on the basis of art. 260ter on organised crime.[150]

Among others, it turned out that in the period between 30 January and 29 March 2015, D had been in contact at least 15 times with N, a dual Swiss/Syrian national, who left for Hatay (Turkey), from Zurich Airport on 4 April 2015, leaving behind his wife and three children, and whose whereabouts are still unknown. On 31 March 2015 the accused had received a phone call in which he had been offered a flight ticket for 4 April 2015 from Zurich to Istanbul, in which the person calling explained that the journey would be "very difficult". On 3 April 2015 he was seen departing from other people at the entrance of the mosque of an Islamic association.[151]

D was arrested at 2.10 p.m. on 7 April 2015 at the gate of Zurich Airport, while he was about to get on board flight number TK 1914 of Turkish Airlines (Zürich-Istanbul). The police found among his belongings a ticket reservation for a flight from Istanbul to Zurich on 7 April 2015, a return flight ticket from Istanbul to Zurich on 14 April 2015 and a hotel booking for one person from 7 to 14 April 2015 in Istanbul.[152]

148 For an analysis see A. Eicker, "Zur Interpretation des Al-Quaida- und IS Gesetzes durch das Bundesstrafgericht im Fall eines zum Islamischen Staat Reisenden – Eine Besprechung des Entscheids des Bundesstrafgerichts" SK.2016.9 vom 15 Juli 2016, *Jusletter* 21. November 2016; A. Eicker, "Das Antreten eines Fluges nach Istanbul als strafbare Unterstützung oder Förderung des 'Islamischen Staats'?" – Besprechung von BGer 6B_948/2016 vom 22. 2. 2017, 2017 (5) *forumpoenale* 351–357. See also a short analysis in R. Arnold, "Il concetto di 'war on terror' e i suoi risvolti penali", 2018 (3) *forumpoenale* (forthcoming).

149 BGer 6B_948/2016, E. 4.2.1.

150 SK.2016.9, Judgment of the Federal Criminal Tribunal of 15 July 2016, at §1.3.1–1.3.3.

151 SK.2016.9, at §1.3.6.

152 SK.2016.9, at §1.7.

D was held in pre-trial detention from 7 to 20 April 2015. He was then interdicted from leaving Switzerland and his passport was seized. From 30 October 2015, he had to announce himself regularly to the police.

The Federal Prosecutor released her indictment on 18 February 2016, charging D with participation in and support of a criminal organisation under art. 260ter CC and art. 2(1) of the Anti-IS (emergency) law and repeated exposure of violence (art. 135 (1) and 1bis CC). The Federal Prosecutor requested two years of detention (suspended), on bail for three years. His lawyer requested his client's acquittal.[153] The trial took place on 14 July 2016 at the seat of the Federal Criminal Tribunal in Bellinzona, Canton Ticino. The judgment was released on 15 July 2016.

THE LEGAL ASSESSMENT

The accused D was acquitted of the charge of repeated exposure of violence (art. 135 (1) and 1bis CC) on the basis of the missing required *mens rea*. Moreover, the FCT observed that the Anti-IS (emergency) Law is *lex specialis* with regard to this provision.[154]

With regard to the other charges, the FCT observed that the accused should have known that every form of "promotion" (*Fördern*) of IS, in particular through a personal engagement, leads further to the murderous activity of the organisation; because of the widespread media reports and propaganda activities of the IS, he should moreover have known that by his conduct he was gravely jeopardising the social values and structures of his homeland.[155]

With regard to the other charges, the FCT concluded that the Anti-IS legislation is *lex specialis* with regard to art. 260ter CC. Both aim at preventively protecting the public security and both require intent. The author must be aware of the fact that he is supporting (*Unterstützen*) the criminal organisation, respectively IS, and acting at least with *dolus eventualis*. It is not necessary, though, that he acted with the intention of supporting the commission of a specific crime. He must nevertheless take into account the fact that the organisation commits violence-based and enrichment crimes. The FCT then held that, with regard to IS, it must be concluded that every judicious adult in the European and Arabic regions knows that IS commits atrocities, since not only all media but also IS itself, via social media, disseminates almost daily this type of information.[156]

The FCT comes to the conclusion that the accused had intentionally undertaken his trip to the boarding phase, i.e. to a point where he was totally in the power of the flight company, with which he had signed a contract of transportation that obligated him to undertake the trip. Only the intervention of the police precluded his departure. Moreover, the information he had received from another

153 SK.2016.9, at §1.
154 SK.2016.9, at 2.6.
155 SK.2016.9, at 4.1.
156 SK.2016.9, at §1.16.

person who had undertaken the jihad trip and his chat of 28 November 2014 with his girlfriend B were unmistakable evidence that he did not want to travel to Istanbul for a holiday, but that this was meant to be a middle stop for his further journey to Syria in order to go to the jihad. Even if it may not be totally excluded that he might have changed his mind voluntarily, this scenario is purely theoretical. The fact that he left behind his pregnant girlfriend reinforces his determination.[157]

The FCT concludes that in the eyes of those potential individuals interested in the jihad who were left behind, the accused, by undertaking his trip, joined the category of the active and thus to be admired ones. For this reason, his conduct comes so close to the criminal conduct of IS that it is to be considered as a form of "promotion" in the sense of art. 2(1) of the Anti-IS Law.[158] The FCT eventually sentenced him to 18 months of detention, suspended on bail for a period of three years.[159]

The accused filed an appeal to the Federal Tribunal, which adjudicated the case on 22 February 2017.[160]

APPRAISAL OF THE JUDGMENT BY THE DOCTRINE L

The FCT judgment, although appraised in its conclusions, has been criticised in the doctrine for its legal reasoning. Professor A. Eicker,[161] for instance, remarks that the indictment was primarily based on the evidence that the accused, by travelling to Turkey (Istanbul), wanted to join the IS-led jihad in Syria and that the intervention of the police was the only reason why he did not carry out his plans.

The accused, however, though admitting his intention to travel to Syria, had contested his intention to join IS. Professor Eicker points out that art. 2(1) of the Anti-IS Law has a preventive goal: its objective is to protect the public security before the occurrence of a crime. The criminal responsibility of the accused, thus, is anticipated in the phase during which this holds conduct that may qualify as support to or promotion of the organisations banned by this law. Pursuant to it, the support, which must occur in Switzerland, may be provided in three different ways:

1 by supporting personally or materially the movement;
2 by organising forms of propaganda for it;
3 by supporting the movement "in other ways" (general clause).

The first form does not require that the accused supports/shares the criminal acts and objectives of the organisation. This is the main difference between the

157 SK.2016.9, at §1.18.
158 SK.2016.9,at §1.18.
159 SK.2016.9,at §§ 1.3 4.4.
160 BGer 6B_948/2016.
161 Andreas Eicker, "Zur Interpretation des Al-Quaïda- und IS-Gesetzes durch das Bundesstrafgericht im Fall eines zum Islamischen Staat Reisenden - Eine Besprechung des Entscheids des Bundesstrafgerichts SK.2016.9 vom 15. Juli 2016", in *Jusletter* of 21 November 2016 (online journal).

scope of application of the Anti-IS Law and art. 260ter (1)(2) CC.[162] The act of supporting is already fulfilled when the author intentionally makes propaganda or behaves in a manner indicated by the movement in the latter's propaganda. By acting in accordance with the indications of the movement, the author contributes to the latter's prolonged existence.[163]

Professor Eicker expresses some legitimate doubts about this approach, since a movement, in this case IS, may be promoting attitudes and behaviours that are fully accepted and acceptable in Muslim countries and that in those contexts do not qualify as criminal conduct.[164] One could imagine, for instance, indications about dress codes. In his view, which is shared by the author, the concept of "supporting" in this context needs to be defined more narrowly, in order to legitimately attach to it some form of criminal responsibility. This is even more necessary under the Anti-IS Law, which, unlike art. 260ter CC, does not require a nexus between the supporting conduct and the movement's objectives.

In this regard, the third form of support is even more problematic. According to the FCT, this (general) clause should only cover those acts that have a certain closeness to the criminal conduct of IS or al-Qaeda. This is important in order to draw a line between sympathising with or admiring a movement, which is not per se a criminally relevant conduct, and "supporting" it in the sense of art. 2(1).[165]

In its judgment, the FCT concludes that by getting on board the plane, the accused had placed his "fate" to travel to Turkey (and then to Syria) in the hands of a third party (the flight company). Thus, he was no longer in the phase of expressing his mere intention to travel: he had already undertaken the journey. There was no way back.[166] He no longer was in the phase of "attempt" or "preparatory acts": he had already started the criminally relevant act.

Professor Eicker observes that what matters is whether, by getting onto the plane, the accused had already acted in a way that qualifies his conduct as "promotion" under art. 2(1) Anti-IS Law. The law requires some closeness between the act of promotion and the criminal activity of IS.[167] In the case at stake this is not so obvious. The accused had booked a hotel in Istanbul (thus neither in Syria nor in Iraq), and a return ticket for the following week. These, in Professor Eicker's view, are ordinary acts undertaken daily by hundreds of people. What makes the difference in this case is that the accused admitted his intention to travel to combat zones located in Syria. It is on this basis that the FCT established the required closeness, at least from a *mens rea* perspective.[168] With regard to the *actus reus*, the fact of becoming someone to be admired by those left behind further fulfils the closeness requirement from the *actus reus* perspective.[169]

162 SK.2016.9, at 1.14.4.
163 SK.2016.9, at 1.14.2.
164 A. Eicker, supra, at 5, Note 12.
165 A. Eicker, supra, at 5, Note 13; SK.2016.9, at 1.14.1 and 1.18.
166 SK.2016.9, at 1.1.18; See A. Eicker, supra, at 5, Note 4.
167 A. Eicker, supra, at 6, Note 15; SK.2016.9, at 1.14.3.
168 A. Eicker, supra, at 6, Note 15; SK.2016.9, at 1.9.
169 SK.2016.9, at 1.18.

As remarked by Professor Eicker, even if the conclusions in the judgment are per se comprehensible, the legal reasoning is not. What remains particularly problematic is the notion of "promotion" under the Anti-IS Law and its compliance with the principle of legal certainty.

The judgment of the Federal Tribunal (FT) of 22 February 2017 (BGer 6B_948/2016)

In its judgment of 22 February 2017, the FCT remarks that the FCT had correctly observed the fact that the general clause contained in art. 2(1) of the Anti-IS Law "promotes their activities in any other way" is somewhat in a "tense" relation with the principle of legal certainty. Even though it is a common practice to use generic terms in the law, if its meaning cannot be ascertained even with the help of the usual methods of interpretation, their use is problematic. In the FT's view, however, the FCT had prevented a violation of the principle of legal certainty by requiring a certain closeness between the conduct considered to be as form of promotion of IS, and the latter's criminal activities.[170]

The FT, by citing inter alia also the critiques raised by Professor Eicker, concludes further that also with regard to the assessment of guilty, the judgment of the FCT is correct. It may be that the fact that the accused was about to get on board the plane does not per se constitute a sufficient closeness between the conduct and the crimes committed by IS (especially since the accused was not travelling to Syria, but had simply booked a flight to Turkey). It is true that the fact of simply sympathising with or admiring criminal or terrorist organisations is not a conduct encompassed by the general clause. Nevertheless, in order to answer the question of which acts may be considered as "promoting" the activities of forbidden organisations, one must undertake an ad hoc analysis. In the FT's opinion, the FCT correctly assumed that "promotion" to IS is also fulfilled when an individual became so influenced by the organisation that he or she would consciously disseminate further its radicalised propaganda or become active. The question, then, is whether this conduct qualifies as "support" (*Unterstützung*) or "promotion" of its activities in any other way (*Förderung*). The FT then comes to the conclusion that the journey of the accused had a propaganda effect, since four days prior to his departure, he was seen greeting people at the mosque of an Islamic association. The fact that he had a return ticket is irrelevant, since he himself admitted his intention to travel further to combat zones in Syria and that he had taken care of its organisation.[171]

Therefore, the FT rejected the appeal and confirmed the judgment of the FCT.

In his follow-up paper on this judgment,[172] Professor Eicker remarks that, like the FCT, the FT also comes to the conclusion that the mere fact of getting on

170 BGer 6B_948/2016, findings at §4.2.1.
171 BGer 6B_948/2016, findings at §4.2.2.
172 Eicker, "Das Antreten eines Fluges nach Istanbul als strafbare Unterstützung oder Förderung des 'Islamischen Staats'?". See also a short analysis in Arnold, "Il concetto di 'war on terror' e i suoi risvolti penali".

board a plane destined for Istanbul may fall under art. 2 (2) of the Anti-IS Law, notwithstanding the problems highlighted by the FT with regard to the principle of legal certainty of this provision, and the notion of "promotion". In his view, the FT missed this opportunity to interpret and distinguish the various forms of conduct encompassed by the provision, in particular the difference between "support" and "promotion".

Hopefully, this uncertainty will be overcome with the adoption of a new article 260sexies in the Swiss Criminal Code, as proposed by the Federal Council in June 2017.

Conclusions

The launching, in 2001, of the so-called "war on terror" has contributed to the rise of an ongoing debate on the qualification of an act of terrorism. As someone once said, this notion may very much vary depending on the beholder's views. From a legal point of view, especially prior to 9/11, major efforts had been undertaken to define so-called sub-forms thereof, such as hijacking, hostage taking, etc.

The use of military force, as opposed to law-enforcement mechanisms, to counteract new movements like IS or al-Qaeda, and the resort by the latter, notwithstanding their common ground with criminal organisations, to military tactics, have further contributed to the confusion reigning in international law as to the applicable legal regime and the status to be attributed to those involved.

This chapter has aimed at illustrating in particular the legal implications, under criminal law, of the "war on terror", with reference to the example of Switzerland. The latter implemented the various UN Security Council Resolutions calling upon states to adopt the necessary means to counter the threat posed by ISIS, and the Convention of the European Council for the prevention of terrorism and its Additional protocol by adopting an Emergency Law outlawing various forms of support and promotion to movements like IS and al-Qaeda. The critiques raised by the FCT and the FT to the Anti-IS Act, in particular with regard to its vagueness and compliance with the principle of legal certainty, in their first judgments addressing alleged members or supporters or promoters of IS, moved the Federal Council to propose a new package of legislative measures, aimed at improving the existing tools and giving more teeth to the law-enforcement authorities in this regard. In particular, art. 260ter (organised crime) of the Swiss Criminal Code should be revised in order to simplify its application, also to terrorist movements, whereas the Anti-IS Law, which was adopted as an Emergency Law by the Parliament, on the proposal of the Federal Council, shall be integrated in the Swiss Criminal Code under the new heading of art. 260sexies CC. At the same time, with the new Law on the Intelligence Services, which came into force on 1 September 2017, the efforts in preventing acts of terrorism by identifying, at an early stage, threats thereof before the opening of criminal proceedings shall also be facilitated.

What is finally to be welcomed, are the Swiss efforts, as highlighted in the Third TETRA (TErrorist TRAcking) Report, to take an interdisciplinary and global approach in the fight against terrorism, trying to identify and solve the problem at its roots and trying to propose solutions with positive mid- and long-term effects (e.g. with regard to de-radicalisation). As observed by the Swiss Minister of Justice Simonetta Sommaruga on 13 October 2017, on the occasion of the meeting of the Schengen Justice Departments and State Departments, a pivotal role in the fight against terrorism shall be played by the exchange of information between the law-enforcement authorities and the intelligence services. Efforts in this direction have proven to be fruitful with the exchanges takin place within TETRA, at domestic level.[173]

All these measures show that acts of terrorism and threats thereof posed by new movements like IS are and shall be counteracted, in the mid- and long term by law-enforcement tools, strengthened by a better exchange of information. The resort of military force may be a short-term solution to be resorted to in self-defence, under the UN Charter, if no other means seem to be available and/or viable. The phenomenon, though, cannot be equated with an "armed conflict". The notion of "war on terror" is an expression that, as remarked by the ICRC, has no legal foundation under international law. Thus, its use should also not lead to a misleading interpretation and application of the rules applicable in times of warfare to ordinary acts of violence.

173 Media Report: "Simonetta Sommaruga am JI Rat: Mit Informationsaustausch gegen Terrorismus", 13.10.2017, online at www.ejpd.admin.ch/ejpd/de/home/aktuell/news/2017/2017-10-13.html.

6 Disrupting terrorist activity

What are the limits to criminal methods of disruption?

Stuart Macdonald and Lord Carlile[1]

Introduction

The UK's CONTEST strategy for countering the threat of terrorism emphasises that prosecution is the UK's preferred method of disrupting terrorist activity.[2] Whilst this prioritisation of prosecution has several benefits – including the fact that imprisonment is more protective of national security than other non-criminal methods of disruption and the level of censure communicated by conviction for a criminal offence – it should, we suggest, be understood as being rooted primarily in the procedural protections and safeguards of the criminal law.[3] Suspects charged with a criminal offence are tried in open court, they have the opportunity to see and respond to the evidence against them, and the burden of proof rests on the prosecution, who must prove their allegations beyond reasonable doubt. These features give the criminal sanction a unique moral authority and legitimacy that other methods of disruption lack.

In furtherance of this commitment to prosecuting suspected terrorists, the UK has enacted a large number of terrorism precursor offences. In this chapter we evaluate this use of the criminal sanction and suggest that there is a need for greater legislative restraint. We develop this argument, in the next section, by first examining three non-criminal methods of disrupting terrorist activity: Terrorism Prevention and Investigation Measures (TPIMs); asset-freezing; and proscription. Whilst each of these powers has been found to be necessary, we outline four sets of concerns about them that explain why they are regarded as less desirable in principle than prosecution. We then turn, in the following section, to terrorism precursor offences. Whilst agreeing that terrorism precursor offences are needed for the sake of prevention, we argue that the wide range of such offences currently

1 The authors would like to thank Lowri Davies for her excellent research assistance during the production of this chapter.
2 HM Government, *CONTEST: The United Kingdom's Strategy for Countering Terrorism* (Cm 9608, The Stationery Office, 2018)
3 The 'priority of prosecution' is discussed further in Stuart Macdonald, 'Prosecuting Suspected Terrorists: Precursor Crimes, Intercept Evidence and the Priority of Security', in Lee Jarvis and Michael Lister (eds), *Critical Perspectives on Counter-terrorism* (Routledge, 2014).

in force in the UK go too far in pursuit of this objective. As a result, the same concerns that apply to the non-criminal methods of disruption apply also to terrorism precursor offences. We argue that this is counter-productive, for it risks undermining the very features of the criminal law that give it its unique moral authority and legitimacy. It is self-defeating to create offences in the name of prioritising prosecution if those same offences undermine the basis on which prosecution is prioritised in the first place.

Non-criminal methods of disruption

In some instances it is not possible to prosecute individuals suspected of involvement in terrorism-related activity; sometimes because there is insufficient admissible evidence (particularly given the UK's self-imposed ban on the use of intercept as evidence in criminal trials[4]); sometimes because there are cogent public interest reasons for not disclosing incriminating admissible evidence in open court (e.g. to retain the cover and ensure the safety of human agents); and, sometimes, because the individual has already been convicted, served his sentence, but is still assessed as posing a threat to national security. In such a situation, CONTEST advocates the use of other methods of disruption that sit outside the criminal justice process. One of these – deportation – applies only to foreign nationals. In this section we focus on three other methods of disruption that apply to domestic and foreign suspected terrorists alike: TPIMs; asset-freezing; and proscription.

Designed to be 'less intrusive, more clearly and tightly defined and more comparable to restrictions imposed under other powers in the civil justice system',[5] TPIMs replaced the previous system of Control Orders in December 2011. According to the Terrorism Prevention and Investigation Measures Act 2011 (hereafter 'TPIMA'), before issuing an individual with a TPIM notice the Home Secretary must first apply to the courts for permission to do so.[6] The permission hearing may take place without the individual concerned being present, without the individual having been notified of the application and without the individual having been given an opportunity to make representations to the court.[7] If permission is granted, a TPIM notice may then be issued and a review hearing is prescribed, at which a Special Advocate represents the interests of the individual concerned (see discussion below).[8] The TPIM notice may contain any of the twelve types of measure listed in schedule 1 of the Act that are considered necessary to prevent or restrict the individual's involvement in terrorism-related activity,

4 HM Government, *Intercept as Evidence* (Cm 8989, The Stationery Office, 2014).
5 HM Government, *Review of Counter-Terrorism and Security Powers: Review Findings and Recommendations* (Cm 8004, The Stationery Office, 2011) 41.
6 TPIMA, s 3(5)(a). An exception exists for cases in which the Home Secretary 'reasonably considers that the urgency of the case requires terrorism prevention and investigation measures to be imposed without obtaining such permission' (s 3(5)(b)).
7 Ibid. s 6(4).
8 Ibid. s 8(4).

such as an overnight residence measure, an exclusion and/or movement directions measure and an electronic communication device measure.[9] Once issued, the TPIM notice lasts for one year, at the end of which the Home Secretary may renew it for a second year if the statutory conditions are still met.[10] At the end of the second year, however, the Home Secretary may only issue a fresh TPIM notice if the individual has been, or is involved in new terrorism-related activity.[11] As of November 2017, there were seven TPIM notices in force.[12] TPIM notices have been used considerably less frequently than Control Orders. In response to the low numbers of TPIM notices in force in 2014 and 2015 a number of amendments were made to TPIMA by the Counter-Terrorism and Security Act 2015 on the recommendation of the then Independent Reviewer of Terrorism Legislation.[13]

In UK law different powers exist for the freezing of terrorist assets.[14] Of these, the Terrorist Asset-Freezing etc. Act 2010 (hereafter 'TAFA') is 'the default option where the unilateral freezing of terrorist assets is concerned'.[15] This Act – which was enacted in response to the judgment of the Supreme Court that the Treasury had acted beyond its powers in seeking to provide for asset-freezing by Order[16] – implements the UK's obligations under UN Security Council Resolution 1373. The Act stipulates a set of prohibitions relating to designated persons, including: dealing with funds or economic resources owned, held or controlled by a designated person;[17] making funds or financial services available to, or for the benefit of, a designated person;[18] and making economic resources available to, or for the benefit of, a designated person.[19] A person is designated either as an automatic consequence of appearing on the EU list drawn up pursuant to Regulation 2580/2001 or on the initiative of the Treasury.[20] Designations last for no more than one year, but may be renewed indefinitely as long as the conditions for designation continue to be met.[21] The Treasury may also make interim

9 Ibid. s 3(4). The other eight types of measure are: travel measure; financial services measure; property measure; association measure; work or studies measure; reporting measure; photography measure; and, monitoring measure.
10 Ibid. s 5(2).
11 Ibid. s 3.
12 Grahame Allen and Noel Dempsey, Terrorism in Great Britain: the Statistics (House of Commons Library, 2018).
13 Ss. 16–20; David Anderson, *Terrorism Prevention and Investigation Measures in 2013: Second Report of the Independent Reviewer on the Operation of the Terrorism Preventions and Investigation Measures Act 2011* (The Stationery Office, 2014).
14 In addition to the Terrorist Asset-Freezing etc. Act 2010 are part II of the Anti-Terrorism, Crime and Security Act 2001 and part 5 and schedule 7 of the Counter-Terrorism Act 2008.
15 David Anderson, *First Report on the Operation of the Terrorist Asset-Freezing etc. Act 2010* (The Stationery Office, 2011) para. 2.3.
16 *HM Treasury v Ahmed* [2010] UKSC 2, [2010] 2 AC 534.
17 TAFA s. 11.
18 Ibid. ss. 12, 13.
19 Ibid. ss. 14, 15.
20 Ibid. s. 1.
21 Ibid. s. 4.

designations, which last for thirty days or until replaced by a final designation (whichever is earlier).[22] These powers are, however, 'lightly used'.[23] Indeed, former Independent Reviewer David Anderson urged that 'consideration continues to be given by all concerned to the greater use of TAFA 2010 as a way of disrupting persons who cannot be prosecuted but in respect of whom financial restrictions are necessary in order to protect the public from terrorism'.[24]

Under the Terrorism Act 2000 (hereafter 'TA 2000'), the Home Secretary may proscribe any organisation that is 'concerned in terrorism'.[25] The Act specifies that an organisation is concerned in terrorism if it commits or participates in acts of terrorism, prepares for terrorism, promotes or encourages terrorism, or is otherwise concerned in terrorism.[26] Seeking to clarify the last of these expressions, the Court of Appeal has held that an organisation that has 'temporarily ceased from terrorist activities for tactical reasons' may be said to be concerned in terrorism, whereas one that has 'decided to attempt to achieve its aims by other than violent means' may not – even if 'the possibility exists that it might decide to revert to terrorism in the future'.[27] If an organisation is concerned in terrorism, the Home Secretary has regard to five factors when deciding whether or not to exercise the discretion to proscribe: the nature and scale of the organisation's activities; the specific threat it poses to the UK; the specific threat it poses to British nationals overseas; the extent of the organisation's presence in the UK; and the need to support other members of the international community in the global fight against terrorism.[28] Once imposed, proscription lasts indefinitely. A proscribed organisation, or any person affected by the organisation's proscription, may apply to the Home Secretary for the organisation to be de-proscribed.[29] If unsuccessful, there exists a right of appeal to the Proscribed Organisations Appeal Commission (POAC).[30] The role of POAC is to determine whether the Home Secretary's refusal was 'flawed', applying the principles of judicial review.[31]

The former Independent Reviewers of Terrorism Legislation Lord Carlile and David Anderson both asserted the importance of these three methods of disruption. TPIMs 'are a useful tool for the protection of the public in the exceptional

22 Ibid. s. 8.
23 David Anderson, *Fourth Report on the Operation of the Terrorist Asset-Freezing etc. Act 2010* (The Stationery Office, 2015) para. 6.1. This report states that, as of 30 September 2014, there were a total of 68 designations and 59 accounts frozen in the UK. The value of the frozen assets was £61,000.
24 Ibid. para. 3.26.
25 TA 2000 s. 3(4).
26 Ibid. 2000 s. 3(5).
27 *Secretary of State for the Home Department v Lord Alton of Liverpool and others* [2008] EWCA Civ 443, [2008] 1 WLR 2341, [38].
28 David Anderson, *The Terrorism Acts in 2011: Report of the Independent Reviewer on the Operation of the Terrorism Act 2000 and Part 1 of the Terrorism Act 2006* (The Stationery Office, 2012) para. 4.6.
29 TA 2000, s. 4.
30 Ibid. 2000, s. 5(2).
31 Ibid. 2000, s. 5(3).

cases where a credible terrorist threat cannot be dealt with by prosecution or deportation'.[32] Asset-freezing has a 'deterrent and disruptive effect'[33] and also fulfils the UK's international obligations. And, whilst proscription may have limited utility in terms of public protection, it is useful in dealing with lower level activity, it supports other countries in their counterterrorism efforts and it deters terrorist organisations from operating in the UK and disrupts their ability to do so.[34] At the same time, however, both have also warned against excessive reliance on these exceptional measures. TPIMs are 'restrictive measures [which] should be imposed only when unavoidable, and as a last resort'.[35] 'Asset-freezes, particularly when imposed on persons at liberty in the UK, are highly disruptive of everyday life; yet the process of judicial challenge, though designed to be as fair as possible, may in some cases be cumbersome, slow and imperfect.'[36] And proscription impinges upon the right of the organisation's members to freedom of expression and association,[37] can cause 'collateral damage' to individuals 'who are not members of the proscribed organisation, but merely of the ethnic community from which the organisation derives its support' and can be of 'propaganda value' to governments 'which seek to repress the organisation in question or the population that it claims to represent, perhaps by violent and unsavoury means of their own'.[38]

There are four sets of concerns about these non-criminal forms of disruption that we wish to highlight for the purposes of this chapter. The first regards the preconditions for the exercise of each of the three powers. For the Home Secretary to issue a person with a TPIM notice and for the Treasury to designate a person for the purposes of TAFA, it must be shown both that the individual is, or has been, involved in terrorism-related activity and that the measure is necessary for purposes connected with protecting members of the public from terrorism.[39] This two-pronged approach – which involves a forward-looking evaluation of necessity as well as a backward-looking question of fact – is in keeping with Noorda's 'autonomy respecting model' of preventive measures, in that it requires 'an individualized and fact-specific assessment of risk' (as opposed to her 'security

32 David Anderson, *Terrorism Prevention and Investigation Measures in 2014: Third Report of the Independent Reviewer on the Operation of the Terrorism Prevention and Investigation Measures Act 2011* (The Stationery Office, 2015) para. 2.12.
33 Anderson, *First Report on the Operation of the Terrorist Asset-Freezing etc. Act 2010*, para. 2.11.
34 Lord Carlile, *Report on the Operation in 2008 of the Terrorism Act 2000 and of Part 1 of the Terrorism Act 2006* (The Stationery Office, 2009) para. 51; Anderson, *The Terrorism Acts in 2011*, para. 4.48.
35 Anderson, *Terrorism Prevention and Investigation Measures in 2014* (n 32) para 2.12.
36 Anderson, *Fourth Report on the Operation of the Terrorist Asset-Freezing etc. Act 2010*, para. 3.13.
37 European Convention on Human Rights, Arts 10, 11.
38 Anderson, *The Terrorism Acts in 2011*, para. 4.42. See also Lee Jarvis and Tim Legrand, 'Legislating for Otherness: Proscription Powers and Parliamentary Discourse' (2016) 42 *Review of International Studies* 558.
39 TPIMA, ss. 3(1), 3(3); TAFA, ss. 2(1)(a), 2(1)(b).

protecting model', which imposes preventive constraints 'on a category of persons defined by certain characteristics, premised on the probability that a member of this category will behave in a certain way irrespective of individual risk assessments').[40] By contrast, the sole requirement for an organisation to be proscribed is that it is concerned in terrorism.[41] This leaves the Home Secretary with an 'extraordinarily wide discretion',[42] particularly given the breadth of the statutory definition of terrorism.[43] Yet the possibility of introducing a necessity test, similar to the one used for TPIMs and asset freezes, has not been accepted.[44]

In addition to the preconditions themselves, the potential invasiveness of these measures has led to concerns being expressed about the required standard of proof. For both asset freezes and proscriptions the standard of proof that applies is that of reasonable belief.[45] This was also the standard that applied to TPIMs when they were first introduced, which marked an increase from the reasonable suspicion threshold that applied to Control Orders. However, following the Counter-Terrorism and Security Act 2015 (and in response to a recommendation of the then Independent Reviewer[46]), the Home Secretary may now only issue a TPIM notice if he is satisfied, on the balance of probabilities, that the individual is, or has been, involved in terrorism-related activity.[47] This increase from the previous standard of reasonable belief is significant since the balance of probabilities is recognised in formal legal terms as the standard of proof in civil litigation and, from a theoretical point of view, the change represents a movement from an approach based on the judgment of the executive to one based on the establishment of facts.[48] Whilst the practical impact of this change may be minimal,[49] adopting an approach based on the establishment of facts does go some way towards increasing the legitimacy of the TPIMs regime.[50]

40 Hadassa Noorda, 'Preventive Deprivations of Liberty: Asset Freezes and Travel Bans' (2015) 9 *Criminal Law and Philosophy* 521, 524–25.
41 TA 2000, s. 3(4).
42 Anderson, *The Terrorism Acts in 2011*, para. 4.4.
43 TA 2000, s. 1. The breadth of the existing definition was criticised by the Supreme Court in *R v Gul* [2013] UKSC 64, [2014] AC 1260.
44 HM Government, *The Government Response to the Annual Report on the Operation of the Terrorism Acts in 2011 by the Independent Reviewer of Terrorism Legislation* (Cm 8494, The Stationery Office, 2013).
45 TAFA, s. 2(1)(a); TA 2000, s. 3(4)
46 Anderson, *Terrorism Prevention and Investigation Measures in 2013*, paras 6.16–6.18.
47 TPIMA, s. 3(1).
48 Adrian Hunt, 'From Control Orders to TPIMs: Variations on a Number of Themes in British Legal Responses to Terrorism' (2014) 62 *Crime, Law and Social Change* 289.
49 In his final annual report on Control Orders, the former Independent Reviewer of Terrorism Legislation Lord Carlile stated that 'most' of the 48 individuals who received Control Orders between 2005 and 2011 would still have received one even if the standard of proof had been the civil standard instead of the lower threshold of reasonable suspicion (Lord Carlile of Berriew, *Sixth Report of the Independent Reviewer Pursuant to Section 14(3) of the Prevention of Terrorism Act 2005* (The Stationery Office, 2011) para. 29). A similar conclusion was reached by David Anderson in respect of TPIMs (Anderson, *Terrorism Prevention and Investigation Measures in 2013*, para. 6.17).
50 Anderson, *The Terrorism Acts in 2011*, para. 4.60.

This leads us to the second set of concerns, which focus on the roles of the executive and judiciary. There have been repeated suggestions that it should be the courts, not the executive, that issue TPIM notices.[51] Those who argue that TPIM notices should be issued by the courts emphasise the impact of TPIMs on an individual's liberty and the independence of the judiciary. Others assert that TPIMs are concerned primarily with national security, which is the responsibility of the executive, and emphasise that the Home Secretary is democratically accountable for the decisions he or she makes in this regard. The existing arrangement – in which the Home Secretary issues TPIM notices but only after first receiving the permission of the courts – is in effect an uneasy compromise between these perspectives. At the same time that he recommended increasing the standard of proof that applies to TPIMs to the civil standard, former Independent Reviewer David Anderson also recommended that the Home Secretary should be required, at a TPIM review hearing, to satisfy the court on the balance of probabilities that the person is, or has been, involved in terrorism-related activity.[52] But whilst this change was supported by the Joint Committee on Human Rights,[53] it was not accepted by the coalition government who reasserted that 'the Home Secretary is best placed to make the decision to impose a TPIM notice'.[54]

In respect of asset freezes and proscription, the courts' role is more limited still. There is no judicial involvement in the process for designating a person under TAFA or the process for renewing a designation.[55] Instead, designated persons have a right of appeal to the High Court.[56] All new designations and renewals are also reviewed by the Asset-Freezing Review sub-Group (AFRG).[57] According to David Anderson, this 'has been effective in focusing minds on whether the statutory tests are still met, and in clearing out dead wood'.[58] Similarly, in respect of proscription there is also no judicial involvement in the proscription process. As noted above, a proscribed organisation, or any person affected by the organisation's proscription, may apply to the Home Secretary for the organisation to be

51 Stuart Macdonald, 'The Role of the Courts in Imposing Terrorism Prevention and Investigation Measures: Normative Duality and Legal Realism' (2015) 9(2) *Criminal Law and Philosophy* 265.

52 Anderson, *Terrorism Prevention and Investigation Measures in 2013*, paras 6.16–6.18.

53 Joint Committee on Human Rights, *Legislative Scrutiny: Counter-Terrorism and Security Bill* (Fifth Report of Session 2014–15, The Stationery Office, 2015) paras 4.11–414.

54 HM Government, *The Government Response to the Report by David Anderson Q.C. on Terrorism Prevention and Investigation Measures in 2014* (Cm 9041, The Stationery Office, 2015).

55 For an overview of these processes, see David Anderson, *Third Report on the Operation of the Terrorist Asset-Freezing etc. Act 2010* (The Stationery Office, 2013) paras 3.10, 3.13.

56 TAFA, s. 26.

57 This was introduced on the recommendation of the Independent Reviewer. See Anderson, *Third Report on the Operation of the Terrorist Asset-Freezing etc. Act 2010* (n 55) para. 3.4.

58 Anderson, *Fourth Report on the Operation of the Terrorist Asset-Freezing etc. Act 2010*, para. 3.2.

de-proscribed.[59] If this application is unsuccessful, there then exists a right of appeal to the Proscribed Organisations Appeal Commission (POAC).[60] Whilst section 5(3) of the TA 2000 states that the principles of judicial review apply at such a hearing, the Court of Appeal has insisted that POAC should apply an intense level of scrutiny to the Home Secretary's decision to proscribe.[61] This mirrors the position in respect of TPIM review hearings (and, previously, Control Orders).[62] In contrast to both asset freezes and TPIMs, however, there is no longer annual review of decisions to proscribe: the Home Secretary will consider de-proscription on application only.[63] This is an 'unsatisfactory situation' not merely because of the cost involved in applying for de-proscription and the fact that proscription lasts indefinitely, but also because some currently proscribed organisations do not appear to meet the legal threshold for proscription since they cannot be said to be currently concerned in terrorism.[64] Indeed, a few may be moribund or even obsolete.

The third set of concerns regards the use of closed material proceedings. During both a TPIM review hearing and an appeal to POAC the court may exclude the individual and his legal representative from the proceedings if doing so is necessary to ensure that information is not disclosed contrary to the public interest.[65] This must now be read in the light of the decision in *Secretary of State for the Home Department v AF* (hereafter '*AF (No 3)*'), in which the House of Lords held that the individual must 'be given sufficient information about the allegations against him to enable him to give effective instructions in relation to those allegations'.[66] The scope of this minimum disclosure requirement has been determined on a case-by-case basis. Whilst the terms of the Control Order in *AF (No 3)* involved significant restrictions on liberty, the High Court held that the minimum disclosure requirement also applied to light-touch Control Orders.[67] It will presumably therefore be held to apply to all TPIM review hearings. The judgment in *AF (No 3)* thus alleviates some of the unease about the use of closed material proceedings in TPIM proceedings, though it remains to be seen whether it will also be held to apply to POAC proceedings and appeals against asset freezes.

59 TA 2000, s. 4.
60 Ibid. 2000, s. 5(2).
61 *Alton* (n. 27).
62 *Secretary of State for the Home Department v MB* [2006] EWCA Civ 1140, [2007] QB 415.
63 David Anderson, *The Terrorism Acts in 2013: Report of the Independent Reviewer on the Operation of the Terrorism Act 2000 and Part 1 of the Terrorism Act 2006* (The Stationery Office, 2014) para. 5.8.
64 David Anderson, *The Terrorism Acts in 2014: Report of the Independent Reviewer on the Operation of the Terrorism Act 2000 and Part 1 of the Terrorism Act 2006* (The Stationery Office, 2015) paras 4.11–4.13.
65 CPR 80.18(1); Proscribed Organisations Appeal Commission (Procedure) Rules 2007, r. 22(1).
66 [2009] UKHL 28, [2010] 2 AC 269, [59] (*per* Lord Phillips).
67 *Secretary of State for the Home Department v BC* [2009] EWHC 2927 (Admin), [2010] 1 WLR 1542.

During closed sessions the individual is represented by a Special Advocate (a practitioner with security clearance appointed by the Attorney General).[68] The Special Advocate may make submissions and cross examine witnesses on behalf of the individual.[69] A study of the relevant cases shows that judges have found the contribution of Special Advocates to be valuable and effective in the protection of the individuals whose interests they represent.[70] Yet the Special Advocates themselves have expressed misgivings about their role. Before the Special Advocate is shown the closed materials he may communicate freely with the individual and the individual's legal representative.[71] Once the Special Advocate has been served with the closed materials, the individual may still communicate with him (in writing and through his legal representative).[72] But the Special Advocate may no longer communicate with the individual, except in two circumstances: first, to acknowledge receipt (in writing) of any communication received from the individual;[73] and, second, following a successful application to the court for authorisation to communicate with the individual or his legal representative.[74] Before the court decides whether to grant authorisation, however, the Home Secretary must be notified of the request and given the opportunity to object.[75] The effect of this, according to evidence provided to the Joint Committee on Human Rights by a group of Special Advocates, was that

> the facility in the Rules to seek the Court's permission to consult with the controlled person was rarely used in practice, partly because such permission was unlikely to be forthcoming in practice if the purpose of the meeting was to discuss anything to do with the closed case, and partly because the Rules require any application for such permission to be served on the Secretary of State, which is not considered tactically desirable because of the risk that it might give away to the opposing party the parts of the closed evidence in relation to which the controlled person does not have an explanation.[76]

68 CPR 80.19; Proscribed Organisations Appeal Commission (Procedure) Rules 2007, r. 9(3).
69 CPR 80.20; Proscribed Organisations Appeal Commission (Procedure) Rules 2007, r. 9(5).
70 This is based on an examination of the relevant case files by one of the current co-authors (Lord Carlile).
71 CPR 80.21(1); Proscribed Organisations Appeal Commission (Procedure) Rules 2007, r. 10(1).
72 CPR 80.21(6)(a); Proscribed Organisations Appeal Commission (Procedure) Rules 2007, r. 10(6)(a).
73 CPR 80.21(6)(b); Proscribed Organisations Appeal Commission (Procedure) Rules 2007, r. 10(6)(b).
74 CPR 80.21(4); Proscribed Organisations Appeal Commission (Procedure) Rules 2007, r. 10(4).
75 CPR 80.21(5); Proscribed Organisations Appeal Commission (Procedure) Rules 2007, r. 10(5).
76 Joint Committee on Human Rights, *Counter-Terrorism Policy and Human Rights: 28 Days, Intercept and Post-Charge Questioning* (19th Report of Session 2006–07, The Stationery Office, 2007) para. 201.

Furthermore, even if permission was sought, 'it would be very likely to be refused because any question that it would assist the Special Advocates to ask is likely to be one from which part of the closed case could be inferred'.[77] It is this restriction on the ability to communicate with the individual that the Special Advocates themselves have described as 'the most significant restriction on the ability of [Special Advocates] to operate effectively'.[78] This – in addition to other concerns including lack of funding and access to justice, the lack of any practical ability to call evidence and the practice of iterative disclosure – led a group of 57 Special Advocates to state that closed materials proceedings 'are inherently unfair; they do not "work effectively", nor do they deliver real procedural fairness'.[79] Yet, following the Justice and Security Act 2013, closed material proceedings may now be employed not only in appeals under TAFA as well as POAC proceedings and TPIM review hearings, but in all civil proceedings.

The final set of concerns regards the proximity of the suspect to an actual act of terrorism. In his report on the operation of TPIMs during 2013, David Anderson drew attention to the fact that the definition of terrorism-related activity in TPIMA was broader than the one in TAFA, and questioned

> whether measures as strong as TPIMs need or ought to be available for use against a person whose connection with an act of terrorism could be as remote as the giving of support to someone who gives encouragement to someone who prepares an act of terrorism. That person is at three removes from terrorism – itself a concept that encompasses more than just politically-motivated violent acts.[80]

Whilst noting that TPIMs had not to that point been sought against 'peripheral figures', he pointed out that there might be a 'temptation to resort to the outer fringes of the [definition]', particularly in a case in which evidence of new terrorism-related activity needs to be found in order to justify issuing a new TPIM notice.[81] The Counter-Terrorism and Security Act 2015 accordingly narrowed the scope of the definition. The revised definition now encompasses: the commission, preparation or instigation of acts of terrorism; conduct that facilitates the commission, preparation or instigation of such acts (or that is intended to do so); conduct that gives encouragement to the commission, preparation or instigation of such acts (or that is intended to do so); and conduct that gives support or assistance to those who are known or believed by the suspect to be involved in the commission, preparation or instigation of acts of terrorism.[82] Some differences

77 Martin Chamberlain, 'Special Advocates and Procedural Fairness in Closed Proceedings' (2009) 28(3) *Civil Justice Quarterly* 314, 322.
78 *Justice and Security Green Paper: Response to Consultation from Special Advocates* (2011) para. 27.
79 Ibid. para. 15.
80 Anderson, *Terrorism Prevention and Investigation Measures in 2013* (n 13) para. 6.14.
81 Ibid. para. 6.15.
82 TPIMA, s. 4(1).

between TPIMA's revised definition of terrorism-related activity and the one used in TAFA do remain; in particular, the TAFA definition is still capable of encompassing individuals who are three steps removed from terrorist acts – such as someone [D1] who lends support to someone else [D2] who facilitates the instigation [by D3] of a terrorist act to be committed by someone else [D4].[83] A further difference is that TAFA's definition does not encompass conduct that gives encouragement to the commission, preparation or instigation of terrorist acts.

In contrast to both TPIMA and TAFA, the TA 2000 does not use the term terrorism-related activity. As explained above, it instead states that an organisation may be proscribed if it is 'concerned in terrorism'.[84] The definition of this term encompasses organisations that are committing, participating in, preparing for or are otherwise (actively) concerned in terrorism.[85] It also encompasses organisations that are promoting or encouraging terrorism, that is are one step removed from terrorist acts.[86] But, whilst it does not extend to organisations that are two or more steps removed, it is expansive in a different sense. Unlike TPIMA, the TA 2000's definition of encouragement mirrors the one used in the encouragement of terrorism offence,[87] and so includes the glorification of (past, present or future) terrorist acts.[88] As will be explained further below, the encouragement of terrorism offence has been criticised.[89] The nebulosity of the concept of glorification in particular gives both the encouragement of terrorism offence and the preconditions for proscription an uncertain and over-inclusive ambit.

Disruption by prosecution: terrorism precursor offences

The criminal law has a preventative, as well as a punitive, function.[90] As Husak states, 'Statutes designed to prevent future harm are neither unusual nor deviant'.[91] In addition to the well-known inchoate offences of attempt,[92] conspiracy[93]

83 TAFA, s. 2(2).
84 TA 2000, s. 3(4).
85 TA 2000, ss. 3(5)(a), (b), (d); *Alton* (n. 27).
86 Ibid. s. 3(5)(c).
87 TA 2006, s. 1.
88 TA 2000, ss. 3(5A)–(5C).
89 John Burton (2008) 37 *Index on Censorship* 115; James Edwards, 'Justice Denied: The Criminal Law and the Ouster of the Courts' (2010) 30 *Oxford Journal of Legal Studies* 725; Sterling A. Marchand 'An Ambiguous Response to a Real Threat: Criminalizing the Glorification of Terrorism in Britain' (2010) 42 *George Washington International Law Review* 123.
90 R.A. Duff, *Criminal Attempts* (Clarendon Press, 1996); Andrew Ashworth and Lucia Zedner, 'Prevention and Criminalization: Justifications and Limits' (2012) 15 *New Criminal Law Review* 542.
91 Douglas Husak, 'Preventive Detention as Punishment? Some Potential Obstacles' in Andrew Ashworth, Lucia Zedner and Patrick Tomlin (eds), *Prevention and the Limits of the Criminal Law* (Oxford University Press, 2013) 185.
92 Criminal Attempts Act 1981, s, 1.
93 Criminal Law Act 1977, s, 1.

and encouraging/assisting crime,[94] there are a number of offences that penalise conduct that creates a risk of harm (such as speeding, drunk-driving and dangerous driving) as well as what Ashworth and Zedner describe as 'substantive offences defined in the inchoate mode'.[95] Alongside these offences there exist a number of pre-inchoate – or precursor – offences. In the specific context of terrorism-related activity, the rationale of these precursor offences is twofold. The first is evidentiary. Offences such as conspiracy and encouraging crime are notoriously difficult to prove. Many terrorist groups observe good communications security, such that 'Clear, understandable exchanges that plainly inculpate those involved are very much the exception'.[96] And even if materials that have evidential value are available, there may be public interest reasons for not disclosing them in open court (such as not exposing other ongoing investigations or revealing agencies' capabilities[97]) and/or the UK's self-imposed ban on the use of intercept as evidence in criminal trials may apply.[98] The second reason is temporal. The offence of attempt only applies if the defendant has performed an act that is 'more than merely preparatory' to commission of the planned full offence.[99] This test has been interpreted to mean that the defendant is not guilty of a criminal attempt until he 'embarks upon the crime proper'.[100] When responding to would-be terrorists, this is regarded as leaving it too late. It is necessary to intervene at an earlier stage: in the words of David Anderson, it is necessary to defend further up the field.[101]

There are a large number of different terrorism precursor offences, found predominantly in the 2000 and 2006 Terrorism Acts. These include: membership of a proscribed organisation;[102] inviting support for a proscribed organisation;[103] wearing the uniform of a proscribed organisation;[104] fund-raising for terrorist purposes;[105] use or possession of money or other property for terrorist purposes;[106] failure to disclose information which might be of material assistance in

94 Serious Crime Act 2007, ss, 44–46.
95 Andrew Ashworth and Lucia Zedner, 'Just Prevention: Preventive Rationales and the Limits of the Criminal Law' in R,A, Duff and Stuart P, Green (eds), *Philosophical Foundations of Criminal Law* (Oxford University Press, 2011) 284. One of the examples they offer is the offence of fraud by false representation (Fraud Act 2006, s. 2), which requires only that the defendant dishonestly made a false representation with the intention of making a gain or causing a loss. It is thus a conduct, not a result, crime since there is no requirement that anyone did in fact make a gain or suffer a loss.
96 *Privy Council Review of Intercept as Evidence* (Cm 7324, The Stationery Office, 2008) para. 52.
97 Ibid. para. 58.
98 HM Government, *Intercept as Evidence.*
99 Criminal Attempts Act 1981, s. 1.
100 *R v Gullefer* [1990] 1 WLR 1063, 1066.
101 David Anderson, 'Shielding the Compass: How to Fight Terrorism Without Defeating the Law' [2013] *European Human Rights Law Review* 233, 237.
102 TA 2000, s. 11.
103 Ibid. s. 12.
104 Ibid. s. 13.
105 Ibid. s. 15.
106 Ibid. s. 16.

preventing a terrorist act;[107] directing the activities of a terrorist organisation;[108] possession of an article for terrorist purposes;[109] collection of information or possession of a document likely to be useful to a terrorist;[110] encouragement of terrorism;[111] dissemination of terrorist publications;[112] preparation of terrorist acts;[113] training for terrorism;[114] and attendance at a place used for terrorist training.[115] A number of criticisms have been levelled at this wide range of offences, including: their often broad and ambiguous wording; the potential they create for intrusive and discriminatory methods of investigation; the severity of the accompanying sentencing powers; the level of overlap between the offences and whether all the offences are actually necessary; and the lack of evidence to support the empirical assumption that the offences have a preventative effect.[116] Our aim, however, is not to argue that terrorism precursor offences should be rejected. As explained above, this stratum of offences is necessary, though it is essential that its scope is carefully justified and circumscribed.[117] Rather, our aim is to draw attention to the potentially self-defeating nature of terrorism precursor offences. This section will show that the criticisms of the non-criminal methods of disruption identified above – the very reasons why those methods are not the option of first resort – may also be applied to the terrorism precursor offences (as currently constituted). This inconsistency threatens to undermine both the rationale for

107 Ibid. s. 38B.
108 Ibid. s. 56.
109 Ibid. s. 57.
110 Ibid. s. 58.
111 TA 2006, s. 1.
112 Ibid. s. 2.
113 Ibid. s. 5.
114 Ibid. s. 6.
115 Ibid. s. 8.
116 Lord Carlile QC and Stuart Macdonald, 'The Criminalisation of Terrorists' Online Preparatory Acts' in Thomas M Chen, Lee Jarvis and Stuart Macdonald (eds), *Cyberterrorism: Understanding, Assessment, and Response* (Springer, 2014); Ian Leader-Elliott, 'Framing Preparatory Inchoate Offences in the Criminal Code: The Identity Crime Debacle' (2011) 35 *Criminal Law Journal* 80; Manuel Cancio Melia and Anneke Petzsche, 'Precursor Crimes of Terrorism' in Genevieve Lennon and Clive Walker (eds), *Routledge Handbook of Law and Terrorism* (Routledge, 2015); Kent Roach, 'The Criminal Law and Its Less Restrained Alternatives' in Victor V. Ramraj, Michael Hor, Kent Roach and George Williams (eds), *Global Anti-Terrorism Law and Policy* (2nd edn, Cambridge University Press, 2012); Clive Walker, *Terrorism and the Law* (Oxford University Press, 2011); Clive Walker, 'Terrorism Prosecution in the United Kingdom: Lessons in the Manipulation of Criminalisation and Due Process' in F. ni Aolain and O, Gross (eds), *Guantanamo and Beyond: Exceptional Courts and Military Commissions in Comparative and Policy Perspective* (Cambridge University Press, 2013).
117 Andrew Ashworth and Lucia Zedner, *Preventive Justice* (Oxford University Press, 2014); Peter Ramsay, 'Democratic Limits to Preventive Criminal Law' in Ashworth, Zedner and Tomlin (eds), *Prevention and the Limits of the Criminal Law*; A.P. Simester, 'Prophylactic Crimes' in G.R. Sullivan and Ian Dennis (eds), *Seeking Security: Pre-Empting the Commission of Criminal Harms* (Hart Publishing, 2012).

prosecution as the measure of first resort and the moral authority and legitimacy of the criminal law.

Whilst the criminal trial requires an individualised assessment of guilt, there are two respects in which terrorism precursor offences dilute the force of the requirement that the prosecution prove its case beyond reasonable doubt. First, some of these offences are intertwined with other, non-criminal methods of disruption, resulting in a degree of hybridity. For example, the offences of belonging to a proscribed organisation and making funds available to a designated person might equally be expressed as belonging to an organisation that the Home Secretary *reasonably believes* is concerned in terrorism and providing funds to a person that the Home Secretary *reasonably believes* (a) has been involved in terrorist activity, and (b) is someone against whom the public requires protection.[118] The civil law underpinning of these offences effectively means that some of the preconditions for a finding of criminal liability do not have to be established to the criminal standard. A similar point applies to the offence of breaching a TPIM notice.[119] Here the focus of the criminal trial will be whether it has been proven, beyond reasonable doubt, that the defendant violated his TPIM notice without reasonable excuse. The question whether the defendant is or has been involved in terrorism-related activity, which the Home Secretary determined was proven to the *civil standard* as part of the process for imposing the TPIM notice, will not be revisited. This use of orders made in civil law proceedings to justify the subsequent imposition of severe criminal penalties – a technique that has been adopted in a number of contexts[120] – led Ashworth to describe civil preventative orders like TPIMs as a 'Trojan horse'.[121]

Second, it is important to recognise that the content of substantive laws can undermine procedural rules in a more general sense.[122] When an offence is defined in very expansive terms, the probative burden that rests on the prosecution is diminished. Indeed, the *actus reus* of a number of precursor offences is defined so broadly that proving this part of the offence will inevitably be straightforward. For example, for the offence of use or possession of money or other property for terrorist purposes all that is required to establish the *actus reus* is that the defendant possessed money or other property.[123] Similarly, the *actus reus* of the offence of preparation of terrorist acts merely requires proof that the defendant engaged

118 TA 2000, s. 11; TAFA, s. 12.

119 TPIMA, s. 23.

120 A.P. Simester and A. von Hirsch, 'Regulating Offensive Conduct through Two-Step Prohibitions' in A. von Hirsch and A.P. Simester (eds), *Incivilities: Regulating Offensive Behaviour* (Hart Publishing, 2006).

121 Andrew Ashworth, 'Editorial: In Favour of Community Safety' [1997] *Criminal Law Review* 769, 770.

122 Victor Tadros, 'Justice and Terrorism' (2007) 10 *New Criminal Law Review* 658; Marianne Wade, 'Fighting Terrorism – the Unprincipled Approach: the UK, the War on Terror and Criminal Law' in Marianne Wade and Almir Maljevis (eds), *A War on Terror? The European Stance on a New Threat, Changing Laws and Human Rights Implications* (Springer, 2010).

123 TA 2000, s. 16(2).

'in any conduct'.[124] In these offences it is clear that the *mens rea* requirement will take centre stage – which gives rise not only to concerns about whether the *mens rea* of these offences is sufficiently stringent (whilst the latter offence requires proof of intention, the former requires only that the defendant had reasonable cause to suspect that the money/property may be used for the purposes of terrorism), but also the potentially invasive and discriminatory methods of investigation that might be employed in order to ascertain a defendant's thoughts in the absence of any overtly incriminating acts. A further example of how the substance of a law might undermine procedural rules is the offence of collection of information or possession of a document likely to be useful to a terrorist.[125] Even though the definition of this offence now has a narrower scope following the gloss added to it by the House of Lords in *R v G*, [126] it remains unnecessary to prove that the defendant had any terrorist purpose or connection.[127] The requirement of proof beyond reasonable doubt can have no bite if there is nothing to prove!

The second and third set of concerns about the non-criminal methods of disruption examined above focused on the limited role of the judiciary and the possibility of closed proceedings. Similar concerns have also been expressed about terrorism precursor offences, notwithstanding the fact that the trial of a defendant charged with such an offence will be held in a criminal court, before an independent judge, with no possibility of closed proceedings. As we have seen, the definitions of these offences are frequently over-inclusive, such that there is a discrepancy between the definition itself and the wrong that is in fact being targeted. The offence of encouragement of terrorism, for example, was targeted at extremists who promote a culture of hate, but is broad enough to also encompass North Korean exiles who criticise their native regime and those 'who express their ability to understand the actions of Palestinian suicide-bombers'.[128] Moreover, terrorism precursor offences cannot be regarded as analogous to offences such as speeding or possession of weapons – i.e. offences of necessitous over-inclusion – since unlike these offences precursor crimes do not seek to guide all citizens away from all of the conduct they encompass. Rather, only some of those who fall within the offence definition will be selected for prosecution. This selection will presumably be based largely on whether the individual in question is deemed to pose a threat to national security. But at trial the issue will be whether the requirements set out in the offence definition are satisfied. The national security considerations that led to the decision to prosecute will sit in the background. So 'Even though the pursuit of security is central to the justification for the law itself, it is not open to challenge by the defendant with respect to his particular case'.[129] For this reason Edwards labels the terrorism precursor offences 'ouster

124 TA 2006, s. 5(1).
125 TA 2000, s. 58.
126 *R v G* [2009] UKHL 13, [2010] 1 AC 43.
127 Jacqueline Hodgson and Victor Tadros, 'How to Make a Terrorist Out of Nothing' (2009) 72 *Modern Law Review* 984.
128 Edwards, 'Justice Denied', 730.
129 Tadros, 'Justice and Terrorism', 688.

offences',[130] since they deprive the trial court of the opportunity to adjudicate on the actions that the offences are targeting.

Lastly, terrorism precursor offences may encompass peripheral figures who are several steps removed from acts of terrorism.[131] Two features of these offences give them this expansive reach. First, a number of the precursor offences target not only would-be perpetrators of terrorists acts and accomplices who facilitate the acts of these would-be perpetrators. They also encompass those who facilitate the acts of accomplices. For example, the offence of encouragement of terrorism encompasses not only the individual (D1) who encourages another (D2) to commit an act of terrorism, but also the person (D1) who encourages another (D2) to instigate an act of terrorism to be committed by someone else (D3) and even the one (D1) who causes another (D2) to publish a statement that encourages another (D3) to instigate an act of terrorism to be committed by someone else (D4). So already the precursor offences may reach those who are up to three steps removed from an act of terrorism. Add to this the second feature, which is that many of the precursor offences can be committed in inchoate form (such as attempting to prepare an act of terrorism or conspiracy to provide training for terrorism) – and in some instances it may even be possible to place one layer of inchoate liability on top of another, so-called double inchoate liability – and at their most extreme the precursor offences may reach those up to five steps removed from a terrorist act![132] This gives them a significantly wider reach than the non-criminal methods of disruption outlined in the previous section.

Conclusion

The features of terrorism precursor offences that we have identified in this chapter create a danger of inappropriate convictions. Here, experience tells us that trial by jury is an important safeguard. For example, 29-year-old medical student Yousif Badri was found not guilty at Glasgow High Court of being involved in conduct with the intention of committing acts of terrorism. The case against him had been based on alleged contact with a terrorist organisation and possession of online materials and a tub of nails.[133] Also, 27-year-old Erol Incedal was convicted of possession of a five-page bomb-making manual but acquitted (following a retrial) on the more serious charge of plotting to mount a Mumbai-style attack on the streets of London.[134] And 18-year-old Waris Ali – who had been accused of

130 Edwards, 'Justice Denied', 732.

131 Macdonald, 'Prosecuting Suspected Terrorists'.

132 Stuart Macdonald, 'Cyberterrorism and Enemy Criminal Law' in Jens David Ohlin, Kevin Govern and Claire Finkelstein (eds), *Cyberwar: Law and Ethics for Virtual Conflicts* (Oxford University Press, 2015).

133 'Aberdeen Student Yousif Badri Cleared of Terror Charges', *BBC News*, 9 October 2015, www.bbc.co.uk/news/uk-scotland-north-east-orkney-shetland-34485501 (last accessed 9 July 2016).

134 Ian Cobain, 'Student Cleared of London Terror Charge after Partially Secret Trial', *Guardian* 26 March 2015, www.theguardian.com/uk-news/2015/mar/26/stu

possessing the *Anarchists' Cookbook* and researching bomb-making techniques online in order to blow up members of the British National Party – was acquitted of possessing an article for a terrorist purpose.[135] Moreover, in more general terms, it has to be remembered that, whilst generally faithful to judicial directions of law, juries have been known to use their verdicts to reject what they perceive as unfairness.[136] However, whilst the possibility of a jury returning a verdict of not guilty is a valuable safeguard, it is important to seek to ensure that those who are not guilty are not prosecuted wherever possible.

There have also been cases in which the appeal courts have demonstrated restraint, by limiting the overly broad interpretation of terrorism offences.[137] For example, the House of Lords used the interpretative obligation under the Human Rights Act 1998 to hold that a defendant pleading the section 11(2) defence on a charge of being a member of a proscribed organisation bears an evidential, not a persuasive, burden.[138] And in *R v G* the House of Lords narrowed the scope of the offence of collection of information or possession of a document likely to be useful to a terrorist, by refining the statute's statement of the offence's *actus reus* and reading into the offence two *mens rea* requirements (although the offence does still retain an overly broad ambit).[139] Examples such as these underscore the importance of legislative restraint when new offences are created. In particular, a high level of culpability should be required for terrorism precursor offences.[140]

dent-cleared-london-terror-secret-trial-erol-incedal-not-guilty (last accessed 9 July 2016).

135 'Teenage Bomb Plot Accused Cleared', *BBC News*, 23 October 2008, http://news.bbc.co.uk/1/hi/england/bradford/7685636.stm (last accessed 9 July 2016).

136 For example: 'Even when my conscience tells me the jury have made a mistake in acquitting the criminal, even then I am triumphant. Judge for yourselves, gentlemen; if the judges and the jury have more faith in *man* than in evidence, material proofs and speeches for the prosecution, is not that faith in *man* in itself higher than any ordinary considerations?' (Anton Chekhov, *The Head Gardener's Story* (Eldritch Press, 1894)).

137 Cf. the judgment of the Supreme Court of Victoria in *Benbrika* [2007–8] Annual Report Supreme Court of Victoria 49–50, in which it was held that the mere viewing of violent extremist online materials demonstrated preparation for terrorism because the resources were used to motivate, desensitise and train members of the allegedly terrorist group. See further Keiran Hardy, 'Violent Extremism Online and the Criminal Trial' in Anne Aly, Stuart Macdonald, Lee Jarvis and Thomas Chen (eds), *Violent Extremism Online: New Perspectives on Terrorism and the Internet* (Routledge, 2016).

138 *Re Attorney General's Reference (No. 4 of 2002)* [2004] UKHL 43, [2005] 1 AC 264.

139 *R v G* (n. 126); Hodgson and Tadros, 'How to Make a Terrorist Out of Nothing'.

140 Carlile and Macdonald, 'The Criminalisation of Terrorists' Online Preparatory Acts'. More specifically, a person should only be held criminally liable for acts they have done, on the basis of what they might have gone on to do in the future, if it can be shown that they intended to do those future acts; and a person should only be held criminally liable for acts they have done, on the basis of what a third party might have gone on to do in the future, if it can be shown that they had some normative involvement in those future acts (see Ashworth and Zedner, *Preventive Justice*; A.P. Simester, 'Prophylactic Crimes' in G.R. Sullivan and Ian Dennis (eds), *Seeking Security: Pre-Empting the Commission of Criminal Harms* (Hart Publishing, 2012).

Whilst offence definitions should be as clear and tightly drawn as possible, it is also important to recognise that it is not possible to neatly dichotomise rules and discretion. Discretion is heavily implicated in the interpretation and application of rules, and rules enter the exercise of discretion.[141] Indeed, as we have argued elsewhere, some proposed rewordings of terrorism precursor offences would be open to more than one possible interpretation, meaning that they might not only fail to narrow the scope of the offence in question but would also involve a sacrifice of legal certainty.[142] So in addition to encouraging greater legislative restraint, it is also necessary to harness the restraining power of extra-legal constraints. In particular, the discretion not to prosecute – vested in the Director of Public Prosecutions or, in some instances, the Attorney General – is a significant procedural protection. Yet at present the exercise of this discretion in the context of terrorism precursor offences is both unpredictable and ill-defined. Guidance should be published that seeks not only to clarify the ambit of individual offences, but also explain how choices should be made between offences in situations where they overlap (especially given the important implications this may have in terms of the maximum applicable sentence).

To conclude, this chapter has highlighted the tension between, on the one hand, the role that terrorism precursor offences play in disrupting terrorist activity and protecting the public and, on the other hand, the temptation to take disproportionate refuge in yet more broadly couched and ill-defined criminal offences. In seeking to resolve this tension, it is essential to be mindful of the reason why we prioritise prosecution in the first place and to endeavour to respect those features of the criminal law that give it its unique moral authority and legitimacy.

141 Denis Galligan, *Discretionary Powers* (Clarendon Press, 1986); Keith Hawkins, 'The Use of Legal Discretion: Perspectives from Law and Social Science' in Keith Hawkins (ed.), *The Uses of Discretion* (Clarendon Press, 1992).

142 Carlile and Macdonald, 'The Criminalisation of Terrorists' Online Preparatory Acts'.

7 Terrorism Law in Canada

Combatting terrorism through the defense of human rights

James C. Simeon

Introduction

The use of violence to advance any political cause is anathema in any liberal democratic society. Indeed, it is contrary to its core values and principles such as freedom of expression and conscience and consensus decision-making, which allows for open discussion and debate on all political issues and concerns and that the most persuasive arguments resolve the questions of the day, provided that they adhere to the rule of law and principles of fundamental justice. Terrorism, the deliberate and random denial of everyone's most fundamental human rights and human dignity, the right to life itself, can only be combatted effectively through the defense and advance of human rights and most effectively, likely, through criminal law and, ultimately, the judgments of the final courts of appeal, and in Canada, the Supreme Court of Canada (SCC).[1]

This chapter will first examine and analyze the manner in which the term terrorism is defined within the Canadian Criminal Code. This will be followed with an examination of some of the most recent and relevant jurisprudence on terrorism by the SCC. The main argument presented here is that the Canadian judiciary has played a crucial role in combatting terrorism through the protection of human rights. The SCC has carefully assessed the statutory provisions of the definition of terrorism and the various legal instruments established in the struggle against terrorism and weighed these against the most fundamental human rights found in the Canadian Charter of Rights and Freedoms[2] to ensure that they do not infringe on an accused's constitutionally entrenched human rights and freedoms. The chapter concludes by arguing that the prosecution of terrorism cases is one of the most effective counter-terrorism strategies available to states and that it is the role of the courts and, especially the SCC, to ensure that the Canadian government, the political executive, does not exceed its legal and constitutional authority and that human rights are upheld and protected to the utmost. Accordingly, the protection and the enhancement of fundamental human rights is absolutely crucial to the national security of any liberal democracy.

1 The Supreme Court of Canada's website is found at www.scc-csc.ca/.
2 Canadian Charter of Rights and Freedoms, Part I of the Constitution Act, 1982, being Schedule B to the Canada Act 1982 (UK), 1982, c. 11.

The Legal Definition of Terrorism in Canada

The current statutory definition of terrorism in Canada originated in the 2001 Anti-terrorism Act (ATA) which amended the Canadian Criminal Code, the Official Secrets Act, the Canada Evidence Act, the Proceeds of Crime (Money Laundering) Act, and other Acts, as well as enacting measures respecting the registration of charities, in an effort not only to counter terrorism but to eradicate it, if at all possible.[3] The Preamble of the ATA recognizes the following key elements with respect to the purposes of the law on terrorism that:

- acts of terrorism constitute a substantial threat to both domestic and international peace and security;
- acts of terrorism threaten Canada's political institutions, the stability of the economy and the general welfare of the nation;
- the challenge of eradicating terrorism, with its sophisticated and trans-border nature, requires enhanced international cooperation and a strengthening of Canada's capacity to suppress, investigate and incapacitate terrorist activity;
- the Parliament of Canada, recognizing that terrorism is a matter of national concern that affects the security of the nation, is committed to taking comprehensive measures to protect Canadians against terrorist activity while continuing to respect and promote the values reflected in, and the rights and freedoms guaranteed by, the Canadian Charter of Rights and Freedoms;
- these comprehensive measures must include legislation to prevent and suppress the financing, preparation, facilitation, and commission of acts of terrorism, as well as to protect the political, social, and economic security of Canada and Canada's relations with its allies.[4]

It should be noted that the ATA was amended in 2015 to include further changes to the Security of Canada Information Sharing Act, the Secure Air Travel Act, the Canadian Criminal Code, the Canadian Security Intelligence Service Act, and the Immigration and Refugee Protection Act.[5] The changes to the Criminal Code are especially relevant here. The amendments to the Criminal Code include creating an offense of knowingly advocating or promoting the commission of terrorism offenses.[6] It further authorizes a judge to order the seizure of terrorist propaganda and when the propaganda is in electronic form to order the deletion of the propaganda from a computer system.[7]

3 Anti-terrorism Act (S.C. 2001, c. 41), assented to December 18, 2001, http://laws-lois.justice.gc.ca/eng/acts/A-11.7/page-1.html. (accessed January 8, 2018).
4 Ibid.
5 Anti-terrorism Act, 2015 (S.C. 2015, c. 20), assented to June 18, 2015, http://laws-lois.justice.gc.ca/eng/AnnualStatutes/2015_20/page-1.html#docCont. (accessed January 11, 2018).
6 Ibid.
7 Ibid.

The legal definition of the crime of terrorism in Canada is found in the Canadian Criminal Code (R.S.C., 1985, c. C-46), Part II-1 – Terrorism, Section 83.01. The provisions laid out therein are quite extensive, covering everything from the definition of terrorism to the financing of terrorism, the freezing, seizing and restraint, and the forfeiture of property, to a hoax regarding terrorist activity, proceedings and aggravated punishment, investigative hearing, and recognizance and conditions.[8]

The legal definition of the crime of terrorism is broken down into two main parts: terrorist activity; and terrorist group. Terrorist activity contains three principal elements: offenses; the motivation; and, the intention. They include the following:

(a) an act or omission that is committed in or outside Canada and that, if committed in Canada, is one of the following offences:[9]

It then goes on to list the 13 functional Conventions and Protocols, negotiated under the auspices of the United Nations, against different types of terrorist acts.[10]

(b) an act or omission, in or outside Canada,

(i) that is committed

(A) in whole or in part for a political, religious or ideological purpose, objective or cause, and

(B) in whole or in part with the intention of intimidating the public, or a segment of the public, with regard to its security, including its economic security, or compelling a person, a government or a domestic or an international organization to do or to refrain from doing any act, whether the public or the person, government or organization is inside or outside Canada, and[11]

Section 83.01 (1)(b)(i)(A) and (B) are the motive clauses of the definition. The offenses listed 83.01 (1)(a) must be committed, in whole or in part, with either a "political, religious or ideological purpose, objective or cause" and it must, in whole or in part, be done with "the intention of intimidating the public or a segment of the public, with regard to its security or … [to compel] a person, a government or a domestic or an international organization to do or to refrain from doing any act" whether they are inside or outside Canada.

Intention incorporates the following elements of section 83.01 (1)(b):

8 Criminal Code (R.S.C., 1985, c. C-46), Part II-1-Terrorism, Section 83.01.

9 Ibid., section 83.01(1)

10 Ibid., 83.01(1)(a)(i)–(x). There are, in fact, 19 international instruments that have been negotiated under the auspices of the UN. See UN, United Nations Action to Counter Terrorism, International Legal Instruments, www.un.org/en/counter terrorism/legal-instruments.shtml (accessed April 26, 2017).

11 Criminal Code (R.S.C., 1985, c. C-46), Part II-1-Terrorism, Section 83.01(1).

(ii) that intentionally
(A) causes death or serious bodily harm to a person by the use of violence,
(B) endangers a person's life,
(C) causes a serious risk to the health or safety of the public or any segment of the public,
(D) causes substantial property damage, whether to public or private property, if causing such damage is likely to result in the conduct or harm referred to in any of clauses (A) to (C), or
(E) causes serious interference with or serious disruption of an essential service, facility or system, whether public or private, other than as a result of advocacy, protest, dissent or stoppage of work that is not intended to result in the conduct or harm referred to in any of clauses (A) to (C),[12]

Section 83.01 (1)(b) is qualified by the following condition:

> and includes a *conspiracy*, attempt or threat to commit any such act or omission, or *being an accessory after the fact* or *counselling* in relation to any such act or omission, but, for greater certainty, does not include an act or omission that is committed during an armed conflict and that, at the time and in the place of its commission, is in accordance with customary international law or conventional international law applicable to the conflict, or the activities undertaken by military forces of a state in the exercise of their official duties, to the extent that those activities are governed by other rules of international law. (*activité terroriste*)[13]

There are two important qualifications that are added to the definition of terrorist activity that includes all those who may be complicit in these types of acts or omissions. This also includes inchoate offences of which the crime of "conspiracy" is a prime example. But it excludes these types of acts or omissions during an armed conflict that is in accordance with customary or conventional international law or that are undertaken by military forces of a state in the exercise of their official duties.

The "terrorist group" part of the definition of the crime of terrorism has two elements to its meaning: (a) an entity that has as one of its purposes or activities facilitating or carrying out any terrorist activity; or (b) a listed entity.[14] The term "entity" is defined as: "***entity*** means a person, group, trust, partnership or fund or an unincorporated association or organization. (*entité*)."[15] And a "listed entity" is defined as: "***listed entity*** means an entity on a list established by the Governor in Council under section 83.05. (*entité inscrite*)."[16] The current list of some 53

12 Ibid.
13 Ibid. (emphasis added).
14 Ibid.
15 Ibid. (emphasis in the original).
16 Ibid.

entities is found at the Government of Canada, Public Safety Canada website.[17] It is also relevant and important to point out that even though it is not a crime to be a listed entity,

> [i]t is an offence to knowingly participate in or contribute to, directly or indirectly, any activity of a terrorist group. This participation is only an offence if its purpose is to enhance the ability of any terrorist group to facilitate or carry out a terrorist activity.[18]

Brief Summary of the Definition of Terrorism

The legal definition of the crime of terrorism in Canada appears to be detailed and thorough and incorporates two main parts, terrorist activity and terrorist group. It also incorporates what is commonly understood to constitute terrorism: an extremely violent politically motivated attack that is intended to incite fear in the society at large in order to influence, through intimidation, the policymakers to a particular course of action. The Canadian definition of the crime of terrorism incorporates international instruments directly in its definition and recognizes terrorist acts can be conducted within Canada or abroad. It also recognizes that in situations of armed conflict that involve the military of the state that is abiding by international law are excluded from the definition of terrorism. It is mindful of the fact that those who are complicit in terrorist activities and terrorist groups are criminally liable for their indirect participation in terrorism. Canada also maintains a list of "entities" that are involved in terrorist activities to help screen out all those who are involved in or support terrorist groups and/or organizations.

It has been noted that the legal definition of terrorism,

> Although broad in scope, or perhaps because of its breadth, the definition of terrorist activity includes certain saving provisions designed to ensure that activities related to lawful armed conflict under international law, advocacy, protest, dissent or work stoppage, or the mere expression of a political, ideological or religious belief, without more, will not be considered "terrorist activity."[19]

Canada, like other states, has its Listed Terrorist Entities or list of Foreign Terrorist Organizations or Proscribed Terrorist Organizations, as they are referred to

17 Government of Canada, Public Safety Canada, Currently listed entities, www.publicsafety.gc.ca/cnt/ntnl-scrt/cntr-trrrsm/lstd-ntts/crrnt-lstd-ntts-en.aspx (accessed April 16, 2017).

18 Government of Canada, Public Safety Canada, Listed Terrorist Entities, www.publicsafety.gc.ca/cnt/ntnl-scrt/cntr-trrrsm/lstd-ntts/index-en.aspx (accessed April 28, 2017).

19 Jennifer Wispinski, "The USA Patriot Act and Canada's Anti-Terrorism Act: Key Differences in Legislative Approach," The Library of Parliament, Parliamentary Information and Research Service, March 31, 2006, https://lop.parl.ca/content/lop/researchpublications/prb0583-e.htm (accessed January 8, 2018).

in other jurisdictions, that are used to screen out all those who directly or indirectly support or are affiliated in some way with terrorist organizations.

Canada, like the United States and other jurisdictions, has incorporated its definitions of terrorism directly within its Criminal Code.[20]

An Act Respecting National Security Matters, 2017

When the new Liberal government, under the leadership of Prime Minister Justin Trudeau, came into office, after its majority electoral victory on October 19, 2015,[21] it undertook an unprecedented consultation on national security,[22] as part of its election commitment to amend the problematic aspects of the 2015 Anti-terrorism Act.[23] The Minister of Public Safety and Emergency Preparedness, Ralph Goodale, introduced new legislation, Bill C-59, An Act respecting national security matters or the National Security Act, on June 20, 2017.[24] One of the central components of this legislation was to amend the Criminal Code in four main ways, such as:

- clarifying the scope of the Advocacy or Promotion of the Commission of a Terrorism Offence (Counselling);
- defining Terrorist Propaganda more clearly;
- increasing a threshold for a Recognizance with Conditions;
- requiring annual reporting on the number of Terrorism Peace Bonds entered into.[25]

20 In the United States, criminal jurisdiction is concurrent between the federal and state governments and, consequently, there are Criminal Codes for the federal governments and 50 state governments. There is one Criminal Code in Canada under the authority of the federal government.

21 Justin Trudeau, Prime Minister of Canada, https://pm.gc.ca/eng/prime-minister-justin-trudeau (accessed January 13, 2018).

22 Government of Canada, Consultation on National Security, www.canada.ca/en/services/defence/nationalsecurity/consultation-national-security.html (accessed January 13, 2018). The public consultation took place from September 8, 2016 to December 15, 2016. For the results of the consultation, see *National Security Consultations: What We Learned*, at Government of Canada, Public Safety Canada, Department of Public Safety and Emergency Preparedness, www.publicsafety.gc.ca/cnt/rsrcs/pblctns/2017-nsc-wwlr/index-en.aspx (accessed January 13, 2018).

23 Government of Canada, "Fulfilling Commitments to Address Former C-51," www.canada.ca/en/services/defence/nationalsecurity/our-security-our-rights/fulfilling-commitments-address-former-c51.html (accessed January 13, 2018).

24 Government of Canada, Department of Justice, National Security, www.justice.gc.ca/eng/cj-jp/ns-sn/index.html (accessed January 13, 2018); Kathleen Harris, "Liberals to Create 'Super' National Security Watchdog as Part of Anti-Terror Overhaul," *CBC News*, June 20, 2017, www.cbc.ca/news/politics/security-terrorism-legislation-1.4168780 (accessed January 13, 2018)

25 Government of Canada, "Fulfilling Commitments to Address Former C51,"www.canada.ca/en/services/defence/nationalsecurity/our-security-our-rights/fulfilling-commitments-address-former-c51.html (accessed January 13, 2018).

These four proposed amendments to the *2015* Anti-terrorism Act are the most germane to the Canadian definition of terrorism and ensuring that the current legislation does not infringe on the Canadian Charter of Rights and Freedoms and, furthermore, that it adheres to the objectives of achieving greater accountability and transparency in counterterrorism measures and the laws of terrorism in general. For instance, "terrorism propaganda" material is defined currently as "any writing, sign, visible representation or audio recording that advocates or promotes the commission of terrorism offences in general or counsels the commission of a terrorism offence."[26] This definition of "terrorist propaganda" has been criticized for being unclear by the May 2017 Report of the Standing Committee on Public Safety and National Security and others. Specifically, the phrase "advocates or promotes the commission of terrorism offences in general" is considered too broad and, with the 2017 National Security Act, will be clarified and revised with a clearer conception of what consists of the "counselling of terrorism offences."[27]

It is also relevant and important to point out that other statutes incorporate "terrorism" within their provisions. For example, the Immigration and Refugee Protection Act (IRPA),[28] at Division 4, Inadmissibility, Section 34, Security, states that,

34 (1) A permanent resident or a foreign national is inadmissible on security grounds for

- **(c)** engaging in terrorism;
- **(d)** being a danger to the security of Canada;
- **(e)** engaging in acts of violence that would or might endanger the lives or safety of persons in Canada; or
- **(f)** being a member of an organization that there are reasonable grounds to believe engages, has engaged or will engage in acts referred to in paragraph (a), (b), (b.1) or (c).

Persons are determined to be inadmissible to Canada on security grounds for "engaging in terrorism" or "engaging in acts of violence that … endanger the lives or safety of persons in Canada" or "being a member of an organization" that engages in terrorism. It is important to note that these provisions not only cover foreign nationals but Canadian permanent residents as well. It is also interesting to point out that while it might not be illegal to be a member of a Listed Terrorist Entity it is, however, a crime to "knowingly participate in or contribute to, directly

26 Criminal Code (R.S.C., 1985, c. C-46), Act current to December 11, 2017 and last amended on October 18, 2018. Section 83.222(3), http://lois-laws.justice.gc.ca/eng/acts/C-46/page-16.html#docCont (accessed January 14, 2018).

27 Government of Canada, "Fulfilling Commitments to Address so Former C-51,"www.canada.ca/en/services/defence/nationalsecurity/our-security-our-rights/fulfilling-commitments-address-former-c51.html (accessed January 13, 2018).

28 Immigration and Refugee Protection Act (S.C. 2001, c. 27), Act current to December 11, 2017 and last amended on October 18, 2017,. http://laws.justice.gc.ca/eng/acts/i-2.5/page-18.html#h-52 (accessed January 13, 2018).

or indirectly, any activity of a terrorist group."[29] What is contentious is whether mere membership in such an organization is sufficient to constitute knowingly participating in or contributing to, directly or indirectly, "any activity of a terrorist group"? However, by virtue of IRPA, s. 34(1)(f), mere membership in a terrorist organization would make a person inadmissible to Canada whether they are a permanent resident or foreign national.

Under Part 2 of IRPA, Refugee Protection, Division 1, Refugee Protection, Convention Refugees and Persons in Need of Protection, Section 98, Exclusion – Refugee Protection, it states:

98. A person referred to in section E or F of Article 1 of the Refugee Convention is not a Convention refugee or a person in need of protection.[30]

For the purposes of exclusion from refugee protection with respect to serious criminality what is most relevant is Article 1F. The 1951 Convention relating to the Status of Refugees does not allow for Convention refugee status from more than one country, as evident from Article 1E. Those who are "engaged in terrorism" either directly or indirect, that is, for being complicit in terrorist activities, can be excluded from refugee protection in Canada.

Some Leading Jurisprudence on Terrorism in Canada

This part of the chapter will analyze some of the recent leading jurisprudence on terrorism in Canada. It will examine how the SCC has used applied and interpreted the Canadian Charter of Rights and Freedoms in the protection of fundamental rights and freedoms to the statutes that define terrorism and, hence, advance the protection of national security.

29 Government of Canada, Public Safety Canada, "Listed Terrorist Entities," www.publicsafety.gc.ca/cnt/ntnl-scrt/cntr-trrrsm/lstd-ntts/index-en.aspx (accessed January 27, 2018).

30 Immigration and Refugee Protection Act (S.C. 2001, c. 27), Act current to December 11, 2017 and last amended on October 18, 2017, http://laws.justice.gc.ca/eng/acts/i-2.5/page-18.html#h-52 (accessed January 13, 2018), Article 1E and 1F of the *1951 Convention relating to the Status of Refugees* state: E. This Convention shall not apply to a person who is recognized by the competent authorities of the country in which he has taken residence as having the rights and obligations which are attached to the possession of the nationality of that country. F. The provisions of this Convention shall not apply to any person with respect to whom there are serious reasons for considering that:

(a) he has committed a crime against peace, a war crime, or a crime against humanity, as defined in the international instruments drawn up to make provision in respect of such crimes;
(b) he has committed a serious non-political crime outside the country of refuge prior to his admission to that country as a refugee;
(c) he has been guilty of acts contrary to the purposes and principles of the United Nations.

Suresh v. Canada (Minister of Citizenship and Immigration)

Manickavasagam Suresh, a Sri Lankan Tamil, arrived in Canada in 1990 and was recognized as a Convention refugee in 1991.[31] In 1995 he was detained by the authorities on the grounds that he was a fundraiser and member of the Liberation Tigers of Tamil Eelam (LTTE), an organization known to be engaged in terrorist activities. The government started proceedings to deport him and he challenged the order for his deportation on various grounds of substance and procedure.

The Supreme Court of Canada laid out the issues in the following manner:

> On the one hand stands the manifest evil of terrorism and the random and arbitrary taking of innocent lives, rippling out in an ever-widening spiral of loss and fear. Governments, expressing the will of the governed, need the legal tools to effectively meet this challenge.
>
> On the other hand stands the need to ensure that those legal tools do not undermine values that are fundamental to our democratic society—liberty, the rule of law, and the principles of fundamental justice—values that lie at the heart of the Canadian constitutional order and the international instruments that Canada has signed. In the end, it would be a Pyrrhic victory if terrorism were defeated at the cost of sacrificing our commitment to those values. *Parliament's challenge is to draft laws that effectively combat terrorism and conform to the requirements of our Constitution and our international commitments.* [32]

The Solicitor General and the Minister of Citizenship and Immigration filed a certificate under section 40.1 of the Immigration Act alleging that Suresh was inadmissible to Canada on security grounds.[33] The section 40.1 certificate was based on the opinion of the Canadian Security Intelligence Service (CSIS) that Suresh is a member of LTTE, which is engaged in terrorist activity in Sri Lanka, and operates in Canada under the auspices of the "World Tamil Movement" (WTM).[34]

A Federal Court judge upheld the section 40.1 certificate finding it to be "reasonable" under section 40.1(4)(d) of the Act.[35] The findings of the Federal Court judge are relevant to the case:

> (1) Suresh had been a member of the LTTE since his youth and is now (or was at the time of Teitelbaum J.'s consideration) a member of the LTTE executive; (2) the WTM is part of the LTTE or at least an organization that supports the activities of the LTTE; (3) Suresh obtained refugee status "by

31 *Suresh v. Canada (Minister of Citizenship and Immigration)*, [2002] 1 S.C.R. 3, 2002 SCC 1, para 1.
32 Ibid., paras 3–4 (emphasis added).
33 Ibid., para. 9.
34 Ibid., para. 10.
35 Ibid., para. 12.

willful misrepresentation of facts" and lacks credibility; (4) there are reasonable grounds to believe the LTTE has committed terrorist acts; and (5) Tamils arrested by Sri Lankan authorities are badly mistreated and in a number of cases the mistreatment bordered on torture.[36]

On September 17, 1997, the Minister notified Suresh that she was considering issuing an opinion that would declare him a danger to Canada under section 53(1)(b) of the Act. This section allows the Minister to deport a refugee on security grounds even where a refugee's "life or freedom" would be threatened upon return.[37] On January 6, 1998, the Minister issued an opinion that Suresh constituted a danger to the security of Canada and should be deported pursuit to section 53(1)(b). He was not given a copy of the Immigration Officer's, Citizenship and Immigration Canada, memorandum nor was he given an opportunity to respond either orally or in writing.[38] No reasons for the opinion were required under section 53(1)(b) and none were provided.[39]

Suresh appealed the Minister's danger opinion at the Federal Court arguing that it was unreasonable and unfair because the procedures under the Act did not require an oral hearing before an independent decision-maker. Moreover, the Act was unconstitutional because it violated sections 7 and 2 of the Canadian Charter of Rights and Freedoms.[40] The Federal Court denied the appeal on all grounds.

Suresh then appealed to the Federal Court of Appeal and his application was again dismissed. Justice Robertson, for the Federal Court of Appeal, held that the right under international law to be free from torture was limited by the country's right to expel those who posed a security risk.[41] He further held that the 1951 Convention relating to the Status of Refugees permits the derogation from the prohibition against deportation to torture and he also held that Canadian statutory law supersede customary international law.[42] In essence, the Federal Court of Appeal upheld the Federal Court's judgment confirming that fundraising to support terrorist violence was not protected under section 2 of the Canadian Charter of Rights and Freedoms and that the provisions of the Immigration Act did not infringe on the constitution and that an oral hearing was not required to assess the risk of torture upon deportation or that the terms "danger to the security of Canada" and "terrorism" were unconstitutionally vague. The Federal Court of Appeal rejected Suresh's argument that section 53(1)(b) of the Act was unconstitutional because it permitted the Minister to expel a refugee to torture. The Court held that while deportation to torture did violate section 7 the right to life, liberty, and security of the person of the Charter, the violation was justified under section 1.

36 Ibid., para. 13.
37 Ibid., para. 15.
38 Ibid., para. 16.
39 Ibid.
40 Ibid., para. 17.
41 Ibid., para. 20.
42 Ibid.

> The objective of preventing Canada from becoming a haven for terrorist organizations was pressing and substantial and the deportation provision was a proportionate response to that objective bearing in mind the limitations on the power of deportation, its use as a measure of last resort and Canada's international obligations to combat terrorism. Expulsion of a refugee who is a danger to the security of Canada would not violate the sense of justice or "shock the conscience" of most Canadians, notwithstanding that the refugee might face torture on return, because Canada would be neither the first nor the last link in the chain of causation leading to torture, but merely an involuntary intermediary.[43]

The alternative other argument was also rejected that, if constitutional, section 53(1)(b) would be in violation of Suresh's section 7 right to security in its application. The administrative decision to deport Suresh properly considered the risk that he posed to Canada and his risk of torture upon return to Sri Lanka, duly noted any mitigating factors, and concluded on balance that it was outweighed by Canada's interest in its security.[44]

In the Supreme Court's analysis, the first question that must be considered is what standard should be adopted with respect to the Minister's decision that a refugee constitutes a danger to the security of Canada.[45] The Court agreed with the Federal Court of Appeal that a deferential approach should be applied to this question. This conclusion is mandated by *Pushpanathan v. Canada (Minister of Citizenship and Immigration)*, [1998] 1 S.C.R. 982, which considers the language of the Act that the Minister must be "of the opinion" that the person constitutes a danger to the security of Canada.[46] The four factors to be considered are: (1) the presence or absence of a clause negating the right of appeal; (2) the relative expertise of the decision-maker; (3) the purpose of the provision and the legislation generally; and (4) the nature of the question.[47] The Court ruled that these factors suggest that Parliament wanted to grant the Minister a broad discretion in issuing a section 53(1)(b) opinion, reviewable only when the Minister makes a patently unreasonable decision.[48]

The principles of fundamental justice are determined by a contextual approach that takes into consideration the nature of the decision to be made.[49] It is one of essentially balancing and as the Court stated in *United States v. Burns, [2001] 1 S. C.R. 283, 2001 SCC 7*, it is inherent in the "balancing process that the outcome may well vary from case to case depending on the mix of contextual factors put in the balance."[50] Deportation to torture requires a careful consideration of a wide

43 Ibid., para. 21.
44 Ibid., para. 22.
45 Ibid., para. 29.
46 Ibid., para. 30.
47 Ibid.
48 Ibid., para. 32.
49 Ibid., para. 45.
50 Ibid.

set of factors and the resulting balance struck will be dependent, at least in part, on the personal situation and circumstances of the potential deportee, the general circumstances, including the danger the potential deportee poses to Canadians and the security of Canada, and the threat of terrorism in Canada.[51] The balance struck will vary on a case-by-case basis.

The Court further notes that determining whether deportation to torture violates the principles of fundamental justice requires balancing Canada's interest in combatting terrorism and the Convention refugee's interest in not being deported to torture.[52] "Canada has a legitimate and compelling interest in combatting terrorism. But, it is also committed to fundamental justice."[53] A key principle of the constitution is "proportionality" and, accordingly, what the Court needs to decide is whether the government's response is reasonable to the threat posed.[54]

The principles of fundamental justice are found in Canadian experience and jurisprudence as well as international law, including, *jus cogens*.[55] From the Canadian experience vantage point, the Court noted that a number of phrases have been used to describe conduct that would violate the principles of fundamental justice. The most frequently used phrase is conduct that would "shock the Canadian conscience."[56] In other words, would it be contrary to Canadian values and notions of fair practice and justice?[57]

The Supreme Court further states that Canadians do not accept that torture is either fair or compatible with justice. Indeed, it notes that, "Torture has as its end the denial of a person's humanity; this end is outside the legitimate domain of a criminal justice system: see, generally, E. Scarry, *The Body in Pain: The Making and Unmaking of the World* (1985), at pp. 27–59. Torture is an instrument of terror and not of justice."[58] The Court concludes that torture is seen in Canada as fundamentally unjust.[59] And it points out that Canadian jurisprudence suggests that the balance will come down to not expelling the person to face torture elsewhere.[60]

As to the international perspective the Court states, "A complete understanding of the Act and the Charter requires consideration of the international perspective."[61] However, the Court also acknowledges that treaty norms are not binding in Canada unless they have been incorporated in Canadian legislation. The Court, however, looks to international law not to discern Canada's binding legal obligations but, rather, to discern the principles of fundamental justice.[62] After a

51 Ibid.
52 Ibid., para. 47.
53 Ibid.
54 Ibid.
55 Ibid., para. 46.
56 Ibid., para. 49.
57 Ibid.
58 Ibid., para. 51.
59 Ibid.
60 Ibid., para. 58.
61 Ibid., para. 59.
62 Ibid., para. 60.

thorough review of the relevant international instruments the Court concludes that "international law rejects deportation to torture, even when national security interests are at stake."[63] Hence, "barring extraordinary circumstances, deportation to torture will generally violate the principles of fundamental justice protected by section 7 of the Charter."[64]

The central concern, according to the Court, is not the legislation, section 53 (1)(b), that permits deportation to torture, and which the Court ruled was not in violation of section 7 of the Charter, but the Minister's obligation to exercise the discretion section 53(1)(b) in a constitutional manner.[65]

Suresh asserted that the phrase "danger to the security of Canada" was unconstitutional because it was vague. The Court ruled that it was not constitutionally vague. The Court ruled that "danger to the security of Canada" is not constitutionally vague and that a fair, large, and liberal interpretation, in accordance with international norms, be accorded to "danger to the security of Canada" in deportation legislation.[66] However, returning a refugee to torture under section 53(1)(b) of the Act, the Court noted, requires evidence of a serious threat to national security. "To suggest that something less than serious threats founded on evidence would suffice to deport a refugee to torture would be to condone unconstitutional application of the Immigration Act."[67] The Court states that the threat must be "serious" in the sense that it should be grounded in "objectively reasonable suspicion based on evidence and in the sense that the threatened harm must be substantial rather than negligible."[68]

Regarding the term "terrorism" found in section 19 of the Immigration Act, the Court ruled that the term provides a sufficient basis for adjudication and, hence, is not unconstitutionally vague.[69] The Court acknowledged that the term "terrorism" is notoriously difficult to define and that they would not endeavor to do so in this decision.[70] Nonetheless, the Court does conclude that even though the term is unsettled this does not mean that they cannot set the proper boundaries of legal adjudication.[71] The Court considers the International Convention for the Suppression of the Financing of Terrorism, GA Res. 54/109, December 9, 1999, that approaches the definitional problem in two ways to be suitable for the task: first, through a functional definition under Article 2(1)(a) that utilizes the definitions of terrorism that is found in nine treaties that cover a range of terrorist activities such as aircraft hijackings, terrorist bombings, and so on; and, second, it supplements the offense-based list with a stipulative definition of terrorism found in Article 2(1)(b).[72]

63 Ibid., para. 75.
64 Ibid., para. 76.
65 Ibid., para. 79.
66 Ibid., para. 85.
67 Ibid., para. 89.
68 Ibid., para. 90.
69 Ibid., para. 93.
70 Ibid.
71 Ibid., para. 96.
72 Ibid.

> Any … act intended to cause death or serious bodily injury to a civilian, or to any other person not taking an active part in the hostilities in a situation of armed conflict, when the purpose of such act, by its nature or context, is to intimidate a population, or to compel a government or an international organization to do or to abstain from doing any act.[73]

The Court argues that this definition catches the essence of what the world understands to be terrorism.[74] It is concluded that this definition is sufficiently certain under the Immigration Act to be workable, fair, and constitutional.[75]

Suresh argued that section 40.1, the Minister's certificate, under the Immigration Act and the order declaring him a "danger to the security of Canada," under section 53(1)(b), on the grounds that he was a member of the LTTE violated his Charter rights to freedom of expression and freedom of association.[76] He argued that he was being deported for being a member of an organization that a Canadian citizen may lawfully join without sanction, and that he was not involved in any terrorist activities in Canada but merely fundraising.[77] He also contended that his membership of the LTTE, which has been or will be involved in terrorism, unjustifiably limits the freedom of Convention refugees to express their views on dissident movements outside the country as well as their freedom of association with other people inside Canada.[78] However, it is established law that section 2 of the Canadian Charter of Rights and Freedoms does not protect expressive or associational activities that constitute violence.[79]

On the point of either contributing to or membership of a terrorist organization the Court makes a distinction between those who would innocently contribute to or become members of a terrorist organization and those who would willing do so. The Court states that section 19 of the Act exempts "persons who have satisfied the Minister that their admission would not be detrimental to the national interest."[80] This allows the person that is a member of a terrorist organization to establish that they will not be detrimental to Canada and their association with this organization was innocent. Thus, the Court concludes that Suresh's section two Charter rights have not been infringed.

Suresh's final argument was that the process that the Minister used to assess his risk to torture, should he be returned to Sri Lanka, were flawed and violated his constitutional rights by exposing him to a risk of torture.[81] This requires an assessment of the procedural protections that the person is entitled to under section 7 of the Charter. These were outlined by Justice L'Heureux-Dubé in *Baker*.

73 Ibid.
74 Ibid., para. 98.
75 Ibid.
76 Ibid., para. 100.
77 Ibid.
78 Ibid.
79 Ibid., para. 107.
80 Ibid., para. 110.
81 Ibid., para. 112.

The Court outlined what procedural protections must be provided that included the consideration of the following factors:

> (1) the nature of the decision made and to meet the duty of fairness: the procedures followed in making it, that is, "the closeness of the administrative process to the judicial process"; (2) the role of the particular decision within the statutory scheme; (3) the importance of the decision to the individual affected; (4) the legitimate expectations of the person challenging the decision where undertakings were made concerning the procedure to be followed; and (5) the choice of procedure made by the agency itself: *Baker*, supra, at paras. 23–27. This is not to say that other factors or considerations may not be involved.[82]

Looking at the statutory scheme, the Court concludes that given its nature it suggests that strong procedural safeguards are required. The Court observes that the procedural safeguards for section 40.1 of the Immigration Act are quite extensive and are designed to help ensure that the Minister's danger certificates are issued fairly and allow for the meaningful participation of the person involved.[83] However, there are no procedural safeguards under section 53(1)(b): no provision for a hearing; no requirement for oral or written reasons; and, no right to appeal.[84]

The Court draws on *Baker* to state that when there is no appeal mechanism and the decision is determinative of the issue then greater procedural safeguards are required.[85] Another factor that must be considered is the right affected. In this instance, the appellant is a Convention refugee and the risk of torture that he will likely face upon return to Sri Lanka, given his membership in the LTTE.[86] "[The principle being] The greater the effect on the life of the individual by the decision, the greater the need for procedural protections to meet the common law duty of fairness and the requirements of fundamental justice under s. 7 of the *Charter*."[87] Given a person who is subject to a section 53(1)(b) opinion may be subjected to torture then the procedural safeguards must be higher. The Court finds that given the government is bound by the 1984 Convention Against Torture, and Other Cruel, Inhuman or Degrading Treatment and Punishment (CAT), it is only reasonable to expect that they would be bound by the provisions of this Convention that the appellant had a right to procedural safeguards.[88] The Court concludes that the choice of procedures under section 53(1)(b) is up to the Minister to decide, but, the principle of the higher the risk to the appellant the stronger the procedural safeguards need to be followed. Accordingly, the Court rules that

82 Ibid., para. 115.
83 Ibid., para. 117.
84 Ibid.
85 Ibid.
86 Ibid., para. 118.
87 Ibid.
88 Ibid., para. 119.

given the procedural protections that are required under section 7 of the Charter, this does not require the Minister to provide for a full hearing or a complete judicial process.[89] However, what is required is more than is provided under the Act for section 53(1)(b) which is none and more than Suresh received. Accordingly, a person facing deportation to torture under section 53(1)(b) "must be informed of the case to be met."[90] This includes full disclosure of documents, save those that entail confidential public security, which implies all materials that the Minister bases his decision on, including the Immigration Officer's memorandum to the Minister.[91]

> Fundamental justice requires that written submissions be accepted from the subject of the order after the subject has been provided with an opportunity to examine the material being used against him or her. The Minister must then consider these submissions along with the submissions made by the Minister's staff.[92]

In addition, when the Minister is relying on the written assurances of a foreign government that a person would not be tortured then the appellant must have an opportunity to present evidence and to make submissions as to the value of those assurances.[93] The Court stipulated that written reasons must be provided for his decision and that the reasons must rationally sustain a finding that there is no substantial ground to believe that the person subject to a section 53(1)(b) declaration will be subjected to torture, execution, or other unusual treatment or punishment. The reasons must also articulate why the Minister has come to the conclusion that the person is a "danger to the security of Canada" as required under the Act.[94] All that would be required on the part of the appellant is to make out a *prima facie* case that there may be a risk of torture upon deportation.[95] Moreover, the Court ruled that section 1 of the Charter does not save the procedural deficiencies of section 53(1)(b) necessary compliance with the requirements of section 7 of the Charter.

As a consequence, the Court ruled that since Suresh made a *prima facie* case that he would face torture upon his return to Sri Lanka, then, he should have been provided the section 7 Charter rights not to be expelled to torture. Hence, the Court remanded the case to the Minister for reconsideration in accordance with the reasons presented in their judgment.[96]

89 Ibid., para. 121.
90 Ibid., para. 122.
91 Ibid.
92 Ibid.
93 Ibid. para. 123.
94 Ibid., para. 126.
95 Ibid., para. 127.
96 Ibid., para. 130.

Application under s. 83.28 of the Criminal Code (Re)

In *Application under s. 83.28 of the Criminal Code (Re)* the Supreme Court of Canada considered the constitutionality of the Investigative Hearing, s. 83.28 of the Canadian Criminal Code.[97] This case is a companion to *Vancouver Sun (Re)*, [2004] 2 S.C.R. 332, 2004 SCC 43 (the "media appeal"), that was released concurrently with *Application under s. 83.28 of the Criminal Code (Re)*. [98] This was the first case in which the Supreme Court of Canada had to address the constitutional validity of the Anti-terrorism Act 2001. It is important to point out that the Anti-terrorism Act 2001 was a legislative response to the 9/11 terrorist attacks in the United States and similar legislative responses that took place in the United States, United Kingdom, and in other countries.[99]

The subject of this appeal dealt with the invocation of s. 83.29 Criminal Code provisions for conducting an "Investigative Hearing" relating to alleged acts of terrorism that took place on June 23, 1985. One was an explosion at Narita Airport in Japan that killed two baggage handlers and injured four others while baggage was being transferred to Air India Flight 301. The other was a second explosion that took place less than one hour later on board Air India Flight 182 that crashed off the west coast of Ireland that killed all 329 passengers and crew. These terrorist attacks were among the most deadly terrorist incidents in modern history and the Air India bombing was the worst terrorist attack involving an aircraft on record until the coordinated attacks that took place in the United States on September 11, 2001.[100]

On May 6, 2003, the Crown brought an *ex parte* application that the appellant attend an Investigative Hearings pursuant to s. 83.28 of the Criminal Code. The British Columbia Supreme Court granted the application and issued an order to gather information on the basis of an affidavit by a member of the RCMP Air India Task Force.[101] The appellant sought leave to challenge the constitutional validity of s. 83.28 of the Criminal Code.

The application to set aside the order was dismissed, and Holmes J. issued reasons on July 21, 2003. However, the judicial Investigative Hearing was adjourned

97 *Application under s. 83.28 of the Criminal Code (Re)* 2004 SCC 42.
98 Ibid., para. 1.
99 Ibid., para. 2.
100 Kent Roach, "The Air India Report and the Regulation of Charities and Terrorism Financing," *University of Toronto Law Journal* (2011), Vol. 61, No. 3, pp. 418–422, wherein it states at p.418: "Until 11 September 2001, the Air India bombings were the world's most deadly act of aviation terrorism." See also World Atlas, World Facts, "Worst Terrorist Attacks in World History," www.worldatlas.com/articles/worst-terrorist-attacks-in-history.html (accessed March 22, 2017); Worst Terrorist Strikes – Worldwide, compiled by Wm. Robert Johnston, updated January 2, 2017, www.johnstonsarchive.net/terrorism/wrjp255i.html (accessed March 22, 2017); Top 5 of Anything, The Top 5 Deadliest Terrorist Attacks in Modern History, https://top5ofanything.com/list/317e8f79/Deadliest-Terrorist-Attacks-in-Modern-History. (accessed March 22, 2017).
101 *Application under s. 83.28 of the Criminal Code (Re)* 2004 SCC 42., p. 262, para. 15.

pending leave to the SCC.[102] On August 11, 2003, leave to appeal was granted by the SCC and the case was heard on December 10 and 11, 2003.[103] The judicial Investigative Hearing was conducted in relation to terrorism offenses related to the two Air India explosions.[104]

The Supreme Court considered five constitutional questions related to s. 83.28 and an additional three other issues related to the conduct of the Investigative Hearing.[105] It began its analysis by considering the purpose of legislation and came to the conclusion that it is the "prosecution and prevention of terrorist offenses."[106] The SCC goes on to note that,

> At its core, s. 83.28 permits the investigation of terrorism offences, at both a pre- and post-charge stage through testimonial compulsion on the part of the named witness. Consequently, the purpose of the provision is to confer greater investigative powers upon the state in its investigation of terrorism offences.[107]

The Court identified two ambiguities in the legislation: the first dealt with the role of counsel; and the second was the threshold for relevance and admissibility related to an Investigative Hearing.[108] The Court further notes its preference is to take a broad purposive interpretative approach to s. 83.28, "which accords with the presumption of constitutional validity" as required by the modern principle of statutory interpretation.[109]

With respect to the role of counsel, the Court deduces that s. 83.28 provides for the "fulsome participation by counsel"[110] in the proceedings. And, for relevance and admissibility the Court finds that,

> Accordingly, the observance of the applicable common law rules of evidence is mandatory. More importantly, the judge is present at the judicial investigative hearing to ensure that the procedure is carried out in accordance with constitutional protections.[111]

Hence, the Court concludes at the interpretive phase that the presumption of constitutionality has not been rebutted.[112]

102 Ibid., p. 263, para. 19.
103 Ibid., para. 20.
104 Ibid., pp. 264–265, para. 21.
105 Ibid., pp. 266–267, Issues, paras 26, 27.
106 Ibid., p. 272, para. 40.
107 Ibid., para. 41
108 Ibid., pp. 273–274, para. 45.
109 Ibid.
110 Ibid., p. 274, para. 47.
111 Ibid., p. 277, para. 53.
112 Ibid., para. 54.

On the issue of retrospectivity and whether s. 83.28 can be applied to events that took place prior to the legislation being passed and proclaimed the Supreme Court finds that "while the judicial investigative hearing may generate information pertaining to an offence (and indeed this is the purpose of the hearing), the hearing itself remains procedural."[113] In conclusion, in its analysis of this issue the Court found that s. 83.28 did not interfere with the substantive rights of the appellant, and, since s. 83.28 is strictly procedural, and the appellant has not rebutted the presumption of immediate application, then s. 83.28 has immediate effect and applies retrospectively to the effects of past events.[114]

With respect to the infringement of s. 7 Charter rights, the Supreme Court notes that the statutory compulsion to testify at a judicial Investigative Hearing engages the liberty interests under of s. 7.[115] Indeed, under s. 83.29 of the Criminal Code those who evade service, fail to attend, or remain at a judicial Investigative Hearing may be imprisoned.[116] In addition, s. 83.28 also encompasses the ordinary laws of contempt of court if the subject of the Investigative Hearing fails to answer questions and the potential liability with respect to perjury offenses.[117]

The appellants contended that s. 83.28 violated their absolute right to silence and their right against self-incrimination.[118] Here the Supreme Court sees the role of the judge in an investigative hearing as pivotal. After underscoring the significance of the independence of the judiciary to Canadian law, the rule of law, and its constitutional foundations, the Court states:

> The function of the judge in a judicial investigative hearing is not to act as "an agent of the state", but rather, to protect the integrity of the investigation and, in particular, the interests of the named person *vis-à-vis* the state.[119]

Accordingly, the Court ruled that, "A failure on the part of a hearing judge to exercise his and her discretion in this manner [to provide the witness with all of the constitutional guarantees of the *Charter*] will constitute a reviewable error."[120] In the companion *Vancouver Sun (Re)* case the Supreme Court ruled that "judicial investigative hearings are to be held presumptively in open court and that the onus was on the Crown to rebut that presumption under the test laid out in *Dagenais v. Canadian Broadcasting Corporation* [1994] 3 S.C.R. 835, and *R. v. Mentuck*, [2001] 3 S.C.R. 442, 2001 SCC 76."[121] The presumptive

113 Ibid., p. 279, para. 60.
114 Ibid., p. 281, para. 66.
115 Ibid., para. 67.
116 Ibid.
117 Ibid.
118 Ibid., p. 282, para. 69.
119 Ibid., pp. 289–290, para. 87.
120 Ibid., pp. 290–291, para. 89.
121 Ibid., p. 291, para. 91.

openness of the judicial Investigative Hearings is a further shield for the independence and impartiality of the judiciary in these proceedings.

The majority opinion in this judgment ruled that the appeal was dismissed that s. 83.28 does not infringe on the Canadian Charter of Rights and Freedoms nor does it infringe on the independence and impartiality of the judiciary.[122] It is important to note that the dissenting opinions of Justices Bastarache and Deschamps and of Justice Binnie were not on the constitutional validity or its possible compromise of judicial independence or impartiality; rather, they were differences of opinion on the necessity of the openness of the judicial Investigative Hearing and whether the circumstances of the current appeal constituted an abuse of process.[123]

R v. Khawaja *and* Sriskandarajah v. United States of America

Mohammad Momin Khawaja was born in Canada and worked as a computer programmer in Ottawa. He got involved with terrorists who were based in London, United Kingdom, and travelled to Pakistan to attend a terrorist training camp. He also provided his terrorist contacts with money, SIM cards, and started building a detonator as part of a fertilizer bomb-plot aimed at London, UK. He was the first person charged under the new terrorism laws under the Canadian Criminal Code.[124]

Suresh Sriskandarajah and Piratheepan Nadarajah were extradited to the United States to stand trial for allegedly trying to purchase surface-to-air missiles, AK-47 assault rifles, electronic equipment, submarine and warship design software, and communications equipment for the Liberation Tigers of Tamil Eelam (LTTE).[125] Both Canada and the United States list the LTTE as a terrorist organization.

R. v. Khawaja [126] and *Sriskandarajah v. United States of America* [127] raised similar legal issues with respect to the definition of terrorism on appeal and were heard conjointly by the Supreme Court of Canada. At trial, Khawaja claimed that several provisions of the Canadian Criminal Code were unconstitutional.[128] The trial judge held that s. 83.01(1)(b)(i)(A), the "motive clause," that states that a

122 Ibid., pp. 296, paras 105–106.

123 Ibid., pp. 296–298, paras 107–112.

124 Paul Burd, "Canada's Terrorism Laws Stand: R v. Khawaja and the Constitutionality of Criminalized Terrorism," *CanLII Connects*, September 26, 2014, http://canliiconnects.org/en/commentaries/29909 (accessed January 27, 2018).

125 Randall Palmer, "SCC Upholds Terrorism Law," *Canadian Lawyer*, December 14, 2012, www.canadianlawyermag.com/legalfeeds/scc-upholds-terrorism-law-4873/ (accessed January 27, 2018); Randall Palmer, "Top Canada court upholds anti-terrorism law in unanimous ruling," Reuters, #World News, December 14, 2012, https://uk.reuters.com/article/uk-terrorism/top-canada-court-upholds-anti-terrorism-law-in-unanimous-ruling-idUKBRE8BD0UQ20121214 (accessed January 27, 2018).

126 *R. v. Khawaja*, 2012 SCC 69, [2012] 3 S.C.R. 555.

127 *Sriskandarajah v. United States of America*, 2012 SCC 70, [2012] 3 S.C.R. 609.

128 Criminal Code, ss. 83.01(1), 83.03(a), 83.18, 83.18(1), 83.18(3)(a), 83.19, 83.2 and 83.21(1).

terrorist activity must be an act or omission committed in whole or in part "for a political, religious or ideological purpose, objective or cause," was a *prima facie* infringement of s. 2(a), (b) and (d) of the Canadian Charter of Rights and Freedoms[129] and that it could not be justified under s. 1 of its provisions.[130] The Court of Appeal found that the trial judge had erred in finding that the motive clause was unconstitutional and stated that "expressive activity that takes the form of violence is not protected under s. 2(b) of the Charter, since violence is destructive of the very values that underlie the right to freedom of expression. For the same reason, threats of violence are not protected by s. 2(b)."[131]

The Canadian Supreme Court considered the constitutionality of the s. 83.18 of the Canadian Criminal Code. The appellants challenged this provision on its vagueness and overbreadth. Writing the unanimous judgment for the Supreme Court, Chief Justice Beverley McLachlin[132] opined that a principle of fundamental justice is that criminal laws cannot be overbroad. The appellants asserted that "the combined effect of the definition of terrorist activity (s. 83.01(1)) and the provisions prohibiting participation in terrorist activity (s. 83.18) result in overbreadth, by criminalizing conduct that creates no risk of harm and is only tenuously connected to Parliament's objective of preventing terrorist activity."[133] "The appellants argue that the law is too broad because it is grossly disproportionate to the objective that it seeks to achieve."[134]

Chief Justice McLachlin considered whether "overbreadth" and "grossly disproportionate" are distinct constitutional doctrines that breech the principles of fundamental justice but decided instead to consider them together without deciding whether they are distinct constitutional doctrines.[135] She applied a three-point analysis in doing so, by: (1) examining the scope of the law; (2) determining the objectives of the law; and (3) asking whether the means selected by the law are broader than necessary to achieve the state's objective and whether the impact of that law is grossly disproportionate to that objective.[136] Chief Justice McLachlin noted that the purpose of the terrorism provisions of the Canadian Criminal Code

129 Sections 2 of the Canadian Charter of Rights and Freedoms (Charter) covers Fundamental Freedoms and subsections (a), (b), and (d) are: (a) freedom of conscience and religion; (b) freedom of thought, belief, opinion and expression, including freedom of the press and other media of communication; and (d) freedom of association.

130 Section 1 of the *Charter*, Guarantee of Rights and Freedoms, states: "The *Canadian Charter of Rights and Freedoms* guarantees the rights and freedoms set out in it subject only to such reasonable limits prescribed by law as can be demonstrably justified in a free and democratic society."

131 *R. v. Khawaja*, para. 17.

132 The new Chief Justice of the Supreme Court of Canada, the Rt. Hon. Richard Wagner, was sworn into office on December 18, 2017. *News Release*, December 18, 2017,https://scc-csc.lexum.com/scc-csc/news/en/item/5699/index.do (accessed January 29, 2018).

133 *R. v. Khawaja*, para. 35.

134 Ibid., para. 38.

135 Ibid., para. 40.

136 Ibid.

is "'to provide a means by which terrorism can be prosecuted and prevented' (*Application under s. 83.28 of the Criminal Code (Re)*, at para 39) – not to punish individuals for innocent, socially useful or causal acts which absent any intent, indirectly contribute to a terrorist activity."[137] This was determined to require a high *mens rea* threshold that includes the person *knowingly* participating in and contributing to a terrorist activity but that their actions must be undertaken *for the purposes of* enhancing the ability of a terrorist group to facilitate or to carry out terrorist activity.[138] At paragraph 48 of the judgment, Chief Justice McLachlin states:

> To convict under s. 83.18, the judge must be satisfied beyond a reasonable doubt that the accused intended to enhance the ability of a terrorist group to facilitate or carry out a terrorist activity. There may be direct evidence of this intention. Or the intention may be inferred from the evidence of the knowledge of the accused and the nature of his actions.

The Supreme Court ruled that the scope of the law under s. 83.18 was much narrower than claimed by the appellants and that it did not include "innocent or socially useful conduct that is undertaken absent any intent to enhance the abilities of a terrorist group to facilitate or to carry out a terrorist activity" or "for conduct that a reasonable person would not view as materially capable of enhancing the abilities of the terrorist group to facilitate or carry out a terrorist activity."[139]

On the question of whether s. 83.18 of the terrorism provisions of the Criminal Code are broader than necessary or have a grossly disproportionate impact on the prosecution or prevention of terrorist activities, it is noted in the judgment that the *actus reus* does not include "conduct that a reasonable person would not view as capable of materially enhancing the abilities of a terrorist group to facilitate carrying out a terrorist act."[140] In addition, the high *mens rea* requirement that involves a "specific intent to enhance the abilities of a terrorist group to facilitate or carry out a terrorist activity"[141] helps to ensure to those who are complicit in terrorist activities are found guilty under this provision of the Criminal Code.

The Crown is required to prove both of these elements beyond a reasonable doubt in order to secure a conviction of anyone charged under these provisions. Chief Justice McLachlin states: "Conduct that meets both of these requirements discloses a non-negligible risk of harm that is sufficiently connected to real or contemplated terrorist activity."[142] Accordingly, the judgment reached was that when the "tailored reach of the section is weighed against the objective, it cannot be said that the selected means are broader than necessary or the impact of the section is disproportionate."[143] Indeed, the court ruled:

137 Ibid., para. 44.
138 Ibid., para. 45.
139 Ibid., para. 53.
140 Ibid., para. 57.
141 Ibid.
142 Ibid.
143 Ibid., para. 62.

> The criminalization under s. 83.18 of a broad range of interactions that have the potential to – and are intended to – materially enhance the abilities of terrorist groups is not grossly disproportionate nor overly broad in relation to the objective of prosecuting, and in particular, of preventing terrorism.[144]

Accordingly, the court concludes that s. 83.18 does not violate Section 7 of the Charter.

The appellants further asserted that the terrorism provisions of the Criminal Code infringe on s. 2 guarantees of freedom of expression, freedom of religion and freedom of association in the Charter. The Supreme Court noted that a law may infringe on a right by either its purpose or its effect.[145] The appellants contended that the terrorism legislation by its very purpose imposes limits on the s. 2 rights in the Charter.

Chief Justice McLachlin ruled that if freedom of expression was not infringed on the facts of this case, then, there would be no basis on which freedom of religion or freedom of association could be infringed. The crucial point being that violent activities are not protected under s. 2(*b*) of the Charter.[146] Although this was acknowledged by the appellants, they argued, nonetheless, that the violence exception should be construed narrowly to include only expressive activity that only involves violence.[147] However, the Supreme Court in a series of previous cases has taken the position that the violence exception under s. 2(*b*) also includes threats of violence. As the court noted in the *Greater Vancouver Transportation Authority*, "violent expression or threats of violence fall outside the scope of the s. 2(*b*) guarantee (para. 28 (emphasis added))."[148]

It is worth noting that Chief Justice McLachlin has firmly taken the position that violence and threats of violence undermine the rule of law and that they take away freedom of choice while undermining freedom of action. Violence, including the threat of violence, Chief Justice McLachlin observed, "undermine the very values and social conditions that are necessary for the continued existence of freedom of expression,"[149] and she goes on to state categorically that, "Threats of violence fall outside s. 2(*b*) guarantee of free expression."[150] The court goes on then to make a finding that the purpose of the law is not an infringement of freedom of expression.[151]

The Supreme Court then considered whether the effect of the law violated freedom of expression. The appellants argued that the s. 83.01(1)(*b*)(i)(A), the "motive clause," is unconstitutional on two grounds:

144 Ibid., para. 63.
145 Ibid., para. 65.
146 Ibid., para. 67.
147 Ibid., para. 68.
148 Ibid., para. 70.
149 Ibid.
150 Ibid.
151 Ibid., para. 75.

(1) it has the effect of chilling the exercise of freedom of expression, freedom of religion, and freedom of association;
(2) it would legitimize law enforcement action aimed at scrutinizing individuals based on their religious, political, and ideological beliefs.[152]

The trial judge accepted these arguments and severed the motive clause from the trial. However, the Court of Appeal disagreed and restored it. On the first point, Chief Justice McLachlin found that the appellants had not demonstrated that the motive clause had a chilling effect on the expression of religious or ideological views. The point was made that the trial judge's finding that there was a chill in the expression of religious and ideological views was, the Supreme Court found, a consequence of the "post-9/11" climate of suspicion rather than from the motive clause in the terrorism legislation.[153]

The Supreme Court observed further that a patently incorrect understanding of the terrorism provisions cannot be a basis for a finding of unconstitutionality.[154] Furthermore, the Supreme Court of Canada also argued that police misconduct, such as profiling based on religion or ideology, is not a chill that is a result of the terrorism legislation.[155] The Supreme Court goes so far as to state that "the impugned provision is clearly drafted in a manner that is respectful of diversity, as it allows for the non-violent expression of political, religious or ideological views."[156]

The Supreme Court ruled that the impugned terrorism provisions within the Criminal Code do not infringe either s. 7 or s. 2 of the Charter. Accordingly, Canada's anti-terrorism laws were found to be constitutionally valid on the basis of these two conjointly heard cases before the SCC.[157]

General Observations Regarding these Leading Cases on Terrorism

What is evident from these leading cases on terrorism in Canada is that the SCC has supported the Canadian government's efforts to combat terrorism while ensuring that they adhered to fundamental human rights and freedoms. The *Suresh* judgment is most notable in this regard. The SCC ruled in *Suresh* that a refugee could be refouled to their country of nationality or former habitual residence to face torture if they were properly determined to be a threat to national security and the Minister did not violate the constitutionally sanctioned procedures of fairness. The collective security interests of Canadian society superseded the human rights of the refugee not to face the likelihood of torture upon their

152 Ibid., para. 76.
153 Ibid., para. 81.
154 Ibid., para. 82.
155 Ibid., para. 83.
156 Ibid.
157 Wendy Zeldin, "Canada: Anti-Terror Law Ruled Constitutional," *Global Legal Monitor*, Library of Congress, December 18, 2012, www.loc.gov/law/foreign-news/article/canada-anti-terror-law-ruled-constitutional/ (accessed January 28, 2018).

return. Further, in their judgment in *Application under s. 83.28* the SCC sanctioned the use of open judicial Investigative Hearings to deduce evidence involving potential and actual acts of terrorism, provided constitutionally guaranteed procedural rights were adhered to. And, in the SCC judgment in *Khawaja*, the definition of terrorism in the Anti-terrorism Act 2001 was found not to be in violation of the Canadian Charter of Rights and Freedoms. This applied, in particular, to the motive clause of the ATA.

Conclusions

From the foregoing, it is evident that the definition of terrorism found in the Canadian Criminal Code is detailed, broad in scope, and thorough in its coverage. The definition includes two main parts: terrorist activities and terrorist groups; and, it has three principal elements: offenses, motivation, and intention. The Canadian government is in the process of amending the most troublesome portions of these provisions found in the current legislation with the introduction of a new 2017 National Security Act. It is also important to stress that mere membership in a terrorist organization is sufficient to make a foreign national or permanent resident inadmissible to Canada under IRPA s. 34(1)(f).

The prosecution of terrorism cases is one of the most effective counter-terrorism strategies employed by states. The SCC has been especially vigilant in ensuring that the Canadian government does not exceed their legal and constitutional authority and that human rights are ensured to the highest degree, thereby ensuring that national security is protected to the maximum degree possible. Hence, the protection and advancement of fundamental human rights is the key to enhancing national security in any liberal democracy.

8 Human rights and anti-terror laws in Australia

George Williams

Introduction

Australia came relatively late to enacting national anti-terror laws. It had no such laws prior to the 11 September 2001 attacks, but afterwards quickly made up time. New legislation of unprecedented reach has been enacted, including laws providing for: restrictions on freedom of speech through new sedition offences and broader censorship rules; detention and questioning for up to a week by the Australian Security Intelligence Organisation (ASIO) of Australian citizens not suspected of any crime; the banning of organisations by executive decision; control orders that can enable house arrest for up to a year; detention without charge or trial for up to 14 days; and warrantless searches of private property by police officers. As these examples demonstrate, powers and sanctions once thought to lie outside the rules of a liberal democracy except during wartime have now become part of the Australian legal system. Not surprisingly, these laws raise important questions about the protection of human rights, and the capacity of the Australian legal system to operate as a significant check and balance in this regard.

These questions have assumed even greater importance as the years have passed. When enacted, Australia's anti-terror laws were typically cast as a temporary, emergency reaction to attacks overseas and the possibility that such indiscriminate violence might be repeated at home. However, it is now clear that Australia's anti-terror laws can no longer be cast as a transient, short-term legal response. This reflects the assessment of the Australian government and its agencies that terrorism remains a persistent threat to the community. The National Terrorism Public Alert System has set its threat level at 'medium', indicating an assessment that a terrorist attack 'could' occur.[1] In 2010, the Australian government reiterated that '[t]he threat of terrorism to Australia is real and enduring. It has become a persistent and permanent feature of Australia's security environment.'[2]

There are many prior examples of Australia's Federal Parliament enacting national security legislation that conferred broad powers on government agencies

1 www.nationalsecurity.gov.au/Securityandyourcommunity/Pages/NationalTerrorismPublicAlertSystem.aspx.
2 Australian Government, *Counter-Terrorism White Paper: Securing Australia—Protecting Our Community* (2010) ii.

and had a significant impact upon individual liberty. Such laws were typically found on the statute books during the First and Second World Wars.[3] However, those conflicts were of more definite duration, and wartime legal measures ceased to operate after the conflict ended. By contrast, Australia's new anti-terror laws have taken on a character of permanence. Indeed, what has been called the 'war on terror' has run now for a longer period than either of those worldwide conflicts, and continues unabated with no likely end in sight. Moreover, while a few Australian anti-terror laws are the subject of 'sunset clauses' that could see them lapse after a specified period of time unless re-enacted, most have effect for an indefinite duration. All this points to the fact that the body of Australian anti-terror laws may be altered in the coming years, but will not likely be repealed.

This means that the inroads made into human rights protection by these extraordinary laws will endure. In doing so, the laws create new precedents, understandings, expectations and political conventions when it comes to the proper limits of government power and the role of the state in protecting human rights. Hence, despite their often exceptional nature, anti-terror measures risk been seen as normal rather than exceptional. This is due both to the passage of time and the fact that anti-terror strategies are now being copied in other areas of the law.

Such questions around the enactment of anti-terror laws are of course not unique to Australia. These laws raise similar issues in many other nations. The Australian context differs though in that Australia is now the only democratic country without a national bill of rights or human rights act.[4] This has had significant implications both for the type of anti-terror laws enacted in Australia, as well as for the post-enactment judicial and other scrutiny of such laws. It means that Australia offers the unique perspective of the making of anti-terror laws within a democratic framework lacking a formal national human rights instrument.

This chapter explores these themes and issues. It begins by asking whether Australia needed to enact national anti-terror laws in the wake of 9/11, and so in doing to make accommodations and compromises with regard to human rights. It then examines the laws actually enacted and the capacity of the Australian legal system to subject those laws to scrutiny on human rights grounds.

Were national anti-terror laws needed?

The absence of national anti-terror laws in Australia prior to 9/11 was unsurprising. Apart from isolated incidents such as the 1978 bombing attack on the Commonwealth Heads of Government Regional Meeting at the Sydney Hilton Hotel, Australia had little direct experience of terrorism. It took the attacks of 9/11 to provide a catalyst for the passing of Australia's first national anti-terror laws.

3 See, e.g., the War Precautions Act 1914 (Cth) and the National Security Act 1939 (Cth), and the various regulations made under those acts.

4 George Williams and Daniel Reynolds, *A Charter of Rights for Australia* (UNSW Press, 2017) 17–18.

It had been argued that Australia did not need such laws, primarily on the basis that terrorism can be dealt with by the existing criminal law.[5] However, that position was not sustainable. Laws were needed to deal with specific aspects of threat posed by terrorism. For example, the nation needed a statutory framework directed to preventing the financing of terrorist acts overseas so as to ensure that Australians do not enable such attacks. New laws were also required on subjects such as the targeting of terrorist organisations.

More broadly, the criminal law in place in 2001 was not sufficient for the task of preventing terrorist attacks. It is not appropriate in the context of terrorism, as is often the case for other types of crime, to primarily apply the force of law once an act has been committed so as to bring the perpetrator to justice. Instead, given the potential for catastrophic damage and loss of life, intervention to prevent terrorism is justified at an earlier point in the chain of events that might lead to an attack. Such prevention can be seen as an act of political pragmatism given the pressing need for Australian governments to take action to protect the community from terrorism. It can also be seen as a measure designed to respect fundamental human rights, including the right to life and to live free of fear.

Anti-terror laws raise important questions as to how early the law should intervene to pin criminal responsibility on actions that may give rise to a terrorist attack. It is arguable that the laws as actually enacted give rise to lengthy jail sentences for preparatory acts too far removed from the actual commission of an act of terrorism. However, this is not a persuasive argument against the existence of anti-terror laws per se, but for their recalibration so as to ensure that they criminalise actions that can be more realistically described as preparation for committing a terrorist act. On the other hand, the argument for appropriate anti-terror laws is not a case for departing from well-accepted principles of criminal law aimed at ensuring outcomes such as the right to a fair trial. Anti-terror laws must be framed in light of such human rights values.

An effective prevention strategy also required laws to confer powers on agencies such as the Australian Federal Police and ASIO. These organisations required legal authorisation to collect information to head off an attack and the power to target not only individuals that might engage in terrorism but also groups or cells of potential terrorists. Again, the issue here is not so much one of justification, but of proportionality. Australia's law-enforcement and intelligence agencies should have sufficient powers to dismantle and prevent threats to the community, but those powers should be carefully tailored to the level of the threat. They should also be subject to strict and transparent safeguards enforced by independent agencies.

Apart from the inadequacy of its existing national laws, Australia was justified in enacting new anti-terror laws after 9/11 in fulfilment of its obligations as a

5 See, e.g., Commonwealth, *Parliamentary Debates*, Senate, 24 June 2002, 2403, where Greens Senator Bob Brown said during debate on the Security Legislation Amendment (Terrorism) Bill 2002 (Cth) package: 'The existing criminal law, with offences such as murder, criminal damage, conspiracy, and aiding and abetting, can and should be used to prosecute and penalise anything that can sensibly be described as terrorism.'

member of the international community. For example, Resolution 1373 of the United Nations Security Council, adopted on 28 September 2001, determined that states shall 'take the necessary steps to prevent the commission of terrorist acts' by ensuring that 'terrorist acts are established as serious criminal offences in domestic laws and regulations'.[6] This gave rise to an obligation on the part of Australia to enact laws directed at this problem. While Australia had criminal laws in place that could have been used to *prosecute* individuals for acts of terrorism, it was unsustainable for Australia to argue that it already had sufficient laws in place directed at the *prevention* of terrorism.

Finally, Australia's anti-terror laws can be seen as having an important moral dimension. In an era punctuated by terrorist attacks starting with New York and Washington and followed by Bali, Madrid, London, Mumbai, Jakarta and elsewhere, it was appropriate that Australia outlawed such forms of political violence. Enacting a specific crime of terrorism signalled that, as a society, Australia rejects the use of violence in the pursuit of a political, religious or ideological goal.

The Australia government and parliament deserves credit for recognising that Australia required new laws directed towards protecting the community from the threat of terrorism. These institutions were correct in their assessment that such laws ought to be directed particularly to the prevention of such acts. In hindsight, Australia's legal system prior to 9/11 reflected complacency about the potential for political violence in Australia and the region. The task then for legislators was not to determine whether anti-terror law should be enacted, but to bring them into being in an appropriate form, including in a way that gave due respect to fundamental human rights

The laws that Australia got

The problem arising from Australia's anti-terror laws is not that they exist, but the extraordinary and far-reaching form in which they were enacted. Australia's response to 9/11 was similar to that of many other countries. It emphasised the need to deviate from the ordinary criminal law – with its emphasis on punishment of individuals after the fact – by preventing terrorist acts from occurring in the first place. The result was a bout of lawmaking that continues to challenge long-held assumptions as to the proper limits of the law, and criminal law in particular, and also accepted understandings of the respective roles of the executive, parliament and the judiciary.

One remarkable feature of Australia's response to terrorism is the sheer volume of lawmaking. In the years since 9/11, Australia's Federal Parliament, and so not including the laws of the states and territories, has enacted 70 anti-terror laws.[7]

6 SC Res 1373, UN SCOR, 56th sess., 4385th mtg, UN Doc S/RES/1373 (28 September 2001), preamble and art. 2(e).

7 This figure is based upon the 54 anti-terror statutes I identified had been enacted in the decade after 9/11 in George Williams, 'A Decade of Australian Anti-Terror Laws' (2011) 35 *Melbourne University Law Review* 1136, 1144. Since that tally, further anti-terror laws have been enacted, with such statutes identified according to the

Most of these laws were made from 11 September 2001 to the fall of Prime Minister Howard's coalition government in November 2007. Over that time, the Federal Parliament enacted 48 anti-terror laws, an average of a new anti-terror statute every 6.7 weeks.

These statistics are eye-catching and, indeed, Australia's output of anti-terror laws exceeds that of nations facing a higher threat level. In a comparative analysis of the anti-terror laws passed in a range of democratic nations, Kent Roach has described Australia's response as being one of 'hyper-legislation' as a result of Australia getting 'caught up in the 9/11 effect'.[8] He found:

> Australia has exceeded the United Kingdom, the United States, and Canada in the sheer number of new antiterrorism laws that it has enacted since 9/11 ... this degree of legislative activism is striking compared even to the United Kingdom's active agenda and much greater than the pace of legislation in the United States or Canada. Australia's hyper-legislation strained the ability of the parliamentary opposition and civil society to keep up, let alone provide effective opposition to, the relentless legislative output.[9]

Australia's national anti-terror laws are striking not just in their volume, but, more significantly, in their reach. For example, Australia's laws:

- define a 'terrorist act' as conduct engaged in or threats made for the purpose of advancing a 'political, religious or ideological cause'.[10] The conduct or threat must be designed to coerce a government, influence a government by intimidation or intimidate a section of the public. The conduct or threat must also cause any of a number of harms, ranging from death and serious bodily harm to endangering a person's life, seriously interfering with electronic systems, or creating a 'serious risk to the health or safety of ... a section of the public'.[11] The definition excludes advocacy, protest, dissent or industrial action so long as there is no intention to cause things such as serious physical harm, death or a serious risk to the health or safety of the public. The

methodology set out in that article. For example: Combating the Financing of People Smuggling and Other Measures Act 2011 (Cth); Aviation Transport Security Amendment (Air Cargo) Act 2011 (Cth); Nuclear Terrorism Legislation Amendment Act 2012 (Cth); Social Security Amendment (Supporting Australian Victims of Terrorism Overseas) Act 2012 (Cth); Aviation Transport Security Amendment (Screening) Act 2012 (Cth); Customs Amendment (Military End-Use) Act 2012 (Cth); Aviation Transport Security Amendment (Inbound Cargo Security Enhancement) Act 2013 (Cth).

8 Kent Roach, *The 9/11 Effect: Comparative Counter-Terrorism* (Cambridge University Press, 2011) 309.

9 Ibid., 310.

10 Criminal Code Act 1995 (Cth) Sch 1 ('Criminal Code') s. 100.1(1) (definition of 'terrorist act', para. (b)).

11 Ibid., s. 100.1(2)(e).

definition is more carefully tailored than others in some nations,[12] but still encompasses liberation movements, such as the struggle of Nelson Mandela against apartheid, the armed resistance in East Timor or those seeking to bring down the Syrian government.

- create a range of new offences, including that of committing a 'terrorist act'.[13] Other provisions create a wide range of offences for conduct preparatory to a terrorist act. These include: providing or receiving training connected with terrorist acts;[14] possessing 'things' connected with terrorist acts;[15] and collecting or making documents likely to facilitate terrorist acts.[16] The penalties are severe. For example, a maximum penalty of life imprisonment is imposed where a person provides or collects funds and is reckless as to whether those funds will be used to facilitate or engage in a terrorist act,[17] or, more generally, where the person does 'any act in preparation for, or planning, a terrorist act'.[18] These offences can be combined with the 'inchoate' offences that apply to other Commonwealth crimes, such as that for attempt or conspiracy. These offences are also committed even if a terrorist act does not occur or the training/thing/document/act is not connected to a specific terrorist act.[19] The offences thus render individuals liable to serious penalties even before there is what would ordinarily be regarded as the formation of criminal intent. It is this predictive approach, exemplified in the doubly pre-emptive offence of 'conspiracy to do an act in preparation for a terrorist act', that gives the offences such an extraordinary reach.
- contain remodelled sedition offences whereby it is an offence punishable by seven years' imprisonment to urge the overthrow of the Constitution or government by force or violence, or to urge interference in parliamentary elections. It is also an offence to urge violence against a group or an individual on the basis of their race, religion or political opinion.[20]
- enable warrantless searches whereby police officers may enter premises without a warrant in order to prevent a thing from being used in connection with a terrorism offence, or where there is a serious and imminent threat to a

12 Ben Golder and George Williams, 'What is "Terrorism"? Problems of Legal Definition' (2004) 27 *University of New South Wales Law Journal* 270; Keiran Hardy and George Williams, 'What is "Terrorism"? Assessing Domestic Legal Definitions' (2011) 16 *UCLA Journal of International Law and Foreign Affairs* 77.
13 Criminal Code s. 100.1(1) (definition of 'terrorist act').
14 Ibid., s. 101.2.
15 Ibid., s. 101.4.
16 Ibid., s. 101.5.
17 Ibid., ss. 103.1(1) (general offence), 103.2(1) (where the funds are collected for or on behalf of a specific person).
18 Ibid., s. 101.6.
19 See ibid., ss. 101.2(3), 101.4(3), 101.5(3), 101.6(2).
20 Ibid., ss. 80.2A–80.2B. These offences were first introduced as 'sedition' offences by the Anti-Terrorism Act (No. 2) 2005 (Cth) sch 7 item 12. They were amended to their current form by the National Security Legislation Amendment Act 2010 (Cth) pt 2

person's life, health or safety.[21] While on the premises, police officers have the power to seize any other 'thing' if they suspect on reasonable grounds that doing so is necessary to protect someone's health or safety, or because the circumstances are 'serious or urgent'.[22]

- provide a longer investigation period for terrorism offences (24 hours) compared with non-terrorism offences (12 hours).[23] In the case of a terrorism offence, the investigating authorities may also apply to a magistrate for up to seven days of 'dead time' if they need to suspend or delay questioning the suspect (for example, while making overseas enquiries in a different time zone).[24]
- enable the proscription, or banning, of organisations by government decree. The Attorney-General can make a written declaration that an organisation is a 'terrorist organisation'.[25] Once a declaration is made, a range of offences apply to individuals who are linked to that organisation, including: directing the activities of a terrorist organisation;[26] intentionally being a member of a terrorist organisation;[27] recruiting for a terrorist organisation;[28] receiving funds from or giving funds to a terrorist organisation;[29] providing 'support' to a terrorist organisation;[30] and associating with a terrorist organisation.[31]
- include a 'preventative detention order' regime in which individuals may be taken into custody, without charge or trial, and detained for a maximum period of 48 hours where this is reasonably necessary to prevent an 'imminent' terrorist act from occurring or to preserve evidence relating to a recent terrorist act.[32] An extended period of detention is then possible under state law up to a maximum of 14 days.[33]
- include a 'control order' regime, in which individuals not suspected of any criminal offence may be subject to a wide range of restrictions that can regulate almost every aspect of their life, ranging from where they work or live, to whom they can talk, where those restrictions are 'reasonably necessary, and reasonably appropriate and adapted, for the purpose of protecting the public from a terrorist act'.[34] A person can even be subject to house arrest. All this

21 Crimes Act 1914 (Cth) s. 3UEA.
22 Ibid., (Cth) s 3UEA(5).
23 Compare ss. 23DB–23DF (terrorism offences) with ss. 23C–23DA (non-terrorism offences).
24 Ibid., s. 23DB(11).
25 In order to make such a declaration, the Attorney-General must be satisfied that the organisation 'is directly or indirectly engaged in, preparing, planning, assisting in or fostering the doing of a terrorist act' or 'advocates the doing of a terrorist act': Criminal Code s. 102.1(2)(a)–(b).
26 Ibid., s. 102.2.
27 Ibid., s. 102.3.
28 Ibid., s. 102.4.
29 Ibid., s. 102.6.
30 Ibid., s. 102.7.
31 Ibid., s. 102.8.
32 Ibid., s. 105.4.
33 See, e.g., Terrorism (Police Powers) Act 2002 (NSW) s. 26K(2).
34 Criminal Code s. 104.4(1)(d).

can occur without a trial, and indeed control orders ignore the concept of guilt and innocence altogether.

- provide extraordinary new powers to ASIO whereby the Director-General of ASIO can apply to the Attorney-General for questioning and detention warrants.[35] A person may be questioned in eight-hour blocks up to a maximum of 24 hours where this would 'substantially assist the collection of intelligence that is important in relation to a terrorism offence'.[36] In addition, a person may be detained for up to a week for questioning where there are reasonable grounds to believe that he or she will alert another person involved in a terrorism offence, not appear before ASIO for questioning, or destroy a record or thing that may be requested under the warrant. It is an offence punishable by five years' imprisonment to refuse to answer ASIO's questions, or to give false or misleading information. These warrants may be issued against non-suspects, including family members, journalists, children between the ages of 16 and 18,[37] and innocent bystanders. It is an offence, while a warrant is in effect and for two years afterwards, to disclose 'operational information' (including 'information that [ASIO] has or had') that a person has as a direct or indirect result of the issue or execution of the warrant.
- provide new powers of electronic surveillance, not only for terrorist suspects, but also for those who the authorities believe are 'likely to communicate' with the person under investigation.[38]
- provide additional powers to the Attorney-General to close down a courtroom from public view where sensitive national security information is likely to be disclosed.[39] That information may then be led against a defendant in summary or redacted form. Decisions as to whether the evidence will be admitted are decided in a closed hearing from which the defendant and even his or her legal representative may be excluded.[40] When deciding whether and in what form to admit the evidence, the judge or magistrate is directed to give 'greatest weight' to the interests of national security over other considerations.[41]
- require that publications, films or computer games that 'advocate' the doing of a terrorist act must be classified as 'Refused Classification'.[42] This includes where the publication, film or computer game 'directly praises the doing of a terrorist act in circumstances where there is a risk that such a praise might have the effect of leading a person (regardless of his or her age or any mental impairment (within the meaning of section 7.3 of the Criminal Code) that the person might suffer) to engage in a terrorist act'.[43]

35 Australian Security Intelligence Organisation Act 1979 (Cth), Part III Div. III.
36 Ibid., ss. 34D–34G, 34R–34S.
37 See the 'special rules for young people' in ibid., s. 34ZE.
38 Telecommunications (Interception and Access) Act 1979 (Cth) s. 46(1)(d)(ii).
39 National Security Information (Criminal and Civil Proceedings) Act 2004 (Cth) s. 31.
40 Ibid., s. 29(3).
41 Ibid., ss. 31(7)(a), (8), 38L(7)(a), (8).
42 Classification (Publications, Films and Computer Games) Act 1995 (Cth), s. 9A.
43 Ibid., s. 9A(b).

As is clear from this list, Australia's new anti-terror laws impact upon a broad range of human rights. The laws are extraordinary in their scope and operation, and so require a high level of justification to support their impact upon fundamental freedoms.

Protecting human rights without a bill of rights

Australia needed new anti-terror laws, but the laws actually enacted reflect major problems of process and political judgement. To a significant degree, this was a result of many of the laws being enacted in haste[44] as a reaction to catastrophic attacks overseas, especially those on 9/11 and in London in 2005, both of which provoked considerable anger, fear and grief in the community.

It is not surprising that at such times people look to their political leaders for a strong response, including action that may actually prove to be disproportionate to the threat due to its impact on democratic liberties. This dynamic is well known, and was well stated by Alexander Hamilton in *The Federalist* (No. 8) in the late eighteenth century:

> Safety from external danger is the most powerful director of national conduct. Even the ardent love of liberty will, after a time, give way to its dictates. The violent destruction of life and property incident to war, the continual efforts and alarm attendant on a state of continual danger, will compel nations the most attached to liberty to resort for repose and security to institutions which have a tendency to destroy their civil and political rights. To be more safe, they at length become willing to run the risk of being less free.[45]

This might be countered, or at least lessened, by strong human rights protection. However, such protection, at least in the form of a formal national human rights instrument, is absent in Australia.

Human rights protection in Australia

Australia lacks anything akin to a national human rights act or bill of rights.[46] Human rights acts have been passed in two sub-national jurisdictions, the

44 See Andrew Lynch, 'Legislating with Urgency –The Enactment of the Anti-Terrorism Act (No 1) 2005' (2006) 30 *Melbourne University Law Review* 747; Andrew Lynch, 'Legislating Anti-Terrorism: Observations on Form and Process' in Victor V. Ramraj et al. (eds), *Global Anti-Terrorism Law and Policy* (Cambridge University Press, 2nd edn, 2012) 151; Greg Carne, 'Hasten Slowly: Urgency, Discretion and Review – A Counter-Terrorism Legislative Agenda and Legacy' (2008) 13(2) *Deakin Law Review* 49.

45 James Madison, Alexander Hamilton and John Jay, *The Federalist Papers* (Penguin, 1987), 112–113.

46 See George Williams and David Hume, *Human Rights under the Australian Constitution* (Oxford University Press, 2nd edn, 2013).

Australian Capital Territory in 2004[47] and Victoria in 2006.[48] These laws are based on the models enacted in New Zealand and the United Kingdom, known as the 'Commonwealth model'[49] or 'parliamentary model'.[50] However, their operation is limited in that they apply only with respect to the particular territory and state laws, and not at all to national laws, including those enacted on the subject of terrorism.

In 2008, a federal inquiry was initiated to determine whether a human rights act should be adopted at the national level. It recommended in the following year that such an act be enacted.[51] However, Australia's federal government rejected this recommendation, and instead proposed a new national human rights framework centred upon enhanced parliamentary scrutiny. As now enacted, the Human Rights (Parliamentary Scrutiny) Act 2011 (Cth) requires bills and legislative instruments to be accompanied by a statement of their compatibility with a number of international human rights conventions.[52] These claims can be examined, and other human rights matters investigated, by a new Parliamentary Joint Committee on Human Rights. The model provides no avenues for judicial enforcement of human rights. There are also no legal consequences should Parliament not properly fulfil the scrutiny function.

A scheme of human rights protection is also absent from the Australian Constitution. The Constitution was drafted at two conventions held in 1891 and 1897–98, and then enacted for Australia by the British Parliament. In *Australian Capital Television Pty Ltd v Commonwealth*,[53] Mason CJ noted the 'prevailing sentiment of the framers that there was no need to incorporate a comprehensive Bill of Rights in order to protect the rights and freedoms of citizens. That sentiment was one of the unexpressed assumptions on which the Constitution was drafted.'[54] Chief Justice Mason's statement reflects the widely held view that the framers intended the human rights of the Australian people to be protected by the common law and the good sense of elected representatives (as constrained by the Westminster system of responsible government).

Instead, the Constitution was designed as a compact between the colonies – as opposed to being a 'people's constitution' – and the focus of the framers was on issues such as defence, nationhood and free trade. According to Lois O'Donoghue,

47 Human Rights Act 2004 (ACT).
48 Charter of Human Rights and Responsibilities Act 2006 (Vic).
49 See Stephen Gardbaum, 'The New Commonwealth Model of Constitutionalism' (2001) 49 *American Journal of Comparative Law* 707.
50 Janet Hiebert, 'Parliamentary Bills of Rights: An Alternative Model?' (2006) 69 *Modern Law Review* 7. See also, e.g., Mark Tushnet, 'The Rise of Weak-Form Judicial Review' in Tom Ginsburg and Rosalind Dixon (eds), *Comparative Constitutional Law* (Edward Elgar, 2011) 321.
51 National Human Rights Consultation Committee, *Report* (2009).
52 See generally George Williams and Lisa Burton, 'Australia's Exclusive Parliamentary Model of Rights Protection' (2013) 34 *Statute Law Review* 58.
53 (1992) 177 CLR 106.
54 Ibid., 136.

a former Chairperson of the Aboriginal and Torres Strait Islander Commission, the Constitution as drafted

> says very little about what it is to be Australian. It says practically nothing about how we find ourselves here – save being an amalgamation of former colonies. It says nothing of how we should behave towards each other as human beings and as Australians.[55]

To the extent that human rights were taken into account by the framers, one concern was to maintain existing race based distinctions. A majority of the constitution's framers considered, for example, that a clause that conferred 'equal protection of the laws' was undesirable because it might protect 'Chinamen, Japanese, Hindoos, and other barbarians' in areas such as employment.[56] The racially discriminatory origins of the Constitution remain evident in s. 25, which recognises that the states can disqualify people from voting because of their race, and s. 51(xxvi), which provides that the Commonwealth Parliament may legislate with respect to the 'people of any race for whom it is deemed necessary to make special laws'.[57]

The Constitution does contain a few, scattered express rights. However, the narrow drafting of these provisions and their constrained interpretation by the High Court of Australia has meant that they have had little (if any) effect. For example, the requirement in s. 80 of the Constitution that '[t]he trial on indictment of any offence against any law of the Commonwealth shall be by jury' has been interpreted by the High Court as conferring on the Commonwealth Parliament the power to itself determine what offences shall be 'on indictment', and thus subject to a jury trial.[58] Similarly, s. 41, which might seem to confer a 'right to vote',[59] has been interpreted as applying only to people who had a right to vote in state elections as at 12 June 1902. The High Court has noted that the 'practical effect of s. 41 is now spent'.[60]

55 Frank Brennan, *Securing a Bountiful Place for Aborigines and Torres Strait Islanders in a Modern, Free and Tolerant Australia* (Constitutional Centenary Foundation, 1994) 18.

56 *Official Record of the Debates of the Australasian Federal Convention: 1891–1898*, vol. 5, *Melbourne 1898*, Legal Books, 1986, 1784 (Dr Quick). See also 1752, where Dr Quick refers to 'people of any undesirable race or of undesirable antecedents'.

57 Prior to 1967, this section included the following phrase: 'other than the aboriginal race in any State'. This phrase by deleted by referendum in 1967. Significantly, whilst the intention of voters in 1967 was to enable the Commonwealth Parliament to make laws benefiting the Aboriginal people, it appears that the s. 51(xxvi) may also enable the Commonwealth Parliament to make laws which *disadvantage* Aboriginal people. See *Kartinyeri v Commonwealth* (*Hindmarsh Island Bridge Case*) (1998) 195 CLR 337.

58 See, for example, *R v Bernasconi* (1915) 19 CLR 629, 637.

59 This section provides that '[n]o adult person who has or acquires a right to vote at elections for the more numerous House of the Parliament of a State shall, while the right continues, be prevented by any law of the Commonwealth from voting at elections for either House of the Parliament of the Commonwealth'.

60 *Snowdon v Dondas* (1996) 188 CLR 48, 71–72 (Brennan CJ, Dawson, Toohey, Gaudron and Gummow JJ).

The most significant constitutional development for the protection of human rights in Australia has been the implication of rights by the High Court from the text and structure of the Constitution. In 1992, the High Court discovered in the Constitution a freedom to discuss matters relating to Australian government, and used this freedom to strike down sections of the Political Broadcasts and Political Disclosures Act 1991 (Cth) which limited political advertising on radio and television during election periods.[61]

Furthermore, Chapter III of the Constitution, which establishes and defines 'federal judicial power' and creates a separation of judicial from legislative and executive powers, has been recognised by the High Court as the source of a number of procedural rights.[62] In *Polyukhovich v Commonwealth*, [63] six of the seven members of the High Court held that the Commonwealth Parliament was constitutionally prohibited from enacting a Bill of Attainder. It was found that a declaration of the guilt of a particular person or class of persons by the Commonwealth Parliament would constitute an improper exercise by the Parliament of judicial power. In the same case, however, the limits of the separation of powers for the implication of rights were also demonstrated. The High Court was unable to reach a consensus as to whether the Australian Constitution prohibits the Commonwealth Parliament from making retrospective criminal laws. To date, the High Court has stopped short of implying substantive rights from the separation of powers provision.[64] For example, in *Kruger v Commonwealth*, [65] five members of the High Court rejected the existence of an implied guarantee of general legal equality in the Australian Constitution.[66]

Challenging anti-terror laws

There is rarely a role for Australian judges in assessing Australia's terrorism laws, and even then not usually on human rights grounds. Courts might only be called upon, for example, to assess as part of the federal division of power whether a counter-terrorism law falls within any of the limited subject-matters on which the Constitution permits the Commonwealth Parliament to make laws (such as with respect to 'the naval and military defence of the Commonwealth' in s. 51(vi)).[67]

61 *Australian Capital Television Pty Ltd v Commonwealth* (1992) 177 CLR 106.

62 In *Re Tracey; Ex parte Ryan* (1989) 166 CLR 518 at 580, Deane J suggested that the separation of judicial from legislative and executive power effected by the Constitution is 'the Constitution's only general guarantee of due process'.

63 (1991) 172 CLR 106.

64 See Michael McHugh, 'Does Chapter III of the Constitution Protect Substantive as Well as Procedural Rights?' (2001) 21 *Australian Bar Review* 235.

65 (1997) 190 CLR 1.

66 *Kruger v Commonwealth* (1997) 190 CLR 1 44–45 (Brennan CJ), 63–68 (Dawson J, with whom McHugh J agreed at 142), 112–113 (Gaudron J), 153–155 (Gummow J).

67 The Commonwealth does not have a general power to legislate with respect to 'crime'. However, the Commonwealth's power to enact key parts of Australia's counter-terrorism legislation was put beyond doubt when the states referred their power over the area to the Commonwealth Parliament under s. 51(xxxvii) of the Constitution.

The courts have developed the common law rules regarding the interpretation of legislation so that the infringement of human rights is minimised. According to Mason CJ and Brennan, Gaudron and McHugh JJ in *Coco v The Queen*:[68] 'The courts should not impute to the legislature an intention to interfere with fundamental rights. Such an intention must be clearly manifested by unmistakeable and unambiguous language.'[69] Hence, 'a statute or statutory instrument which purports to impair a right to personal liberty is interpreted, if possible, so as to respect that right'.[70] The limits of this method of judicial review in protecting human rights are clear. The Commonwealth Parliament may legislate to abrogate any human right if it merely states its intention to do so 'by unmistakeable and unambiguous language'. There is no mechanism through which to analyse whether such abrogation is appropriate.

The 'rule of law' has also been recognised by the High Court to be an 'assumption'[71] underpinning the Commonwealth Constitution. In Australia, the rule of law is given expression through the judicial review of government action. The High Court's decision in *Australian Communist Party v Commonwealth*[72] demonstrates that while the *effect* of courts applying the rule of law in particular cases may be to protect human rights, there remains limited scope in Australia for the *direct* application of human rights to invalidate legislation. This case concerned legislation enacted by the Commonwealth Parliament as part of its attempt to eliminate communism in Australia. The recitals to the Communist Party Dissolution Act 1950 (Cth) provided that the act was 'necessary, for the security and defence of Australia and for the execution and maintenance of the Constitution and of the laws of the Commonwealth'.[73] The act:

- declared the Australian Communist Party to be an unlawful association;[74]
- enabled the Governor-General to declare other organisations whose, in his or her opinion, 'continued existence ... would be prejudicial to the security and defence of the Commonwealth or to the execution or maintenance of the Constitution or of the laws of the Commonwealth';[75] and
- applying a similar test, enabled the Governor-General to declare any person to be a 'Communist'.[76]

Such declarations resulted in the dissolution of an organisation and prohibited a person from holding office in the Commonwealth public service or industries

68 (1994) 179 CLR 427.
69 Ibid., 437.
70 *Re Bolton; Ex parte Beane* (1987) 162 CLR 514, 523 (Brennan J).
71 *Australian Communist Party v Commonwealth* (1951) 83 CLR 1, 193 (Dixon J).
72 Ibid.
73 Communist Party Dissolution Act 1950 (Cth), recital 9.
74 Ibid., s. 4.
75 Ibid., s. 5.
76 Ibid., s. 9.

declared by the Governor-General to be vital to the security and defence of Australia.

The High Court held that the Dissolution Act was invalid in its entirety. However, the finding of invalidity did not depend upon the act having breached any constitutional guarantee protective of human rights. Instead, the High Court found that the Dissolution Act did not fall within any of the heads of Commonwealth legislative power. In particular, the High Court refused to accept the statement in the recitals that it fell within the defence power because it was necessary for 'the security and defence of Australia'. It reached this conclusion because sections of the act imposed 'legal consequences on a legislative or executive opinion which itself supplies the only link between the power and the legal consequences of the opinion'.[77] The attempt by the Commonwealth Parliament in these sections to determine the scope of its own legislative power – by enabling the Governor-General to decide what organisations or persons were 'prejudicial to the security or defence of the Commonwealth' – breached the maxim that 'a stream cannot rise higher than its source'.[78] In other words, it is for the courts rather than the Commonwealth Parliament to determine the scope of the latter's legislative powers under the Constitution.

The *Communist Party Case* reflects the importance for the protection of rights of a legal culture based upon the rule of law and enforced by an independent judiciary. However, it also demonstrates the limitations of relying only upon the structural features of the Constitution – for example, limitations derived from federalism or the separation of judicial powers – to protect human rights. In many cases, there may simply be no constitutional remedy for the violation of human rights, such as discrimination on the basis of race or sex. Furthermore, even where legislation that violates human rights is challenged, the case is rarely litigated or adjudicated upon within a human rights framework. Instead, complainants are forced to rely upon the structural features of the Constitution to argue their case. This can transform concerns over human rights in Australia into debate about the respective powers of the Commonwealth and the states or about whether the courts are being asked to exercise 'judicial' power, leaving little or no room for concepts that are central to an effective human rights discourse.

The constitutional challenge to Australia's control order regime in *Thomas v Mowbray* [79] highlights these deficiencies. Division 104 of the Criminal Code empowers the Australian Federal Police to seek an order imposing restrictions, prohibitions and/or obligations upon an individual (for example, that he or she may not communicate with certain people or must reside at a particular address). Such an order may be made if an 'issuing court' is satisfied, on the balance of probabilities, that the control order would substantially assist in preventing a terrorist act or that the subject of the control order provided training to or received training from a terrorist organisation.[80] Control orders are problematic:

77 *Australian Communist Party v Commonwealth* (n. 61) 261 (Fullagar J).
78 Ibid., 258 (Fullagar J).
79 (2007) 233 CLR 307.
80 Criminal Code Act 1995 (Cth) s. 101.4(1).

> They illustrate the tension in employing the law as a tool of preventative policy. They challenge the traditional purpose of legal regulation. Under neither order is there a need for a person to have been found guilty of, or even be suspected of committing, a crime. Yet both orders enable significant restrictions on individual liberty. This is more than a breach of the old 'innocent until proven guilty' maxim: it ignores the notion of guilt altogether.[81]

However, *Thomas v Mowbray* was not argued before the High Court on the basis that the control order regime violated human rights. It was argued that: (a) the legislation did not fall within the scope of the defence power, external affairs power or implied nationhood power in the Constitution; and (b) the conferral of a power upon judicial officers to issue control orders violated Chapter III of the Constitution (either because it is a non-judicial power or, if the power is judicial, the legislation authorises the exercise of that power in a manner contrary to Chapter III). It, therefore, came as no surprise that human rights were not given a prominent place in any of the five separate judgments of the majority, which rejected both of the complainant's arguments. Comments made by Gleeson CJ in relation to (b) above demonstrate a perception on the part of the majority that human rights were principally the domain of the legislative and executive branches of government:

> An argument, as a matter of policy, that legislation for anti-terrorist control orders ought to be subject to some qualification in aid of the human rights of people potentially subject to such orders is one thing. An argument that the making of such orders should be regarded as totally excluded from the judicial function is another.[82]

No other member of the majority made any reference to human rights in their judgment. By contrast, the dissenting judgment of Kirby J is exceptional for its willingness to take human rights (and international law) into account: 'The Australian Constitution should be read, so far as the text allows, in a way that is harmonious with the universal principles of the international law of human rights and not destructive of them.'[83] He found that the control order regime was invalid because it 'directly encroaches upon rights and freedoms belonging to all people both by the common law of Australia and under international law'.[84]

The High Court (in addition to giving little consideration to human rights) deferred to the executive's assessment of the level of the threat posed by terrorism and what action is necessary to prevent terrorism. This is important because the scope of the defence power is not fixed – it 'waxes and wanes' according to the

81 Andrew Lynch and George Williams, *What Price Security? Taking Stock of Australia's Anti-Terror Laws* (UNSW Press, 2006), 42.
82 (2007) 233 CLR 307, 329.
83 Ibid., 441.
84 Ibid., 380.

nature of the threat to Australia at any particular time. The Commonwealth submitted to the court that there were nine 'factors' which, taken together, demonstrated something 'new and evil which Australia has to defend [itself] against'.[85] These factors included: the ready availability of explosive substances, the dependency of Australia on certain types of infrastructure and the importance that it places on 'iconic structures', the particular vulnerability of public transport (especially trains) to attack and the growth of fanatical ideological movements that compass the destruction of Western civilisation. Callinan J described these factors as 'blindingly obvious', and further noted that they 'render attempts to draw analogies with historical atrocities, as grave and frightening to their contemporary targets as they may have been, unconvincing'.[86]

The final point that must be noted about the decision in *Thomas* is the attitude shown by the majority judges towards the High Court's decision in the *Communist Party* case. One recurring theme in the majority judgments in *Thomas* was an attempt to narrow the principle upon which the *Communist Party Case* was decided. During questioning of counsel for the Commonwealth, Gleeson CJ stated that '[t]he *Communist Party Case* did not decide that the government could not protect the country against communism. The *Communist Party Case* was a decision about facts … About evidence.'[87]

The dismissive attitude of the majority is most clearly apparent in the decision of Callinan J. He stated of the evidence in *Thomas v Mowbray* that there was 'an abundance of uncontradicted, cogent, factual and notorious matter, having the character of constitutional and other facts upon which this Court may and should act'.[88] By contrast, in the *Communist Party Case* 'the Commonwealth sought to rely … factually solely on the allegations made in the preamble to the [Act]'.[89] He concluded from this that the 'particular principle, properly identified and understood,' for which the *Communist Party Case* stands is simply that 'it is for the courts, and not the Parliament to have the final say on whether legislation is within constitutional power or not'.[90] Justice Kirby, in dissent, was scathing of comments such as these:

> I did not expect that, during my service, I would see the *Communist Party Case* sidelined, minimised, doubted and even criticised and denigrated in this Court. Given the reasoning expressed by the majority in these proceedings, it appears likely that, had the Dissolution Act of 1950 been challenged today, its constitutional validity would have been upheld. This is further evidence of the unfortunate surrender of the present Court to demands for more and more

85 Ibid., 396.
86 Ibid., 490.
87 Transcripts of Proceedings, *Thomas v Mowbray* (High Court of Australia, Gleeson CJ, 20 February 2007).
88 (2007) 233 CLR 307, 486.
89 Ibid.
90 Ibid., 503.

governmental powers, federal and state, that exceed or offend the constitutional text and its abiding values.

Consequences

Legally protected human rights standards can provide a yardstick against which to assess the making of new anti-terror laws. Even then, they may prove to be only of limited benefit in the face of what can be overwhelming political and community pressure, in the aftermath of a terrorist attack, for 'tough laws' that 'do whatever it takes' to stop a future terrorist attack. A more significant benefit of human rights protection may therefore be that it can provide a trigger and mechanism for post-enactment analysis. This is a means by which overbreadth in anti-terror laws in other democratic nations can be reassessed, and on occasion remedied. Such a winding back may occur as a result of judicial decisions or through a fresh assessment by a government recognising the value and importance of protecting democratic freedoms.

Such a call was taken up in the lead-up to the 2010 UK general election. Counter-terrorism reform was identified as a priority by the Liberal Democrats and the Conservative Party and then formed part of the coalition agreement between them.[91] In 2011, the new coalition government announced a comprehensive review of the UK's anti-terror and security powers. Home Secretary Theresa May declared the government was 'committed to reversing the substantial erosion of civil liberties' produced by the UK's terrorism laws:

> I want a counter-terrorism regime that is proportionate, focused and transparent. We must ensure that in protecting public safety, the powers which we need to deal with terrorism are in keeping with Britain's traditions of freedom and fairness.[92]

The results of this review were published in 2011. It was found that some of the UK's counter-terrorism measures were 'neither proportionate nor necessary'.[93] As a result, the government announced a suite of proposals designed to 'liberalise' its counter-terrorism laws to 'correct the imbalance … between the State's security powers and civil liberties' and make those powers more targeted.[94] A key component of this reform was the abolition of control orders and their replacement with Terrorism Prevention and Investigation Measures (TPIMs).[95] Australia has gone through no like process of political recalculation and review, despite the fact that its control order regime, which remains in place unamended, is based upon the now-repealed UK regime.[96]

91 UK Government, *The Coalition: Our Programme for Government* (2010), 11, 24.
92 'Rapid Review of Counter-terrorism Powers', *Press Release*, 13 July 2010.
93 UK Government, *Review of Counter-terrorism and Security Powers: Review Findings and Recommendations*, 5.
94 Ibid., 3.
95 Ibid., 5.
96 See generally Lisa Burton and George Williams, 'What Future for Australia's Control Order Regime?' (2013) 24 *Public Law Review* 182.

The result in Australia is a body of anti-terror laws that in key respects undermines democratic freedoms to a greater extent than the laws of other comparable nations, including nations facing a more severe terrorist threat. For example, it would be unthinkable, if not constitutionally impossible, in nations such as the United States and Canada to restrict freedom of speech in the manner achieved by Australia's new censorship laws which enable publications, films or computer games to be banned according to the possible reaction of a person suffering a mental impairment. It would also not be possible to confer a power upon a secret intelligence agency, like that conferred on ASIO, to question and detain for up to a week non-suspect citizens.

A central challenge in enacting anti-terror laws is how best to ensure the security of the nation while also respecting the liberty of its people. In democratic nations, the answer is usually grounded in legal protections for human rights. In Australia, the answer is provided almost completely by the extent to which political leaders are willing to exercise good judgement and self-restraint in the enactment of new laws. This is not a check or balance that has proved effective in Australia when it comes to the enactment of anti-terror laws.

The future

Many Australians assume that Australia's anti-terror laws are subject to sunset or other clauses and so will depart the statute book when the immediate emergency is over. This indeed was the experience of the like laws enacted during the First and Second World Wars, but, unlike those conflicts, the 'war on terror', like the war on drugs, is a misnamed conflict without a conceivable end. As a result, with rare exceptions where sunset clauses may yet expire sometime in the future,[97] the Australia's new anti-terror laws will operate in perpetuity unless action is taken.

The problem is not necessarily one of the misuse of anti-terror laws. Indeed, some laws, such as ASIO's detention power, have never been, and may never be, used. In such cases, the problem lies in how such extraordinary powers are becoming seen as normal, and so applied elsewhere.[98] An example is the extension of the control order regime from our national anti-terror legislation to so-called anti-bikie laws.[99] In South Australia, former Premier Mike Rann justified this by saying: "We're allowing similar legislation to that applying to terrorists, because

97 See generally Nicola McGarrity, Rishi Gulati and George Williams, 'Sunset Clauses in Australian Anti-Terrorism Laws' (2012) 37 *Adelaide Law Review* 307.

98 See Nicola McGarrity and George Williams, 'When Extraordinary Measures Become Normal: Pre-Emption in Counter-Terrorism and Other Laws' in Andrew Lynch, Nicola McGarrity and George Williams (eds), *Counter-Terrorism and Beyond: The Culture of Law and Justice after 9/11* (Routledge, 2010) 131; Gabrielle Appleby and John Williams, 'The Anti-Terror Creep: Law and Order, the States and the High Court of Australia' in Andrew Lynch, Nicola McGarrity and George Williams (eds), *Counter-Terrorism and Beyond: The Culture of Law and Justice after 9/11* (Routledge, 2010) 150.

99 For example, Serious and Organised Crime (Control) Act 2008 (SA).

[bikie groups] are terrorists within our community."[100] Laws of this kind are now spreading throughout the country, and are also encouraging the revival of offences for guilt by association and consorting. The danger is that the exceptional powers granted to combat terrorism will increasingly be used by state governments to prosecute the law and order debate. They are becoming part of the state legislators' toolbox for demonstrating to the community how they are tough on crime.

While there has been little political backing for revising Australia's anti-terror laws, there is no shortage of analysis and official reports on the subject. In 2013, two long-awaited, independent reports commissioned by the Commonwealth were released that deal with major parts of the laws, and recommend very significant change. One report was convened by the Council of Australian Governments (COAG) to review a long list of powers and offences.[101] The committee was led by Anthony Whealy QC, a retired judge from the NSW Court of Appeal, and included senior state and federal police officers.[102] The other report was prepared by a leading New South Wales barrister, Bret Walker SC.[103] He was appointed in 2011 as Australia's first Independent National Security Legislation Monitor, and as such was charged generally with reviewing the operation, effectiveness and implications of these laws, including by having regard to Australia's international obligations under international human rights agreements.[104] His term ended in 2014.

Walker had significant advantages in preparing his report. The COAG Review was rushed for time, whereas Walker's conclusions are the culmination of more than a year and a half of discussion and analysis. The Federal Parliament also gave Walker special powers. He could question agencies such as the Australian Federal Police and ASIO, and has access to classified information such as their case files.

Both reports recognise the danger posed to the community by terrorism. Walker identifies 'investigation and particularly surveillance' as 'by far the most effective powers' to meet this threat.[105] The problem is that the Federal Parliament has granted the police and ASIO powers that go considerably beyond this. Both the COAG and Walker reports come to the same conclusion: in many respects, Australia's anti-terror laws are unnecessary, go too far and lack appropriate safeguards. It is clear from these reports that many of these laws need urgent repair or even repeal.

100 ABC Radio National, 'South Australia's Plans to Obliterate Outlaw Bikie Gangs', *The Law Report*, 6 May 2008 (Mike Rann), www.abc.net.au/radionational/programs/lawreport/south-australias-plans-to-obliterate-outlaw-bikie/3254212.

101 Council of Australian Governments, *Review of Counter-terrorism Legislation* (2013).

102 The membership of the review committee can be found here: www.coagctreview.gov.au/committee/Pages/default.aspx.

103 Walker B, *Independent National Security Legislation Monitor Declassified Annual Report* (2013).

104 *Independent National Security Legislation Monitor Act 2010* (Cth) s. 8.

105 Walker B, *Independent National Security Legislation Monitor Declassified Annual Report* (2013), 4.

The reports have a lot in common. Both undertake a careful, forensic analysis of some of Australia's most contentious laws, and find aspects of them wanting. For example, the reports recommend the abolition of preventative detention orders, by which a person can be held without charge for up to 14 days. The COAG Review also examines offences directed at terrorism. It finds that many apply far too widely, such as one that permits a person to be jailed for up to 15 years for 'possessing a thing' connected with a terrorist act. It finds that offences such as this should be tightened, and in other cases it recommends repeal, such as for the broad-ranging offence of associating with a terrorist organisation.

Walker finds that the control order regime is 'not effective, not appropriate and not necessary'.[106] He recommends that it be abolished, or at least rewritten to apply only to people convicted of a terrorism offence who remain a danger to the community. By contrast, the COAG Review recommends that the control orders be retained, but only with a range of significant new safeguards.

The controversial law that grants ASIO an extraordinary power to question and detain in secret for up to a week Australian citizens not suspected of any crime also receives attention. Walker recommends that ASIO retain the power to gather intelligence by questioning people about their knowledge and links to terrorism. However, he finds that the agency should lose its power to detain.

Walker's report and the COAG Review strip away any pretence that Australia has the right laws in place to protect the community from terrorism. The reports reveal that many of these laws are ineffective or unnecessary. Some are also dangerous in how they undermine important human rights and democratic values, such as freedom of speech, the right to a fair trial and the presumption of innocence.

It is clear that the Federal Parliament has much work to do to fix Australia's anti-terror laws. The manner in which the COAG and Walker reports were made public was not a promising start. They were released to the public at 5 p.m. on federal budget day in May 2013. This also happened to be the last possible day allowed for releasing the Walker report, which the government had received in late 2012. Releasing the reports in this way meant that they and their recommendations were buried under the analysis and media attention bestowed on the budget. Leaving the release to the last minute also meant there was no chance that they could be acted on prior to the September 2013 federal election.

It might have been thought that the election period would at least provide an opportunity for the major parties to indicate how they would respond to these reports in the next Parliament. However, rather than do so, both sought to avoid providing a concrete answer. When pressed to do so by the Law Council of Australia, the governing Labor Party stated that 'a re-elected federal Labor Government will carefully consider the reports before reaching a final position on the substance of the recommendations',[107] while the opposition coalition said that it would 'carefully consider' the recommendations in Walker's report, but otherwise

106 Ibid.
107 Law Council of Australia, *Key Legal Issues: 2013 Federal Election Responses* (2013) 16.

had 'no plans to make material alterations to the anti-terrorism legislation introduced under the former coalition Government following the September 11, 2001 attacks'.[108] Such responses hardly amounted to clarion calls for reform, or even a preparedness to acknowledge the major deficiencies in Australia's anti-terror laws identified by the Commonwealth's own independent inquiries. This is reflected in a lack of action by the coalition government since its victory at the 2013 election. It has not sought to remedy any of the deficiencies identified with Australia's anti-terror laws. In fact, it's only significant initiative has been to introduce legislation to repeal the office of the Independent National Security Legislation Monitor.[109]

Conclusion

Australia was right to enact new anti-terror laws in the wake of the 9/11 attacks. Such laws were needed to ensure that the legal system offered protection to the community by preventing terrorist attacks from occurring. Passing new anti-terror laws also enabled Australia to live up to its international obligations and signalled that as a nation Australia rejects such forms of political violence.

In the years since 9/11, the Federal Parliament has enacted many new anti-terror laws. This has given rise to a large and remarkable new body of legislation providing for powers and sanctions that were unthinkable prior to the 2001 attacks. Indeed, the rhetoric of a '*war* on terror' reflects the nature and severity of the laws enacted in response to the threat. While these laws were often cast as a transient response to an exceptional set of events, it is now clear that the greater body of this law will remain on the Australian statute books for the foreseeable future.

This poses a long-term challenge for the Australian legal system and human rights protection. While new anti-terror laws were needed, the laws actually enacted diverge in too many respects from the laws that Australia should have achieved. The result is a body of enactments that is creating new understandings of the normal limits of the law in Australia. This is broadening the extent to which it is considered acceptable for Australian law to sanction extraordinary powers or outcomes, such as detention without charge or the silencing of speech.

Australia's new anti-terror laws expose structural problems with Australia's system of law. That system is dependent upon an effective parliamentary process and a culture of respect among political leaders when it comes to democratic values, rule of law principles and human rights. Anti-terror laws reveal how many of the bedrock principles of Australian democracy are actually only assumptions and conventions within the political system rather than hard legal rules that demand compliance. The laws reveal the capacity of politicians and the Federal Parliament to contravene these values and, in doing so, to create new and problematic precedents for the making of other laws.

108 Ibid.
109 Independent National Security Legislation Monitor Repeal Bill 2014 (Cth).

9 The legacy of apartheid and South Africa's struggle to contain contemporary forms of terrorism and violent extremism*

Martin Ewi and Willem Els

Introduction

Since 2002, South Africa has not experienced a major terrorist attack. The country, however, remains in a state of alert and consternation. Recent criminal and terrorist activities, notably the spate of kidnappings,[1] incidences involving explosives,[2] foiled terrorist attacks,[3] violent attacks at mosques,[4] and recruitment of some South Africans into the Islamic State's caliphate,[5] as well as the alleged presence of terrorist cells in the country,[6] have exposed South Africa's vulnerability to the current global threat of terrorism and violent extremism. A series of warnings by foreign governments[7] about potential terrorist attacks in South Africa have

1 See, for example, C. Pieterse, Kidnapping danger growing, News24, 27 May 2018, www.news24.com/SouthAfrica/News/kidnapping-danger-growing-20180527-2, accessed 31 July 2018.

2 See, for example, L. Daniel, Bomb blasts reported near Durban July, The South African, 8 July 2018, www.thesouthafrican.com/bomb-blasts-reported-near-durban-july/, accessed 31 July 2018.

3 See, for example, Planned terror attack in SA foiled – spy cables, News24, 26 February 2015, www.news24.com/SouthAfrica/News/Planned-terror-attack-on-SA-foiled-spy-cables-20150226, accessed 30 July 2018; and N. Onishi, South Africa charges twins over plot to attack U.S. embassy and join ISIS, New York Times, 11 July 2016, www.nytimes.com/2016/07/12/world/africa/south-africa-islamic-state.html, accessed 31 July 2018.

4 R. Davis, Second deadly mosque attack leaves South Africa reeling, Daily Maverick, 15 June 2018, www.dailymaverick.co.za/article/2018-06-15-second-deadly-mosque-attack-leaves-south-africa-reeling/, accessed 31 July 2018.

5 See, for example, ISIS recruiting in SA – report, News24, 23 November 2014, www.news24.com/SouthAfrica/News/ISIS-recruiting-in-SA-report-20141123, accessed 30 July 2018.

6 For an assessment of the threat of terrorism including domestic and foreign terrorist threats, see R. C. Cachalia and A. Schoeman, Violent extremism in South Africa: Assessing the current threat, ISS Southern Africa Report, No. 7, May 2017. See also K. Shillinger, Al-Qaida in southern Africa: The emergence of a new front in the war on terrorism, Armed Forces Journal, 1 February 2006, http://armedforcesjournal.com, accessed 18 October 2016.

7 Many of the warnings have been issued by the United States' and British governments. See, for example, C. Williams, Terror threats and turmoil: A bad time for US–South Africa relations, The Conversation, 9 June 2016, https://theconversation.

generated a great deal of debate and, to some extent, panic among South Africans, many of whom have cast doubt about the capability of the South African government to deal with a potential terrorist threat. To some extent, the public, influenced by a stream of misleading media reports, and insufficient communication from government, has shown little or limited knowledge about South Africa's counterterrorism measures and the institutions of government that work tirelessly to avert the threat. The principal objective of this chapter is to fill this information void. It seeks to investigate and evaluate the measures taken by government and the current framework for countering terrorism and violent extremism in South Africa. Of foremost importance is the need to understand how the South African government is organized internally to counter the prevailing threat of terrorism and violent extremism. In this context, this chapter is intended to identify and provide an overview of the systems, procedures and the governmental agencies responsible for the interception, investigation, prosecution, adjudication and policy coordination on matters relating to counterterrorism and the countering of violent extremism.

Research methodology, scope and limitations

This chapter is based on a desktop literature review and a field study designed in the form of qualitative semi-structured interviews with experts and practitioners. The purpose of the field study was to empirically investigate through the perception of those dealing with the issue at different levels, the claim that violent extremism poses a threat to South Africa, and to critically evaluate the country's responses and capabilities to deal with the threat of violent extremism. The field study consisted of 40 interviews conducted over a two-month period in September and October 2016. Interviewees were chosen on the basis of their familiarity with the topics of terrorism and violent extremism. The criteria for sampling of the population were carefully selected to ensure broad representation of expertise, gender and discipline. To this end, the 41 respondents were drawn from different backgrounds and included civil society; relevant government departments, including the South African Police Service (SAPS), Department of International Relations and Cooperation (DIRCO), State Security Agency (SSA) and the South African National Defence Force (SANDF); ex-service men; security analysts and experts; academia; journalists, members of the diplomatic corps, community and student leaders. Due to the sensitive nature of the topic, most respondents chose to remain anonymous.

The literature review included media reports, court documents on cases that have been prosecuted and academic research on extremist groups in South Africa. The field study was conducted in Gauteng, notably in Johannesburg and Pretoria. The data collected from the field study was in the form of perception and experts' analyses.

com/terror-threats-and-turmoil-a-bad-time-for-us-south-africa-relations-60804, accessed 10 June 2016; UK authorities issue travel warning to those visiting South Africa, eNCA news, 22 February 2018, www.enca.com/south-africa/uk-authorities-issue-travel-warning-to-those-visiting-south-africa, accessed 30 July 2018.

The scope of this chapter is limited to current South Africa's post-9/11 responses to terrorism and violent extremism, and the institutional mechanisms existing at the time it was going to print. In order to establish the context of current responses, as well as demonstrate continuation or consistency and inconsistency in Pretoria's endeavours, this chapter begins with a brief overview of the historical evolution of South Africa's approach and responses to terrorism and violent extremism.

Historical evolution of South Africa's responses to terrorism

While terrorism[8] has a long history, violent extremism in its current conceptual meaning is a relatively new term in South Africa. It is therefore important to state at the outset of this chapter that there exists no specific legislation and formal institution dedicated to the issue. It is used in this chapter in view of its close links[9] with terrorism and the belief that counterterrorism measures are relevant to countering violent extremism (CVE).[10]

Terrorism has been one of the most contested issues in South African politics and government responses to it have been shaped by its changing patterns in South Africa and the world at large. The advent of the armed struggle in 1961 brought to the fore two competing forms of terror – state sponsored and revolutionary terrorism.[11] The interplay between the two or what Michael Schmidt refers to as 'the dirty war' was so profound that Schmidt asserts that 'terrorism built our democracy'.[12] Since the advent of democracy in 1994, the threat of terrorism has shifted from what was regarded as a domestic threat posed by PAGAD and far-right Afrikaner groups between 1996 and 2000, to what is now perceived as a global or foreign threat posed by international terrorist groups such as the Islamic State of Iraq and Syria (ISIS), al-Qaeda, al Shabaab and Boko Haram, in

8 Terrorism in this chapter means an act that violates the criminal laws of a country or a legal entity, which is calculated to cause harm and fear to the population or segment thereof. For a full definition, see Articles 1 and 3 of the OAU Convention on the Prevention and Combating of Terrorism, adopted in Algiers, Algeria in 1999. See electronic version: https://au.int/en/treaties/oau-convention-prevention-and-combating-terrorism, accessed 10 June 2016.

9 Violent extremism is believed to be the ideological mindset that inspires terrorist activities or leads individuals to commit terrorist acts. For a comprehensive discussion on the links between terrorism and violent extremism, see, for example, UNDP, Journey to Extremism in Africa: Drivers, Incentives and the Tipping Point for Recruitment (UNDP, 2017).

10 For a comprehensive understanding of violent extremism and countering violent extremism (CVE), see, for example, Organization for Security and Co-operation in Europe, Preventing Terrorism and Countering Violent Extremism and Radicalization that Lead to Terrorism: A Community-Policing Approach (OSCE, 17 March 2014), www.osce.org/atu/111438, accessed 29 June 2017.

11 See, for example, D.J. Whittaker (ed.), The Terrorism Reader—Fourth Edition (Routledge, 2012), 271.

12 See M. Schmidt, Drinking with ghosts: The aftermath of apartheid's dirty war, www.hsrc.ac.za/en/events/events/drinking-with-ghosts-launch (16 October 2016).

the post 9/11 period. This shift in trends and manifestations of terrorism has also affected the terrorism threat perception in South Africa. While terrorism was considered a serious threat to the state during the years between 1996 and 2000, since 9/11 the threat has been generally perceived to be low or non-threatening.[13] This section attempts to provide a brief historical experience of South Africa's response to terrorism, as a background to understanding the dynamics of the country's current responses to and the policy and institutional architecture for the fight against terrorism and the phenomenon of violent extremism.

The term terrorism is believed to have gained currency in South African political parlance in the 1960s – a decade often believed to have laid the genesis of the armed struggle against apartheid. Prior to that various appellations were used to refer to some of the offences that were later characterized as 'terroristic' in the 1967 Terrorism Act. Among these included acts of sabotage, conspiracy, treason, riots, communist activities, disruption of law and order, and other criminal conducts, which were mostly associated with resistance to apartheid. Terroristic crimes were therefore regarded as the gravest criminal offences, which were punishable by the severest of penalties or what was referred to as the 'supreme penalty' (death penalty).

The apartheid government responded to these perceived terroristic acts through a rule of law-based approach that saw the adoption of a series of repressive and draconian laws and gave law-enforcement agencies vast powers to enforce them. Between 1906 and 1990, more than 35 of such laws had been passed to deal with crimes that were regarded as terroristic in nature. These included the 1912 Riotous Assemblies Act, 1917 Criminal Procedure and Evidence Act No. 31, 1922 Strike Condonation Act, 1950 Suppression of Communism Act No. 44, 1952 Criminal Sentences Amendment Act No. 33, 1953 Public Safety Act, 1953 Criminal Law Amendment Act No. 8, 1960 Unlawful Organisation Act No. 34, 1962 Sabotage Act General Laws Amendment Act No. 76, 1963 General Law Amendment Act No. 37, 1968 Dangerous Weapons Act No. 71, 1972 Security Intelligence and State Security Council Act No. 64 and 1976 Internal Security Amendment Act No. 791992.[14]

Because the stability and sustainability of the apartheid regime depended on the maintenance of law and order, there was therefore strict enforcement of security-related laws. As Mzukisi Njotini rightly points out, these legislative acts were conceived and executed on the basis of the principle of *salus reipublicae suprema lex*, which held that the safety and well-being of the state was the supreme or highest law, and therefore gave the state unfettered powers to enforce the law even at the expense of human rights,[15] and the erosion of civil and political

13 Most of those who responded to the field questionnaire indicated that they see the threat of terrorism to be low, and only a few respondents saw it to be threatening or serious.

14 For a comprehensive list of apartheid laws see The history of separate development in South Africa, South African History Online, www.sahistory.org.za/article/apartheid-legislation-1850s-1970s, accessed 10 October 2016.

15 See Mzukisi Niven Njotini, Anti-terrorism measures in South Africa: Suspicious transaction reporting and human rights, African Human Rights Law Journal, Vol. 15:2, 2015, 528.

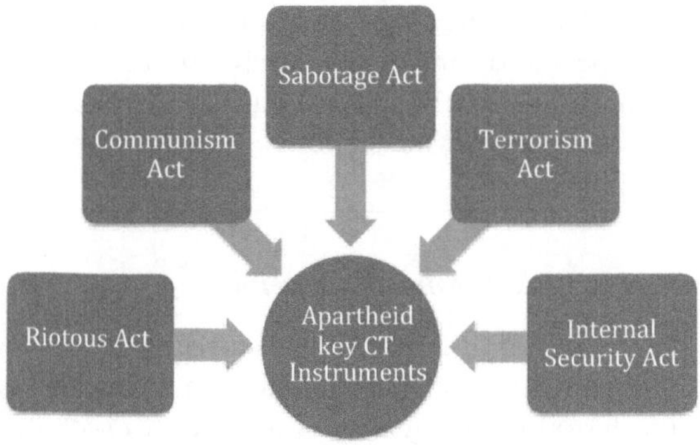

Figure 9.1 **Principal terrorism laws under apartheid**

liberties in South Africa.[16] The far-reaching impact of these laws is captured by Dale McKinley in his observation that laws were 'used to try and crush all political, social, economic and cultural resistance to the apartheid state'.[17]

As a result, hundreds of people were prosecuted and convicted pursuant to the abovementioned legislative acts. The most famous of these prosecutions was the so-called 'Rivonia Trial', which took place at the Pretoria Supreme Court, and is commonly described as 'the trial that changed South Africa'.[18] This was due to its harsh sanctions against key leaders of the African National Congress (ANC), including Nelson Mandela, who was sentenced to life imprisonment.[19]

The 1967 Terrorism Act did not create any specific mechanism for its implementation, though by law, it was the foremost responsibility of the police. The apartheid machinery for combatting terroristic acts, however, included the Supreme Court, the Executive Branch (the State President and the Cabinet) and all the security apparatus. These included the South African Defence Force (SADF), created in 1912; the South African Police (SAP), formed in 1913; and the State Security Council (SSC), formed in 1972 (previously called the Security

16 This is further corroborated by Leonard Thompson, who has observed that these repressive laws gave the police vast powers to arrest people without trial and detain them indefinitely in solitary confinement, without revealing their identities and without giving them access to anyone except government officials. The government could ban any organization, prohibit the holding of meetings of any sort and prevent organizations from receiving funds from abroad. See Leonard Thompson, A History of South Africa, Fourth Edition (Yale University Press, 2014), 199.

17 Dale T. McKinley, State security and civil-political rights in South Africa, Strategic Review for Southern Africa, Vol 35:1, June 2013, 120. See electronic version: www.questia.com/library/p3957/strategic-review-for-southern-africa, accessed November 16, 2016.

18 See, for example, Rivonia Trial 1963–1964, South African History Online, www.sahistory.org.za/topic/rivonia-trial-1963-1964, accessed 10 October 2016.

19 See Douglas O. Linder, The Nelson Mandela (Rivonia) Trial: An account, http://law2.umkc.edu/faculty/PROJECTS/FTRIALS/mandela/mandelaaccount.html, accessed 19 June 2016.

Branch,[20] formed in 1947). There were also numerous coordination committees, particularly at the operational and policy levels. At least 18 interdepartmental security coordinating committees were operational by 1978. The SSC served as an advisory body on security policies and strategies to the state president and was also represented in the cabinet.[21]

President Nelson Mandela's response to terrorism

The transition from apartheid to democracy was most remarkable in the legal field, where many of the apartheid laws were repealed and/or amended. In the post-1994 dispensation, terrorism emerged once again as a major threat to the new democracy, when PAGAD and the far-right Afrikaner groups escalated their attacks in the wake of Mandela's administration. For a leader who had spent 27 years in prison for politically motivated charges of terrorism (or acts of sabotage) and was blacklisted by foreign governments including the United States and the United Kingdom,[22] the threats posed by PAGAD and far-right Afrikaner groups tested not only the nation but also Mandela's own personal resolve and integrity. For Mandela, the most serious of these was the threat from the far right or what he called the 'ultra right-wing' because their activities were leading South Africa in a path of 'race war'.[23] Earlier in 1993, Mandela had warned that, if the 'right-wing tries to unleash a civil war they will be crushed by the democratic forces'.[24] When PAGAD escalated in 1996,[25] as a vigilante group to fight what was perceived as a chronic problem of gangsterism and drugs,[26] Mandela initially resisted

20 The Security Branch here refers to the body responsible for coordinating security and intelligence during apartheid and not the unit in the police that was formed in the post-apartheid era.
21 See, for example, M Hough, The concept of a national security strategy: The case of the United States and South Africa, Strategic Review for Southern Africa, Vol. XXVIII/2, November 2006, 9–10.
22 See, for example, K. Roach, Canada's response to Terrorism, in V.V. Ramraj, M. Hor and K. Roach (eds), Global Anti-Terrorism Law and Policy (Cambridge University Press, 2005), 515.
23 Statement by Nelson Mandela on the ultra right-wing's threats of civil war issued on 26 November 1993, www.mandela.gov.za/mandela_speeches/1993/931126_threats.htm (16 October 2016).
24 Ibid.
25 Although PAGAD is generally believed to have been formed in 1995, it was formally introduced to both the South African public and the international community in August 1996, following the shocking killing of Mr Rashaad Staggie, a notorious drug lord in Cape Town. See Abdulkader Tayob, The function of Islam in the South African political process: Defining a community in a nation, in Abdulkader Tayob and Wolfram Weisse (eds), Religion and Politics in South Africa: From Apartheid to Democracy (Waxmann, 1999), 21. See also Bill Dixon and Lisa-Marie Johns, Gangs, Pagad & the state: Vigilantism and revenge violence in the Western Cape, Violence and Transition Series, Vol. 2, May 2001.
26 The problem of gangsterism was so entrenched in the Cape that some researchers on the topic estimated that there were about 80,000 active gang members belonging to some 137 gangs. See, for example, Rachel Monaghan, One merchant, one bullet: The

pressure or, as David Africa put it, his administration 'was reluctant to assign the label of terrorism to any group'. As a result, the administration was accused of inaction and for being dismissive of the existence of a home-grown violent extremism.[27]

The first response of the administration was to negotiate with PAGAD. This was, however, short-lived due to PAGAD's intransigency, internal split, frequent leadership turnover, disputed controlled by Qibla[28] and the continuation of deadly bombings.[29] It became evident that any effective response to PAGAD would also have to use force. Security operations began in earnest early in 1996, when a joint team of the new South African Police Service (SAPS) and the new South African National Defence Force (SANDF) responded to PAGAD's activities in the greater Cape Town area.[30] In May 1996, the National Crime Prevention Strategy was launched. It proposed a broad framework, which integrated local communities into police crime prevention strategies. In October 1997, Mandela held several policy and strategic meetings with cabinet ministers and heads of the security forces to further decide on the administration's response to PAGAD.[31]

The result was a strong focus on an intelligence-led, integrated and coordinated approach. A series of high-profile operations included a high-density security force deployed in a crime prevention operation codenamed 'Operation Recoil', which resulted in a record arrest of 7,437 suspects between October 1997 and January 1998.[32] Other successful operations included 'Operation Saladin' (1998), 'Operation Good Hope' (1999), 'Operation Crackdown' (2000) and 'Operation Lancer' (2001).[33] What was most successful in the fight against PAGAD, as with the far-right Afrikaners, was that Mandela was able to isolate the group from

rise and fall of PAGAD, Journal of Low Intensity Conflict & Law Enforcement, Vol. 12:1, 2004, 2.

27 See D. Africa, Countering ideological support for terrorism: A South African case study, in A. Aldis and G.P. Herd (eds), The Ideological War on Terror: Worldwide Strategies for Counter-Terrorism (Routledge, 2007).

28 The role played by Qibla (a radical Islamic organization) in PAGAD remains highly contested. Some views suggest that PAGAD was hijacked by Qibla, which took over control of the vigilante group (PAGAD), others suggest that Qibla had very little influence. For a comprehensive discussion of the role of Qibla within PAGAD, see A. Desai, The cape of good dope? A post-apartheid story of gangs and vigilantes, A joint study by the Centre for Civil Society and the School of Development Studies, University of KwaZulu-Natal, 2004; see electronic version: ccs.ukzn.ac.za/files/Desai%20Pagad%20Research%20Report.pdf, accessed 10 August 2016.

29 For more details on the negotiation and its shortcomings, see B. Gilder, Songs and Secrets: South Africa from Liberation to Governance (Jacana Media (Pty) Ltd, 2012), 313–316.

30 See H. Boshoff and M. Schönteich, South Africa's operational and legislative responses to terrorism, in J. Cilliers and K. Sturman (eds), Africa and Terrorism, Joining the Global Campaign, ISS Monograph 74, July 1, 2002, 44.

31 Ibid.

32 Ibid.

33 Ibid.

Muslim communities in Cape Town,[34] which as Barry Gilder noted remained 'well integrated into South African society at all levels', and that the 'Muslim community in the Western Cape and its leadership did not support the tactics of PAGAD'.[35] In a 2004 report to the United Nations Security Council Counter-Terrorism Committee (CTC) pursuant to Security Council Resolution 1373 (2001), the South African government stated that, 'The multi-disciplinary law enforcement approach, highlighted by Operation Good Hope, led to numerous seizures of illegal weapons', and isolation of extremist elements within PAGAD, who committed acts of terrorism.'[36] This multidimensional approach, which combined hard security responses and soft strategies that relied on community support proved effective in defeating PAGAD.[37]

Understanding South Africa's post-9/11 responses to terrorism and violent extremism

The 9/11 attacks occurred at a time when the domestic threat of terrorism had receded. Nonetheless, South Africa joined the chorus of states in condemning 9/11 and showing solidarity with the United States.[38] Though Pretoria was in no mode to reawaken sleeping dogs at home, it also could not afford to show indifference to the global war on terror that ensued led by the United States, a key partner. Pretoria was also critical of some aspects of the war on terror, particularly the invasion of Iraq and the tendency for the terrorism discourse to infuriate and potentially isolate certain communities based on the belief by some in the West that Islam was the source of modern terrorism. After 9/11, the threat perception of terrorism in South Africa shifted from domestic threat posed by local groups such as PAGAD and far-right Afrikaner groups to foreign groups such as al-Qaeda, Islamic State of Iraq and Syria (ISIS), Boko Haram and al Shabaab, which

34 See A. Tayob, Race, ideology, and Islam in contemporary South Africa, in R.M. Feener (ed.), Islam in World Cultures: Comparative Perspectives (ABC-CLIO, Inc, 2004), 279.

35 Gilder, Songs and Secrets, 313–314.

36 See Letter dated 27 February 2004 from the Chairman of the Security Council Committee established pursuant to resolution 1373 (2001), Ambassador Inocencio F. Arias, concerning counter-terrorism addressed to the President of the Security Council, Security Council document, S/2004/170, dated 2 March 2004 (English), 26–27.

37 It is not clear whether PAGAD was ever destroyed or they just ceased violent attacks against government's agencies and ordinary citizens. A leaked document of the National Intelligence Agency, entitled Ministerial Brief, bearing an update on risk assessment of PAGAD, dated 22 October 2009, alleged that PAGAD carried out acts of intimidation in which two people were killed by gunshots, and that PAGAD collected and provided to SAPS crime-related information. For details see A.J. Pius, Spy cables: Inside South Africa's spy agency, Al Jazeera, 25 February 2015, http://america.aljazeera.com/articles/2015/2/25/spy-cables-inside-south-africas-spy-agency.html, accessed 25 September 2016.

38 See, for example, C MacFarlane, Terrorism in South Africa, Prehosp Disaster Medicine, 18/2, April–June 2003, 133–134, www.ncbi.nlm.nih.gov/pubmed/15074496 (19 October 2016).

were previously believed not to be associated with terrorism in South Africa.[39] This shift in perception was first signalled, at least officially, in President Thabo Mbeki's State of the Nation Address in February 2003. In that speech, the president, while condemning the new threat of global terrorism, averred that 'no normal South African has any reason to resort to force to communicate his or her views'.[40] Indeed, the president's statement was remarkably consistent with a similar statement he had made in 2001, in which he unequivocally condemned 9/11. 'As we share the grief of the bereaved and seek to comfort those who are maimed', he apprised fellow South Africans, 'this we must say, that as a civilized people we condemn this act of terrorism unreservedly and will do everything we can to ensure that our own society does not give birth to the ugly and repugnant formations that committed wilful mass murder in New York and Washington'.[41] The president seemed to suggest that this was a foreign phenomenon, which should be prevented by all costs from having any roots in South Africa. Through this policy perception, terrorism was seen to be distant or a faraway threat from South Africa. Several years later, President Jacob Zuma echoed the same policy sentiments. In his reaction to terrorist attacks in Europe, Africa and the Middle East, the president stated:

> The most prevalent cause of the current trend of terrorism and the breeding ground for violent extremism is primarily the result of unabated war and conflict in a region [Middle East] where, for a very long time, there has been a preference for military action instead of political solutions. Other factors, including socio-economic ones, interference by outside parties and the pursuance of the regime change doctrine has also played a significant role in perpetuating the ongoing cycle of conflict and instability. The lack of progress on political dialogue and the absence of a sustainable long-term solution have created the space for terrorist groups such as ISIS, Al-Qaeda and the others

39 The extent of the threat posed by these foreign groups to South Africa remained highly contested. While foreign intelligence agencies saw it to be high or even serious, the State Security Agency did not see the threat as such. Another contentious issue relates to whether al-Qaeda, ISIS, al Shabaab and other foreign terrorist groups have a presence in South Africa. While South African Intelligence has not established such presence, foreign intelligence agencies alleged that these groups, particularly al-Qaeda and ISIS, have a presence. For more discussion on this, see Rahul Radhakrishnan and Wil Jordan, Cables reveal S Africa at odds with allies on al-Qaeda, Al Jazeera, 25 February 2015, www.aljazeera.com/news/2015/02/spy-cables-reveal-south-africa-odds-allies-al-qaeda-shabab-guardian-russia-fsb-150225144344673.html, accessed 18 January 2017.

40 See State of the Nation Address of the President of South Africa, Thabo Mbeki, Houses of Parliament, Cape Town, 14 February 2003, www.gov.za/state-nation-address-president-south-africa-thabo-mbeki-houses-parliament-cape-town-14-february-2003, accessed 6 January 2017.

41 Cited in Scott Firsing, South Africa's role in the United States-led war against Islamic extremism, Foreign Policy Journal, 23 July 2011, www.foreignpolicyjournal.com/2011/07/23/south-africas-role-in-the-united-states-led-war-against-islamic-extremism/view-all/, accessed 25 August 2016.

associated with them to exploit divisions for the furtherance of their distorted beliefs.[42]

What influenced this shift in the perception of terrorism were several factors including the end in PAGAD's attacks and a significantly diminished threat from the far-right Afrikaner groups, the globalization of the al-Qaeda brand of terrorism and the proliferation of new groups such as Boko Haram, ISIS and al Shabaab. The immediate and long-term consequence of this foreign perception of terrorism was that an issue, which from 1996 to 2000 was viewed as a serious security threat and considered a priority for government action, suddenly assumed a low profile, even at a time when other countries were upgrading their threat level as a result of the global trend.

The field survey conducted for this study found that the low threat perception was not just a perception held by government, but that there was also popular support for it.[43] Indeed the majority of the 41 people interviewed believed that terrorism does not pose a serious threat to South Africa,[44] at least not on the same scale as ordinary crime and organized crime including drug trafficking and money laundering. Recent strategic policy documents indicate that there is no specific threat to South Africa beyond what exists as a general threat globally. As a result, the government has consistently dismissed allegations or warnings issued by foreign intelligence agencies about potential terrorist attacks in South Africa, even when such intelligence warnings indicate that the target is not South Africa per se but foreign interests, especially American and European interests in the country. It is worthy of note that the threat posed by foreign terrorist groups should not only be assessed from their capability to carry out attacks in South Africa, but also the threat they pose to South Africans abroad. Indeed, South African citizens are increasingly being targeted abroad by terrorist organizations in Mali, Yemen, Somalia, Nigeria, Syria and Iraq.[45]

42 See President Jacob Zuma: Global challenges: Terrorism and refugee crisis, Remarks by President Jacob Zuma at Working Dinner of G20 Leaders on the topic Global Challenges: Terrorism and Refugee Crisis Antalya, Turkey, 15 November 2015, www.gov.za/speeches/president-jacob-zuma-working-dinner-g20-leaders-global-challenges-terrorism-and-refugee, accessed 10 November 2016.

43 Hough provides a noteworthy distinction between government and public perceptions. The government uses statistics as indicators, while the public bases its views on perceptions, actual experiences and media reports. See Michael Hough, Criminal terror in RSA, ISSUP Bulletin, vol. 2, 2007, 9. See electronic version: http://repository.up.ac.za/handle/2263/3736?show=full, accessed 6 January 2017.

44 Of the 41 people interviewed, 30 of them stated that the threat of terrorism to South Africa is low.

45 For example, just to name a few: in 2011, AQIM kidnapped Mr Stephen McGown in Timbuktu, Mali, in May 2013 al-Qaeda kidnapped South African couple Yolande and Pierre Korkie in Yemen, released Yolande six months later and killed Pierre eighteen months later; In 2010, South African couple Bruno and Debbie were kidnapped by Somali pirates and were only released in 2012; in March 2015, Boko Haram killed two South Africans helping Nigerian soldiers; and in 2017, a South African journalist working with Gift of the Givers was kidnapped in Syria.

Despite this low-level perception of the threat, South Africa has nonetheless joined the global war on terrorism, even if its role has not been conspicuous. The government has cooperated with foreign governments including the United States, the United Kingdom, Israel and other key actors in the global fight against terrorism to track down and arrest terrorist suspects in South Africa. In addition, the government has prosecuted individuals suspected of terrorism and taken both executive and legislative measures to combat the threat of terrorism to South Africa. The legal responsibility or the legitimacy of government action against terrorism is derived from the country's constitution. In its Chapter II, the constitution promulgates the Bill of Rights, which enunciates certain fundamental human, political and civil rights that government must safeguard, and in Article 41 (1)(a) and (b), the constitution obligates the government to preserve the peace, national unity and indivisibility of the Republic, and secure the well-being of the people of the Republic, respectively. It is therefore in pursuit of this constitutional responsibility that South Africa's actions against terrorism may be understood. This section discusses some of the policy and legislative measures taken by the South African government to prevent and combat the threat of global terrorism.

Viewed against its historical experience and the social and political sensitivities attached to the notion of terrorism, government responses to it have been somewhat ambivalent.[46] This ambivalence has been spurred by the need, on the one hand, to safeguard national security and, on the other hand, the need to preserve the unity and integrity of the rainbow nation as a democracy. The South African government has therefore been extremely sensitive to the tendency of the post-9/11 counterterrorism global politics to offend and marginalize certain religious and social groups, as well as the recourse to force or the militaristic approach of some governments. As a result, the government has distanced itself from the militaristic paradigm or non-diplomatic and non-criminal justice responses to terrorism. This section discusses some of the policy and legislative measures taken by the South African government to prevent and combat the threat of global terrorism.

Underpinning policy dictates of the South African response

South Africa's response to terrorism has been premised on the fundamental needs to fulfil its constitutional duties and its international law obligations. In the words of Thabani Masuku, a South African legal expert, 'Post-apartheid South Africa's approach to terrorism has both mirrored the international stance and been designed to respond to the numerous instances of urban terrorism.'[47] Consequently, as

46 To further shed light on this, see Hussein Solomon's discussion on South Africa's ambiguous response to terrorism arising from what he calls 'the dictates of the political correctness approach and a harsh reality which contradicts this'. See Hussein Solomon, Terrorism and counterterrorism in South Africa, Journal of the Middle East and Africa, Vol. 1:1, 2010, 115–116.

47 T. Masuku, Reflections on South Africa's Approach to Terrorism, CHRI News, February 2002, www.humanrightsinitiative.org/publications/nl/articles/south_africa/reflections_on_sa_approach_to_terrorism.pdf, accessed 30 August 2016.

mentioned earlier, the measures adopted by the government have been heavily influenced by the Constitution of the Republic (Act No. 108 of 1996) and international law, particularly the 19 universal counterterrorism instruments and relevant United Nations resolutions, as well as the General Assembly Global Counterterrorism Strategy and the Secretary-General's Action Plan for the Prevention of Violent Extremism. The role plays by international law cannot be overstated. As a common law country, international law is an integral part of the South African legal system and Article 39(1) of the Constitution underscores this linkage by obligating South African courts, tribunals and other forums, that they (a) must promote the values that underlie an open and democratic society based on human dignity, equality and freedom; (b) must consider international law; and (c) may consider foreign law. In *State v Henry Emomotimi Okah*, one of the grounds for establishing the jurisdiction of the Court was by virtue of South Africa's signatory and party to various universal conventions related to terrorism, further emphasizing the importance of South Africa's international obligations in the country's jurisprudence.[48] There exists no specific single policy document in the open sources, in which the South African policy approach to terrorism is described. Documents such as South Africa's Counterterrorism Strategy and National Intelligence Estimates, which are believed to contain details of the government's policy, remain watertight confidential policy papers, which provide a strategic direction for government responses to terrorism. These two documents provide important information on prime threats and how to mitigate them, and identify departments responsible for implementing different aspects.

The South African government's current approach to terrorism may be described as non-direct engagement and non-confrontational with terrorist groups. The policy is also heavily focused on prevention, in order to safeguard the prevailing status quo in South Africa, which, despite much rhetoric has not witnessed a major terror attack since 2002. This means that, while the government strongly condemns terrorism in all its aspects and manifestations, it does not go about directly confronting individuals or groups accused of terrorism if such groups have not directly committed terrorist or any other criminal acts in South Africa. This policy is underpinned by a number of key principles, which have guided South Africa's response to terrorism in the post-1994 era, as well summarized by Ismail Vadi:[49]

- a commitment to take all lawful measures to prevent acts of terror and to bring to justice those who are involved in terrorism;
- a commitment to upholding the rule of law;
- a commitment never to resort to any form of general and indiscriminate repression;

48 See judgment by the South Gauteng High Court, Johannesburg, on the matter between the State and Henry Emomotimi Okah, 2013.

49 See Ismail Vadi, Terrorism, public policy and democracy in South Africa, Strategic Review for Southern Africa, Vol. 29:1, May 2007, 53–54. See electronic version: www.questia.com/read/1G1-167107937/terrorism-public-policy-and-democracy-in-south-africa, accessed 9 October 2016.

- a commitment to defending and upholding the freedom and security of all its citizens;
- a commitment to respecting its international obligations with respect to combating terrorism;
- a commitment to protect foreign citizens from terror attacks in South Africa;
- a commitment to cooperate with the host government to investigate a terrorist incident involving South Africans abroad;
- a commitment not to make any concessions that could encourage extortions by terrorists and not to allow its territory to be used as a haven to plan, direct and support acts of terror. On this basis of this commitment, the government has adopted a policy of non-negotiation and non-payment of ransom to terrorist groups; and
- a commitment to cooperate with the international community in the fight against terrorism and to support citizens who are victims of terrorism.

An approach built on multilateralism

Multilateralism is both a foreign policy orientation and a strategy to achieve the unwritten policy of non-confrontation and non-direct engagement with terrorist groups. As a part of this policy, the government has aligned itself with the Palestinian people and sees the lack of consensus on the Palestinian problem as the cause of global terrorism. There are two main approaches to the application of this policy – the external and internal dimensions. Externally, the emphasis has been on multilateralism through the auspices of multilateral institutions such as the United Nations (UN), African Union (AU) and many others. This policy is premised on a strong conviction that 'international cooperation is a prerequisite for countering terrorism and other forms of transnational crime'.[50] In this regard, South Africa has emphasized the centrality of the role of the UN.[51] As President Zuma stated, 'Given the attacks in Europe and several other acts of terror in Africa and the Middle East, collective global action against all forms of terrorism under the auspices of the United Nations is imperative. Addressing the root causes of terrorism is also critical.'[52]

50 See South Africa in the United Nations Security Council (2007–2008), a report produced by the Department of Foreign Affairs, February 2009, 16. Electronic version: www.southafrica-newyork.net/pmun/PDF/bookletb5.indd.pdf, accessed 16 October 2016.

51 This is a key feature or the central pillar of South Africa's post-1994 foreign policy framework on terrorism, initiated under Mandela, elaborated under Mbeki and strengthened under Zuma. See, for example, Department of International Relations and Cooperation (DIRC), President Mbeki to Lead South African Delegation to the 58th Session of the United Nations General Assembly New York, United States of America Monday, 22 September 2003–Wednesday, 24 September 2003, www.dirco.gov.za/docs/2003/ticad0926.htm, accessed 18 October 2016.

52 See President Jacob Zuma: Global challenges: Terrorism and refugee crisis, Remarks by President Jacob Zuma at Working Dinner of G20 Leaders on the topic Global Challenges: Terrorism and Refugee Crisis Antalya, Turkey, 15 November 2015, www.

To this end, the government has taken an active part in the adoption of counterterrorism resolutions, strategies, conventions, protocols and other legal instruments in the UN and AU. For example, South Africa participated actively in the discussion leading to the adoption of the UN Global Counter-Terrorism Strategy in 2006, and advocated the inclusion and strengthening of the human rights aspects of the strategy. As the South African delegate put it, 'South Africa wished to see a focused implementation of section V on Human Rights and International Law to ensure that human rights were at the centre of the counter-terrorism strategy.'[53] The government also utilized its very first non-permanent seat at the United Nations Security Council (UNSC) in 2007–2008 to condemn specific terrorist attacks, improve safeguards for human rights and legal due process in counterterrorism, and renew the mandates of the Counter-Terrorism Committee, al-Qaeda and Taliban Sanctions Committee and the 1540 Committee on proliferation of weapons of mass destruction by non-state terrorist actors.[54] During its second mandate at the UNSC in 2011–2012, South Africa continued to promote counterterrorism, when it was assigned to chair the 'Terrorism and Weapons of Mass Destruction Committee', which looks at the threat of non-state actors acquiring WMDs.[55]

The government has also used multilateral institutions to respond to some specific terrorist groups. This is the approach it has adopted in its response to Boko Haram, for example. Here South Africa was among the countries that requested that the issue of Boko Haram be addressed within the framework of the AU and for the latter to play a more visible role.[56] In addition, South Africa has used its membership of the African Union Peace and Security Council (AUPSC) to highlight poverty and unemployment as drivers of violence and terrorism, and advocated engagement between affected AU members on issues of terrorism on the continent, as well as called for the operationalization of existing mechanisms aimed at assisting the AU to address the challenges of terrorism, such as the AUPSC's Subcommittee on Counter Terrorism.[57] It has also supported other

gov.za/speeches/president-jacob-zuma-working-dinner-g20-leaders-global-challenges-terrorism-and-refugee, accessed 10 November 2016.

53 See verbatim report of the 99th plenary meeting of the General Assembly, General Assembly Adopts Resolution on Strategy to Counter International Terrorism, 8 September 2006, www.un.org/press/en/2006/ga10488.doc.htm.

54 See South Africa in the United Nations Security Council (2007–2008), a report produced by the Department of Foreign Affairs, February 2009, 16. Electronic version: www.southafrica-newyork.net/pmun/PDF/bookletb5.indd.pdf, accessed 16 October 2016.

55 See the New Age, South Africa's Second Term in the United Nations Security Council, 11 January 2011, www.saiia.org.za/opinion-analysis/south-africas-second-term-in-the-united-nations-security-council, accessed 19 August 2016.

56 See, for example, Condemn Boko Haram and calls for President Goodluck Jonathan to provide clear leadership, ANC Youth League, 21 May 2014, www.ancyl.org.za/docs/pr/2014/pr0521.html, accessed 10 September 2016.

57 See Department of International Relations and Cooperation (DIRCO) Annual Report 2014–2015 Financial Year, 9 & 80.

multilateral responses to terrorism such as the regional Taskforce to defeat the Lord Resistance Army (RCI-LRA),[58] African Union Mission in Somalia (AMISOM), and the African and UN missions in Mali.

This external counterterrorism policy seems to have strong backing from South Africans. The field study revealed that most South Africans believe that there is a correlation between foreign policy and vulnerability to terrorism. As a result, many seem to associate the low threat perception or the fact that no major terrorist attack has occurred in South Africa since the strings of terrorist bombings in Soweto in October and November 2002, for which the Boeremag or the far-right Afrikaner groups were suspected,[59] to effective government policy. According to one interviewee, 'The policy of non-engagement with terrorist groups is keeping this country safe.'[60] Another stated that the kind of attacks that occurred in Belgium (Brussels) and France (Nice) cannot occur in South Africa, and that the likelihood of an attack is remote, because of the policy of tolerance, inclusiveness and the fact that South Africa accepts people of all persuasions.[61]

There was also a strong view that the historical link between the struggle against apartheid in South Africa and the Palestinian struggle, as well as the strong ties between the two, constitute a factor that makes an attack in South Africa unlikely.[62] For many of those who felt that an attack from a violent extremist group such as al-Qaeda or ISIS was unlikely, the belief was that the far-right Afrikaner groups posed a more serious threat and were more likely to attack.[63] There were others who felt that there was nothing special about South Africa, and that an attack from violent extremist groups was possible[64] and only a matter of time.[65] The key South African actors for the external dimension of the fight against terrorism are DIRCO and the Foreign Branch of the State Security Agency (SSA). This means that the focus is on policy and intelligence.

The internal dimension of the application of the policy of non-engagement is premised on a criminal justice approach that is anchored on an uncompromising

58 Ibid., 80.

59 See, for example, Henri E. Cauvin, Series of bombings shake Soweto, killing one, The New York Times, 31 October 2002, www.nytimes.com/2002/10/31/world/series-of-bombings-shake-soweto-killing-one.html, accessed 16 August 2016; see also Boeremag bomb blasts rock Soweto and Bronkhorstspruit, South African History Online, 30 October 2002, www.sahistory.org.za/dated-event/boeremag-bomb-blasts-rock-soweto-and-bronkhorstspruit, 16 August 2016; Six sought over Soweto bombings, BBC News, 10 November 2002, http://news.bbc.co.uk/2/hi/africa/2437861.stm, accessed 29 November 2016.

60 Interview with Professor Michael Hough, retired professor, University of Pretoria and former editor of Strategic Review for Southern Africa, on 4 November 2016.

61 Interview with a senior staff from the Department of International Relations and Cooperation, on 22 September 2016.

62 Interviews with a second senior staff of DIRCO on 4 October 2016.

63 Interviews with two academic and community representatives on 21 September 2016.

64 See, for example, interview with Roland Henwood, lecturer, University of Pretoria, on 20 September 2016.

65 Interviews with Jasmine Opperman on 29 September 2016, and with representatives of SAPS on 4 October 2016.

rule of law. This approach seeks to detect, intercept, investigate, prosecute, deter and prevent any potential terrorist attack whether from foreign or domestic terrorist entities. The fight against terrorism internally covers a wide range of areas and actors, and includes legislative and operational responses to terrorism. These are discussed in the subsequent sections below.

Non-payment of ransom to terrorist groups

One of the underpinning principles of the South Africa's counterterrorism policy is non-direct negotiation with and non-payment of ransom to terrorist groups. It's a controversial principle, which as Neumann explains is based on the democratic practice of never giving in to violence or to those who use non-democratic or non-political methods to pursue their objectives.[66] It is also believed that negotiating with terrorists legitimizes their methods and undermines the efforts of actors, who pursue political change through peaceful means.[67] In practice, this policy has been demonstrated in a number of cases, including the kidnapping of a South African couple by Somali pirates in 2010,[68] the kidnapping of a South African citizen by al-Qaeda in the Islamic Maghreb (AQIM) in 2011,[69] the kidnapping of a South African couple in Yemen by al-Qaeda in the Arabian Peninsula (AQAP)[70] and the kidnapping of a South African journalist in Syria in January 2017.[71] In all of these cases, the government refused to pay a ransom or to have any direct negotiation with the kidnappers, and instead opted for diplomatic efforts with host countries to free the hostages. Strict compliance and consistency with this policy has, however, been interrogated by analysts who claim that there have been exceptions to the rule. For example, the *New York Times*, citing 'a retired European intelligence official', reported that a ransom of '3.5 million euros (about $4.2 million)'[72] was paid for the release of Mr Stephen McGown, a South African national kidnapped by AQIM in 2011, and held in captivity until his

66 Peter R. Neumann, Negotiating with terrorists, Foreign Affairs, January/February 2007, www.foreignaffairs.com/articles/2007-01-01/negotiating-terrorists, accessed 30 June 2016.

67 Ibid.

68 See South Africa couple freed from Somali pirates, BBC News, 21 June 2012, www.bbc.com/news/world-africa-18532305, accessed 19 March 2016.

69 See Baba Ahmed, South African and Swede kidnapped in Mali, Mail&Guardian, 26 November 2011, https://mg.co.za/article/2011-11-26-south-african-and-swede-kidnapped-in-mali, accessed 17 April 2016.

70 See Ebrahim Ebrahim, No word on SA couple kidnapped in Yemen, News24, 21 June 2013, www.news24.com/SouthAfrica/News/No-word-on-SA-couple-kidnapped-in-Yemen-20130621, accessed 24 July 2016.

71 J. Bornman, 'Proof of life' of kidnapped SA photojournalist Shiraaz Mohamed received, News24, 9 January 2018, www.news24.com/SouthAfrica/News/proof-of-life-of-kidnapped-sa-photojournalist-shiraaz-mohamed-received-20180109, accessed 3 August 2018.

72 R. Callimachi and S. Chan, Hostage held by Al Qaeda in Mali for 5 years is freed, New York Times, 3 August 2017, www.nytimes.com/2017/08/03/world/africa/mali-stephen-mcgown-south-africa-al-qaeda.html, accessed 3 August 2018.

release on 29 July 2017. According to the *New York Times* article, the ransom payment was negotiated through the South African non-profit, Gift of the Givers Foundation,[73] which had been involved in similar negotiations for the release of South African hostages. The government denied paying any such ransom. In her response to the question of ransom, the South African Minister of Foreign Affairs, Maite Nkoana-Mashabane, stated that 'The South African government does not subscribe to payment of ransoms', and 'That's why I focused on the work we have been doing in the past six years: campaigning, engaging with governments, and with the captors the way we know how. That's what we have been doing. And that's what we can confirm.'[74]

South African strategy against terrorism and violent extremism

As already mentioned, the South African Counterterrorism Strategy is under public embargo and the content is not known to the public. It is also to be recalled that no specific framework has been adopted by the government to deal with the problem of violent extremism. The draft Prevention and Combating of Hate Crimes and Hate Speech Bill, which could address some of the issues of radicalization, is yet to be finalized. Although many of the counterterrorism arsenals mentioned in this chapter may be relevant and applicable to countering violent extremism, it is, however, necessary to address the specific threats posed by the latter, especially issues related to radicalization, which are often overlooked in counterterrorism policies. The field study revealed that the Counterterrorism Strategy was significantly influenced by the United Nations' Global Counter-terrorism Strategy and that it was designed and premised on the four pillars of the UN Global Counterterrorism Strategy.[75] These pillars include: (1) measures to address the conditions conducive to the spread of terrorism; (2) measures to prevent and combat terrorism; (3) measures to build states' capacity to prevent and combat terrorism and to strengthen the role of the United Nations system in this regard; and (4) measures to ensure respect for human rights for all and the rule of law as the fundamental basis of the fight against terrorism. This provides valuable insight into the nature of NCTS. It is also indicative that human rights, international cooperation, interagency coordination and intelligence are key aspects of NCTS. It is likely that NCTS has been informed by the 1995 National Crime Prevention Strategy (NCPS), which was equally designed around four pillars including (1) criminal justice process; (2) reducing crime through environment design; (3) public values and education; and (4) transnational crime.[76] The NCPS was based on a fundamentally new approach by government. In particular, it

73 Ibid.
74 Ibid.
75 Interviews with representative of DIRCO on 4 October 2016, and with a former official of the SSA. A representative of the SSA also confirmed the existence of the Strategy and its implementation.
76 See National Crime Prevention Strategy, Summary, www.gov.za/documents/national-CRIME-prevention-strategy-summary#2, accessed 16 August 2016.

requires the development of wider responsibility for crime prevention and a shift in emphasis from reactive 'crime control'; which deploys most resources towards responding after crimes have already been committed, towards proactive 'crime prevention' aimed at preventing crime from occurring at all.[77] The NCTS could benefit from this proactive approach, particularly if South Africa is to maintain the current status quo of non-terrorist attacks. Any counterterrorism strategy for South Africa should include aspects of violent extremism. Such a strategy should target recent trends in radicalization leading to recruitment in terrorist organization.

Mapping the key areas of the response architecture

In order to fully understand the existing architecture for the prevention and combatting of terrorism in South Africa, it is important to begin the discussion by examining its reach or scope. In recognition of the multifaceted threat posed by terrorism and violent extremism, South Africa has responded with a wide range of measures. Figure 9.2 summarizes some of the key areas of South African responses to terrorism and violent extremism.

The figure demonstrates nine major areas of counterterrorism activities in South Africa. Although some areas have had more priority, such as intelligence, immigration and border control, human rights, financial measures (including money laundering), and legislative measures, considerable measures have been taken to enforce certain standards. These areas are identified and provided under international and regional conventions, protocols, and other legal instruments for the prevention and combatting of terrorism; as well as UN resolutions such as the watershed Security Council resolution 1373 (28 September 2001). They are therefore considered to be pivotal in the fight against terrorism. Table 9.1 summarizes the key legislative texts that provide the legal and policy bases of the South African response to terrorism and violent extremism.

Combatting the financial aspects of terrorism has been underlined by various international instruments, as one of the critical areas for defeating terrorism. Although South Africa does not possess an anti-money laundering instrument, as most countries do, it has quite a number of financial legislative acts and regulations that deal with aspects of money laundering and the financing of terrorism. In its first report to the CTC in 2002, South Africa indicated that the applicable legislation included those financial measures outlined in Table 9.1 above and Internal Security Act No. 74 of 1982.[78] These legislative acts cover various aspects of suppressing the financing of terrorism including powers for asset forfeiture and freezing. The main institution here is the Financial Intelligence Centre (FIC), which monitors financial activities. FIC, or FICA (Financial Intelligence Centre

77 Ibid.

78 See letter dated 27 December 2001 from the Chairman of the Security Council Committee established pursuant to resolution 1373 (2001) concerning counter-terrorism addressed to the President of the Security Council, Ambassador Jeremy Greenstock, United Nations document, S/2001/1281 dated 8 January 2002 (Original: French), 3–5.

Figure 9.2 **Major areas of South African CT/CVE actions**

Act) as it is often referred to, does not have enforcement powers but provides information and support to the police, especially on financial investigations.

Implementation of international sanctions

The report also mentioned the Banks Act No. 94 of 1990 (Section 7(1)(a), as constituting South Africa's framework for implementation of UN sanction regimes:

Intelligence measures

Since Operation Good Hope in 1999, intelligence has remained the backbone of South Africa's response to terrorism. Respondents to the field study highlighted the crucial role of intelligence in keeping South Africa safe from terrorism. The gathering and dissemination of intelligence in South Africa is a responsibility shared by four security institutions: SANDF (Defence Intelligence), investigative

Table 9.1 Applicable legislations in core CT areas

No.	*Area of Action*	*Key Measures*	*Comments*
1	Legislation	Protection of Constitutional Democracy Against Terrorist and Related Act No. 33 of 2004 (POCDATARA)	Principal CT legislation that criminalizes terrorism and defines its numerous offences
		Prohibition of Mercenary Activities and Regulation of Certain Activities in Country of Armed Conflict Act No. 27 of 2006	Prohibits foreign fighters and the provision of training or military service to parties in armed conflicts abroad
		Regulation of Foreign Military Assistance Act No. 15 of 1998	Prohibits any person within South Africa and elsewhere from rendering any foreign military assistance to any person unless with explicit authorization from NCACC
2	Financial Measures	Financial Intelligence Centre Act (FICA) of 2001	Establishes the South African equivalence of Financial Intelligence Unit (FIU), and provides for measures and tools for dealing with money laundering crimes
		Prevention of Organised Crime Act No. 121 of 1998	Deals with crime syndicates and creates money laundering offences offenders could face up to life imprisonment and a fine up 1 billion Rand in penalties It also provides for confiscation of proceeds of crime
		Prevention and Combating of Corrupt Activities Act No. 12 of 2003	
		Anti-Corruption Commission Bill	Establishes the Anti-Corruption Commission and the Special Operation Unit

		Currency and Exchange Act No. 9 of 1933	Empowers the Minister of Finance to instruct authorized dealers to freeze funds and financial resources and block accounts held in South Africa and prohibits the movement of capital into and out of South Africa
		Money Laundering and Terrorist Financing Control Regulations of 2002	Set out regulations for financial and business institutions to prevent money laundering
		Exchange Control Regulation Act of 1961	
		Non-Profit Organisation Act No. 71 of 1997	
		Proceeds of Crime Act No. 76 of 1996	
		Banks Act No. 94 of 1990	
		Income Tax Act No. 58 of 1962	
3	Intelligence	General Intelligence Act No. 11 of 2013	
		National Intelligence Service Act No. 65 of 2002	
		National Strategic Intelligence Act No. 39 of 1994	
		Protection of Information Act No. 84 of 1982 (as amended in 2003)	Prohibits access to and disclosure of certain information or places
4	Immigration and Border Control	Immigration Amendment Act No. 13 of 2011	
		Immigration Act No. 13 of 2002	
		Preventing and Combating of Trafficking in Persons Act No. 7 of 2013	
		Civil Aviation Offences Act No. 10 of 1972	
		Alien Control No. 96 of 1991	

(*Continued*)

Table 9.1 (Continued)

No.	*Area of Action*	*Key Measures*	*Comments*
5	Firearms and Non-proliferation of Weapons of Mass Destruction	Non-proliferation of Weapons of Mass Destruction Act No. 87 of 1993	
		Armament Development and Production Act No. 57 of 1968	
		Arms and Ammunition Act No. 75 of 1969	
		Explosives Act No. 26 of 1956	
		National Convention Arms Control Act No. 41 of 2002	
		Dangerous Weapons Act No. 15 of 2013	
		Firearms Control Act No. 60 of 2000	
6	Human Rights	Constitution of the Republic 1996 (as amended in 2013)	Chapter II promulgates the Bill of Rights that government must enforce and cannot derogate even in counterterrorism
		Human Right Commission Act No. 54 of 1994	Establishes the Human Rights Commission and provides for matters connected to the protection of human rights
		Abolition of Corporal Punishment Act No. 33 of 1997	Prohibits the death penalty
		Prevention and Combating of Torture of Persons Act No. 13 of 2013	Prohibits torture and other cruel and inhumane treatment of persons in South Africa
7	International Cooperation	International Cooperation in Criminal Matters Act No. 75 of 1996	Provides for mutual legal assistance and facilitate the provision of evidence, the execution of sentences in criminal cases, and the confiscation and transfer of the proceeds of crime between South Africa and foreign states
		The Extradition Act No. 67 of 1962	Defines South Africa's jurisdiction and the bases on which extradition could be granted or denied
		Extradition Amendment Act No. 77 of 1996	

8	Investigation and Prosecution	South African Police Service Act No. 41 of 1995	
		South African Police Service Amendment Act 41 of 1997	
		Independent Police Investigative Directorate Act 1 of 2011.	
		Institution of Legal Proceedings against certain Organs of State Act 40 of 2002	
		Witness Protection Act No. 112 of 1998	Provides for the placement of witnesses and related persons under protection, and establishes the Office of Witness Protection
		Civil Proceedings Evidence Act No. 25 of 1965	
		Investigation of Serious Economic Offences Amendment Act No. 46 of 1995	
		National Prosecuting Authority Act, 32 of 1998	
		Criminal Law (Forensic Procedures) Amendment Ac, of 2013 (DNA Act).	Provides for procedures and guidelines for the collection, analysis and use of DNA evidence
9	Ratification of International Instruments	Ratification of 13 of the 19 UN and international instruments (68.42%)	
		Ratification of relevant AU instruments	
		Ratification of relevant SADC instrument	
10	Cybersecurity	Electronic Communications and Transactions Act … 25 of 2002	
		National Cybersecurity Policy Framework (NCPF)	Provides for an integrated cyber security legal framework for the Republic
		The Criminal Procedure Act, 1977	Applicable to the investigation of cybercrimes
		Draft Cybercrime and Cybersecurity Bill	Creates offences and imposes penalties which have a bearing on cybercrime

division of the SAPS (Crime Intelligence), the State Security Agency (SSA) and the National Intelligence Agency (NIA). Table 9.1 provides a list of the legislative and regulatory measures taken in the area of intelligence. The coordination of intelligence is entrusted to the National Intelligence Coordinating Committee (NICOC). This is perhaps the most important intelligence outfit in South Africa. It comprises SANDF, SAPS, the State Security Agency (SSA) and Office of the President. There has been confusion surrounding the new SSA and its relationship with the previous intelligence outfits. On its website, it is indicated that the SSA is to incorporate into its structures the following:[79]

- The National Intelligence Agency (NIA)
- The South African Secret Service (SASS)
- The South African National Academy of Intelligence (SANAI)
- The National Communications Centre (NCC)
- The Office for Interception Centres (OIC)
- Electronic Communications Security (Pty) Ltd (COMSEC)

In its report to the CTC, the government indicated that NICOC works on 'a 24-hour alert Centre at the National Intelligence Agency and an operation Centre at the South Africa Secret Service (SASS)'. According to the report, 'The South African National Early Warning Centre (NEWC) is situated in NICOC, and is linked to the operational centres of the various South African intelligence and law-enforcement agencies. The NEWC therefore provides a coordinated early warning response to any domestic or foreign issue requiring the urgent attention of the South African government. These issues include incidents or threats of terrorism.'[80] Respondents to the field survey highlighted the fact that NICOC functions effectively through a growing number of inter-departmental working groups.[81]

Other intelligence bodies include the South Africa National Academy of Intelligence

Intelligence Services Council on Conditions of Service

Firearms and non-proliferation of weapons of mass destruction

South Africa has passed a number of legislative acts to govern and control the circulation of firearms including dangerous weapons, which could be acquired by terrorists. The main legislative and regulatory acts are indicated in Table 9.1. The National Conventional Arms Control Committee (NCACC) is a committee of government established in terms of Act No. 41 of 2002. The Committee

79 See SSA website: www.ssa.gov.za/AboutUs.aspx (24 October 2016).

80 See letter dated May 4, 2006 from the Chairman of the Security Council Committee established pursuant to resolution 1373 (2001) concerning counter-terrorism addressed to the President of the Security Council, Ellen Margrethe Løj, Security Council document, S/2006/281 dated 19 May 2006, 13.

81 This point was made by respondents still actively employed in government and those who previously worked in government but have recently retired.

functions within the framework the National Conventional Arms Control Act 41 of 2002 (NCAC Act) and the Constitution. As provided by law the NCACC provides regular reports to the cabinet, parliament and the UN on conventional arms control.[82]

International cooperation

Internal coordination and international cooperation constitute an important pillar in South Africa's fight against terrorism. Internally, DIRCO has a key responsibility to coordinate the activities of an Interdepartmental Working Group on Counter-Terrorism. This Working Group brings together all the key actors to discuss regularly the threat of terrorism and violent extremism. The applicable legislative and regulatory acts are summarized in Table 9.1. Cooperation is expansive and covers many sectorial issues and disciplines including police (INTERPOL), intelligence, defence and security. In its 2002 report to the CTC, the government stated that, 'The South African Police Service co-operates internationally in respect of the exchange of criminal information and police co-operation, including the use of Interpol channels', and that the Police has concluded police co-operation agreements, which without mentioning terrorism specifically, can be used to obtain co-operation in terrorism investigations.[83] In this context, SAPS has concluded several mutual legal assistance agreements to facilitate cooperation on criminal matters. The expansiveness of this cooperation is evident in South Africa's participation in regional arrangements. South Africa has prioritized the harmonization of legislation in the Southern African region in its cooperation within the frameworks of the Southern African Development Community (SADC) and the Southern African Regional Police Chiefs Cooperation (SARPCCO). Although the threat of terrorism within the region is generally perceived to be low,[84] many of the borders in the region are porous.[85] Counterterrorism has been an emerging issue and South Africa has played a visible role in driving that agenda. President Jacob Zuma was the Chair of SADC when the Regional Counter-Terrorism Strategy was negotiated and adopted in August 2015, with the help of the United Nations Counter-Terrorism Committee Executive Directorate (CTED) and the African Centre for the Study and Research on Terrorism

82 See Department Justice, National Conventional Arms Control Committee (NCACC) statement on South African arms sales regulation, 6 August 2009, www.gov.za/national-conventional-arms-control-committee-ncacc-statement-south-african-arms-sales-regulation.

83 Letter dated 18 July 2002 from the Chairman of the Security Council Committee established pursuant to resolution 1373 (2001) concerning counter-terrorism addressed to the President of the Security Council, Ambassador Jeremy Greenstock, Security Council document S/2002/792 dated 19 July 2002, p. 22.

84 The general impression during the field interview was that the threat of terrorism within the region is low but border porousness remains a big threat.

85 See The porous border problem, The Southern Times, 28 November 2011, http://southernafrican.news/2011/11/28/the-porous-border-problem/, accessed 25 October 2016.

(ACSRT).[86] The Strategy provides a solid framework for operational regional collaboration on preventing terrorism. South Africa's commitment to regional cooperation is also indicative of the political will Pretoria has shown towards ratifying key regional instruments for extradition and mutual legal assistance. SARPCCO has also provided a strategic framework for strengthening police-to-police cooperation and standardization of practical counterterrorism skills through training.[87]

Human rights

The South African Bill of Rights, which is described as the cornerstone of South Africa's democracy, imposes an obligation on the government to respect, protect, promote and fulfil the rights in the Bill of Rights.[88] The protection of human rights in the fight against terrorism is not therefore a matter of choice but a constitutional responsibility. In pursuit of this, the government has been a staunch supporter of human rights at home and abroad. It is a party to all the major human right regimes at the regional, continental and international levels. For a list of the applicable human rights measures see Table 9.1. Some critiques have questioned the government's commitment and effective implementation of South Africa's human rights regimes in its counterterrorism practices. Such critiques often cite a number of cases, such as *Jeebhai & Others v Minister of Home Affairs & Others* [89] and *Mohamed v. President of the Republic of South Africa,* [90] as demonstrating inconsistencies or discrepancies in the government's pronouncements and enforcement.

Foreign terrorist fighters (FTF)

During the field research, there was an acknowledgement of the growing number of South Africans travelling to Syria to join ISIS. Respondents were, however, split on their estimates of how many South Africans have left to fight for ISIS, and how many may have returned. Conservative estimates from those who deal with the issue on a regular basis put the figure between 50 and 100. This indicates the

86 See, for example, United Nations, Facilitating the Development of Regional Counter-Terrorism Strategies, www.un.org/counterterrorism/ctitf/en/uncct/facilitating-development-regional-counter-terrorism-strategies, accessed 8 October 2016.
87 See South African report to the CTC 2006, 14.
88 See Chapter (2) Subsection 7(3).
89 In this case, Mr Khalid Rashid, a Pakistani national, was arrested and deported to Pakistan in secret without respecting due process. For details, see M. N. Njotini, Anti-terrorism measures in South Africa, 532–534.
90 In the case, the South African Constitutional Court unanimously ruled that the deportation of Mr. Khalfan Khamis Mohamed (accused of the 1998 embassy bombings in Kenya and Tanzania) to the United States without securing an assurance that he would not be subjected to the death penalty was a violation of his constitutional and statutory rights. For details, see M. O. Mhango, Taking human rights higher in the fight against terrorism in South Africa, Michigan State Journal of International Law, Vol. 19/1, 2010, 106–107.

extent to which South Africans are accepting ISIS propaganda through social media. Field respondents, particularly those in government, stated that the approach has been to step up intelligence and monitoring of vulnerable individuals. This means that there is no overt government response to the problem of South Africans traveling to Syria to join ISIS. The applicable framework includes the Prohibition of Mercenary Activities and Regulation of Certain Activities in Country of Armed Conflict Act No. 27 of 2006, which makes it unlawful for South Africans to participate, train, or provide any support directly or indirectly to a party in conflict in foreign countries;[91] Regulation of Foreign Military Assistance Act No. 15 of 1998, prohibiting South Africans from providing military assistance to parties to a conflict in foreign territories; and relevant provisions in POCDATARA.

Cyberterrorism

With increased terrorist activities on social media, including the recruitment of South African youth, there is a need for mechanisms and for efforts to focus on how best to effectively police or govern the cyberspace without impinging on human and civil rights of ordinary South Africans. The applicable legislative acts are summarized in Table 9.1.

Universal counterterrorism instruments

As part of its response to terrorism, South Africa has taken an active part in the enforcement of the existing universal counterterrorism instruments. Of the 19 conventions and protocols, the government has ratified and/or acceded to 13 of them. This represents 68.42 per cent. These include: 1963 Convention on Offence and Certain Other Acts Committed on Board Aircraft; 1970 Convention for the Suppression of Unlawful Seizure of Aircraft; 1971 Convention for the Suppression of Unlawful Acts against the Safety of Civil Aviation; 1973 Convention on the Prevention and Punishment of Crimes against International Protected Persons, including Diplomatic Agents; 1979 International Convention against the Taking of Hostages; 1980 Convention on the Physical Protection of Nuclear Material; 1988 Protocol for the Suppression of Unlawful Acts of Violence at Airports Serving International Civil Aviation; 1988 Convention for the Suppression of Unlawful Acts against the Safety of Maritime Navigation; 1988 Protocol for the Suppression of Unlawful Acts against the safety of Fixed Platforms Located on the Continental Shelf; 1991 Convention on the Marking of Plastic Explosives for the Purpose of Detection; 1997 International Convention for the Suppression of Terrorist Bombing; 1999 International Convention for the Suppression of the Financing of Terrorism; 2005 International Convention for the Suppression of Acts of Nuclear Terrorism. Figure 9.3 show the trends in Southern Africa and the position of South Africa.

91 See Subsections 1, 2, 3, 4 and 5 of the Prohibition of Mercenary Activities and Regulation of Certain Activities in Country of Armed Conflict Act No. 27 of 2006.

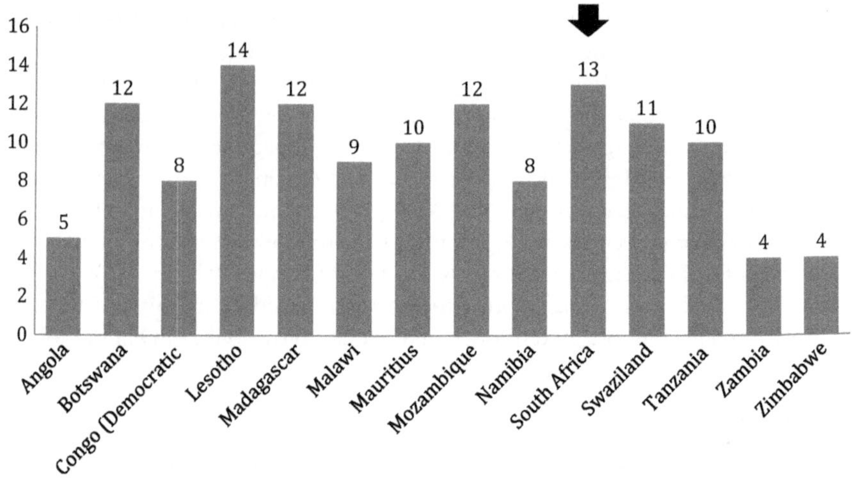

Figure 9.3 **Ratification of universal counterterrorism instruments in Southern Africa**

Machinery for responding to a terrorist attack in South Africa

The response to terrorism is first and foremost the responsibility of the South African Police Service (SAPS) with respect to a criminal justice response, particularly investigation and prosecution. The Police Directorate for Priority Crime Investigation (DPCI), also referred to as the Hawks, has a special Counter-Terrorism Unit that monitors and investigate terrorist cases. The police annual report for 2015 indicates that there were 130 police operations related to terrorism. The State Security Agency (SSA) leads on intelligence and serves as the eyes of the nation on counterterrorism. The Department of Defence or the SANDF provides both strategic and operational support to the police and the SSA. When a terrorist attack occurs, however, the machinery for a national response is similar to or the same as the national structure for disaster management. Figure 9.4 is a summary representation of how a terrorist attack is managed in South Africa.

The legislative framework

The Protection of Constitutional Democracy Against Terrorist and Related Activities Act No. 33 of 2004 (POCDATARA) represents one of the most comprehensive counterterrorism legislations in Africa. The Act evolved from the 1982 Internal Security Act, which provided a definition of terrorism, that many saw to be limited because it was largely motivated by the domestic threat of terrorism. POCDATARA was the new name given to the 2000 Antiterrorism Bill, which had been drafted in 1999 by SAPS, and reviewed and subsequently published for public comments by the South African Law Commission (SALC) as Discussion Paper 92, on 29 September 2000.[92] The bill received

92 See electronic version at the SALC website: http://salawreform.justice.gov.za/dpapers.htm, accessed 15 January 2017.

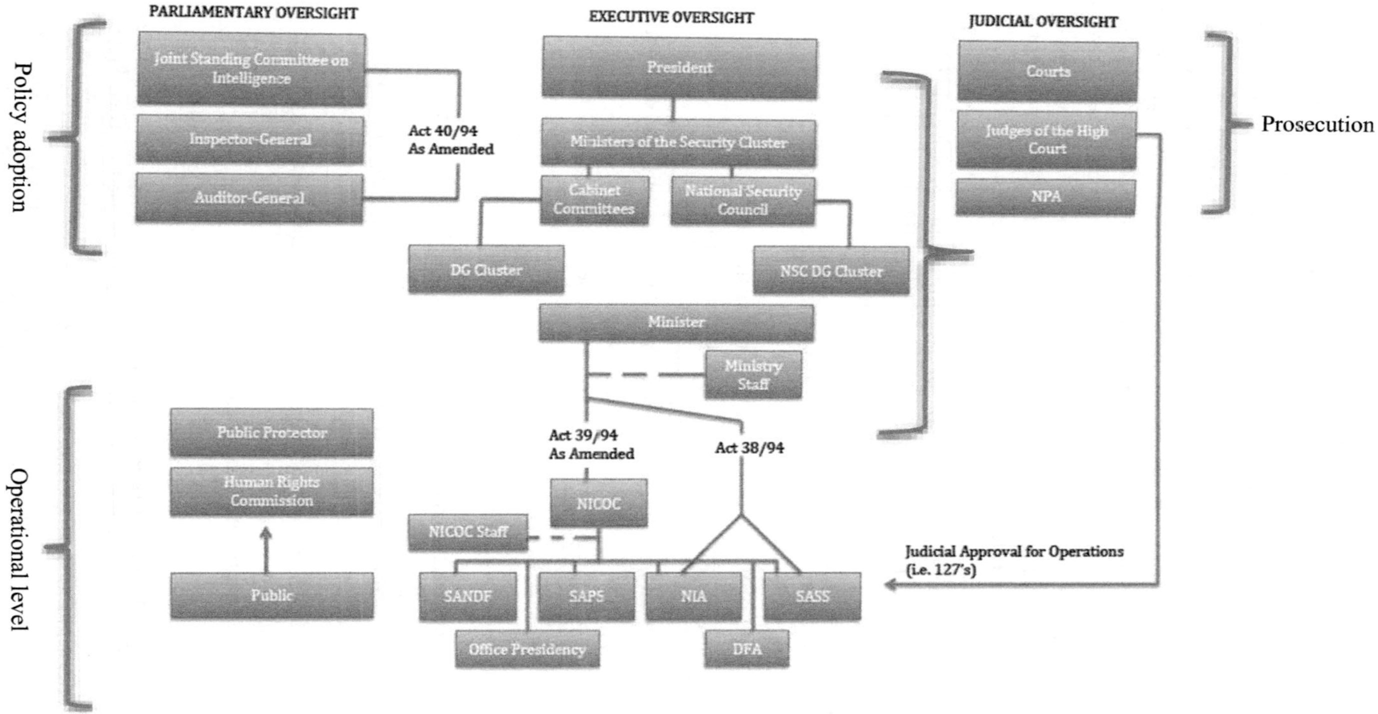

Figure 9.4 **CT/CVE architecture**

over 5,000[93] comments and was met with serious opposition from civil society and human rights groups, which stopped the bill from being adopted.[94] During its debate at the National Assembly in 2003, the Antiterrorism Bill was renamed POCDATARA. Previous legislations against terrorism such as the 1967 Terrorism Act and the Internal Security Act[95] were too state-centric, repressive and aimed essentially at protecting the apartheid regime. In POCDATARA, the legislators saw an opportunity to craft a mechanism by the people and for the people. POCDATARA also represented a recognition by the legislators that the new democracy remained susceptible to acts of terrorism. The fight against terrorism was therefore rooted in constitutionalism, with the primary objective of safeguarding democracy, territorial integrity, values and the fabric of social cohesion in South Africa. POCDATARA also sought to give Parliament oversight role in government's counterterrorism actions.

Following its passage by the National Assembly and the Council of Provinces, in 2004, POCDATARA was signed into law by the President in November 2004 and subsequently entered into force in 2005. POCDATARA was the first major South Africa's response to 9/11. Its key objectives are to provide for:[96]

(I) measures to prevent and combat terrorist and related activities;
(II) terrorist-related offences;
(III) implementation of international instruments against terrorism;
(IV) a mechanism to comply with United Nations Security Council Resolution 1373; and
(V) measures to prevent and combat the financing of terrorist and related activities.

The most revolutionary feature of the Act is Article 1(XXV), which defines a terrorist activity as follows:[97]

a any act committed in or outside the Republic, which –

i involves the systematic, repeated or arbitrary use of violence by any means or method;
ii involves the systematic, repeated or arbitrary release into the environment or any part of it or distributing or exposing the public or any part of it to –

(aa) any dangerous, hazardous, radioactive or harmful substance or organism;
(bb) any toxic chemical; or
(cc) any microbial or other biological agent or toxin;

93 Ibid.
94 See Katrin Kokott, The Impact of 9/11 on the South African Anti-Terrorism Legislation and the Constitutionality thereof (Master Thesis supervised by Nico Steytler), November 2005.
95 The Internal Security Act was repealed by POCDATARA.
96 These objectives are stated in the chapeau to the preamble of the Protection of Constitutional Democracy Against Terrorist and Related Activities Act 33 of 2004.
97 See Article 1(XXV).

iii endangers the life, or violates the physical integrity or physical freedom of, or
iv causes serious bodily injury to or the death of, any person, or any number of persons;
v causes serious risk to the health or safety of the public or any segment of the public;
vi causes the destruction of or substantial damage to any property, natural resource, or the environmental or cultural heritage, whether public or private;
vii is designed or calculated to cause serious interference with or serious disruption of an essential service, facility or system, or the delivery of any such service, facility or system, whether public or private, including, but not limited to –
viii (aa) a system used for, or by, an electronic system, including an information system;

(bb) a telecommunication service or system;
(cc) a banking or financial service or financial system;
(dd) a system used for the delivery of essential government services;
(ee) a system used for, or by, an essential public utility or transport provider;
(ff) an essential infrastructure facility; or
(gg) any essential emergency services, such as police, medical or civil defence services;

ix causes any major economic loss or extensive destabilisation of an economic system or substantial devastation of the national economy of a country; or
x creates a serious public emergency situation or a general insurrection in the Republic, whether the harm contemplated in paragraphs (a) (i) to (vii) is or may be suffered in or outside the Republic, and whether the activity referred to in subparagraphs (ii) to (viii) was committed by way of any means or method; and

b which is intended, or by its nature and context, can reasonably be regarded as being intended, in whole or in part, directly or indirectly, to –

i threaten the unity and territorial integrity of the Republic;
ii intimidate, or to induce or cause feelings of insecurity within, the public, or a segment of the public, with regard to its security, including its economic security, or to induce, cause or spread feelings of terror, fear or panic in a civilian population; or
iii unduly compel, intimidate, force, coerce, induce or cause a person, a government, the general public or a segment of the public, or a domestic or an international organisation or body or intergovernmental organisation or body, to do or to abstain or refrain from doing any act, or to adopt or abandon a particular standpoint, or to act in accordance with certain principle.

The key attributes of the act include a definition of what constitutes a terrorist activity in Section 1, provision of terrorist offences and offences associated or connected with terrorist activities in section 3 – covering the commission of the act, the means and methods used, and the outcome of the act, provision of terrorist specific convention offences covering the 12 universal counterterrorism instruments and the OAU Convention for the Prevention and Combating of Terrorism in Article 4, offences related to harbouring or concealment of persons committing specified offences in Article 11, provision of penalties ranging from five years to life imprisonment and which can be judged as severe – imprisonment for a period up to life imprisonment or a fine ranging from 250,000 Rand to 10 million Rand in Article 18. The act seems to cover all major areas though its definition was criticized to be too broad and too vague.[98] In addition, POCDATARA also creates offences relating to hoaxes and auxiliary or inchoate offences such as conspiracy, incitement, attempt, conspiracy and inducing another person to commit an offence under the act.[99]

Several criticisms levied against earlier drafts by human rights groups, who saw the definition as too vague as it could criminalize and classify as terrorist activities unprotected strikes or protests, and other forms of industrial action,[100] forced the drafters to exempt in the definition of a terrorist activity 'any act which is committed in pursuance of any advocacy, protest, dissent or industrial action and which does not intend the harm contemplated in paragraph (a)(i) to (v) of that definition, shall not be regarded as a terrorist activity within the meaning of that definition'.[101] This explicit exemption from the definition of protest and public demonstration was critical for the passage of POCDATARA, particularly from the human rights and civil society perspective. The definition was widely criticized by civil society and human rights groups for being overly broad and encompassing aspects that would not normally fall within the purview of terrorism.

Conclusion

This chapter has discussed the evolution of South Africa's response to terrorism and violent extremism, as well as the applicable policy framework and institutions. There is no doubt that the existing legislative and regulatory framework is largely adequate. A key observation, however, is the disparity in the treatment of the different areas of the fight against terrorism and violent extremism. One of the main weaknesses of the existing framework is that it is not up to date in some core areas. For example, it does not take into account the concepts of radicalization

98 See, for example, A. Stoppard, South African anti-terror bill draconian, Global Issues, 26 June 2003, www.globalissues.org/article/432/south-african-anti-terror-bill-draconian, accessed 13 June 2016.

99 See Articles 13 and 14 of POCDATARA

100 See 'Controversial' anti-terrorism bill passed, IOL News, 12 November 2004, www.iol.co.za/news/politics/controversial-anti-terrorism-bill-passed-226834, accessed 13 June 2016.

101 See Article 1(XXVI)((3) of POCDATARA.

and violent extremism. Although it addresses some of the issues involved in the foreign terrorist fighters (FTFs) phenomenon, the framework is silent on how to deal with FTF returnees. As a result, South Africans FTFs who went to Syria returned to a country that had no strategy to deal with them. The Henry Okah case also demonstrated some of the legal lacunae in POCDATARA, particularly in relation to its applicability to situations involving terrorist acts committed in foreign countries by foreigners resident in South Africa. Analysts like Devon Kudsen have pointed out that part of the problem of POCDATARA is that, after 11 September 2001, legislation on terrorism has been largely externally driven, notably through the United Nations Counter-Terrorism Committee and donor governments.[102] Indeed, the adoption of the Security Council's landmark resolution 1373 on 28 September 2001 under Chapter VII of the UN Charter, heralded new counterterrorism measures globally, including in Africa, as countries tried to show that they were meeting their obligations under international law. This is important in understanding the sweeping provisions of POCDATARA, which in many respects were inspired by resolution 1373 and the existing 12 universal counterterrorism instruments at the time.

Practical implementation of the various legislative and regulatory acts remains perhaps a far cry for South Africa. The established working groups only operate at the policy level. When it comes to practical intervention, there are hardly synergies and cooperation among law-enforcement units, such as the Hawks, the SAPS, the SSA and the National Prosecuting Authority (NPA). Another impediment to practical implementation is the ongoing brain or skills drain within the law-enforcement agencies. This is particularly acute with SSA and the Hawks, where many skilled officers continue to vacate their positions either due to forced resignations or retirement without replacements. This has left behind a huge capacity void, particularly in the areas of intelligence gathering and analysis, investigation and crime scene intervention, to the extent that one interviewee noted that 'the capacity void was so huge that it was impossible to imagine how South Africa can mount a successful response to an attack in the magnitude of the Nice terror attack in France, which killed 84 people in July 2016'.[103] As a result, only a handful of law-enforcement officers are available at any given time for terrorist-related crimes.

Recommendations

In order to overcome some of the abovementioned challenges, the government should undertake the following actions:

102 See Devon Knudsen, A new wave of African counterterrorism legislation: contextualizing the Kenyan security laws, Georgetown Journal of International Affairs, 11 June 2015, http://journal.georgetown.edu/a-new-wave-of-african-counterterrorism-legislation-contextualizing-the-kenyan-security-laws/, accessed 30 November 2016.

103 Interview with an interviewee in SSA on 14 September 2016.

- establish an integrated national counter-terrorism center to replace the existing units set up in each department, and to bring all specialised counter-terrorism activities and capacities together. The Centre should be anchored on a bomb database, investigation and intelligence.
- increased focus and more resource investment on improving implementation of the existing legislative and regulatory acts;
- immediately address the void in human capital through training and recruitment within the core law enforcement agencies;
- acquire the latest technological equipment for counterterrorism and violent extremism;
- strengthen transparency and public communication on law enforcement agencies' counterterrorism activities, and educate the public on its role in preventing and countering the threat of violent extremism;
- increase practical collaboration with foreign governments including those in the frontline in the fight against terrorism and violent extremism with a view to acquire latest intelligence and trends in the phenomenon; and
- increase and broaden cooperation with communities and civil society groups and think tanks in the prevention and countering violent extremism.

* This study was funded under the Danish contribution to the Institute for Security Studies

10 Indian counterterrorism and the influence of the Global War on Terror

Harsh V. Pant and Ivan Lidarev

India has been a major victim of terrorism. It has suffered massive terrorist attacks, such as the 2008 Mumbai attacks, and has witnessed dramatic terrorist assaults on its political leadership, such as the 1991 assassination of former Prime Minister Rajiv Gandhi and the 2001 attack on India's Parliament. India's terrorism predicament is exceptional. It is the target not only of a shockingly diverse array of terrorists, including Maoist Naxalites, rebels in its Northeast, Khalistani separatists, insurgents in Kashmir and jihadi militants, but also of the largest campaign of state-sponsored terrorism[1] in the world, orchestrated by its arch-enemy Pakistan.

Recent years have confronted Delhi with new and increasingly complex terrorist challenges. A domestic Islamist terrorist movement has emerged in India, while international terrorist organizations, such as al-Qaeda and Islamic State of Iraq and Syria (ISIS), have increasingly focused their attention on India. At the same time, India's old problems with Pakistan-sponsored terrorism in Kashmir and beyond have persisted. This situation has meant that the terrorist threat that India faces has been grave even by international standards. According to the 2016 Global Terrorism Index, India ranks eight in the world on terrorism impact, just after Somalia and before Egypt and Libya.[2]

In the face of this unprecedented challenge, it is important to understand how India has responded to terrorism. To do so this chapter examines two key issues: India's approach to counterterrorism and how the Global War on Terror (GWOT) has influenced this approach. We argue that India has adopted a localized, defensive, law and order approach to counterterrorism. This approach

1 Some authors have made a distinction between state-supported and state-sponsored terrorism, on the basis that the two categories represent different levels of state support for terrorists. However, this chapter will not make such a distinction because it is often difficult to determine precisely the level of support a state gives to a terrorist organization. See Timothy D. Hoyt, "The War on Terrorism: Implications for South Asia", in *South Asia in World Politics*, ed. Devin Hagerty (Lanham, MD: Rowman & Littlefield, 2005), 281.

2 *Global Terrorism Index (GTI) 2016: Measuring and Understanding the Impact of Terrorism* (Institute for Economics and Peace, 2016), 10, accessed 3 February 2017, http://economicsandpeace.org/wp-content/uploads/2016/11/Global-Terrorism-Index-2016.2.pdf.

defines terrorism primarily as a law and order issue to be handled by India's internal security and legal apparatus, seeks to defend the Indian homeland by making it more resilient to terrorist attacks and harder to assault, and restricts counterterror operations to India's borders. This approach has evolved in response to various attacks over the years but still remains underdeveloped and incoherent due to domestic politics and bureaucratic resistance. The GWOT has affected India's fight against terror by allowing Delhi to draw on America's rich counterterror experience and by influencing India's domestic debate on terrorism, civil liberties and human rights in the direction of expanding the domestic space within which India's government can craft tougher counterterrorism policies.

This chapter will first provide an overview of the terrorism challenges that India faces. Subsequently, it will examine the evolution of Indian counterterrorism policy and its institutional set-up. Finally, this study will analyse how the GWOT has impacted on India's fight against terror and its domestic debate on terrorism, civil liberties and human rights. Before proceeding, however, it is important to make two points of clarification. First, while India faces various terrorist threats, this chapter will focus only on Islamist terrorism because it is the target of the US-led GWOT, the subject of this volume, and, arguably, the greatest non-conventional security challenge facing India. Second, this chapter will not engage with the complex but often unproductive discussion on how to define terrorism and counterterrorism. A notoriously difficult and controversial task, the search for a definition of terrorism has produced numerous but widely divergent definitions,[3] with the historian Walter Lacquer counting more than one hundred definitions by 1999.[4] Hence, for practical purposes this study loosely defines terrorism as violence perpetrated, threatened or promoted by non-state actors to attain political objectives, while counterterrorism is defined as the political, intelligence or military activities designed to prevent terrorism or limit its destructive impact.

Islamist terrorism in India

Islamist terrorism has posed a serious and increasingly multifaceted threat to India for the last three decades. This threat first emerged in the late 1980s, when a Pakistan-supported insurgency erupted in Kashmir. While this insurgency was partially motivated by local grievances,[5] it was soon overtaken by Pakistan-supported Islamist groups, manned by veterans from the Afghan war, which

3 For an overview of the discussion on defining terrorism see Joseph S. Tuman, *Communicating Terror: The Rhetorical Dimensions of Terrorism* (New Delhi: Sage, 2003), 2–4. For a discussion of the meaning of terrorism and its historical evolution see Bruce Hoffman, *Inside Terror* (New York: Columbia University Press, 2006), 1–43

4 Walter Laqueur, *The New Terrorism: Fanaticism and the Arms of Mass Destruction* (New York: Oxford University Press, 1999), 6

5 The insurgency emerged in response to the disputed 1987 state election in Jammu and Kashmir and New Delhi's hardline policies in its aftermath. See Stephen M. Saideman, "At the Heart of the Conflict: Irredentism and Kashmir", in *The India–Pakistan Conflict: An Enduring Rivalry*, ed. T.V. Paul (Cambridge: Cambridge University Press, 2005), 216. For a more comprehensive treatment of the social, political and ideational origins of the insurgency in Kashmir see Sumit Ganguly, *The Crisis in*

infiltrated Kashmir and turned it into the main battleground between Islamist terrorism and the Indian state.

In the meantime, in the early 1990s, India saw the emergence of a home-grown Islamist terrorist threat outside Kashmir. With the backdrop of communal tensions between Hindus and Muslims following the 1992 destruction of the Ayodhya mosque, Dawood Ibrahim, the Muslim don of the D-Company mafia syndicate, organized the 1993 Mumbai blasts, with the likely support of Pakistan.[6]

India during the last three decades has faced various Islamist terrorist organizations, which can be broadly divided into three large categories: Pakistan-based terrorist groups, home-grown terrorist groups and international terrorist organizations.[7]

Pakistan-based terrorist groups have been the oldest and most lethal Islamist terror threat to India. Based in Pakistan and benefitting from substantial ISI[8] support, these groups aim to overthrow Indian rule in Kashmir and unify it with Pakistan, although some also pursue a broader Islamist agenda. However, with the improvement of India's counterinsurgent operations in Kashmir and the diminishing strategic returns of supporting the insurgency, groups like Lashkar-e-Taiba (LeT) and Jaish-e-Mohammed (JeM) have expanded their operational zone beyond Kashmir to unleash terror in India's heartland. The Jammu and Kashmir Liberation Front (JKLF) was the first major Pakistan-based[9] terror group, although due to its support for Kashmir independence and nominally secular orientation ISI soon sidelined it to make way for Islamist groups[10] such as Hizb-ul-Mujahideen (HM). A highly centralized organization based in Pakistan but primarily staffed by Kashmiris, HM has run training camps in Pakistan-administered Kashmir (PAK) and has boasted a large force under its command, as many as 10,000 militants in the early 1990s.[11] Arguably the leading driver of violence in Jammu and Kashmir since 1990, the group has recently attracted a following among radicalized Kashmiri youths due to the efforts of its charismatic commander Burhan Wani, whose assassination by Indian forces in 2016 provoked massive unrest in Kashmir.[12] In contrast with the Kashmir-focused HM, LeT and JeM

Kashmir: Portents of War, Hopes of Peace (New York: Cambridge University Press, 2008).

6 Prem Mahadevan, *The Politics of Counterterrorism in India: Strategic Intelligence and National Security in South Asia* (New York: I.B. Tauris, 2012), 97

7 This division is made for classification and analytical purposes only and should not be regarded as absolute.

8 The Directorate General for Inter-Services Intelligence or just Inter-Services Intelligence (ISI) is Pakistan's premier intelligence agency.

9 Please note that JKLF has changed its home base several times over the years but for the period under study, from the late 1980s onward, it has been Pakistan-based.

10 Surinder Kumar Sharma and Anshuman Behera, *Militant Groups in South Asia* (New Delhi: Institute for Defence Studies and Analyses, Pentagon Press, 2014), 46–48

11 Josy Joseph, "Hizbul now biggest militant group", *The Hindu*, 28 March 2016, accessed 10 February 2017, www.thehindu.com/news/national/hizbul-now-biggest-militant-group/article7646317.ece.

12 R. Meenakshi, "Kashmir on the Boil: A Timeline", *The Hindu*, 21 July 2016, accessed 10 February 2017, www.thehindu.com/news/national/Kashmir-on-the-boil-a-timeline/article14596369.ece.

operate on Indian territory both inside and outside Kashmir. Founded in 1986 as an Islamist educational outfit involved in the Afghanistan war, LeT is a multifaceted Islamist organization which has combined jihad against India and the West with rigorous educational and charitable activities.[13] Often regarded as the most trusted of ISI's terrorist proxies, LeT, under its long-time leader Hafiz Muhammad Saeed, operates a number of training facilities for militants and is believed to have been involved in the 2001 Indian Parliament attack (with JeM)[14] and the 2008 Mumbai attacks (with IM).[15] A player on both the Indian and the global jihadi stage, LeT has close contacts with a number of militant organizations, including al-Qaeda, the Haqqani network and the Indian Mujahideen with which it has extensively cooperated. JeM is yet another Pakistan-based group which was founded, under ISI orders, by HuM militants freed by India after an Indian Airlines plane hijacking in 1999.[16] Active in Kashmir, the Indian heartland, Afghanistan and even Pakistan itself,[17] JeM is known to cooperate closely with al-Qaeda, Indian Mujahideen (IM) and LeT. It has been suspected of carrying out a number of attacks, including the 2001 Indian Parliament attacks (together with LeT),[18] the Indian consulate bombing in Mazar-e-Sahrif (2016),[19] the Pathankot attack (2016) and the Uri attack (2016),[20] the first two likely aimed at blocking any potential improvement in Indo-Pakistani relations.[21]

Home-grown terrorist groups are the second type of terrorist organization that threaten India's security. Usually motivated by grievance against the Indian state and India's Hindus, these groups threaten India with the rise of a potentially massive domestic jihadi movement. While indigenously formed, such Islamist groups have received support, training and shelter both from Pakistan's ISIS and from Pakistani-based terrorist groups, such as LeT and JeM. The first such group

13 Stephen Tankel, *Storming the World Stage: The Story of Lashkar-e-Taiba* (New York: Columbia University Press, 2011), 33–44.
14 "2001 Parliament Attack", *Times of India*, 25 October 2016, accessed 10 February 2017, http://timesofindia.indiatimes.com/event/2001-Parliament-attack/articleshow/55053711.cms.
15 Stephen Tankel, *The Indian Jihadist Movement: Evolution and Dynamics* (Washington, DC: National Defense University Press, 2014), 6.
16 Antoine Sfeir, *The Columbia World Dictionary of Islamism* (New York: Columbia University Press, 2008), 269
17 For example, JeM was implicated in the murder of the American journalist Daniel Pearl in Karachi in 2002 (see Sfeir, *The Columbia World Dictionary of Islamism*, 279).
18 "2001 Parliament Attack", *Times of India*.
19 "Afghanistan: Terrorists Gunned Down after 25-Hour Gunfight at the Indian Consulate in Mazar-e-Sharif", *The Indian Express*, 5 January 2016, accessed 11 February 2017, http://indianexpress.com/article/india/india-news-india/afghanistan-3-militants-killed-in-attack-outside-indian-consulate/.
20 "Pathankot Attack: NIA Files Charge Sheet Against Jem Chief Masood Azhar", *The Times of India*, 19 December 2016, accessed on 23 February 2017, http://timesofindia.indiatimes.com/india/pathankot-attack-nia-files-chargesheet-against-jem-chief-masood-azhar/articleshow/56059873.cms.
21 Bruce Riedel, "Blame Pakistani Spy Service for Attack on Indian Air Force Base", *The Daily Beast*, 5 January 2016, www.thedailybeast.com/articles/2016/01/05/blame-pakistani-spy-service-for-attack-on-indian-air-force-base.html.

was the D-Company which orchestrated the 1993 Mumbai attacks and, after moving to Pakistan, enabled its ISI backers to use its criminal network to recruit terrorists.[22] The Student Islamic Movement of India (SIMI) is another home-grown group which began as a legitimate Muslim student organization in Uttar Pradesh but gradually become radicalized and turned to terrorism.[23] A key recruitment source for the LeT, which had supported it since the mid-1990s, SIMI has been massively reduced in recent years due to police action.[24] An offshoot of SIMI,[25] IM is viewed as the most dangerous domestic terrorist group in India, at present. It has established a wide network across much of India and has benefitted from extensive training by ISI and close contacts with the Bangladesh-based HUJI, its parent organization SIMI[26] and with LeT, turning it into the key domestic Indian terrorist organization through which LeT and ISI have operated in India.[27] IM has been involved in the 2008 Jaipur bombing,[28] the 2008 Ahmedabad bombing, the 2011 Mumbai serial blasts[29] and perhaps the 2013 Hyderabad attack, among others.[30]

Large international terrorist organizations are the newest type of Islamist group to face India, which has long elicited little attention from such organizations. Since 2014, India has become a target of the two largest international terrorist organizations, al-Qaeda and Islamic State (IS), which are competing to radicalize Indian Muslims and unleash terror on Indian soil. In 2014, al-Qaeda announced the formation of a south Asian affiliate, al-Qaeda in the Indian Subcontinent (AQIS), which reportedly unified different South Asian terror groups under the leadership of an experienced Pakistani militant.[31] AQIS has launched a magazine, *Resurgence*, [32] and its propaganda has specifically targeted Indian Muslims by stoking discontent against the alleged oppression they face at the hands of Hindus and the government of Prime Minister Narendra Modi.[33] AQIS has carried out a

22 Tankel, *The Indian Jihadist Movement: Evolution and Dynamics*, 3.
23 Ibid., 3–5.
24 Amit Kumar, "Islamist Terrorism in India: Is the State Prepared to Combat Terror?", *in Asian Strategic Review 2016 Terrorism: Emerging Trends*, ed. S.D. Muni Vivek Chadha, Institute for Defence Studies and Analyses (New Delhi: Pentagon Press, 2016), 263
25 Tankel, *The Indian Jihadist Movement*, 5–6
26 IM's contacts with SIMI have been so close that some analysts speak of a "SIMI–IS complex". Kumar, "Islamist Terrorism in India", 263
27 Sharma and Behera, *Militant Groups in South Asia*, 127–129.
28 Ibid., 127.
29 Tenkel, *The Indian Jihadist Movement*, 8.
30 Ibid.
31 Abdul Basit, "Asim Umar 'New Kid on the Block'?," *Counter Terrorist Trends and Analysis* 6, 19 (2014): 8–12, www.rsis.edu.sg/wp-content/uploads/2014/07/CTTA-November14.pdf
32 Thomas Joscelyn, "Analysis: Al Qaeda's 'Resurgence' focuses on Indian Subcontinent", *The Long War Journal*, 23 October 2014, www.longwarjournal.org/archives/2014/10/al_qaedas_resurgence-2.php.
33 Alistair Reed, *Al Qaeda in the Indian Subcontinent: A New Frontline in the Global Jihadist Movement?* The International Centre for Counter-Terrorism – The Hague. ICCT Policy Brief, No. 1 (2016), 9

number of assaults in Pakistan and Bangladesh but has failed to attack India, although arrests of three of its members in Delhi[34] and contacts with the IM[35] indicate that it has infiltrated India. Islamic State has also increasingly posed a threat to India, although it has not managed to carry out an attack on Indian soil by the time of this writing. In 2015, soon after announcing the founding of its Khorasan province, which included Afghanistan and Pakistan, IS unveiled a map demonstrating its plans to conquer India before 2020.[36] It has also stepped up its efforts to recruit Indian Muslims, with over 50 Indians travelling to its camps in Afghanistan and dozens leaving Indian states like Kerala to join the IS in Syria and Iraq.[37] The group's propaganda arm has also published recruitment videos featuring its Indian fighters and has promised to avenge alleged atrocities against Muslims in Kashmir, Ayodhya and Gujarat.[38] There are also a number of signs that the IS has been active inside India, from sightings of IS flags in Kashmir[39] to IS-related activities online.[40] Indian authorities have also arrested IS operatives, propagandists and recruits, including members of IS's likely India franchise, the *Junud-ul-Khalifa-e-Hind*, which operated across five Indian states and, under IS orders, was in the process of preparing attacks.[41] It is likely that IS's footprint on the subcontinent would grow in the future as its fighters return from its shrinking territory in Syria and Iraq.

The unprecedented variety, lethality and persistence of these groups testifies to the fact that India faces a massive terrorist threat. In response, India has evolved a

34 Ibid., 15–16
35 Dharmendra Tiwari, "IM affiliation with Al-Qaeda Indian Subcontinent", *Mumbai Mirror*, 26 December 2015, http://mumbaimirror.indiatimes.com/mumbai/crime/IM-affiliation-with-Al-Qaeda-Indian-Subcontinent/articleshow/50328283.cms.
36 "ISIS Map of Areas It Wants to Take Over by 2020 Includes India", *Times of India*, 10 August 2015, accessed 13 February 2017, http://timesofindia.indiatimes.com/india/ISIS-map-of-areas-it-wants-to-take-over-by-2020-includes-India/articleshow/48425666.cms.
37 Anirudh Bhattacharyya, "Indians in Iraq and Syria Joining al Qaeda, Not Just Islamic State", *Hindustan Times*, 18 July 2016, accessed 8 February 2017, www.hindustantimes.com/world-news/indians-joining-al-qaeda-more-than-is-in-iraq-and-syria/story-ssF2ggWqBKs7NOEiJ9RpgL.html.
38 Praveen Swami, "Coming to Avenge Babri, Muzaffarnagar, Gujarat, Kashmir: IS Video", *Indian Express*, 25 May 2016, accessed 21 February 2017, http://indianexpress.com/article/india/india-news-india/avenge-babri-isis-video-islamic-state-indian-mujahideen-2811574/.
39 "Flags of ISIS, Pakistan Hoisted in Kashmir", *Hindustan Times*, 12 June 2015, accessed 21 February 2017, www.hindustantimes.com/india/flags-of-isis-pakistan-hoisted-in-kashmir/story-2YG3E3RKVSDw2LiDBkQXtO.html.
40 T.A. Johnson, "In a First, West Bengal Engineer to Stand Trial for (IS) Terror Online", *The Indian Express*, 13 May 2016, accessed 21 February 2017, http://indianexpress.com/article/india/india-news-india/west-bengal-engineer-to-stand-trial-for-isis-terror-online-2798009/.
41 Animesh Raoul, "How Islamic State Gained Ground in India Using Indigenous Militant Networks", *Terrorism Monitor*, 14, 9, 29 April 2016, https://jamestown.org/program/how-islamic-state-gained-ground-in-india-using-indigenous-militant-networks/.

specific approach to counterterrorism and a complex institutional set-up to implement it.

The evolution of counterterrorism in India

India's response to the threat of terrorism in the last thirty years has been regularly criticized as reactive, piecemeal and poorly organized. Indeed, New Delhi has often hastily adopted counterterrorism polices in reaction to major attacks only to see them gradually wither away. Nevertheless, in response to a series of spectacular attacks, particularly the 2001 Parliament attack and the 2008 Mumbai attacks (also known as 26/11), as well as the launch of the GWOT after 9/11, India has gradually evolved a more comprehensive approach to counterterrorism. The resulting approach, albeit still underdeveloped, can be described as relatively localized (i.e. limited primarily to India's borders), law-enforcement counterterrorism strategy which emphasizes defence.

In the 1990s, India faced divergent terrorist threats in Punjab, the Northeast, Kashmir and Mumbai, which inevitably produced counterterrorist strategies tailor-made to counter each of them and, hence, prevented the emergence of a unified Indian approach to counterterrorism. Hence, Indian counterterrorism in the 1990s was poorly coordinated and often piecemeal, with the major exception of Kashmir.

In Kashmir the thinking about terrorism was dominated by a dual approach based on counterinsurgency and political process. The counterinsurgent element of this strategy relied, on the one hand, on overwhelming military domination of the affected areas which aimed to stop infiltration and eliminate insurgents[42] and, on the other, on a "hearts and mind" policy which sought to win the support of the local population through operations such as "Op Sadhbhavana"[43] and through lavish government spending.[44] However, as India's prevailing thinking on counterinsurgency held that the military cannot address the insurgent threat without a political solution,[45] Delhi sought to offer a political process in Kashmir that would allow the Muslim population to express its political concerns. In this spirit, Delhi promised maximum autonomy to Kashmir, a promise that enabled assembly elections in the restive state in 1996.[46] The Indian government also

42 BhashyamKasturi, "Indian Army's Counter-Insurgency Operations in J&K", *Indian Defence Review*, 3 June 2012, accessed 28 February 2017, www.indiandefencereview.com/news/indian-armys-counter-insurgency-operations-in-jk-i/.

43 See Arpita Anant, "Counterinsurgency and 'Op Sadhbhavana' in Jammu and Kashmir", *IDSA Occasional Paper* No. 19 (2011), www.idsa.in/system/files/OP_CounterinsurgencyKashmir.pdf.

44 Shankkar Aiyar, "Great sop story", *India Today*, 14 October 2002, accessed on 3 February 2017, http://indiatoday.intoday.in/story/jammu-and-kashmir-most-pampered-state-in-india/1/218463.html.

45 Rajesh Rajagopalan, "Evolution of the Indian Army's Counterinsurgency Doctrine", in *India's National Security: A Reader*, ed. Kanti P. Bajpai and Harsh V. Pant (Oxford: Oxford University Press, 2013).

46 Praveen Swami, "Towards Greater Autonomy", *Frontline*, 16, 15, 17–30 July 1999, www.frontline.in/static/html/fl1615/16150360.htm.

negotiated with some insurgents on ceasefire terms and on conducting peace talks,[47] and even sought to engage with Pakistan in 1999 and 2001.

Outside Kashmir in the 1990s, India did not formulate a clear counterterrorism strategy but responded with haphazard measures that mostly emphasized law enforcement. This approach reflected the fact that the terrorism India faced at the time was sporadic and often reflected communal tensions between Hindus and Muslims that could not be addressed by counterterrorism. The 1993 Mumbai bombings proved to be a key event for Indian counterterrorism in the 1990s. The attacks prompted measures such as joint coastal patrols by Maharashtra and Gujarat to prevent arms smuggling by the D-Company,[48] attempts to organize a coastal security system[49]and efforts to stop infiltration through India's borders. The attacks also led to a drive to improve information sharing between intelligence services and state police forces, and to a massive crackdown on ISI agents and militants which yielded valuable intelligence that India used to prevent pre-planned attacks.[50] Just as important, India sought the assistance of foreign intelligence and security agencies in identifying the Pakistani connection in the attack, in the hope of putting international pressure on Islamabad, with little success.[51] Nevertheless, as there was little institutional or doctrinal change, the post-1993 counterterrorism drive soon lost its momentum. For the rest of the 1990s, India primarily relied on local law-enforcement forces in its fight against terrorism and did not fundamentally change its counterterrorism approach in spite of terrorist incidents such the 1998 Coimbatore bombings and the 1999 Indian Airlines hijacking.

The year 2001 marked the beginning of a new period in the evolution of Indian counterterrorism. The 2001 Indian Parliament attacks profoundly shook India and inaugurated a series of massive assaults on India's heartland, such as the 2005 Delhi attacks, the 2006 Mumbai train bombings and the 2008 Mumbai attacks. The 9/11 terrorist attacks also shocked India and deeply affected its fight against terror, a topic discussed later. This massive upsurge in terrorism prompted Delhi to initiate major reforms in all aspects of its counterterrorism. The only major exception was Kashmir, where the existing counterinsurgency strategy largely continued with an added emphasis on winning the support of the local population, emphasis codified in official doctrine in 2004 and 2006.[52]

The shocking 2001 Indian Parliament attack convinced India that it needs to reform its counterterrorism apparatus. The result was the adoption of the

47 "Kashmir Talks Make Progress", BBC News, 3 August 2000, accessed on 5 February 2017, http://news.bbc.co.uk/1/hi/world/south_asia/864336.stm.

48 Pushpita Das, "Coastal Security Arrangement: A Case Study of Gujarat and Maharashtra Coasts", *IDSA Occasional Paper* No. 6 (November 2009): 15, www.idsa.in/system/files/OP_CoastalSecurityArrangement.pdf.

49 Mahadevan, *The Politics of Counterterrorism in India*, 149.

50 Ibid., 171.

51 Vikram Sood, "The India Intelligence System: Meeting the Challenges of a New World", in *Handbook of Indian Defence Policy: Themes, Structures and Doctrines*, ed. Harsh V. Pant (New York: Routledge, 2016), 343–343

52 Anant, "Counterinsurgency and 'Op Sadhbhavana'".

Prevention of Terrorism Act (POTA), a relatively tough terrorism law that was repealed in 2004, as well as a renewed but unsuccessful push to found a multi-agency centre to combat terrorism. Delhi also hastened to implement many of the intelligence recommendations made after the Kargil War (1999), including the establishment of a Defence Intelligence Agency (DIA)[53] which gathers intelligence on Kashmir insurgents, among other tasks. Even more important, following the 2001/2002 Indo-Pakistani standoff prompted by the Parliament attack, India became better aware of the limits of its ability to coerce Pakistan militarily in response to terrorist attacks and the risks and costs of conflict with its nuclear-armed rival. These lessons have constrained India's response to terrorism ever since and have shaped Delhi's adoption of a law and order approach to counterterrorism instead of a military one. Similarly, Delhi's discovery of the limits of US pressure on Pakistan – Washington forced Islamabad to ban JeM and LeT but was unable to force their dismantling[54] – convinced India again that a diplomatic, international strategy of addressing terrorism is unfeasible.

The 26/11 attacks, a series of "comprehensive failures from the point of view of India's security establishment",[55] which had clues about the impeding attack but did not act on them,[56] had an even deeper impact on Indian counterterrorism. The attacks and the shambolic response of the authorities spectacularly revealed the intelligence, coordination and operational weaknesses of Indian counterterrorism and prompted a series of reforms. Institutionally, Delhi decided to establish a National Investigation Agency (NIA) to investigate terrorism, a National Counter Terrorism Centre (NCTC) to lead its counterterrorism efforts, and a National Intelligence Grid to coordinate intelligence sharing, although of these three only NIA has materialized at the time of this writing.[57] Legislatively, India added a special terrorism amendment to the Unlawful Activities (Prevention) Act (UAPA), which incorporated the tougher elements of the repealed POTA, and passed the Central Industrial Security Force (Amendment) Bill 2008, which enabled the Central Industrial Security Force (CISF) to provide security to private industrial establishments.[58] Operationally, Delhi set up four regional special forces hubs, in Kolkata, Hyderabad, Chennai and Mumbai, in order to

53 Sood, "The India Intelligence System", 338

54 Stephen Tankel, *Jihadist Violence: The Indian Threat* (Washington, DC: Wilson Center, 2013), 25.

55 Ajai Sahni, "The Uneducable Indian", *Outlook*, 1 December 2008, accessed 1 February 2017, www.outlookindia.com/website/story/the-uneducable-indian/239084.

56 Mahadevan, *The Politics of Counterterrorism in India*, 149–150; Suhasini Haidar, "U. S., U.K., India Had Many Leads but Failed to Stop 26/11", *The Hindu*, 22 December 2014, accessed on 17 February 2017, www.thehindu.com/news/national/deadly-nearmisses-in-spycraft-history-resulted-in-2611/article6715736.ece.

57 Sood, "The India Intelligence System", 338.

58 "Government Sanctions 500 CISF Men for Tata Projects in Gujarat, Odisha", *The Economic Times*, 24 September 2015, accessed 3 February 2017, http://economictimes.indiatimes.com/news/defence/government-sanctions-500-cisf-men-for-tata-projects-in-gujarat-odisha/articleshow/49090894.cms.

respond faster to terrorist attacks.[59] India made plans to expand its coastal security infrastructure[60] and improve its surveillance capabilities[61] in cities and on key sites,[62] plans that were implemented slowly and partially. Whereas the effort to improve Indian counterterrorism after 26/11 initially gained momentum, it gradually petered out and reforms stalled. Since then, there has been little change in India's approach to counterterrorism, although Delhi's response to the Uri attack in 2016[63] and hints that the NCTC[64] might be revived suggest that changes might be under way.

How can we classify India's counterterrorism approach outside Kashmir?[65] Ami Pedahzur, drawing on the literature on counterterrorism, identifies four counterterrorism models: defensive, reconciliatory, criminal justice and war models.[66] Using this matrix, it is clear that India has adopted the criminal justice model, also known as the law and order model, which conceptualizes terrorism as a crime and employs the internal security apparatus and the criminal justice system to fight it. After all, India has regularly marshalled legislation to prosecute terrorists, has relied on its police forces, primarily state police, as its first line of defence against terrorists and has mostly assigned responsibility for counterterrorism to its domestic security agencies. Delhi has also adopted elements of the defensive model, which defends the country both by making it a harder target for terrorists and by managing better the response to terrorist attacks. This defensive thinking can be detected in India's attempt to improve the security of key sites, prevent

59 "NSG Gets Fourth and Final Regional Hub in Mumbai", *The Hindu*, 24 February 2012, accessed 3 February 2017, www.thehindu.com/news/national/nsg-gets-fourth-and-final-regional-hub-in-mumbai/article2925072.ece.

60 Abhijit Singh, "8 Years After the 26/11 Mumbai Attacks: A Review of India's Coastal Security", *The Diplomat*, 29 November 2016, accessed on 1 March 2017, http://thediplomat.com/2016/11/8-years-after-the-2611-mumbai-attacks-a-review-of-india s-coastal-security/.

61 "4,717 CCTV Cameras Go Live Across Mumbai", *Hindustan Times*, 3 October 2016, accessed on 1 March 2017, www.hindustantimes.com/mumbai-news/4-717-cctv-cameras-go-live-across-mumbai/story-eSz18Aa82HeXHwrwj4Sk6L.html.

62 "300 Hi-Tech Cameras to be Installed in Parliament", News18, 29 January 2009, accessed on 1 March 2017, www.news18.com/news/india/300-hi-tech-camera s-to-be-installed-in-parliament-307431.html.

63 Shruti Singh, "Avenging Uri: How India Conducted Surgical Strikes in Pakistan-Occupied Kashmir", *India Today*, 29 September 2016, accessed on 3 February 2017, http://indiatoday.intoday.in/story/surgical-strikes-pakistan-uri-attack-indian-arm y-loc/1/776103.html.

64 "NCTC May Be Revived Soon: Official", *India Today*, 14 October 2016, accessed on 3 February 2017, http://indiatoday.intoday.in/story/nctc-may-be-revived-soon-offi cial/1/787173.html.

65 Kashmir is a special case because in it India faces not only terrorism but a massive insurgency. This counterinsurgency has prompted Delhi to adopt the militarized counterinsurgency strategy discussed above, strategy which is fundamentally different from India's approach to Islamist terrorism in other parts of the country. Hence, it is not included in this characterization of India's counterterror approach.

66 Ami Pedahzur, *The Israeli Secret Services and the Struggle against Terrorism* (New York: Columbia University Press, 2009), 2–3.

infiltration, and respond faster and more efficiently to attacks. The war model hardly applies to India, as it does not fight terrorists militarily, outside Kashmir. The reconciliatory model also does not describe Indian counterterrorism. Whereas India has negotiated with insurgents in Kashmir and in the Northeast and has even struck a deal with Islamist hijackers in 1999, it has refrained from renouncing its struggle with Islamist terrorists and switching to a policy of reconciliation and political compromise with them.

In short, New Delhi's approach to fighting terror can be described as defensive, law and order-based and localized, that is limited to India's homeland. This approach stands in contrast with the war model approach adopted by the US in the GWOT, which employs military force to launch deadly strikes against terrorists across borders. However, as India faces the militarily powerful, nuclear-armed Pakistan, which hosts most terrorists who attack India, the US approach poses too many risks for escalation for Delhi to adopt.

India's counterterrorism set-up

India boasts a large but highly fragmented institutional set-up for counterterrorism which includes a number of central and state institutions with overlapping responsibilities. As a result, India has many tools to fight terror but its counterterrorism efforts have suffered from poor coordination, institutional rivalry, and unclear division of labour and inability to concentrate resources, resulting in the underfunding and understaffing of institutions. The fits and starts in the evolution of Indian counterterrorism described above is one major culprit for this situation. India's federal constitution is another, as it postulates that the maintenance of law and order, including terrorism, is the responsibility of states.[67] Hence, counterterrorism in India has been divided between national and state agencies.

At the state level, the police forces of each of the twenty-nine states and seven union territories within India are tasked with the operational and intelligence fight against terrorism, a dispensation jealously guarded by states who fear loss of power to the central government. It is these regular law and order forces, often poorly trained, badly equipped and underfunded, that usually react first to terrorist attacks. Fortunately, some states also boast dedicated Anti-Terrorism Squads (ATS), such as the C-60 squad in Maharashtra and the Greyhounds in Andhra Pradesh,[68] which have played an important role during terrorism attacks such as 26/11 but have also drawn criticism about alleged abuses. However, this state police model does not apply to the whole of India, as in restive parts of the country, such as Kashmir and the Northeast, counterterrorism is handled primarily by the army or India's Home Ministry.

At the national level, India has a number of institutions that are responsible for counterterrorism. Traditionally, India's Intelligence Bureau (IB), its chief domestic intelligence agency under the Home Ministry, and the Research and Analysis

67 The Government of India, *The Constitution*, Part XXII, Seventh Schedule, 1950, 320.
68 Kumar, "Islamist Terrorism in India", 272.

Wing (RAW), Delhi's external intelligence agency, have been tasked with collecting intelligence on terrorism, inside and outside the country respectively.[69] In addition, following 26/11, India established the National Investigation Agency (NIA) as the primary national counterterrorism institution with powers both of investigation and arrest, although the latter power was abandoned in the face of opposition from states.[70] Reportedly, the NIA has been insufficiently staffed and very slow in prosecuting cases.[71] India's military intelligence services, the Defence Intelligence Agency, the Intelligence Directorates General of the Armed Forces and the intelligence agencies of the different military branches also gather terrorism-related intelligence, particularly tactical information pertaining to counterterrorism operations in Kashmir.[72] Other parts of India's vast intelligence apparatus, such as the Directorate of Revenue Intelligence (DRI) and the Central Bureau of Investigation (CBI), are also occasionally involved in gathering intelligence on terrorists. The plans to set up the NCTC, to coordinate intelligence gathering across central and state intuitions, and the related initiative for a National Intelligence Grid (NATGRID), to connect the databases of twenty-one separate agencies,[73] have not borne fruit at the time of this writing.[74] Finally, the Ministry of External Affairs also runs a division on terrorism that deals with the legal and diplomatic aspects of counterterrorism and manages India's joint working groups on counterterrorism with other countries.[75]

To operationally combat terrorists, India relies on several counterterrorist forces, apart from state police forces and state ATS which have the primarily responsibility for counterterrorism. To assist state police, Delhi can deploy paramilitary forces such the Central Reserve Police (CRP), which plays an important counterinsurgency role in Kashmir,[76] and the Border Security Force, which protects Indian borders from infiltration and weapons smuggling.[77] India can also deploy the National Security Guard (NSG), a commando special force, modelled on the UK's SAS, which is devoted specifically to counterterrorism and is deployed only in exceptional circumstances.[78] Following 26/11, NSG has established

69 Vandana Asthana, "Cross-Border Terrorism in India, Counterterrorism Strategies and Challenges", ACDIS Occasional Paper, University of Illinois (June 2010): 5.
70 Mahadevan, *The Politics of Counterterrorism in India*, 198.
71 Kumar, "Islamist Terrorism in India", 273–274.
72 B. Raman, "Counter-Terrorism: The Indian Experience", South Asia Analysis Group Paper No. 649, 4 January 2003, accessed on 28 February 2017, www.southasiaanalysis.org/paper649.
73 Kumar, "Islamist Terrorism in India: Is the State Prepared to Combat Terror?", 273.
74 Sood, "The India Intelligence System", 338
75 Raman, "Counter-Terrorism: The Indian Experience".
76 Nerender Kumar, "Paramilitary Forces and Central Armed Police Forces of India: Punching Below Their Capabilities", in *Handbook of Indian Defence Policy: Themes, Structures and Doctrines*, ed. Harsh V. Pant (New York: Routledge, 2016), 372–373.
77 Kumar, "Paramilitary Forces and Central Armed Police Forces of India", 369–370.
78 "Organization and History", National Security Guard, accessed 21 February 2017, www.nsg.gov.in/organisation_history.html.

regional hubs in Kolkata, Hyderabad, Chennai and Mumbai.[79] In addition, Delhi can rely on its Central Industrial Security Force (CISF), which provides security for airports and critical infrastructure.[80] Naturally, India can also deploy its military to fight terrorists as a last resort, as it has done in Kashmir where the army has played the leading counterterrorism role since 1990.[81]

In terms of legislation, a key but often underappreciated aspect of counter-terrorism, India has a relatively weak counterterror legislative infrastructure and still lacks a comprehensive national law on terrorism.[82] India's main terrorism law is the Unlawful Activities (Prevention) Act (UAPA) of 1967, initially designed to protect the integrity and the sovereignty of the state. Following 26/11, UAPA was amended to include a definition of "terrorist act", long pre-trial detention and new terrorism offences[83] in 2008, as well as terrorism financing in 2013.[84] New Delhi has adopted specifically anti-terrorist legislation before, including the lapsed Terrorist and Disruptive Activities (Prevention) Act (TADA) of 1985 and the Prevention of Terrorism Act (POTA), which was passed after the 2001 Indian Parliament attack but repealed in 2004 in response to minority and human rights concerns.[85] In Kashmir, the Armed Forces (Jammu & Kashmir) Special Powers Act adopted in 1990 deals with terrorist and militant activities.[86]

As the previous two sections demonstrate, while there has been improvement in recent years, India's counterterrorism still suffers from fragmentation, lack of strategy and poor implementation. The root causes of these weaknesses include tensions between the federal government and states, bureaucratic resistance, electoral politics which threaten politicians with a backlash if counterterrorism is seen as targeting minority groups, and the sheer difficulty for governments to stay focused on counterterrorism reform in the face of other pressing challenges. Prem Mahadevan identifies four major causes of India's counterterrorism failures: 1) lack

79 "NSG Gets Fourth and Final Regional Hub in Mumbai", *The Hindu*, 24 February 2012, accessed 3 February 2017, www.thehindu.com/news/national/nsg-gets-fourth-and-final-regional-hub-in-mumbai/article2925072.ece.
80 Bhupinder Singh, "Counter-Terrorism: Background and Mechanisms", *CLAWS Journal* (Winter 2007): 48.
81 Asthana, "Cross-Border Terrorism in India", 5.
82 However, there are comprehensive state laws on terrorism in some Indian states, such as the Karnataka Control of Organized Crime Act and the Maharashtra Control of Organized Crime Act (MCOCA). "Bill Gets Muscle to Fight Terror, Organized Crime," *Times of India*, 30 July 2009, accessed on 11 February 2017, http://timesofindia.indiatimes.com/city/bengaluru/Bill-gets-muscle-to-fight-terror-organized-crime/articleshow/4835392.cms.
83 Srijoni Sen et al., "Anti-Terror Law in India: A Study of Statutes and Judgements, 2001–2014", Vidhi Centre for Legal Policy, 2015, 7–8, accessed on 1 February 2017, https://static1.squarespace.com/static/551ea026e4b0adba21a8f9df/t/5575b428e4b08898ef56bc60/1433777192655/150531_Vidhi+Terrorism+Report_Final.pdf.
84 Ibid.
85 Arjun Subramaniam, "Challenges of Protecting India from Terrorism", *Terrorism and Political Violence*, 24: 3 (2012): 410.
86 Sen et al., "Anti-Terror Law in India", 8.

of political consistency, which produces frequent ad hoc changes in counterterror measures; 2) lack of political consensus in fighting terror, due to domestic or international resistance; 3) lack of operational capacity as a result of insufficient funding and manpower; 4) lack of operational coordination between the different state and national security services.[87]

In sum, India has made progress in fighting terror, but if it wants to achieve better results and overcome its counterterrorism faults, it needs some significant reforms.

India and the GWOT

The 9/11 terrorist attacks and the GWOT that they unleashed was an important milestone in India's fight against terrorism. India's lonely fight against Islamist terrorism became part of a much larger global struggle, turning countries such as the US and the UK into allies. This meant that India not only could count on the moral support of the West in its own struggle against terrorism, but could also receive a much more sympathetic hearing about Pakistan's support for terror and use it to put pressure on Islamabad. More practically, the GWOT has allowed India to improve its own struggle with terror by enhancing counterterror cooperation and intelligence sharing with the US and by replicating some of the US's successful counterterrorism practices and institutions. In addition, the US's unrelenting targeting of terrorism financing and of al-Qaeda and the Taliban has weakened anti-Indian terror groups. Domestically, the GWOT and the major terrorist attacks that struck India from 2001 onward increased Delhi's ability to push for harder counterterrorism measures domestically.

India's immediate response to the 9/11 terrorist attacks was to offer the US unprecedented support in its GWOT, including airbases for operations in Afghanistan.[88] Initially, this support bore fruit as Washington designated LeT and JeM terrorist organizations,[89] labelled Dawood Ibrahiman international terrorist[90] and even forced Pakistan's government to ban LeT and JeM.[91] Nevertheless, Delhi soon found out, to its disappointment, that there were limits on how much the US was willing to antagonize Pakistan, a key partner in the GWOT and in Afghanistan. Washington's reluctance to pressure Pakistan or alienate it by cooperating too closely with India on counterterrorism and Afghanistan emerged as a major constraint on Indo-American cooperation. Nonetheless, as US–Pakistani relations deteriorated, especially after the 2011 Abbotabad raid, US–India counterterrorism cooperation regained some of its momentum.

87 Mahadevan, *The Politics of Counterterrorism in India.*
88 Hoyt, "The War on Terrorism", 286.
89 B. Raman, "Indo-U.S. Counter-Terrorism Cooperation: Past, Present and Future", in *US–Indian Strategic Cooperation into the 21st Century: More than Words*, ed. Sumit Ganguly, Andrew Scobell and Brian Shoup (New York: Routledge, 2006), 167.
90 Ibid.
91 Hoyt, "The War on Terrorism", 287.

Beyond the immediate steps prompted by the 9/11 attacks, the GWOT has had three long-term effects on India's fight on terrorism.

First, the GWOT inaugurated a new era of counterterrorism cooperation between India and the US. This cooperation, eulogized by President Obama and Prime Minister Modi as "a defining counter-terrorism partnership for the 21st century",[92] has been institutionalized in a number of key initiatives and agreements. The most important such initiative is the 2010 Counterterrorism Cooperation Initiative (CCI) which aims to promote intelligence sharing and capacity building between the two sides in a wide range of areas, such as transport security, terrorist financing, cybersecurity, port and border security, and special units training.[93] Other joint initiatives include the Homeland Security Dialogue, launched in 2011, which has focused on ensuring access to both sides' terrorist databases among other issues, as well as the US–India Counterterrorism Joint Working Group (JWG) which, although inaugurated in 2000,[94] has seen a major boost in cooperation after 9/11 and 26/11. In addition, US and India have issued a number of declarations on counterterror cooperation, such as the 2015 US–India Joint Declaration on Combatting Terrorism,[95] and have signed several agreements to promote such cooperation. For instance, the 2016 Intelligence Sharing Agreement[96] has focused on facilitating terrorist screening, a very sensitive question after it was revealed that American intelligence had not shared all relevant information they had prior to the 26/11 attacks.[97] The 2015 Memorandum of Understanding on terrorism financing is another important bilateral agreement in an area in which Washington can share with India its extensive experience. Furthermore, the US has provided counterterrorism and counterinsurgency training to Indian forces, either as part of Washington's Anti-Terrorism Assistance Program,[98] or as part of joint military training; 2016 witnessed a fine example of such cooperation when American Special Forces trained India's prime counterterrorism force, the NSG commandos.[99] In spite of these developments, the full potential of US–India counterterrorism cooperation is yet to be realized.

92 Kathleen Hicks et al., *U.S.–India Security Cooperation: Promise and Progress for the Next Administration*, Center for Strategic and International Studies (CSIS) (Lanham, MD: Rowman & Littlefield, 2016), 45.

93 "India, U.S. Sign Counter-Terrorism Initiative", *The Hindu*, 23 July 2010, accessed on 13 February 2017, www.thehindu.com/news/national/India-U.S.-sign-counter-terrorism-initiative/article16207465.ece.

94 Raman, "Indo-U.S. Counter Terrorism Cooperation", 160.

95 "U.S.–India Joint Declaration on Combatting Terrorism", U.S. Embassy and Consulates in India, 23 September 2015, accessed on 17 February 2017, https://in.usembassy.gov/u-s-india-joint-declaration-on-combatting-terrorism/.

96 "Documents Signed/Finalized in the Run Up to the Visit of Prime Minister of India to the US", Ministry of External Affairs, Government of India, 7 June 2016, accessed on 17 February 2017, http://mea.gov.in/bilateral-documents.htm?dtl/26878/Documents_signedfinalized_in_the_run_upto_the_visit_of_Prime_Minister_of_India_to_the_US.

97 Haidar, "U.S., U.K., India had many leads but failed to stop 26/11".

98 Asthana, "Cross-Border Terrorism in India", 18.

99 Sushant Singh, "India–US Anti-Terror Cooperation: For the First Time, NSG Commandos Train with US Special Forces", *The Indian Express*, 2 November 2015,

Second, US intervention in Afghanistan, the only major GWOT battleground where Delhi and Washington actively stand on the same side, has deeply influenced India's war on terror. Afghanistan has long been important to India, not only because it has served as an incubator for Islamist fundamentalism in South Asia, to which terrorist groups like LeT trace their origins, but also because it is a key staging ground in which terrorists train and prepare attacks on India, particularly on Jammu and Kashmir, with the aid of ISI and their local Taliban and al-Qaeda allies.[100] Against this background, the US invasion of Afghanistan has substantially reduced the pressure on India in Kashmir,[101] pressure that would likely return if Afghanistan slips back into chaos. As a result, India has supported, albeit in a wavering manner, the struggle to build a stable, democratic Afghanistan, free from Islamist fundamentalists. However, fearful of provoking a Pakistani reaction, Delhi has left the counterinsurgency and military support for Kabul to the US and allies and has focused on soft engagement with Afghanistan. Delhi has spent $2 billion in aid to Kabul, pledged another billion, helped Afghanistan with training and institution building, and completed a number of key infrastructure projects, such as the Salma Dam and the 218 km Zaranj-Delaram road.[102] In terms of security engagement, in 2011 India and Afghanistan signed a Strategic Partnership Pact, as part of which India has trained Afghan officers and policemen in Indian institutions.[103] Kabul has also requested military hardware on several occasions, but Delhi has consistently refused, until 2016 when it provided four Mi-25[104] helicopters to Afghanistan, a gesture that might indicate a shift in India's position on security cooperation. Finally, Afghanistan has been a major theatre in which India has confronted terrorism, with attacks on the Indian Embassy in Kabul (2008) and on Indian consulates in Herat (2014), Jalalabad (2016) and Mazar-e-Sharif (2016).[105]

Third, India's own fight against terrorism has benefitted from US experience during the GWOT in two ways. At one level, the GWOT has helped India approach terrorism in new ways instead of treating it as an exclusively law and

accessed on 13 February 2017, http://indianexpress.com/article/india/india-news-india/india-us-anti-terror-cooperation-for-the-first-time-nsg-commandos-train-with-us-special-forces/.

100 This point is amply proven by the fact that the Kashmir insurgency erupted in 1989, almost immediately after the Soviet withdrawal from Afghanistan.

101 This reduction can be traced to the decline of the total number of fatalities in Kashmir which peaked in 2001 and has fallen dramatically since then, year after year, until 2013, and still remains low at the time of this writing. "Fatalities in Terrorist Violence, 1988–2017", South Asia Terrorism Portal, accessed on 17 February 2017, www.satp.org/satporgtp/countries/india/states/jandk/data_sheets/annual_casualties.htm.

102 Harsh V. Pant, *India's Afghan Muddle: A Lost Opportunity* (Noida, Uttar Pradesh: HarperCollins, 2014), 61–62

103 Ibid., p. 85.

104 "Afghans Push India for More Arms, Despite Pakistan's Wary Eye", Reuters, 22 August 2016, accessed on 13 February 2017, www.reuters.com/article/us-afghanistan-india-defence-idUSKCN10X29W.

105 There are also reports that ISI has been paying the Haqqani network to assassinate Indians in Afghanistan. Pant, *India's Afghan Muddle*, p. 81.

order issue or as a facet of Indo-Pakistani relations. Washington's militarized, offensive approach to fighting terror has fostered a debate about whether India can also pursue such a strategy. This debate, which intensified after the US's raid on Abbottabad in 2011,[106] likely played a role in India's unprecedented decision to launch surgical strikes against militants in Pakistan, following the Uri attack in September 2016.[107] More significantly, the GWOT has focused Indian attention on American counterterrorism models that can be replicated in India, while simultaneously increasing the pressure on Delhi to sort out its counterterrorism. Hence, Delhi has modelled its still nascent NCTC on the US institution of the same name and has made efforts to unify its different security databases in a NATGRID, an echo of Washington's intelligence-sharing reforms after 9/11. The use of US models extends to legislation. POTA clearly reproduced some of the stringent provisions of US's Patriot Act, legislation which the Indian government evoked as a precedent for POTA,[108] and included such innovations as special terrorism courts, partly modelled on the American military tribunals for prosecuting terrorists established after 9/11.[109]

The GWOT and India's debate on terrorism, civil liberties and human rights

The GWOT has also impacted on India's often heated and highly divisive debate on terrorism, civil liberties and human rights. The GWOT's narrative of an international struggle against the deadly threat of jihadi terrorism and the necessity to impose severe security measures and limits on civil liberties to prevail in it has affected the debate between the proponents of a harder approach to terrorism and its opponents. Predictably, this narrative has strengthened the case of India's counterterrorism hawks, who have long pushed for tougher anti-terror legislation and difficult reforms in the face of determined political opposition. Nevertheless, as India has historically witnessed regular abuse of special powers, such a narrative

106 Manoj Joshi and Dipanjan Roy Chaudhuryi, "Does India Have Might to Launch Abbottabad-Like Strike to Get Dawood Ibrahim?", *India Today*, 6 May 2011, accessed on 13 February 2017, http://indiatoday.intoday.in/story/does-india-have-might-to-launch-abbottabad-like-mission/1/137255.html; and Gulam Jeelani, "India Capable of Surgical Strikes Like US: Army Chief", *Hindustan Times*, 4 May 2011, accessed on 13 February 2017, www.hindustantimes.com/india/india-capable-of-surgical-strikes-like-us-army-chief/story-y8zWH0fD3OzFjxauK7VrhP.html.

107 Shruti Singh, "Avenging Uri: How India Conducted Surgical Strikes in Pakistan-Occupied Kashmir", *India Today*, 29 September 2016, accessed on 3 February 2017, http://indiatoday.intoday.in/story/surgical-strikes-pakistan-uri-attack-indian-army-loc/1/776103.html.

108 Manas Mohapatra, "Learning Lessons from India: The Recent History of Antiterrorist Legislation on the Subcontinent", *Journal of Criminal Law and Criminology*, 95 (Fall 2004): 333.

109 Jayanth K. Krishnan, "India's 'Patriot Act': POTA and the Impact on Civil Liberties in the World's Largest Democracy', *Articles by Maurer Faculty*, Indiana University Maurer School of Law, Paper 379 (2004), 280.

and the measures it promotes have inevitably increased the fears that counterterrorism would be used to undermine the rule of law, persecute political opponents and oppress minorities, particularly Muslims. Naturally, political considerations about mobilizing different vote banks and regulating the balance of power between Delhi and the states have played a major role in this debate, which has mostly revolved around terrorism-related legislation.

The GWOT narrative, with its imagery of a global crusade against the scourge of terrorism, has enabled India's government to present its own fight against terror as part of a global struggle that requires tougher counterterror policy. This effect can be witnessed in the way India's government justified the two toughest pieces of anti-terror legislation since 2001, POTA and the UAPA Amendment of 2008. In its introduction POTA states that "terrorism has now acquired global dimensions and has become a challenge to the entire world" as a justification for its adoption.[110] The UAPA Amendment justifies its proposals by citing various UN counterterror resolutions, including UN Security Council Resolution 1373 adopted after 9/11 which requires all states to take hard measures against terrorist organizations.[111] The GWOT narrative has also allowed the Indian government to deflect criticism that its counterterrorism policy undermines Indian democracy by citing the uncompromising counterterror measures of the US. Thus, POTA's controversial provisions were justified with the US Patriot Act, on which it is modelled, while India's special terrorism courts were defended as a version of the American special military tribunals for terrorists. Finally, the US's GWOT narrative and its emphasis on the necessity of major centralizing reforms to effectively fight terror has strengthened the case of counterterrorism reforms in the face of opposition from bureaucracies, states and politicians.

Predictably, the push to introduce harder counterterror legislation with the aid of the GWOT narrative has met with fierce opposition from human rights activists and minority groups, just as in the West. These groups have criticized India's counterterror legislation as a threat to democratic freedoms and the rule of law and an invitation for abuse and human rights violations against minorities. POTA, which some Indian states outright refused to implement,[112] was criticized as a law that dispenses with the presumption of innocence,[113] undermines due process[114] and violates privacy.[115] Critics also portrayed POTA as an instrument of oppression against political opponents, fears that concentrated on the case of Vaiko, a

110 Quoted in B. Jagannatham and G. Haragopal, "Terrorism and Human Rights: Indian Experience with Repressive Laws", *Economic and Political Weekly*, 44, 28, 11 July 2009, 81.

111 The Unlawful Activities (Prevention) Amendment Act 2008.

112 Including Karnataka, Manipur, Madhya Pradesh, and Assam. Asthana, "Cross-Border Terrorism in India", 14.

113 "Open Letter to Law Minister Jana Krishnamurthi about the Forthcoming Trial of Abdul Rehman Geelani and Three Others", Amnesty International, 8 July 2002, accessed on 13 February 2017, www.amnesty.org/en/documents/asa20/010/2002/en/.

114 Jagannatham and Haragopal, Terrorism and Human Rights", 82

115 Ibid.

Tamil politician and MP who was charged under the law, allegedly for political reasons.[116] The UAPA Amendment has also provoked strong criticism for many of the same reasons. Moreover, the amendment has drawn the ire of rights groups because it expands the definition of terrorist act[117] and allows the banning of political organizations on terrorism charges, thus giving a "dangerous tool in the hands of officials who seek to oppress peaceful critics and minority communities"[118] according to Human Rights Watch. Allegations that anti-terror legislation and the whole GWOT/counterterrorism narrative target Indian Muslims and expose them to persecution and discrimination have long plagued Delhi.[119]

In general, the GWOT's narrative has expanded the space for tougher counterterrorism legislation and has strengthened hawks in India's debate on terrorism, civil liberties and human rights. Nevertheless, the opposition to the narrative and to stronger counterterrorism has also had an impact, as it has pushed the government to refine its approach to terror and learn the limits of how much it can restrict civil liberties and human rights. POTA is a good example of this effect. From its inception POTA's draft faced criticism that it does not adequately protect journalists from terrorism charges, criticism that prompted its amendment, while the political abuse of the law led the president to appoint review committees to monitor its unbiased application.[120] Finally the law was repealed, only to see many of its provisions incorporated in the more moderate and better-crafted UAPA Amendment. In short, criticism against POTA limited its worst effects and eventually made way for a better version of the same legislation. As the example demonstrates, GWOT played an important role in the gradual emergence of a more balanced approach to counterterrorism, human rights and civil liberties in India.

Conclusion

As a major target of Islamist terrorism India has stood at the forefront of the GWOT. However, as India's terrorist threat has come primarily from local groups, either home-grown or Pakistan-based, Delhi has refrained from combatting global terrorism on the international stage, as the US and Britain have done. Instead,

116 Nilanjana Bhaduri Jha, "Charges against Vaiko", *Times of India*, 11 July 2002, accessed on 17 February 2017, http://timesofindia.indiatimes.com/india/Charges-against-Vaiko/articleshow/15665836.cms.

117 "Back to the Future: India's 2008 Counterterrorism Laws", Human Rights Watch (July 2010), 5–8, www.hrw.org/sites/default/files/reports/india0710webwcover_0.pdf.

118 "India: Reject Amendments to Counterterrorism Law", Human Rights Watch, 14 December 2012, accessed on 17 February 2017, www.hrw.org/news/2012/12/14/india-reject-amendments-counterterrorism-law.

119 Suchitra Vijayan, "Islamic Difference and Radicalisation", *The Hindu*, 7 January 2015, accessed on 17 February 2017, www.thehindu.com/opinion/op-ed/comment-article-islamic-difference-and-radicalisation/article6760854.ece.

120 J. Venkatesan, "POTA Ordinance Empowers Review Committees", *The Hindu*, 29 October 2003, accessed on 18 February 2017, www.thehindu.com/2003/10/29/stories/2003102908090100.htm.

India has fought in the Global War on Terror by waging its own "local war on terror".

In this "local war on terror", long predating the GWOT, Delhi has evolved, in fits and starts, a defensive, localized, law-and-order approach to counterterrorism. This approach –underdeveloped and constrained by a fragmented institutional set-up and political factors – has benefitted considerably from the GWOT. The GWOT has allowed Delhi to draw on America's rich counterterror experience through cooperation and the adoption of American counterterror models and practices. It has also affected India's debate on civil liberties, human rights and terrorism by helping to expand the domestic space within which India's government can craft tougher counterterrorism policies. While Indian counterterrorism has been influenced by the GWOT, it has retained its defensive, localized, law-and-order character and, hence, has remained distinct from the counterterrorism model adopted by the US in the GWOT.

But would India change its approach to counterterrorism? After all, Indian counterterrorism has produced few successes and has neither checked home-grown terrorism, nor persuaded Pakistan to cease its support for terrorists. The resulting frustration has pushed Delhi to experiment with a more muscular counterterror policy, for instance after the Uri attacks in 2016. Moreover, the terrorist threat that India faces is changing. Global terrorist organizations, such as al-Qaeda and IS, now target the subcontinent, while militants returning from the Middle East threaten to revitalize India's home-grown Islamist movement. It is not readily evident if Indian counterterrorism policy as it stands at present can effectively address these threats.

For all its evolution and progress over the years, Indian counterterrorism increasingly stands at a crossroads. What road it takes will determine its place in the GWOT.

Index

Note: bold page numbers indicate tables; italic page numbers indicate figures; numbers preceded by *n* refer to footnotes.

For Product Safety Concerns and Information please contact our EU representative GPSR@taylorandfrancis.com Taylor & Francis Verlag GmbH, Kaufingerstraße 24, 80331 München, Germany

Batch number: 10725973

Printed by Printforce, the Netherlands